VISUAL QUICKSTART GUIDE

PRO TOOLS 6

FOR MACINTOSH AND WINDOWS

Steven Roback

Peachpit Press

Visual QuickStart Guide
Pro Tools 6 for Macintosh and Windows
Steven Roback

Peachpit Press
1249 Eighth Street
Berkeley, CA 94710
510/524-2178
800/283-9444
510/524-2221 (fax)

Find us on the World Wide Web at www.peachpit.com.
To report errors, please send a note to errata@peachpit.com.

Peachpit Press is a division of Pearson Education.

Editor: Rebecca Gulick
Production Editor: Hilal Sala
Contributing Writers: Douglas Murray and Greg Gordon
Illustrator: Stephen Dampier
Copy Editor: Wade Newbern
Compositor: Owen Wolfson
Indexer: Karin Arrigoni
Cover Design: The Visual Group
Cover Production: Nathalie Valette

Notice of Rights

Notice of Liability

Trademarks

ISBN 0-321-21315-7

9 8 7 6 5 4 3 2 1

Printed and bound in the United States of America

To Bart,

My companion and humming helper,
who sat at my feet through the long,
tortuous nights. "Maow, raow, gabaow."

Acknowledgments

First, I want to re-extend my gratitude to all the folks who helped create the first edition of this book, *Pro Tools 5: Visual QuickStart Guide*: Missy Roback, Rebecca Gulick, Claudia Curcio, Paul Foeckler, Dusty DiMercurio, Thad Brown, Marjorie Baer, and Kelly Ryer. Your hard work, insight, and encouragement are present throughout this new edition.

For this second edition, *Pro Tools 6: Visual QuickStart Guide*, Rebecca Gulick deserves a solar system-sized thank you: Congratulations on the new addition to your family, and thanks for overseeing the birth of this book as well. I also want to thank Cliff Colby for hanging in there with me during the difficult early days. Your negotiation skills are impressive.

Claudia Curcio and the folks at Digidesign deserve another ovation as well. Your support was absolutely critical. Thanks again for coming through when it mattered and for providing me (and the contributors) with the necessary materials in an ultra-timely fashion.

Thanks also to Douglas Murray for contributing Chapter 19 and lending your sound-for-video expertise to this project. And thanks to Greg Gordon and Matt Donner for updating Chapters 17 and 18 and bailing me out of the MIDI vortex.

TABLE OF CONTENTS

INTRODUCTION

Pro Tools is a computer-based audio recording system that runs on Macintosh and Windows operating systems. Pro Tools TDM systems are considered the de facto standard for hard-disk audio recording in professional studios worldwide. Digidesign now offers a range of increasingly popular Pro Tools LE systems, which are designed for use in home studios and project studios.

Pro Tools' popularity is due, in part, to its successful migration of a traditional recording studio environment to the computer realm. It's also famous for its powerful recording, editing, mixing, automation, and real-time DSP effects.

What is Pro Tools LE?

Pro Tools LE is the software that comes with several of Digidesign's hard-disk audio recording systems, including Digi 002, Digi 002 Rack, Digi 001, Mbox, and Audiomedia III. These systems are designed primarily for use in home recording studios and project studios, or, in the case of the Digi 002 Rack and Mbox, to be taken on the road.

Pro Tools LE software is nearly identical to its higher-end Pro Tools TDM software counterpart. The main difference is how each version of Pro Tools handles DSP (digital signal processing): Pro Tools TDM systems include PCI cards with built-in DSP processing chips; Pro Tools LE systems rely entirely on the host computer's CPU for all DSP-processing tasks. Because Pro Tools LE systems are host-based, the number of tracks and plug-ins you can use simultaneously depends on your computer's CPU power. Generally speaking, faster computers perform better.

Sessions created with Pro Tools LE are compatible with Pro Tools TDM systems. This means that you can record tracks using a modest Pro Tools LE system, and then, when you're ready, take them to a studio and mix them on a Pro Tools TDM system. Because Pro Tools LE software is so similar to the TDM version, upgrading to the higher-end system has almost no learning curve.

Who should use this book?

This book is for musicians, engineers, producers, composers, soundtrack creators, film and video producers, music supervisors, broadcasters, Webcasters, students, audiophiles, MP3 addicts, vicarious listeners, and anyone else who wants a simple, clear, and complete explanation of how to use Pro Tools digital audio software. While this book focuses on Pro Tools 6.1 LE, the vast majority of

software features discussed herein apply to all Pro Tools systems, including Pro Tools 5 LE, Pro Tools TDM, and Pro Tools Free. (For more information on Pro Tools Free, see www.digidesign.com.)

What's in this book?

This book contains comprehensive, step-by-step instructions on most aspects of Pro Tools 6.1 LE, including hardware setup, recording and playback, editing, mixing, effects plug-ins, automation, file management, MIDI, and CPU performance. I've also included recording-related sidebars to inspire you and help you make better-sounding recordings.

Structured like a recording session, this book includes the following sections:

Part I: Getting Started with Pro Tools LE. This section covers setting up your Pro Tools LE system. You'll also learn the basics of Pro Tools software, and the layout of the Mix and Edit windows.

Part II: Recording in Pro Tools. This section teaches you how to record and play back audio in Pro Tools. You'll learn how to create new sessions, and how to work with tracks.

Part III: Audio File Management. This section introduces you to Pro Tools' file management features. You'll learn basic functions, such as locating, importing, exporting, and backing up your audio files. You'll also learn how to use DigiBase, Pro Tools' new, comprehensive file-management utility.

Part IV: Editing Audio. This section shows you how to edit audio in Pro Tools. You'll learn how to select and move audio regions, and how to save time using edit playlists. You'll also learn a few advanced features such as creating fades and crossfades, and repairing waveforms.

Part V: Mixing Audio. This section covers mixing audio in Pro Tools. You'll learn about stereo imaging and audio signal flow, as well as how to add effects using real-time DSP plug-ins. You'll also learn how to automate a mix and how to bounce a final mix down to disk.

Part VI: MIDI Sequencing. This section introduces Pro Tool's MIDI sequencing features. You'll learn how to record, edit, and play back MIDI in Pro Tools.

Part VII: Getting the Most from Pro Tools. This section provides an overview of using Pro Tools to work with sound in digital video. It also suggests ways to maximize Pro Tools LE's performance. You'll learn how to set memory buffers and memory-intensive functions to achieve the best results during recording, editing and mixing, and you'll see how making tracks and other items inactive can free up valuable CPU power. You'll also learn how to use DSP plug-ins efficiently, and how to squeeze extra space out of your hard drive.

Appendices and Glossary. Appendix A shows you how to connect Digi 002, Digi 002 Rack, Digi 001, Mbox, and Audiomedia III hardware to your studio. Appendix B presents complete descriptions of all Pro Tools 6.1 preferences. A glossary provides a list of Pro Tools–specific and general recording terms.

About the sidebars

I've included a few sidebars to help you understand some important recording concepts. In creating these sidebars, I tried to present simple topics that I wish I had at my fingertips when I first started recording. Some of these topics include mic placement, gain staging, and monitoring a mix.

How to use this book

If you're new to Pro Tools, use this book as a visually oriented instructional manual to step you through each phase of the recording process. If you're already familiar with Pro Tools, use this book as a visual reference guide to quickly refresh your memory. Either way, there's lots of Pro Tools information within.

What's new in Pro Tools 6 LE ?

Pro Tools 6 LE (and TDM) is an entirely revamped version of Pro Tools, designed from the ground up specifically for Mac OS X's powerful and stable Unix-based operating environment. Pro Tools 6 LE software supports all currently available Pro Tools LE hardware systems, including Digi 002, Digi 002 Rack, Digi 001, Mbox, and Audiomedia III.

Building on the strong recording features of Pro Tools 5 LE, Pro Tools 6 LE adds several thoughtfully conceived new features that make working in Pro Tools easier, more creative, and a lot more fun. Pro Tools 6.0 LE (for Mac OS X only), includes the following new features:

- New windows and user interface
- DigiBase file management utility
- New editing features
- Relative Grid Mode
- Suspend Grid Mode
- Playback Cursor Locator
- Horizontal and vertical Selector tool
- New MIDI features

INTRODUCTION

◆ Groove Quantize

◆ New MIDI Services

◆ More MIDI tracks (up to 256)

◆ Flatten and Restore MIDI Performance

◆ MIDI Time Stamping

◆ Trim Tool

◆ Pencil Tool

◆ Floating MIDI windows

◆ Virtual MIDI Pro Tools Inputs

◆ New Plug-ins and processing features

◆ iLok plug-in copy protection

◆ New DigiRack Click plug-in

◆ New plug-ins including DigiRack Chorus, Flanger, Multi-Tap delay, Ping-Pong delay, Pitch Shift; and D-Verb

◆ Inserting plug-ins during playback

◆ Track height enhancements

◆ Zoom Toggle Track Height

◆ Track height toggle with arrow keys

◆ 32 Voiceable Tracks (Digi 001, Mbox, and Audiomedia III)

◆ Increased track count (up to 128 audio tracks, 128 auxiliary inputs, 64 master faders, and 256 MIDI tracks)

◆ Inactive Tracks

◆ Time Trimmer (region time compression/expansion)

◆ Commands Focus Shortcuts (enables single key commands)

◆ QuickTime DV Playback

As of this writing, Pro Tools 6.0 (Mac OS X only) has been updated to Pro Tools Version 6.1, which runs on both Mac OS X and Windows XP. Pro Tools 6.1 incorporates the features introduced in Pro Tools 6.0 and adds the following new features:

◆ Up to 32 levels of undo

◆ DigiBase browser displays OMF video metadata

◆ Advanced Authoring Format (AAF) with DigiTranslator 2.0

◆ New plug-ins and processing features

◆ New DigiRack plug-ins interface

◆ New DigiRack ReWire plug-in

◆ Waves Time Shifter and TC/E Plug-in Preference

◆ Support for DigiTranslator 2.0 on Digi002 and Digi 002 Rack

◆ DV Toolkit Option for Pro Tools LE

◆ Scroll wheel navigation of Pro Tools windows

For more information on the new features in Pro Tools 6.1 LE, see Digidesign's Web site at www.digidesign.com.

Additional information

For additional information on Pro Tools LE, Pro Tools TDM, or Pro Tools Free, see Digidesign's Web site at www.digidesign.com. The site offers a wealth of information on all Pro Tools-related topics, including download-able software updates and product manuals, product support, and upgrade plans.

INTRODUCTION

A (Very) Brief History of Multi-Track Recording

Thomas Edison invented the world's first recording and playback machine in 1877. But it wasn't until the 1930s, when renowned guitarist and electronics innovator Les Paul began overlaying multiple guitar tracks on acetate discs, that multi-track recording was born.

Les Paul: Recording Pioneer

Paul's contributions to the development of multi-track recording cannot be overstated. In 1949, he adapted a rare Magnetophone tape machine to create sound-on-sound recording—better known as overdubbing. Along the way, Paul literally invented most of the audio gear used in recording studios today, including equalizers, delays, reverbs, and many other audio effects processing devices.

Paul's experimentation with close-up miking techniques also left a lasting impact on vocal production. In 1951 he produced two widely acclaimed, million-selling songs, *How High the Moon* and *Mockin' Bird Hill*, which featured beautifully layered overdubs of his wife, vocalist Mary Ford.

The Beatles: A Multi-Track Revolution

By the 1960s, four-track tape machines were available, but it wasn't until producer George Martin and The Beatles began churning out four- and eight-track masterworks like *Rubber Soul*, *Revolver*, *Sgt. Pepper's Lonely Hearts Club Band*, and *Abbey Road* that the true creative potential of multi-track recording became widely apparent.

Between 1966 and 1970, the Beatles applied all of their energy to studio recording, and in the process, wrote the book on pop music recording. Things that today sound like ordinary elements of pop music—feedback, multiple vocal and guitar overdubs, backwards instruments, tape delays (flange), exotic instruments (sitar)—were used for the first time by Martin and The Beatles as they explored the limits of multi-track recording.

Eno and the Wizard

By the 1970s and '80s, recording on 16-and 24-track tape machines had become the professional standard. Musicians and producers such as Todd Rundgren and Brian Eno quickly took advantage of the expanded track count. Rundgren's 1973 album *Wizard/A True Star* showed the potential of multi-track recording in the hands of an artist with great musical inventiveness. The album features a stirring mix of electric guitars, pianos, organs, synthesizers, vocals, and percussion, strung together with surprising crossfades and creatively applied effects.

continues on next page

INTRODUCTION

A (Very) Brief History of Multi-Track Recording *continued*

Inspired by ambient pioneer John Cage, Brian Eno took multi-track into the realm of chaos theory. Eno used random analog tape loops to create unpredictable ambient soundscapes. His use of randomness to generate sonic atmospherics—best exemplified in his 1975 album *Another Green World* and his *Ambient* series—shows how random sound combinations can create a striking sense of place. Eno's evocative multi-track production has inspired a generation of musicians and producers across many genres of music, from rock and psychedelia to hip-hop and trance.

Today, recording on 24-track analog tape is still considered an excellent, if expensive, way to record.

Digital Audio: Bringing the Studio Home

Recording audio to a computer hard disk is now commonplace in professional studios. Perhaps the most important innovation of hard-disk recording is the ability to edit audio using a graphic interface. Computer editing has given musicians, engineers, and producers new freedom to move, shape, and rearrange sounds in virtually unlimited combinations.

Advances in digital recording have also led to an explosion in the number of home-based recording studios (often called *project studios*). Now anyone with a home computer can take advantage of the once prohibitively expensive features of recording studios, including effects processing and mix automation.

Part I:
Getting Started
with Pro Tools LE

Setting Up Your Pro Tools LE System

1

In this chapter, I'll introduce you to Digidesign's rapidly expanding line of Pro Tools LE hardware systems, including Digi 002, Digi 002 Rack, Mbox, Digi 001, and Audiomedia III. I'll cover each system's hardware specs, as well as basic hard drive and memory requirements. I'll also touch on the capabilities of Pro Tools 6 LE software, including how many channels of recording and playback the software supports with each system.

If you're using Pro Tools Free, which doesn't require any hardware, skip ahead to *Chapter 2: Software Basics*. At press time, Digidesign claims to have no plans for a free version of Pro Tools 6. For more information on Pro Tools Free, see the Digidesign Web site at www.digidesign.com.

Understanding Pro Tools LE Hardware Systems

Pro Tools LE is the software component of Digidesign's entry- to mid-level hard-disk recording systems. Pro Tools LE systems are economical and easy to set up, making them well suited for home and project studios. Unlike Digidesign's pro-level TDM systems (which have their own processing chips), Pro Tools LE systems use the host computer's CPU for all processing tasks. As a result, the number of tracks available during a Pro Tools LE session depends on the host computer's processing speed.

Each Pro Tools LE hardware system offers a unique audio interface with different *I/O* (input and output) options. All Pro Tools LE hardware systems require Pro Tools LE software. Pro Tools LE hardware systems include the following:

Digi 002: Digi 002 is a FireWire-based Pro Tools LE system, with its own mixing board–like control surface. The system features four built-in mic preamps, eight channels of analog I/O, eight channels of ADAT optical I/O, and two channels of S/PDIF digital I/O. Digi 002 supports sample rates up to 96kHz.

Digi 002 Rack: Digi 002 Rack is a rack-mountable version of Digi 002, without the control surface. The unit's compact, FireWire-based design makes it suitable for live situations or small project studios. Like the original, the Digi 002 Rack has four built-in mic preamps, eight channels of analog I/O, eight channels of ADAT optical I/O, and two channels of S/PDIF digital I/O, and supports sample rates up to 96kHz.

Digi 001: Digi 001 consists of an audio interface and a PCI card. The system includes two built-in mic preamps, eight channels of analog I/O, eight channels of ADAT optical I/O, and two channels of S/PDIF digital I/O.

Mbox: Mbox is a two-channel digital audio interface for USB computers. It includes two built-in Focusrite mic preamps, two channels of analog I/O, and two channels of S/PDIF digital I/O. Mbox also includes two analog line inserts for outboard effects processing.

Audiomedia III: Audiomedia III is a PCI card that offers two channels of analog I/O and two channels of S/PDIF digital I/O. The card, which was sold both separately and with Digidesign's Toolbox systems, has been discontinued, yet it remains popular with home studio owners. Audiomedia III does not include a separate audio interface; thus, a separate mixer or mic preamp is recommended.

Table 1.1 shows the capabilities of each Pro Tools LE system.

Table 1.1

Pro Tools LE System Capabilities

SYSTEM TYPE	MONO TRACKS OF SIMULTANEOUS PLAYBACK	NUMBER OF RECORDING/ PLAYBACK CHANNELS	A/D CONVERSION	D/A CONVERSION
Digi 002 (and Digi 002 Rack)	32	up to 18 in/18 out (at 48kHz), 10 in/10 out (at 96kHz)	24-bit	24-bit
Digi 001	32 (Pro Tools 6.0 or higher)	up to 18 in/18 out	24-bit	24-bit
Mbox	32 (Pro Tools 6.0 or higher)	up to 2 in/2 out	24-bit	24-bit
Audiomedia III	32 (Pro Tools 6.0 or higher)	up to 4 in/4 out	18-bit	18-bit

System Requirements

Recording digital audio requires lots of processing power. Because Pro Tools LE systems rely on the host computer's CPU for all processing tasks, you'll want the fastest computer possible. The faster your computer, the more tracks of audio you can record and the more real-time effects you can add to a mix.

Running Pro Tools 6 LE Systems on Mac OS X

On Macintosh computers, Pro Tools 6 LE systems require Mac OS X. Thus, to run a Pro Tools 6 LE system, you'll need a qualified Macintosh computer running Mac OS X, as follows:

To run Digi 002 and Digi 002 Rack on Mac OS X:

You need one of the following:

- Apple Power Mac G4 (AGP Graphics, Single and Dual Processor models)
- Apple PowerBook G4
- iMac G4 (LCD Flat Screen)
- iBook ("Ice White" Dual-USB Models)

Plus the following:

- Pro Tools LE 6.02 (or later)
- Mac OS 10.2.5 or 10.2.6
- 384 MB RAM minimum (512 MB recommended)
- CD-ROM drive
- Color Monitor (1024 X 768 minimum)
- Apple QuickTime 6.1
- Qualified ATA/IDE or FireWire disk drive(s) (recommended)

To run Digi 001 and Audiomedia III on Mac OS X:

You need:

- Apple Power Mac G4 (AGP Graphics, Single and Dual Processor models)

Plus the following:

- Pro Tools LE 6.01 (or later)
- Mac OS 10.2.3, 10.2.4, 10.2.5, or 10.2.6
- 384 MB RAM minimum (512 MB recommended)
- CD-ROM drive
- Color Monitor (1024 X 768 minimum)
- Apple QuickTime 6.0 or 6.1
- Qualified ATA/IDE, SCSI, or FireWire disk drive(s)
- One available PCI slot

To run Mbox on Mac OS X:

You need one of the following:

- Apple Power Mac G4 (AGP Graphics, Single and Dual Processor models)
- Apple PowerBook G4
- iMac G4 (LCD Flat Screen)
- iBook ("Ice White" Dual-USB Models)

Plus the following:

- Pro Tools LE 6.01 (or later)
- Mac OS 10.2.3, 10.2.4, 10.2.5, or 10.2.6
- 384 MB RAM minimum (512 MB recommended)
- CD-ROM drive
- Color Monitor (1024 X 768 minimum)
- Apple QuickTime 6.0 or 6.1
- Qualified ATA/IDE, SCSI, or FireWire disk drive(s)
- One available built-in USB port

Memory and Disk Matters

Recording multiple tracks of 24-bit digital audio can devour hard drive space. For instance, a mono audio track recorded at 24-bit resolution and 44.1kHz sample rate consumes 7.5 MB of RAM per minute; the same track recorded at 16-bit, 44.1kHz consumes 5 MB per minute. **Table 1.2** shows how quickly your disk can fill up with audio files.

If you're strapped for disk space, consider recording at 16-bit resolution. Otherwise, acquire additional hard drives for your system.

Up to Speed

Make sure you use the fastest drive possible. A slow hard drive will limit the number of tracks you can record and the quality of audio playback. When selecting a hard drive, be sure it meets the following requirements:

◆ ATA/IDE, SCSI, or FireWire drive

◆ 3-MB data transfer rate (minimum)

◆ 7,200-rpm drive spin speed

◆ 10-ms seek time (minimum average)

For optimal SCSI performance, consider getting an Ultra Wide SCSI drive with an Ultra Wide SCSI accelerator card.

Managing Hard Drive Space

It's important to efficiently manage your hard drive space. You don't want to run out of space in the middle of a session, or worse, in the midst of recording a live track.

Pro Tools' Disk Space window can help you manage your hard drive space. When you complete a session, use the Compact function to keep your audio files lean. For more on compacting files, see *Chapter 8: File Management Basics*.

The RAM Rule

Having adequate RAM helps ensure a smooth running system. Make sure you have the minimum amounts recommended—and consider adding more. Remember, you can never have too much RAM.

Table 1.2

Hard Drive Space Requirements

# OF TRACKS, LENGTH	16-BIT/44.1KHZ	16-BIT/48KHZ	24-BIT/44.1KHZ	24-BIT/48KHZ	24-BIT/96KHZ
1 track (mono), 1 minute	5 MB	5.5 MB	7.5 MB	8.2 MB	17.2 MB
2 tracks (stereo), 5 minutes	50 MB	55 MB	75 MB	83 MB	172 MB
24 tracks, 1 minute	120 MB	132 MB	180 MB	198 MB	412.8 MB
24 tracks, 5 minutes	600 MB	662 MB	900 MB	991 MB	2064 MB
24 tracks, 60 minutes	7 GB	7.8 GB	10.5 GB	11.6 GB	24.2 GB

Running Pro Tools 6.1 LE Systems on Windows XP

With the release of Pro Tools 6.1, you can now run Pro Tools LE systems on Windows XP. (Pro Tools LE 6.1 does not support Windows 98, Me, 2000, NT, 95, or 3.1).

To run Digi 002 and Digi 002 Rack on Windows XP:

You need one of the following:

◆ Intel Pentium 4 or Xeon (2GHz or faster)

◆ AMD AthlonXP 2000+ CPU (or faster)

Plus the following:

◆ Windows XP Professional or Home Edition (Service Pack 1 required)

◆ Pro Tools LE 6.1 for Windows XP

◆ 384 MB RAM (512 MB or higher recommended)

◆ CD-ROM drive

◆ Color monitor (1024 X 768 minimum)

◆ Apple QuickTime 6.0.2 (or higher)

◆ A 1394 ("FireWire") controller/interface

◆ Qualified ATA/IDE, SCSI, or FireWire disk drive

To run Digi 001 and Audiomedia III on Windows XP:

You need one of the following:

◆ Intel Pentium 4 or Xeon (1.3 GHz or faster)

◆ Intel Pentium III (500 MHz or faster)

◆ AMD AthlonXP (all speeds supported)

◆ AMD Athlon Thunderbird (all speeds supported)

Plus the following:

◆ Windows XP Professional or Home Edition (Service Pack 1 required)

◆ Pro Tools LE 6.1 for Windows XP

◆ 384 MB RAM (512 MB or higher recommended)

◆ Color monitor (1024 X 768 minimum)

◆ CD-ROM drive

◆ Apple QuickTime 6.0.2 (or higher)

◆ 1394 ("FireWire") controller/interface

◆ Qualified ATA/IDE, SCSI, or FireWire disk drive

◆ One available PCI Slot

SYSTEM REQUIREMENTS

To run Mbox on Windows XP:

You need one of the following:

◆ Intel Pentium 4 or Xeon
(1.3 GHz or faster)

◆ Intel Pentium III (500 MHz or faster)

◆ AMD AthlonXP (all speeds supported)

◆ AMD Athlon Thunderbird
(all speeds supported)

Plus the following:

◆ Windows XP Professional or Home
Edition (Service Pack 1 required)

◆ Pro Tools LE 6.1 for Windows XP

◆ 384 MB RAM (512 MB or higher
recommended)

◆ CD-ROM drive

◆ Color monitor (1024 X 768 minimum)

◆ Apple QuickTime 6.0.2 (or higher)

◆ Qualified ATA/IDE, SCSI, or FireWire disk

◆ One available built-in USB port

For additional information on requirements
for running Pro Tools LE on Windows XP, see
Digidesign's Web site at
www.digidesign.com.

About Pro Tools 5 LE Systems on Mac OS 9 and Windows

If you're using Mac OS 9 or versions of
Windows other than Windows XP, you can
still run Pro Tools LE systems, in many
cases, with Pro Tools 5 LE software.

Connecting System Hardware

Before you can begin recording, you must properly connect your Pro Tools LE system to your computer. Digi 001 and Audiomedia III systems also require installation of a PCI card. For instructions on installing PCI cards, see the Getting Started guide provided with your system.

To connect Digi 002 and Digi 002 Rack:

1. Connect the FireWire cable that came with your system into either of the two FireWire ports on the back panel of the Digi 002.

2. Do one of the following, depending on your system configuration:

   ▲ Connect the other end of the FireWire cable into an available FireWire port on your computer.

   ▲ Plug the other end of the FireWire cable into an available FireWire port on a FireWire hard drive connected to your computer.

To connect Mbox:

◆ Connect a USB cable to the USB port on the Mbox and to any available USB port on your Macintosh.

To connect Digi 001:

1. Insert the Digi 001 PCI card into an open PCI slot inside your Macintosh or Windows computer.

2. Connect the card to the Digi 001 I/O box interface using the included Digi 001 cable.

To connect Audiomedia III:

◆ Insert the Audiomedia III PCI card into an open PCI slot inside your Macintosh or Windows computer.

For more information on installing system hardware, see the documentation accompanying your Pro Tools LE system.

For instructions on connecting your studio to your Pro Tools LE system, see *Appendix A: Connecting Your Studio.*

Installing Pro Tools LE Software

Now that you've connected your Pro Tools LE hardware, you're ready to install your Pro Tools LE software.

If you're a Macintosh user, insert the Pro Tools LE installation CD and double-click the Install Pro Tools LE icon. Follow the on-screen instructions.

If you're a Windows user, insert the Pro Tools LE installation CD, open the Installer folder, and double-click the Setup program.

For detailed instructions on installing and configuring Pro Tools LE on a Macintosh or Windows computer, see the *Getting Started* guide that came with your system.

SOFTWARE BASICS

Now that you've connected your Pro Tools LE hardware, you're no doubt itching to lay down some tracks. But first, you'll need to familiarize yourself with some Pro Tools LE software basics and configure your system.

This chapter will explain Pro Tools sessions. I'll introduce you to the key elements of a session, including session files, audio files, audio and MIDI tracks, waveforms and regions, playlists, channels, and I/O Setup.

Lastly, I'll show you how to configure your Pro Tools LE hardware and allocate your computer's CPU resources for optimal performance.

Understanding Sessions

Figure 2.1 A Pro Tools LE session file icon.

A Pro Tools *session* is the virtual workspace in which you record audio. Think of it as a recording studio inside your computer: It contains all the elements you need to record, edit, process, mix, master, and store audio recordings.

Before you begin recording in Pro Tools, it's a good idea to acquaint yourself with the following basic elements of a Pro Tools session.

What is a session file?

When you start a new Pro Tools project, you create a new *session file*. A session file maps all the elements in a session, including audio files, MIDI data, edits, and mix information (**Figure 2.1**). A session file is stored in a Session folder.

You can edit a session and save it as a new session file. This lets you save multiple versions of a project, as well as easily back up your editing and mixing work. For more information on Pro Tools sessions, see *Chapter 4: Starting a New Session.*

Pro Tools File Types

Pro Tools generates several file types, which you can quickly import and export between sessions. The file types include:

◆ **Session file:** This file stores all session information including audio files, MIDI data, edits, and mix information.

◆ **Audio file:** Audio recorded into a session is stored as an audio file. You can import and export audio in a number of file formats (see the *Compatible Audio File Formats* sidebar).

◆ **MIDI file:** This file stores MIDI data recorded on MIDI tracks in a Pro Tools session.

◆ **I/O Settings file:** You can import and export I/O configurations as I/O Settings files for use in future sessions.

◆ **Fade file:** Fades and crossfades for a session are saved as Fade files. They are stored in the Fade Files folder inside the Session folder.

◆ **Plug-in Settings files:** You can save the current settings of any RTAS plug-in and apply them to future uses of that plug-in.

Figure 2.2 Audio file icons.

Figure 2.3 An Audio Files folder inside a Session folder.

What is an audio file?

When you record audio into a Pro Tools session, it's saved on your hard disk as an *audio file* (**Figure 2.2**). Audio files are stored in the Audio Files folder within the Session folder (**Figure 2.3**).

Audio files are listed in the Audio Regions list and are displayed as waveforms on separate tracks within the Pro Tools Edit window (**Figure 2.4**).

Figure 2.4 Audio files are represented by waveforms. The Audio Regions list (right side of Edit window) shows session audio files.

Compatible Audio File Formats

Pro Tools LE lets you record audio in these file formats:

◆ Macintosh: SDII, WAV, and AIFF

◆ Windows: WAV and AIFF

Pro Tools LE also lets you import and export audio in these formats:

◆ Macintosh: SDII, SDI, WAV, MP3, and Sound Resource (AIFL)

◆ Windows: SDII, SDI, WAV, AIFF, MP3, and WMA (Windows Media)

For more information on audio files, see *Chapter 4: Starting a New Session* and *Part III: Audio File Management*.

What are audio and MIDI tracks?

A Pro Tools *track* is where audio, MIDI, and automation data is recorded and edited. When you record audio into a session, it's displayed as a waveform on an *audio track* in the Edit window (**Figure 2.5**).

Similarly, when you record MIDI into Pro Tools, the MIDI data is displayed on a *MIDI track* in the Edit window (**Figure 2.6**).

Audio tracks in Pro Tools LE can be mono or stereo. (Pro Tools TDM systems also support multi-channel, surround-sound formats.)

Figure 2.5 An audio track in the Edit window.

Figure 2.6 A MIDI track in the Edit window.

What are waveforms and regions?

Audio files are displayed as *waveforms* in the Pro Tools Edit window (**Figure 2.7**). A waveform is a graph of an audio signal's sound pressure level (in decibels) versus time.

A waveform's appearance will vary depending on the audio source. Drums, for instance, will have sharp peaks and valleys that represent the sudden attack and decay of a drum hit (**Figure 2.8**). Instruments with softer attacks and longer decays, such as keyboards or vocals, will generally have smoother waveform shapes (**Figure 2.9**).

Figure 2.7 Audio waveforms in the Edit window.

Figure 2.8 A waveform of a drum part. The sharp peaks and valleys indicate the fast attack and decay of a drum hit.

Figure 2.9 A waveform of a keyboard part. Its smooth shape indicates the slow attack and decay of a keyboard.

A region is a visual representation—usually a waveform—of a parent audio file stored on disk. A region can be any length—from an entire audio file to a single verse, hook, bar, or note. You can create a region by selecting a segment of a larger region in a track (**Figure 2.10**). A selected region points to that segment of the original audio or MIDI data on your hard disk.

Once you create a region, you can perform various operations on it. For example, you can easily copy, loop, and arrange regions in playlists to create new song structures (**Figure 2.11**).

Whole file audio region

Selected audio region

Figure 2.10 A selected audio region. You can create smaller regions from larger ones.

Figure 2.11 Use the Duplicate or Repeat command to copy an audio region multiple times and create a drum loop.

Figure 2.12 The Playlist Selector pop-up menu.

Figure 2.13 An audio channel strip in the Mix window.

What is a playlist?

A *playlist* is a group of regions arranged on a single audio or MIDI track. You can create several different playlists on a given track and use the Playlist Selector pop-up menu to choose which one to play (**Figure 2.12**). You can then easily switch between them on the fly during a mix.

A playlist can include a single region or multiple regions. It can include the same sound, such as regions from a vocal or guitar part, or different sounds, such as individual sound effects.

✔ Tip

- Playlists can help you save hard disk space. By using several copies of an audio region in a playlist, you can repeat a section of an audio file multiple times without taking up additional disk space.

What is a channel?

The term *channel* has two separate but related meanings in Pro Tools. The first refers to the actual physical inputs and outputs of the Pro Tools system. For example, the Digi 001 I/O box has 18 channels each of input and output. (See *Chapter 1: Setting Up Your Pro Tools LE System.*)

A channel also refers to a mixer strip in the Pro Tools Mix window, which is called a *channel strip* (**Figure 2.13**). Channel strips let you control the mix functions of a track, such as level, mute, pan, and sends. Channel strips will vary slightly depending on whether the track is an audio track, MIDI track, auxiliary input, or master fader.

What is an I/O Setup?

The way that audio is routed in, out, and through a recording system is called a *signal path*. In Pro Tools you can create many different configurations of a signal path. Each configuration is called an I/O Setup.

The I/O Setup dialog box (**Figure 2.14**) lets you create I/O Setups. You can assign track inputs and outputs, inserts, and internal buses for routing to internal plug-ins or external hardware effects.

You can also export and import I/O Setup configurations as I/O Settings files. This lets you save your favorite I/O Setups and reuse them in future sessions.

✔ Tip

■ Pro Tools LE includes default I/O Setups, so you can quickly begin recording. For more information on I/O Setup, see *Chapter 4: Starting a New Session*.

Figure 2.14 The I/O Setup dialog box.

Figure 2.15 Choose Playback Engine from the Setups menu.

Figure 2.16 The Playback Engine dialog box.

Figure 2.17 Select an audio buffer size for host processing tasks from the H/W Buffer Size pop-up menu.

Configuring Your Pro Tools 6 LE System

When you first launch Pro Tools LE, you'll need to allocate your host computer's CPU resources, and select Pro Tools LE hardware settings from within the program.

For information on launching Pro Tools LE, see the *Getting Started Guide* that comes with your Pro Tools LE system.

Allocating CPU resources

Pro Tools LE systems use the host computer's CPU to process all audio recording, playback, mixing, and effects processing. The program provides the following adjustable parameters, which let you allocate your CPU's resources for optimal performance of these tasks.

Hardware Buffer Size

The Hardware Buffer Size (H/W Buffer Size) determines the amount of hardware cache used for host processing tasks, including audio and MIDI track playback, mix automation, and RTAS plug-in processing. Higher buffer sizes allow for more audio processing and RTAS effects. Lower buffers decrease monitoring latency.

To set the Hardware Buffer Size:

1. Choose Setups > Playback Engine (**Figure 2.15**).

   The Playback Engine dialog box appears (**Figure 2.16**).

2. From the H/W Buffer Size pop-up menu, select the audio buffer size (in samples) (**Figure 2.17**).

3. Click OK.

CPU Usage Limit

The CPU Usage Limit controls the percentage of CPU resources allocated to Pro Tools host processing tasks. Higher CPU Usage Limit settings reserve more processing power for Pro Tools and are useful for playing back large sessions or adding more RTAS effects.

To set the CPU Usage Limit:

1. Choose Setups > Playback Engine.

   The Playback Engine dialog box appears.

2. From the CPU Usage Limit pop-up menu, select the percentage of CPU processing you want to allocate to Pro Tools (**Figure 2.18**).

3. Click OK.

DAE Playback Buffer Size

Digidesign Audio Engine (DAE) is Digidesign's real-time operating system for digital recording systems. Running in the background and directing traffic between Pro Tools and the computer's CPU, DAE provides much of the digital recording, effects processing, mix automation, and MIDI functionality of Pro Tools.

The DAE Playback Buffer Size determines the amount of memory allocated within DAE to manage disk buffers. Smaller buffer sizes can improve playback and recording initiation speed, but performance can become unreliable on slower hard drives. Large buffer sizes will let you make more edits but may cause time lags to occur before playback or recording begins.

To set the DAE Playback Buffer Size

1. Choose Setups > Playback Engine.

   The Playback Engine Dialog Box appears.

2. From the DAE Playback Buffer pop-up menu, select a playback buffer size (**Figure 2.19**).

3. Click OK.

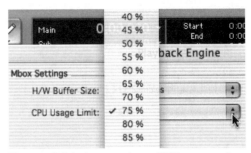

Figure 2.18 Select a percentage of CPU resources to allocate to host-processing tasks.

Figure 2.19 Select a playback buffer size from the DAE Buffer Size pop-up menu.

Figure 2.20 Choose Hardware Setup from the Setups menu.

Figure 2.21 The Digi 001 Hardware Setup Dialog box.

Figure 2.22 Select a sample rate from the Sample Rate pop-up menu.

Configuring system hardware

The Hardware Setup dialog box in the Setups menu lets you select your system's default sample rate, clock source, and input format. (Input format options vary somewhat, depending on which Pro Tools LE hardware system you are using.)

Default Sample Rate

The Hardware Setup dialog box displays the current session's default sample rate. You cannot change the default sample rate of an open session. The default sample rate setting is available in the Hardware Setup dialog box only when no session is open (after the Pro Tools application has been launched).

You can also set the default sample rate via the New Session dialog box when you create a new session.

To change the default Sample Rate:

1. Close the current session. If necessary, launch Pro Tools LE from the application icon. Make sure no session is open.

2. Choose Setups > Hardware Setup (**Figure 2.20**).

   The Hardware Setup Dialog box appears (**Figure 2.21**).

3. From the sample rate pop-up menu, select a sample rate (Digi 002, Digi 002 Rack, and Digi 001) (**Figure 2.22**).

   or

   Select the sample rate by clicking the desired Sample Rate button (Mbox) (**Figure 2.23**).

4. Click OK.

Figure 2.23 Click the desired sample rate in the Mbox Hardware Setup dialog box.

CONFIGURING YOUR PRO TOOLS 6 LE SYSTEM

Clock Source

The Hardware Setup dialog box lets you select a Clock Source for your system. When recording analog signal directly into Pro Tools, you'll generally want to use Internal as the clock source.

When recording digital signal into Pro Tools from an external digital device, you'll generally want use the external digital device as the clock source.

All Pro Tools LE hardware systems accept SPDIF/RCA external digital devices as the clock source. Additionally, Digi 002 and Digi 002 Rack accept ADAT Optical (or "Lightpipe") and Optical S/PDIF external digital devices as the clock source.

Figure 2.24 Select the desired clock source in the Clock Source pop-up menu. Use Internal when recording analog signal into Pro Tools.

To select the Clock Source:

1. Choose Setups > Hardware Setup.
   The Hardware Setup dialog box appears.

2. From the Clock Source pop-up menu, select the desired clock source (Digi 002, Digi 002 Rack, and Digi 001) (**Figure 2.24**).
   or
   Select the clock source by clicking the desired Clock Source button (Mbox).

3. Click OK.

Figure 2.25 The Digi 002, Digi 002 Rack, and Digi 001 Hardware Setup dialog box lets you set ADAT optical, Optical SPDIF, and SPDIF/RCA digital input formats.

Figure 2.26 The Digi 001 Hardware Setup dialog box lets you adjust input gain on Channels 3–8, and insert a high-pass filter (for reducing low-end noise) on Input Channels 1–2.

Input Formats

The Hardware Setup dialog box lets you select the audio input format for your system. The input format options available in the Hardware Setup dialog box differ, depending on the Pro Tools LE system.

When recording from a digital source into Pro Tools, it is necessary to select the appropriate digital input format. The Digi 002, Digi 002 Rack, and Digi 001 Hardware Setup dialog box lets you select ADAT optical, Optical SPDIF, and SPDIF/RCA (**Figure 2.25**). Selecting an input format is only necessary when connecting a digital input to these systems.

The Digi 001 Hardware Setup dialog also lets you adjust the input gain on Analog Inputs 3–8 and insert a high-pass filter on Mic/Line Inputs 1–2 (**Figure 2.26**).

If you're an Mbox user, you'll need to choose between analog or digital input formats. The Mbox Hardware Setup dialog box lets you set Input Channels 1–2 to Analog or SPDIF/RCA digital format.

To set the Input Format:

1. Choose Setups > Hardware Setup.
   The Hardware Setup dialog box appears.

2. When recording from a digital source, select the desired digital input format (Digi 002, Digi 002 Rack, and Digi 001) (**Figure 2.27**).

   or

   In the Channel 1–2 Input box, select either analog or SPDIF/RCA digital format (Mbox) (**Figure 2.28**).

3. Click OK.

For more information on Input Formats, see the *Getting Started Guide* that came with your Pro Tools LE system.

Figure 2.27 When recording from a digital source into Digi 002, Digi 002 Rack, or Digi 001, select the appropriate digital input format.

Figure 2.28 When using Mbox, set Channel 1–2 inputs to either Analog or SPDIF/RCA digital input formats.

THE MIX AND
EDIT WINDOWS

3

Most of the action in Pro Tools takes place in two main windows: the Mix window and the Edit window. Learning the layout and features of these windows will help you master Pro Tools' recording and editing features.

In this chapter, I'll introduce you to the main features of the Mix window, including channel strips, track controls, sends, inserts, and inputs and outputs.

You'll learn the layout of the Edit window, too. I'll point out important editing features such as Zoom buttons, Edit modes, Edit tools, and the Audio Regions list. The latter is an invaluable tool for managing your audio files.

The Mix Window

If you're familiar with an analog mixing board, you'll recognize the Pro Tools Mix window (**Figure 3.1**). It looks just like a hard-wired mixer, but it's more flexible.

Figure 3.1 The Pro Tools Mix window.

Each track in a Pro Tools session is displayed in the Mix window as a channel strip (**Figure 3.2**). Channel strips have controls for inserts, sends, inputs and outputs, volume, panning, mute, solo, automation, and record-enable.

There are four types of channel strips: audio tracks, auxiliary inputs, master faders, and MIDI tracks (**Figure 3.3**). All channel strips except MIDI tracks can be mono or stereo (**Figure 3.4**).

Audio track channel strip *Auxiliary input channel strip* *Master fader channel strip* *MIDI track channel strip*

Stereo channel strip

Mono channel strip

Figure 3.2 An audio track channel strip in the Mix window.

Figure 3.3 Channel strips. Each track type (audio, auxiliary input, master fader, and MIDI) has a slightly different channel strip.

Figure 3.4 Mono and stereo audio track channel strips.

THE MIX WINDOW

Audio track channel strips

Audio track channel strips (**Figure 3.5**) provide controls for audio volume, pan, solo, mute, record-enable, and automation. They also let you route channel inputs and outputs, sends, and inserts.

Inserts view

Sends view

Input selector

Output selector

Automation Mode selector

Pan slider

Pan indicator

Solo/Mute buttons

Record-Enable button

Voice selector

Output Window button

Volume fader

Level meter

Group ID indicator

Track Type indicator

Volume/Peak/Delay indicator

Track name

Track Comments view

Figure 3.5 An audio track channel strip.

THE MIX WINDOW

Figure 3.6 Select File > New Track.

To create an audio track channel strip:

1. Select File > New Track, or Shift-Command-N (Mac) or Shift-Control-N (Windows) (**Figure 3.6**).

   The New Track dialog box appears (**Figure 3.7**).

2. Select Mono or Stereo from the pop-up menu (**Figure 3.8**).

3. Select Audio Track from the pop-up menu (**Figure 3.9**).

4. Enter the number of tracks and click Create.

Figure 3.7 The New Track dialog box.

Figure 3.8 Select Mono or Stereo from the pop-up menu.

Figure 3.9 Select Audio Track from the pop-up menu.

MIDI track channel strips

MIDI track channel strips (**Figure 3.10**) provide controls for volume, pan, solo, mute, and automation. You can also make MIDI patch assignments and MIDI channel assignments through this strip.

To create a MIDI track channel strip:

1. Select File > New Track.
   The New Track dialog box appears.

2. Select MIDI Track from the pop-up menu (**Figure 3.11**).

3. Enter the number of tracks and click Create.

MIDI Input selector
MIDI Output selector
Automation Mode selector
MIDI Pan slider
MIDI Pan Indicator
Solo/Mute buttons
Record-Enable button
Output Window button
MIDI volume fader
MIDI velocity meter
Group ID indicator
Track Type indicator
MIDI Volume indicator
Track name
Track Comments view

Figure 3.10 A MIDI track channel strip.

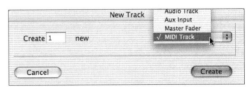

Figure 3.11 Select MIDI Track from the pop-up menu.

THE MIX WINDOW

Auxiliary input channel strips

Auxiliary input channel strips (**Figure 3.12**) are similar to audio track channel strips, but they accept input only from internal bus or hardware sources.

You can use an auxiliary input to create an *effects loop*, in which audio is routed to an auxiliary input, and an effect (such as EQ, compression, or reverb) is added. The *effects return* is then routed to the main mix. For more information on effects loops, see *Chapter 14: Adding Effects to a Mix*.

You can also use auxiliary inputs to create submixes. This lets you consolidate multiple tracks of audio onto one channel strip. For more information on submixes, see *Chapter 13: Mixing Basics*.

To create an auxiliary input channel strip:

1. Select File > New Track.
   The New Track dialog box appears.

2. Select mono or stereo from the pop-up menu.

3. Select Auxiliary Input from the pop-up menu (**Figure 3.13**).

4. Enter the number of auxiliary inputs and click Create.

Figure 3.12 An auxiliary input channel strip.

Figure 3.13 Select Auxiliary Input from the pop-up menu.

Master fader channel strips

Master fader channel strips (**Figure 3.14**) let you control the output level of the main mix. You can also use them to control output levels for submixes, bus paths, sends, and inserts.

To create a master fader channel strip:

1. Select File > New Track.

   The New Track dialog box appears.

2. Select Mono or Stereo from the pop-up menu.

3. Select Master Fader from the pop-up menu (**Figure 3.15**).

4. Enter the number of master faders and click Create.

✔ Tips

■ The inserts section of a master fader is always post-fader. This means that the inserts occur in the signal path after the track's fader. (The inserts section of audio tracks and auxiliary inputs is always pre-fader.)

■ Post-fader inserts are convenient for adding an effect, such as an aural exciter or dither, to the main mix. But avoid the temptation to add compression or other dynamic effects to the main mix. Compression can make a mix sound boxy, and it can also remove audio information that a mastering engineer may want to more precisely sculpt using EQ and other effects. Compression can also change the overall level of a mix and create audible inconsistencies between mixes.

Post-fader insert

Figure 3.14 A stereo master fader channel strip.

Figure 3.15 Select Master Fader from the pop-up menu.

THE MIX WINDOW

Inserts view

Sends view

Track controls (always open)

Track Comments view

Figure 3.16 The view of a fully expanded channel strip.

Viewing channel strips

You can expand or contract the view of a channel strip according to your needs (**Figure 3.16**). A fully expanded channel strip displays:

◆ Track controls (always open)

◆ Sends

◆ Inserts

◆ Track comments

To view an expanded channel strip:

◆ Select Display > Mix Window Shows > All (**Figure 3.17**).

To view a narrow channel strip:

◆ Select Display > Narrow Mix Window (**Figure 3.18**).

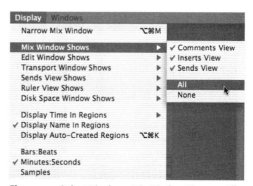

Figure 3.17 Select Display > Mix Window Shows > All.

Figure 3.18 Select Display > Narrow Mix Window.

Track controls

Channel strips in the Mix window offer track controls for recording and playing back audio and MIDI tracks (**Figure 3.19**). Audio and MIDI track channel strips have the following track controls:

Input Selectors: Input selectors let you route audio inputs or internal buses to an audio track or auxiliary input (**Figure 3.20**). Available inputs depend on your I/O Setup configuration.

Output Selectors: Output selectors let you route audio to any available audio output or internal bus (**Figure 3.21**). Available outputs depend on your I/O Setup configuration.

Automation Mode: The Automation Mode selector lets you control how track automation is written and played back. You can choose from Auto Off, Auto Read, Auto Write, Auto Touch, and Auto Latch modes. For more information on automation modes, see *Chapter 15: Automating a Mix*.

Pan Slider: The Pan slider controls the balance of a track between left and right output channels. Pan sliders appear on the channel strips of stereo tracks, or mono tracks routed to a stereo output.

Pan Indicator: The Pan Indicator shows you the left and right output balance of a track. Pan values range from <100 (full left) to >100 (full right).

Solo: The Solo button mutes all tracks except the soloed track. This lets you monitor a track by itself. You can solo multiple tracks simultaneously.

Mute: The Mute button silences a track. You can mute multiple tracks simultaneously.

Record-Enable: The Record-Enable button puts audio and MIDI tracks into Record-Ready mode. Once a track is record-enabled, click the Record button, and then the Play button in the Transport window to start recording.

Figure 3.19 Track controls for an audio track channel strip in the Mix window.

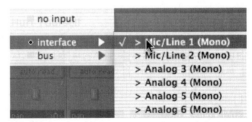

Figure 3.20 Input selectors let you route audio input.

Figure 3.21 Output selectors let you route audio output.

THE MIX WINDOW

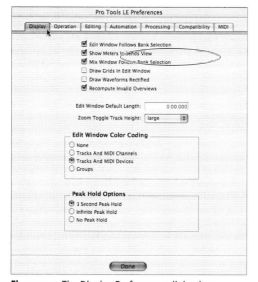

Figure 3.22 Select Setups > Preferences.

Figure 3.23 The Display Preferences dialog box.

Figure 3.24 Choose a Peak Hold option.

Voice Selector: In Pro Tools 6 LE, the Voice selector lets you toggle between Auto voice selection and Off. When set to Auto voice selection, Pro Tools automatically assigns voices to a track. When set to Off, a track's voice assignment remains unchanged.

Volume Fader: The Volume fader controls the monitor volume of a track in playback, as well as the monitor volume of a track in record.

Level Meter: The Level meter displays an audio signal's volume level as it's recorded to the hard disk. It also displays a signal's volume level as it's played back from the hard disk.

The color of the Level meter light indicates the status of the audio signal: Green indicates nominal (safe) levels, yellow indicates pre-clipping, and red indicates clipping.

Volume/Peak/Delay Indicator: The Volume/Peak/Delay indicator shows the current volume input level, the most recent peak playback level, and on TDM systems, the delay time in samples incurred by a TDM plug-in on that channel. Command-click (Macintosh) or Control-click (Windows) the indicator to switch between level, peak, and delay.

Track Name: When you create a track with the New Track command, it's automatically given a track name.

✔ Tips

■ Use the Pro Tools Preferences window to adjust a Peak Hold setting for the Track Level meter. This will help you monitor input and output levels. Select Setups > Preferences (**Figure 3.22**). Click the Display tab (**Figure 3.23**). Choose from three Peak Hold settings: 3 Second Peak Hold, Infinite Peak Hold, or No Peak Hold (**Figure 3.24**).

continues on next page

THE MIX WINDOW

■ Pro Tools remembers both record and playback fader levels for each audio track. Linking these faders in the Pro Tools Preferences window will keep them from changing position when you record-enable a track. Select Setups > Preferences, click the Operation tab, and then select the Link Record and Play Faders checkbox (**Figure 3.25**).

Figure 3.25 Select the Link Record and Play Faders checkbox in the Operation Preferences dialog box.

■ To rename a track, double-click the track name at the bottom of a channel strip. A dialog box appears (**Figure 3.26**). Enter the new track name and click OK.

Figure 3.26 The Rename Track dialog box.

What Are Safe Modes?

You can put certain track controls into Safe mode. This disables the control and protects your work from inadvertent technical mishaps. Safe modes include:

Record Safe: Disables Record-Enable button. To toggle Record Safe mode, Command-click (Macintosh) or Control-click (Windows) the Record-Enable button.

Solo Safe: Disables Solo button. To toggle Solo Safe mode, Command-click (Macintosh) or Control-click (Windows) the Solo button.

Automation Safe: Suspends automation recording. You can toggle outputs, sends, and plug-ins into Automation Safe mode to prevent you from overwriting previously recorded automation (**Figure 3.27**).

Automation Safe button

Figure 3.27 The Automation Safe button prevents you from overwriting previously recorded automation.

The Sends view

Sends let you route audio to an internal bus or external output for effects processing or submixing. The Mix window's Sends view (**Figure 3.28**) lets you assign five mono or stereo sends per audio track or auxiliary input.

Figure 3.28 The Sends view.

To show the Sends view:

◆ Select Display > Mix Window Shows > Sends View.

Output parameters for sends include level, pan, mute, and pre- and post-fader. To control send parameters, you can use either the Sends Output window (**Figure 3.29**) or the individual send controls (**Figure 3.30**) that appear within the Sends view.

To open a Sends Output window:

◆ Click any Send button. This opens a Sends Output window.

To open individual send controls:

1. Select Display > Sends View Shows.

2. Select a send (Send A through Send E) (**Figure 3.31**). Individual send controls appear in the Sends View section.

For more information on Sends, see *Chapter 14: Adding Effects to a Mix*.

Figure 3.29 A Sends Output window.

Figure 3.30 Individual send controls.

Figure 3.31 To display individual send controls, select Display > Sends View Shows. Then select a send (Send A through Send E).

Figure 3.32 The Inserts view.

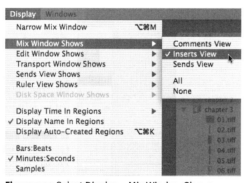

Figure 3.33 Select Display > Mix Window Shows > Inserts View.

Figure 3.34 Click an assigned Insert button to show its Effects Plug-in window.

The Inserts view

Inserts let you add effects on individual channel strips. The Inserts view (**Figure 3.32**) lets you access five pre-fader inserts per audio track or auxiliary input. You can assign internal software effects and external hardware effects to inserts.

To show the Inserts view:

◆ Select Display > Mix Window Shows > Inserts View (**Figure 3.33**).

The Inserts view also gives you access to Effects Plug-in windows.

To show an Effects Plug-in window:

◆ Click an assigned Insert button (**Figure 3.34**). The assigned Effects Plug-in window opens.

The Track Comments view

The Track Comments view shows any comments entered into the Track Name/ Comments dialog box.

To show the Track Comments view:

◆ Select Display > Mix Window Shows > Comments View (**Figure 3.35**).

Figure 3.35 To show the Track Comments view, select Display > Mix Window Shows > Comments View.

THE MIX WINDOW

The Show/Hide Tracks list

The Show/Hide Tracks list (**Figure 3.36**) in the Mix window displays the names of all the tracks in the current session. You can show or hide a track by selecting or deselecting it, and you can rearrange tracks by dragging them up or down.

The Show/Hide pop-up menu at the top of the list gives you options for showing or hiding tracks (**Figure 3.37**).

The Mix Groups list

The Mix Groups list (**Figure 3.38**) in the Mix window shows all the groups in a session. You can enable a group by highlighting its name in the list.

The Mix Groups pop-up menu at the top of the list lets you create new groups; display edit groups or mix groups; and suspend or delete groups (**Figure 3.39**).

✔ Tip

■ If a hidden track is part of a group, operations performed on the group will be performed on the hidden track as well. Disable groups with hidden tracks to avoid making unwanted changes. For information on enabling and disabling groups, see *Chapter 5: Working with Tracks.*

Figure 3.36 The Show/Hide Tracks list.

Figure 3.37 The Show/Hide pop-up menu.

Figure 3.38 The Mix Groups list.

Figure 3.39 The Mix Groups pop-up menu.

The Edit Window

The Edit window (**Figure 3.40**) gives you a visual read-out of audio, MIDI, and automation data against a timeline. It also offers tools for selecting, viewing, and arranging this recorded data. In addition, the Edit window features tools for managing audio files and MIDI files.

Zoom buttons   Edit tools   Event Edit area   Location indicators   Grid/Nudge/ Cursor values   Audio Waveform view   Audio Regions list

Edit Mode buttons

Tab to Transients

Link Selections button

Show/Hide Tracks list

Edit Groups list

Audio track

MIDI track

Master fader track

Auxiliary input track

Selected audio region

MIDI Notes view

MIDI Regions list

Volume Automation view

Figure 3.40 The Pro Tools Edit window.

Viewing the Edit window

The Edit window displays the same channel strips as in the Mix window, with a few additional features outlined below. You can expand the Edit window to view the full channel strips, but they are displayed horizontally, not vertically.

To view expanded channel strips in the Edit window:

◆ Select Display > Edit Window Shows > All. The expanded channel strip view appears (**Figure 3.41**).

For more information on channel strips, see *The Mix Window* section earlier in this chapter.

✔ Tips

■ Edit Window channel strips, unlike Mix Window channel strips, include an I/O (Input/Output) View, which shows track input and output assignments. You can hide the I/O View to conserve track viewing space. To show or hide the I/O View: Select Display > Edit Window Shows > I/O View.

■ To toggle between the Mix and Edit windows, press Command-Equal (=) (Macintosh) or Control-Equal (=) (Windows).

Figure 3.41 An expanded channel strip in the Edit window.

Track name button

Playlist Selector button

Record-Enable button

Mute button

Solo button

Track Height Selector button

Track View Selector button

Automation Mode Selector button

Figure 3.42 The Edit window track controls.

Figure 3.43 The Playlist selector.

Figure 3.44 The Track Height selector.

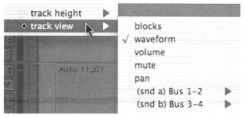

Figure 3.45 The Track View selector.

Track controls

Most of the Edit window's track controls (**Figure 3.42**) are identical to those in the Mix window. For information on Record-Enable, Solo, Mute, Automation Mode Selector, and Track Name, see the Track Controls (Mix Window) section earlier in this chapter.

In addition to the above track controls, the Edit window contains the following:

Playlist Selector: The Playlist selector lets you create and manage multiple *edit playlists* on each track (**Figure 3.43**).

An edit playlist is a snapshot of the current arrangement of regions on a track. Edit playlists give you the flexibility to experiment with region editing ideas. For more information on playlists, see *Chapter 2: Software Basics,* and *Chapter 10: Editing Basics.*

Track Height Selector: The Track Height Selector lets you adjust the vertical size of a track. You can select from Mini, Small, Medium, Large, Jumbo, and Extreme (**Figure 3.44**). In Pro Tools 6, you can now toggle back and forth between track height settings.

Track View Selector: Although you'll mainly use the Waveform view, the Track View Selector lets you see a visual read-out of other track information. On audio tracks you can select from blocks, volume, pan, mute, send level, send mute, and send pan (**Figure 3.45**).

THE EDIT WINDOW

Edit modes

The Edit window's four Edit Mode buttons (**Figure 3.46**) let you choose how regions are moved in the window. You can select from the following modes:

Shuffle: Shuffle mode automatically snaps a region to the end of another region. For instance, if you select an audio region and delete it, the region to the right snaps to the region on the left.

Spot: Spot mode lets you move a selected region to an exact time location. When you move a selected region in Spot mode, the Spot dialog box opens (**Figure 3.47**). This lets you enter a new start time for the selected region.

Slip: Slip mode lets you move regions freely in a track, with few limitations. In Slip mode you can overlap regions or separate regions with space (silence).

Grid: Grid mode lets you snap selected regions to a user-defined time grid.

✔ Tip

■ To switch between edit modes, use the following function keys: F1 (Shuffle), F2 (Slip), F3 (Spot), F4 (Grid).

For more information on Edit modes, see *Chapter 10: Editing Basics.*

Figure 3.46 The Edit Mode buttons.

Figure 3.47 The Spot Mode dialog box. Move a selected region by entering a new start time.

Figure 3.48 The Zoom buttons.

Figure 3.49 Memory Location dialog box. Press Enter on the numeric keypad to set a new memory location.

Zoom buttons

The Edit window's Zoom buttons (**Figure 3.48**) let you zoom quickly in and out of audio and MIDI tracks. Zoom buttons include:

Horizontal Zoom In/Out: Zooms in and out horizontally on a track. Option-click (Macintosh) or Alt-click (Windows) either Horizontal Zoom button to restore the previous zoom level.

Vertical Zoom In/Out (audio): Zooms in and out vertically on audio tracks. Option-click (Macintosh) or Alt-click (Windows) either Vertical Zoom button to restore the previous zoom level.

Vertical Zoom In/Out (MIDI): Zooms in and out vertically on a MIDI track. Option-click (Macintosh) or Alt-click (Windows) either Vertical Zoom button to restore the previous zoom level.

Zoom Presets: You can save up to five horizontal zoom presets. Command-click (Macintosh) or Control-click (Windows) on any Zoom Preset button to save the current horizontal zoom value.

✔ Tip

■ You can save zoom settings in the Memory Location dialog box (**Figure 3.49**) when you enter a memory location. You'll find details for setting memory locations in *Chapter 10: Editing Basics.*

THE EDIT WINDOW

Edit tools

The Edit window's Edit tools (**Figure 3.50**) let you select, audition, view, and move regions. The tools include:

Figure 3.50 The Edit tools.

Zoomer: The Zoomer tool lets you zoom in quickly on a track. To zoom in horizontally, click or drag the Zoomer tool. To zoom in horizontally and vertically, press Command (Macintosh) or Control (Windows) while dragging.

Standard Trimmer: The Standard Trimmer tool lets you quickly expand or condense a region. To use it, click or drag near the start or end point of the region.

Time Trimmer: The Time Trimmer tools lets you expand or compress a region by dragging its start or end points. The Time Trimmer uses the Time Compression/Expansion AudioSuite plug-in to create a new file. For more information on AudioSuite plug-ins, see the *DigiRack Plug-Ins Guide.*

Selector: The Selector tool lets you make a selection anywhere on a track by clicking and dragging. To adjust the length of a selection, Shift-click or Shift-drag with the Selector. To extend an edit selection to other tracks, Shift-click with the Selector in the desired tracks.

Time Grabber: The Time Grabber tool lets you select and move regions anywhere within a track or between tracks by clicking and dragging. To move a region with the Time Grabber, select a region and drag it to a new location.

Separation Grabber: The Separation Grabber tool lets you separate and move a region within or between tracks. To separate regions, click on a selected region with the Separation Grabber.

THE EDIT WINDOW

Figure 3.51 Run the Scrubber tool over an audio region to scrub audio.

Custom Note Duration

Figure 3.52 The Pencil Tool pop-up menu.

Figure 3.53 The Smart tool lets you use several Edit tools simultaneously.

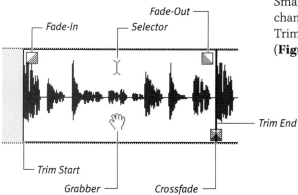

Fade-Out

Fade-In

Selector

Trim End

Trim Start

Grabber

Crossfade

Figure 3.54 The Smart tool automatically changes between the Selector, Grabber, and Trimmer tools as you move your cursor over a region. You can also create fades with the tool.

Scrubber: The Scrubber tool lets you audition or *scrub* audio regions. Scrubbing—a term borrowed from analog recording—refers to running the tape manually back and forth over the playback head. Scrubbing is useful for locating edit points that might be difficult to find visually. To scrub a track, click and drag the Scrubber tool over an audio region (**Figure 3.51**).

Pencil: The Pencil tool lets you insert MIDI notes, edit MIDI note velocities, draw automation and controller events, and repair audio waveforms at the sample level. Clicking the Pencil tool summons its pop-up menu (**Figure 3.52**), which lets you choose from five Pencil shapes.

You can also use the Pencil tool as an eraser to delete notes, program changes, and sysex events. Press Option (Macintosh) or Alt (Windows) to change the Pencil tool to an Eraser.

Smart Tool: The Smart tool (**Figure 3.53**) lets you use several Edit tools without having to switch between them. As you move the Smart tool within a region, it automatically changes between the Selector, Grabber, and Trimmer, and lets you create fades as well (**Figure 3.54**).

THE EDIT WINDOW

✔ Tips

- Use the Grabber pop-up menu (**Figure 3.55**) to choose between the Time Grabber and Separation Grabber. Clicking the Grabber tool summons the pop-up menu. The Time Grabber is the default Grabber tool.

- Use the Trimmer pop-up menu (**Figure 3.56**) to choose between the Standard Trimmer and the Time Trimmer. Clicking the Time Trimmer tool summons the pop-up menu. The Standard Trimmer is the default Trimmer tool.

- Use the following function keys to select and/or toggle Edit tools: F5 (Zoomer), F6 (Standard Trimmer), F7 (Selector), F8 (Time/Separation Grabber), F9 (Scrubber), F10 (Pencil), F6 and F7 simultaneously (Smart tool).

Figure 3.55 The Grabber Tool pop-up menu.

Figure 3.56 The Trimmer pop-up menu.

THE EDIT WINDOW

Figure 3.57 The Event Edit area showing the start time, end time, and length of an audio region selection.

The Event Edit area

The Edit window's Event Edit area (**Figure 3.57**) displays the start point, end point, and length of a selected region or note. The selection indicators display a selection in minutes and seconds, bars and beats, or samples, depending on the current time format of the Main Time Scale (see *Location Indicators* later in this chapter).

When you select a MIDI note, the right side of the Event Edit area displays MIDI note attributes such as pitch, attack velocity, and release velocity. You can change the value of a selection indicator or note attribute by entering a new value in its field.

✔ Tip

■ Press slash (/) on the numeric keypad to select the start field and to navigate from field to field. Press Enter to accept a new value.

THE EDIT WINDOW

Location indicators

The location indicators (**Figure 3.58**) display the current play position in both the Main Time Scale and Sub Time Scale.

The Main Time Scale is the primary time format of your session (see time formats, below). The Sub Time Scale is an additional timing reference that can be useful with synchronization. To change the time format of either scale, click the pop-up menu to the right of its field (**Figure 3.59**).

You can choose from these time formats:

◆ Bars:Beats

◆ Minutes:Seconds (Min:Secs)

◆ Samples

✔ Tip

■ Press Equal (=) on the numeric keypad to select the Main Time Scale in the location indicator. Press period (.) to navigate the indicator's time fields; press Enter to go to a new location.

Main time scale

Sub time scale

Figure 3.58 Location indicators show the Main Time Scale and Sub Time Scale.

Figure 3.59 Click the Location Indicator pop-up menu to change the Main and Sub Time Scale time formats (Bars:Beats, Min:Secs, or Samples).

THE EDIT WINDOW

Grid   0:01.000 ▼ | Nudge   0:00.010 ▼ | Cursor   1:26.938   ▶| 1758949

Figure 3.60 The Grid value, Nudge value, and Current Cursor location value.

Figure 3.61 Select a new Grid value or time format using the Grid Value pop-up menu.

Grid/Nudge values, Current Cursor display

The Edit window also provides fields for quickly entering Grid and Nudge values during editing. The Current Cursor display gives you information about the location of the cursor.

Grid Value: The Grid Value field (**Figure 3.60**) lets you define the size of the grid used in Grid mode. You can define a Grid value that matches the time format currently used by the Main Time Scale, or select a different time format from the pop-up menu to the right of the field (**Figure 3.61**). For more information on using grids, see *Chapter 10: Editing Basics*.

Nudge Value: The Nudge Value field lets you define the distance you can nudge a selected region with the plus and minus keys on the numeric keypad. Use the pop-up menu to the right of the field to select a nudge value. For more information on the Nudge feature, see *Chapter 10: Editing Basics*.

Cursor Location: The Cursor Location field displays the location of the cursor in the same time format as the current Main Time Scale.

Cursor Value: The Cursor Value field displays information about the cursor location based on the current track view. For instance, Volume view shows a dB value, Note view shows a MIDI note value, and Velocity view shows a velocity value.

THE EDIT WINDOW

The Edit Groups list

Much like the Mix Groups list in the Mix window, the Edit Groups list (**Figure 3.62**) displays all the edit groups in a session. You can enable or disable a group by selecting its name in the Groups list. Highlighted groups are enabled.

To create a new group, or suspend or delete groups, use the Edit Groups pop-up menu at the top of the list. For more information on groups, see *Chapter 5: Working with Tracks*.

The Audio Regions list

Audio regions in a session appear in the Audio Regions list (**Figure 3.63**). You can drag an audio region from the list onto any audio track.

The Audio Regions list has an indispensable pop-up menu (**Figure 3.64**), which lets you import, sort, compact, and delete audio files. For more information on handling audio files, see *Chapter 8: File Management Basics*.

Figure 3.62 The Edit Groups list.

Figure 3.63 The Audio Regions list.

Figure 3.64 The Audio Regions List pop-up menu lets you import, sort, compact, and delete audio files.

The MIDI Regions list

MIDI regions in a session appear in the MIDI Regions list (**Figure 3.65**). You can drag MIDI regions from the list onto any MIDI track.

The MIDI Regions list also has a pop-up menu, which includes features for importing and managing MIDI regions (**Figure 3.66**).

Figure 3.65 The MIDI Regions list.

Figure 3.66 The MIDI Regions List pop-up menu.

Part II: Recording in Pro Tools

STARTING A
NEW SESSION

When you start a new project in Pro Tools, you start a new *session*. A Pro Tools session is analogous to a session in a real-world recording studio: It contains all the elements you need to record, edit, process, mix, master, and store audio recordings.

This chapter tells you how to start a new Pro Tools session from scratch. First, I'll show you how to create a new session, and how to configure basic parameters such as sample rate, bit depth, audio file type, and I/O Setup.

Then, we'll look more closely at I/O Setups. You'll learn how to define new signal paths and map channels, and how to save your I/O Setups to use in later sessions. I'll also cover how to create new session templates and discuss sharing sessions between Pro Tools LE and Pro Tools TDM systems.

Creating a New Session

Each time you create a new session, Pro Tools places a new Session folder (**Figure 4.1**) on your hard drive. This folder contains a Session file, an Audio Files folder, and a Fade Files folder (**Figure 4.2**).

All audio files recorded or imported during a Pro Tools session are stored in the Audio Files folder. All fades and crossfades created during a session are stored in the Fade Files folder. Audio files and other basic session elements are discussed in *Chapter 2: Software Basics*.

When you create a new session, the New Session dialog box appears (**Figure 4.3**). Here, you can name the session and set session file parameters, such as audio file type, sample rate, bit depth, and I/O Settings.

Figure 4.1 A Pro Tools Session folder.

Figure 4.2 The contents of a Pro Tools Session folder: a Session file, an Audio Files folder, and a Fade Files folder.

Figure 4.3 The New Session dialog box.

Figure 4.4 Choose File > New Session.

Figure 4.5 Select the session audio file format.

To create a new session:

1. Choose File > New Session (**Figure 4.4**).

2. Choose the destination hard drive for your session. (Make sure you're using a dedicated audio hard drive.)

3. If you want to create cross-platform session and audio files, select Enforce Mac/PC Compatibility (Macintosh) or Enforce PC/Mac Compatibility (Windows).

4. Select the session audio file format (**Figure 4.5**).

5. Select a sample rate (44.1kHz, 48kHz, or 96kHz) and a bit depth (16- or 24-bit). (For more information see the sidebar, *What Are Sample Rate and Bit Depth?* later in this chapter.)

6. Select the I/O settings for the session.

7. Name the session and click Save.

✔ Tip

- Windows doesn't support Sound Designer II (SDII) sessions. For best cross-platform compatibility, set the file type to WAV.

Opening a session

Use the Open Session dialog box to open existing sessions. Pro Tools will automatically scan the session directory for the associated audio and fade files.

If the number of tracks in a session exceeds the maximum number of voices available on your system, those extra tracks are opened set to *voice off.*

To open an existing session:

1. Choose File > Open Session.

   The Open Session dialog box appears (**Figure 4.6**).

2. Select a session and click Open.

✔ Tip

■ Use the DigiBase Workspace browser to quickly locate and open a session file (**Figure 4.7**). Double-click the session file icon to open it. For more information on DigiBase see *Chapter 9: Managing Audio Files with DigiBase.*

Saving a session

The Save Session command saves the changes you make to a session, writing over the previously saved version of the session file. The Save Session command cannot be undone.

To save a session:

◆ Choose File > Save Session.

✔ Tips

■ Save your session frequently. You don't want to lose detailed mix, edit, or automation data because of a computer crash or inexplicable technical mishap.

■ Saving a session does not automatically back up an audio file. Be sure to back up your audio files separately.

Figure 4.6 The New Session dialog box.

Figure 4.7 The DigiBase Workspace browser lets you quickly locate and open your Pro Tools session file.

File	Edit	AudioSuite	MIDI	Movie

New Session...   ⌘N
Open Session...   ⌘O
Close Session   ⇧⌘W
Save Session   ⌘S
Save Session As...
Save Session Copy In...
Revert to Saved...
Bounce to Disk...

New Track...   ⇧⌘N
Group Selected Tracks... ⌘G
Duplicate Selected Tracks ⌥⇧D
Split Selected Tracks Into Mono
Make Selected Tracks Inactive
Delete Selected Tracks...

Figure 4.8 Choose File > Revert to Saved.

Reverting to a previously saved session

If you want to discard changes that you have made to a session file and subsequently saved, use the Revert to Saved command. Revert to Saved recalls the last saved version of a session.

To revert to the last saved version of a session:

◆ Choose File > Revert to Saved (**Figure 4.8**).

✔ Tip

■ You can speed up session saves and disk bounces by reducing the disk cache size in the Memory Control panel to 512K (Macintosh only).

What Are Sample Rate and Bit Depth?

Sample rate, measured in kilohertz (kHz), is the number of times per second that sound wave information is gathered, or *sampled*, during the digital audio recording process. In Pro Tools, you can record at sample rates of 44.1kHz, 48kHz, and 96 kHz, depending on the system.

The sample rate used to record a sound determines the recording's frequency range and, thus, its accuracy. For this reason, higher sample rates generally produce more accurate audio record-ings. A basic rule of digital audio, the *Nyquest Theorem*, states that the sample rate must be twice the value of a sound's highest frequency for that sound to be accurately reproduced. For example, CD audio is sampled at 44.1kHz, while the human hearing range extends to only 20kHz. Having the sample rate at twice the highest frequency of human hearing ensures that all of a sound's *overtones* (high-frequency components of a sound) within the range of human hearing will be recorded. Recording at a sample rate of 48kHz or 96kHz, ensures even greater accuracy.

Bit depth (also known as *bit resolution*) is the number of bits used to describe each individual sample taken during recording. For example, if you're recording at 24-bit resolution and a sam-ple rate of 44.1kHz, there will be 44,100 individual 24-bit representations of the sound recorded each second. That's a lot of data! Pro Tools let you record audio at both 16 and 24 bits.

Although higher sample rates and bit depths generally produce more accurate recordings, they also consume more disk space. In fact, 24-bit resolution requires 50 percent more hard disk space than 16-bit resolution.

If you're low on disk space, recording at 16-bit/44.1kHz (CD audio) is a good option: It sounds good, it saves disk space, and it eliminates the need for any sample-rate or bit-depth conversion process, which can degrade digital audio. For more information on sample rate, bit depth, and file sizes, see Table 1.2 in *Chapter 1: Setting Up Your Pro Tools LE System*.

The Save Session As command

The Save Session As command lets you rename a copy of a session. It closes the current session and leaves the renamed copy open. The Save Session As command duplicates session files only—it does not duplicate audio or fade files.

To rename a session:

1. Choose File > Save Session As.

2. Enter a new name for your session and click Save.

   The renamed session document is saved in the Session folder along with the original session. Any new audio files that you record in the renamed session are stored in the same Audio Files folder created with the original session.

✔ Tip

■ The Save Session As command is useful for developing sessions in successive stages: You can save a session at any stage, and continue working on a renamed copy.

The Save Session Copy In command

The Save Session Copy In command (**Figure 4.9**) lets you save a copy of the current session file, along with its audio files, fade files, plug-in settings files, and movie or video files. You can also designate a new session file format, audio file format, bit depth, and sample rate for the session copy.

The Save Session Copy In command is useful for changing the sample rate or bit depth of a session. It's also useful for generating session files and audio files for use on a different Pro Tools system, or operating system platform.

The Save Session Copy In command does not close the original session—the original session remains the open and active session.

Figure 4.9 Choose File > Save Session Copy In.

Figure 4.10 The Save Session Copy In dialog box.

Figure 4.11 Select a session format.

Figure 4.12 Select session parameters, including audio file format, bit depth, and sample rate.

Figure 4.13 Select Items to Copy.

To save a session copy in a new location:

1. Choose File > Save Session Copy In.

   The Save Session Copy In dialog box appears (**Figure 4.10**).

2. If you want to create session and audio files that can be used in both the Macintosh or Windows version of Pro Tools, select Enforce Mac/PC Compatibility (Macintosh) or Enforce PC /Mac compatibility (Windows).

3. Choose a destination and type a name for the new session file.

4. Select the session format for the session copy (**Figure 4.11**). Select "Latest" to save the session copy in Pro Tools 6 format.

5. Select the session parameters (audio file format, bit depth, and sample rate) for the session copy (**Figure 4.12**).

6. Select the Items to Copy to the new session (**Figure 4.13**).

7. Click Save to save the session in the new location.

✔ Tip

- A Pro Tools session can use mixed audio file types. If your original session uses mixed file types, the Save Session In command will not convert audio files unless you specify that they be converted. Sessions with mixed audio file types require more processing power, and can thus reduce system performance.

Closing a session

You can work on only one session at a time in Pro Tools. The Close Session command closes the current session, leaving the Pro Tools application open so you can create or open another session.

To close a session:

◆ Choose File > Close Session.

The current session closes, leaving the Pro Tools application open.

Quitting Pro Tools

Pro Tools will prompt you to save changes you've made to a session before it quits.

To quit a session on Mac OS:

◆ Choose File > Quit.

To quit a session on Windows:

◆ Choose File > Exit.

Creating an I/O Setup

A *signal path* refers to the way that audio is routed in, out, and through a Pro Tools session. A signal path can have many different configurations. For instance, you may want to bus audio to a DSP plug-in, or output audio to an external hardware effect. This signal path configuration is called an I/O Setup. For more on I/O Setup, see *Chapter 2: Software Basics.*

Using the I/O Setup dialog box

The I/O Setup dialog box (**Figure 4.14**) lets you create I/O Setups. Use this checkerboard-like dialog box to define track inputs and outputs, inserts, and bus paths. You can save your definitions as I/O Settings files for use with later sessions. (See *Importing and Exporting I/O Settings Files* later in this chapter.)

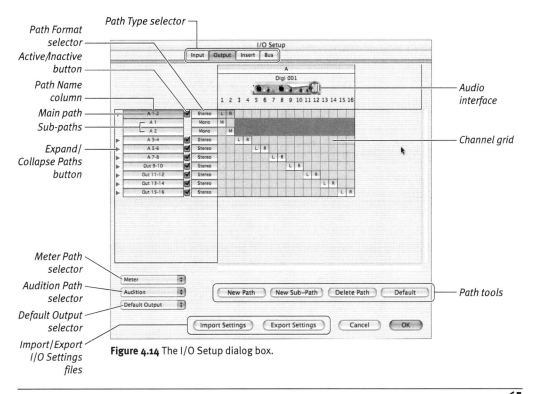

Figure 4.14 The I/O Setup dialog box.

To open the I/O Setup dialog box:

1. Make sure your audio interface is enabled and configured properly in the Hardware Setup dialog box.

2. Choose Setups > I/O Setup (**Figure 4.15**). The I/O Setup dialog box appears. Its parameter controls include the following:

    Path Type Selector: The Path Type selector lets you choose a path type (input, output, insert, or bus).

    Expand/Collapse Paths Button: The Expand/Collapse Paths button lets you expand the path name to show sub-paths associated with a main path.

    Path Name Column: The Path Name column displays the current path name. Enter a new name in the field to rename a path.

    Active/Inactive Button: The Active/Inactive button lets you turn a path on or off.

    Path Format Selector: The Path Format selector lets you choose a format (mono or stereo) for each path.

    Channel Grid: The Channel grid lets you map out paths between the I/O interface and channels in a session.

    Path Tools: Path tools let you customize paths. Path tools include New Path, New Sub-Path, Delete Path, and Default.

    Default Output Selector: The Default Output selector lets you set the default output assignments for new tracks.

    Audition Path Selector: The Audition Path selector lets you pre-configure Audio Regions list previewing.

    Meter Path Selector (Pro Control only): The Meter Path selector lets you set the paths displayed across the Pro Control Output meters.

Figure 4.15 Choose Setups > I/O Setup.

What Is Gain Staging?

It's all too easy to accumulate noise on your recordings when levels are set too high or too low. *Gain staging* can help you keep your recordings clean.

A *gain stage* is any point in an audio signal path where the audio signal is amplified (boosted) or attenuated (cut). The volume knob on your stereo, for instance, is a gain stage. Likewise, every amp, preamp, fader, and effect in your Pro Tools system is a gain stage. The process of setting all gain stages in a system to their optimal values is known as gain staging.

Before you begin recording or mixing, check the levels on each gain stage in your system. Start by optimizing your audio source input levels; then optimize levels on all inserts, sends, and outputs. Avoid *clipping* audio signals (making them too loud), which can produce notoriously unpleasant digital distortion.

For more information on audio input levels, see *Chapter 6: Getting Ready to Record.*

CREATING AN I/O SETUP

Figure 4.16 Main path stereo outputs and corresponding sub-path mono outputs.

Figure 4.17 Click a path type tab (Input, Output, Insert, or Bus).

Figure 4.18 Choose a path format (Mono or Stereo).

Defining new paths

The I/O Setup dialog box lets you define main paths and sub-paths. *Main paths* are logical groupings of inputs, outputs, inserts, or buses, such as a stereo (two-channel) output. *Sub-paths* are signal paths within the main path. For example, a main path stereo output has two mono sub-paths (**Figure 4.16**).

You can define new main paths and sub-paths in the I/O Setup dialog box.

To create a new path:

1. Choose Setups > I/O Setup.

2. Click a path type tab (Input, Output, Insert, or Bus) (**Figure 4.17**).

3. Click the New Path button, or press Command-N (Macintosh) or Control-N (Windows).

   Or, select a main path and click the New Sub-Path button.

4. Double-click the Name field and enter a path name. (The path names appear globally in Pro Tools' track-routing selectors.)

5. Choose a format (mono or stereo) from the Path Format selector (**Figure 4.18**).

6. Configure other path types (Input, Output, Insert, or Bus).

7. Click OK.

✔ Tip

■ You don't need to configure the I/O Setup before you begin recording—Pro Tools' default I/O Setups are adequate for most basic recording situations. As you expand your system, however, you'll likely want to experiment with new I/O Setups.

CREATING AN I/O SETUP

Mapping channels

Once you've defined a path, you can map it in the I/O Setup dialog box's channel grid (**Figure 4.19**). Channel mapping is subject to these limitations:

◆ No two main output paths, insert paths, or main bus paths can partially or completely overlap.

◆ A new output or bus path must be entirely independent of other paths, or it must be a sub-path completely contained within a main path.

◆ Output and insert paths can overlap, but they cannot be used at the same time.

To map channels:

1. Select a main path or sub-path (**Figure 4.20**).

2. In the row for the selected path, click in the grid column under the audio interface and channel (**Figure 4.21**).

Re-mapping channels

You can move individual assignments to different channels and redefine a path.

To re-map channels in a path:

◆ Drag the channel to the new location in the grid (**Figure 4.22**).

Other channel assignments automatically move (shuffle) to accommodate the dragged channels.

Figure 4.19 The I/O Setup dialog box's channel grid.

Figure 4.20 Select a main path or sub-path.

Figure 4.21 Map channels in the channel grid.

Figure 4.22 Re-map a channel by dragging it to a new location in the grid.

Figure 4.23 Inactive paths are italicized.

Figure 4.24 Click the Active/Inactive button.

Making paths active or inactive

Paths can be active (on) or inactive (off). You can switch paths between these states on single tracks or session-wide.

To toggle a track path assignment between active and inactive:

◆ In either the Mix or Edit window, Command-Control-click (Macintosh) or Control-Start-click (Windows) on a track Input, Output, Insert, or Send selector.

Inactive paths are italicized and grayed-out in the track path selectors (**Figure 4.23**).

To toggle a global path assignment between active and inactive:

1. Choose Setups > I/O Setup.

2. Select a path type tab (Input, Output, Insert, or Bus).

3. Click the Active/Inactive button (**Figure 4.24**).

✔ Tip

■ Active paths use system resources. Make paths inactive whenever possible to conserve CPU power and improve system performance.

CREATING AN I/O SETUP

About I/O Settings files

When you start a session, you can choose from several I/O Setup configuration options:

◆ **Default I/O Setups:** These Pro Tools factory pre-sets give you useful basic main path and sub-path definitions.

◆ **Custom Presets:** You can store and recall custom presets using the import and export features of the I/O Setup dialog box.

◆ **Last Used:** The most recent I/O Setup configuration is saved as a Last Used settings file (**Figure 4.25**).

Importing and exporting I/O Settings files

You can import and export I/O Setup configurations as I/O Settings files. This lets you save I/O Setups for reuse.

To export and save an I/O Setup configuration:

1. Click Export Settings in the I/O Setup dialog box (**Figure 4.26**).

2. Name and save the settings file (**Figure 4.27**).

Figure 4.25 The Last Used settings file.

Figure 4.26 Click Export Settings to save I/O Settings files.

Figure 4.27 Name and save the settings file.

Figure 4.28 Click Import Settings to import a settings file.

To import an I/O Settings file:

1. Click Import Settings in the I/O Setup dialog box (**Figure 4.28**).

2. Select the desired settings file in the dialog box. Click OK.

3. You'll be asked if you want to delete the existing unused paths.

4. Select one of the following:

   Yes if you want to delete existing paths. This re-maps the original session path definitions to your current audio interface.

   No if you don't want to delete existing paths. This adds session paths to the current I/O Setup.

Initializing I/O Setup

Before Pro Tools recognizes a new I/O Setup as valid, each path must have a name, a format (mono or stereo), and a valid channel mapping. See *Mapping Channels* earlier in this chapter for channel mapping requirements.

To set the current I/O Setup configuration:

◆ Click OK in the I/O Setup dialog box.

Creating Custom Session Templates

You can create a custom session template that retains all the parameters of a session, including mixer configurations, track setups, signal path routing, track views, and preference settings. This saves you the hassle of recreating your studio setup each time you start a new session.

Creating Macintosh session templates

You can create a session template on the Macintosh by saving a session as a *stationery pad*. Once you do this, the session acts as a template that you can open and save just as you would a normal session.

To create a custom session template on Mac OS:

1. Configure your session parameters as desired.

2. Choose File > Save Session.

3. Name the session and click Save.

4. Close the session.

5. Locate the session file that you just saved.

6. Click once on the file to select it.

7. Choose File > Get Info.
   A File Information window appears.

8. Click the Stationery Pad checkbox to save the file as a template, and then close the window (**Figure 4.29**).

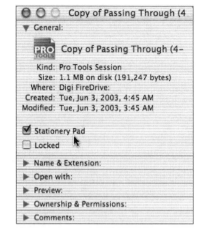

Figure 4.29 To save a file as a template: Choose File > Get Info, and click the Stationery Pad checkbox.

Copy of Passing Through

Figure 4.30 Double-click the session previously saved as a stationery pad.

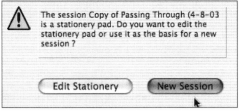

The session Copy of Passing Through (4-8-03) is a stationery pad. Do you want to edit the stationery pad or use it as the basis for a new session?

Edit Stationery   New Session

Figure 4.31 Choose whether to edit the session template, or start a new session.

To open a custom session template on Mac OS:

◆ Double-click a session that was previously saved as a stationery pad (**Figure 4.30**).

or

1. Select File > Open Session.

   The Open Session dialog box appears.

2. Double-click the session that was previously saved as a stationery pad.

   You are prompted to either edit the session template or start a new session (**Figure 4.31**).

3. Choose Edit Stationery if you want to edit the session template.

   or

   Choose New Session.

   This creates a new Session folder containing a new session file (based on the template), with a new Audio Files folder and a new Fade Files folder.

CREATING CUSTOM SESSION TEMPLATES

Creating Windows session templates

You can create a Windows session template by making a session file a Read Only document.

To create a custom session template on Windows:

1. Configure the session parameters as desired.

2. Choose File > Save Session.

3. Name the session and click Save.

4. Close the session.

5. Locate the session file that you just saved.

6. Right-click the file and choose Properties.

7. Under Attributes, deselect Archive and select Read Only.

To open a custom session template on Windows:

1. Double-click the session icon.

   or

   Select File > Open Session.

2. Double-click the session template icon.
   When you first save the session, Pro Tools asks you to rename it. Your original session template remains unchanged.

✔ Tip

- To modify a session template in Windows, reopen its properties, deselect the Read Only option and select the Archive option. Make your modifications, then reopen its properties and change it back to a Read Only file.

Sharing Sessions Between Pro Tools LE and Pro Tools TDM

Sessions created on Pro Tools TDM systems will run on Pro Tools LE systems. However, because LE systems have less processing capabilities than TDM systems, the following limitations apply:

◆ All tracks beyond the first 24 tracks, including inactive tracks, are discarded.

◆ Multi-channel surround tracks are discarded.

◆ Assignments to buses beyond 16 become inactive.

◆ Input and output paths that do not apply to LE systems are discarded.

◆ TDM plug-ins with RTAS equivalents are retained; those without equivalents become inactive.

WORKING
WITH TRACKS

A track is a designated space in a recording system that's assigned to carry a single audio signal. Tracks let you direct the flow of audio into your system, through DSP effects, and then back out to your ears and/or mix-down machine. Every audio or MIDI signal that comes into Pro Tools is routed to a track.

This chapter will show you how to work with tracks in Pro Tools. I'll discuss the four basic track types—audio tracks, auxiliary inputs, master faders, and MIDI tracks—and then show you how to create them and assign inputs and outputs.

I'll also discuss some of Pro Tools' track-viewing features, such as adjusting track height and color-coding track waveforms, which can help you reduce monitor clutter and eye strain.

Finally, you'll learn how to create and work with groups of tracks in the Mix and Edit windows.

About Track Types

Pro Tools includes four types of tracks (**Figure 5.1**):

Audio tracks: Audio tracks control recorded or imported audio files.

Auxiliary inputs: Auxiliary inputs let you add mono or stereo effects to bused signals. They're also useful for submixes and other audio-routing tasks.

Master faders: Master faders control the level of a session's main outputs. They're also useful for inserting effects on the main mix.

MIDI tracks: MIDI tracks store MIDI note, instrument, and controller data.

Each track type has a corresponding channel strip, which appears in the Mix and Edit windows. Tracks that handle audio (audio tracks, auxiliary inputs, and master faders) can be formatted for either mono (one-track) or stereo (two-track).

Macintosh computers also allow movie tracks, which display a picon (picture-icon) overview of imported QuickTime movies (**Figure 5.2**). The closer you zoom in on the track, the more frames you see. Movie tracks appear only in the Edit window.

For more information on track types and channel strips, see *Chapter 3: The Mix and Edit Windows.*

Figure 5.1 Pro Tools track types: audio, auxiliary inputs, master faders, and MIDI.

Figure 5.2 A movie track in the Edit window.

Figure 5.3 The New Track dialog box.

Figure 5.4 Select a track type from the Track Type pop-up menu.

Figure 5.5 Select Mono or Stereo from the Track Format pop-up menu.

Creating New Tracks

The New Track command lets you create mono or stereo audio tracks, as well as MIDI tracks. (Pro Tools TDM systems also let you create multi-channel tracks.)

To create a new track:

1. Choose File > New Track, or press Shift-Command-N (Mac) or Shift-Control-N (Windows).

   The New Track dialog box appears (**Figure 5.3**).

2. Select a track type from the Track Type pop-up menu (**Figure 5.4**).

3. Select Mono or Stereo from the Track Format pop-up menu (**Figure 5.5**).

4. Enter the number of new tracks, and click Create.

✔ Tip

■ If you want a new track to appear next to a specific track, click on that track's name. If you want a track to appear last in a session, make sure no track names are selected.

CREATING NEW TRACKS

79

Naming Tracks

When you create new tracks, Pro Tools, by default, names them according to their track type, and then appends them with consecutive numbers. For example, if you create two new audio tracks, the default names will be Audio 1 and Audio 2 (**Figure 5.6**).

You can rename tracks and also add comments for each track.

To rename a track or add comments:

1. In the Mix or Edit window, double-click the track name (**Figure 5.7**).

   The Track Name/Comments dialog box appears.

2. Type a new track name (**Figure 5.8**).

3. Type comments for the track in the Comments text box.

4. Click the Previous or Next button to rename another displayed track.

5. When you're finished, click OK.

Understanding audio file and region names

Audio files and regions are named after the track on which they're recorded. For example, when you record audio on a track called Keyboard, the audio file written to disk will be called Keyboard_01. The appended digits refer to the *take number* (**Figure 5.9**). In addition, when you separate an audio file into regions, a region name appears in the Audio Regions list with a second set of digits that refers to the *region number* (**Figure 5.10**).

When you record stereo tracks, the audio files and region names for the left and right channels are appended with .L and .R suffixes, respectively.

Figure 5.6 Default track names.

Figure 5.7 Double-click the track name to rename the track.

Figure 5.8 The Track Name/Comments dialog box.

Figure 5.9 An audio file in the Audio Regions list. The appended digits refer to the take number.

Figure 5.10 Audio regions in the Audio Regions list. The second set of digits refers to the region number.

NAMING TRACKS

Figure 5.11 The Input Selector pop-up menu lets you assign input from audio interface channels or internal buses.

Figure 5.12 The Output Selector pop-up menu lets you assign output to audio interface channels or internal buses.

Assigning Audio Track Inputs and Outputs

After you've created a new audio track in Pro Tools, it's important to properly route audio in and out of the track. You can assign audio track inputs and outputs using either Mix or Edit window channel strips.

Audio tracks and auxiliary inputs let you assign audio input from audio interfaces and internal buses (**Figure 5.11**). In turn, you can assign outputs from audio tracks and auxiliary inputs to audio interfaces and internal buses (**Figure 5.12**).

When you create new tracks for a session, they're automatically assigned inputs in ascending order. For example, if you're using a Digi 001 audio interface and you create two new mono audio tracks, they'll be assigned Mic/Line 1 and Mic/Line 2, respectively (**Figure 5.13**). Similarly, if you create two new stereo tracks, they'll be assigned consecutive stereo input pairs: Mic/Line 1-2 and Analog 3-4 (**Figure 5.14**).

Outputs are automatically assigned to the first output pair, or according to the I/O Setup.

The inputs, outputs, and buses available to tracks are defined as *paths* in a session's I/O Setup. You can use a default I/O Setup or create your own in the I/O Setup dialog box. For instructions on creating a customized I/O Setup, see *Chapter 4: Starting a New Session*.

Figure 5.13
New mono audio tracks with automatically assigned consecutive inputs: Mic/Line 1 and Mic/Line 2.

Figure 5.14
New stereo audio tracks with automatically assigned consecutive input pairs: Mic/Line 1-2 and Analog 3-4.

To assign an audio track input:

1. Display track inputs and outputs by
   selecting one of the following:

   Display > Mix Window Shows > I/O
   View.

   or

   Display > Edit Window Shows >
   I/O View.

2. In the Mix or Edit window, click the
   track Input selector, and choose from
   the available audio interface channels
   and buses (**Figure 5.15**).

   Select No Input to remove all the input
   assignments on that track.

Figure 5.15 Select an audio interface channel or
internal bus from the Input selector.

ASSIGNING AUDIO TRACK INPUTS AND OUTPUTS

What is a Bus?

Much as a city bus picks up people from many different stops and delivers them to a bus
depot, an audio *bus* carries audio signals from many different tracks and delivers them to a
single destination track.

Buses are used mainly to *send* audio signals from one or more audio tracks to a single auxiliary input, where a DSP effect is added. A bus lets you add the same effect to many different
tracks simultaneously. For example, to add the same reverb to a vocal track and guitar track,
you'd bus them to the same auxiliary input where both signals would be treated by the same
reverb plug-in. (In this case, the bus would be called a *reverb send*.)

You can also use buses to create *submixes*. Submixes let you control multiple tracks of audio
from a single track. For example, submixes can be useful for making headphone mixes for
performers. They can also help simplify mixing tasks by bringing multiple groups of tracks—
such as basic rhythm tracks, vocals, guitars, or strings—under the control of a single fader.

Bus 1–2 (Stereo)
> Bus 2 (Mono)
> Bus 1 (Mono)
Bus 3–4 (Stereo)
> Bus 3 (Mono)
> Bus 4 (Mono)
Bus 5–6 (Stereo)
> Bus 5 (Mono)
> Bus 6 (Mono)
Bus 7–8 (Stereo)
> Bus 7 (Mono)
> Bus 8 (Mono)
Bus 9–10 (Stereo)
> Bus 9 (Mono)
> Bus 10 (Mono)
Bus 11–12 (Stereo)
> Bus 11 (Mono)
> Bus 12 (Mono)
Bus 13–14 (Stereo)
> Bus 13 (Mono)
> Bus 14 (Mono)
Bus 15–16 (Stereo)
> Bus 15 (Mono)
> Bus 16 (Mono)
Bus 17–18 (Stereo) – path n/a
> Bus 17 (Mono) – path n/a
> Bus 18 (Mono) – path n/a
Bus 19–20 (Stereo) – path n/a
> Bus 19 (Mono) – path n/a
> Bus 20 (Mono) – path n/a
Bus 21–22 (Stereo) – path n/a
> Bus 21 (Mono) – path n/a
> Bus 22 (Mono) – path n/a
Bus 23–24 (Stereo) – path n/a
> Bus 23 (Mono) – path n/a
> Bus 24 (Mono) – path n/a

no output
• interface ▶
bus ▶

Audio 1   Audio 2

Figure 5.16 Select an audio interface channel or internal bus from the Output selector.

To assign an audio track output:

1. Display track inputs and outputs by selecting one of the following:
   Display > Mix Window Shows > I/O View.
   or
   Display > Edit Window Shows > I/O View.

2. In the Mix or Edit window, click the track Output selector and choose from the available audio interface channels and buses (**Figure 5.16**).
   Select No Output to remove all the output assignments on that track. The playlist becomes dimmed on tracks with no output assignments.

✔ Tip

■ Use the No Output option with care. Assigning an audio track, auxiliary input, or master fader to No Output erases pan and plug-in automation.

Viewing Tracks

Pro Tools give you many different ways to view tracks in a session. These viewing options help you mix and edit more quickly and efficiently.

Hiding and showing tracks

The Show/Hide Tracks list (**Figure 5.17**), located in both the Edit and Mix windows, displays all the tracks in a session. You can show or hide a track by selecting or deselecting its name. A hidden track will continue to play normally as part of the session.

The Show/Hide pop-up menu (**Figure 5.18**) gives you options for showing or hiding tracks. You can show/hide tracks according to track type, group, or name.

If a hidden track is a member of an active group, performing edits on other group members in the Edit window will not affect the hidden track. In the Mix window, however, performing operations other than record-enable on group members *will* affect the hidden track.

To hide a track:

◆ Click a highlighted track name in the Show/Hide Tracks list (**Figure 5.19**).

To show a track:

◆ Click a track name that is not highlighted in the Show/Hide Tracks list.

To hide all tracks:

1. Click the Show/Hide button at the top of the Show/Hide Tracks list.

2. From the pop-up menu, choose Hide All Tracks.

Figure 5.17 The Show/Hide Tracks list.

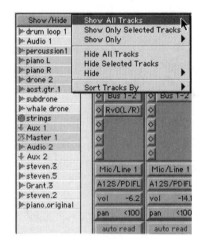

Figure 5.18 The Show/Hide pop-up menu.

Figure 5.19 Click a highlighted track name to hide a track.

VIEWING TRACKS

Figure 5.20 Select a track type from the Show/Hide pop-up menu.

Figure 5.21 The Narrow Mix window.

To show all tracks:

1. Click the Show/Hide button at the top of the Show/Hide Tracks list.

2. From the pop-up menu, choose Show All Tracks.

To show tracks by track type:

1. Click the Show/Hide button at the top of the Show/Hide Tracks list.

2. From the pop-up menu, choose Show Only.

3. Select a track type (**Figure 5.20**).

Adjusting the track size

Pro Tools provides several ways to adjust track sizes. In both the Mix and Edit windows, you can expand channel strips to display the Inserts, Sends, Input/Output, and Track Comments views. The Mix window also lets you choose between narrow and wide channel strip views. The Edit window gives you a wide range of preset track height views, including Mini, Small, Medium, Large, Jumbo, and Extreme.

For more information on viewing tracks in the Mix and Edit windows, see *Chapter 3: The Mix and Edit Windows*.

To view the narrow Mix window:

◆ Select Display > Narrow Mix window. The Narrow Mix window appears (**Figure 5.21**).

VIEWING TRACKS

To change the track height view in the Edit window:

1. Press the Track Height Selector button.

   The Track Height pop-up menu appears.

2. Select a track height.

   or

1. Click in the ruler at the far left of any track's playlist.

   The Track Height pop-up menu appears (**Figure 5.22**).

2. Select a track height.

   or

1. Place the edit cursor in the track.

2. Press Control–Up Arrow key to increase the track height. Press Control–Down Arrow key to decrease the track height.

Figure 5.22 The Track Height pop-up menu.

Zoom toggling track height

Pro Tools 6 lets you increase zoom level and track height with a single keystroke. You can set the default zoom toggle track height in the Display preferences.

To use Zoom Toggle:

1. Make a selection on one or more tracks.

2. Press Control-E (Macintosh) or Start-E (Windows).

   or

   With Commands Focus enabled, press E.

   The selection is zoomed in at the default zoom toggle track height.

VIEWING TRACKS

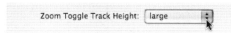

Figure 5.23 The Zoom Toggle Track Height selector in the Display Preferences.

Figure 5.24 The Edit Window Color Coding options in the Display Preferences window.

To set the default Zoom Toggle Track Height:

1. Choose Setups > Preferences.

2. Click on the Display Preferences tab.

3. Select a default track height from the Zoom Toggle Track Height selector (**Figure 5.23**).

For more information on using zoom tools, adjusting track heights, and expanding channel strip views, see *Chapter 3: The Mix and Edit Windows* and *Chapter 10: Editing Basics.*

Color-coding tracks

Color-coding is handy for differentiating tracks in the Edit window. You can assign colors using the Edit Window Color Coding options in the Display Preferences window (**Figure 5.24**). Select from these options:

None: Turns off color assignments to waveforms.

Tracks and MIDI Channels: Assigns colors to waveforms according to the track number and MIDI channel assignment.

Tracks and MIDI Devices: Assigns colors to waveforms according to the track number and MIDI device type.

Groups: Assigns colors to waveforms according to the group ID.

For more information on viewing tracks in the Mix and Edit windows, see *Chapter 3: The Mix and Edit Windows.*

VIEWING TRACKS

Using Track Controls

Track controls on audio and MIDI channel strips let you control level, pan, mute, solo, record-enable, and automation (**Figure 5.25**). For more information on channel strips, see *Chapter 3: The Mix and Edit Windows*.

You can open an Output window (**Figure 5.26**) by clicking a channel strip's Output window button (**Figure 5.27**). Output windows contain the same track controls as channel strips, but they are larger and can float independently over the Mix and Edit windows. This gives you quick access to track controls while you're mixing and editing. For more information on Output windows, see *Chapter 13: Mixing Basics*.

Figure 5.25 The audio channel strip track controls.

Figure 5.26 The audio channel strip Output window.

Figure 5.27 The Output Window button on the audio channel strip.

Figure 5.28 The Mute button.

Figure 5.29 The Solo button.

Figure 5.30 Deselect the Latch Solo Buttons option in the Operation Preference window.

Muting and soloing tracks

Mute and *solo* turn tracks off and on. The Mute button silences a track. The Solo button mutes all tracks except the soloed track, so you can audition tracks separately during playback. You can mute and solo multiple tracks simultaneously.

To mute a track:

◆ Click the Mute button on a track (**Figure 5.28**).

The track is silenced.

To solo a track:

◆ Click the Solo button on the track.

The button is highlighted and all other tracks are muted (**Figure 5.29**).

When you solo more than one track, they're usually *latched,* which means each soloed track is added to the mix. But Pro Tools also lets you unlatch solo buttons, so you can solo just one track at a time.

To unlatch solo buttons:

1. Choose Setups > Preferences.

2. Click the Operation Window tab.

3. Deselect the Latch Solo Buttons option (**Figure 5.30**).

4. Click Done.

For more information on mute, solo, volume level, pan, record-enable, automation, and other track controls, see *Chapter 3: The Mix and Edit Windows.*

USING TRACK CONTROLS

Grouping Tracks

By grouping tracks, you can perform operations on multiple tracks simultaneously. For example, you can group tracks so that their faders move together and their relative volumes are maintained. Or, you can make edits across multiple tracks.

Pro Tools lets you create up to 26 groups. It also lets you create nested groups (subgroups within groups). Grouping affects the following track parameters:

- Volume levels
- Solos
- Mutes
- Automation modes
- Send levels
- Send mutes
- Track view
- Track height
- Editing functions

Grouping does not affect these parameters:

- Record-enable
- Panning
- Send panning
- Output assignments
- Creating plug-in instances

To create a group:

1. Shift-click the tracks that you want to include in the group (**Figure 5.31**).

2. Choose File > Group Selected Tracks. The New Group dialog box appears (**Figure 5.32**).

3. Enter a name for the group and choose a group ID (a letter from a to z) from the pop-up menu (**Figure 5.33**).

4. Choose a group type (Edit, Mix, or Edit and Mix).

5. Click OK.
   The new group is added to the Groups list.

Figure 5.31 Shift-click the tracks you want in a group.

Figure 5.32 The New Group dialog box.

Figure 5.33 Choose a group ID (from a to z).

GROUPING TRACKS

Figure 5.34 The Groups list.

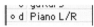

Figure 5.35 A filled-in circle means all members of a group are currently selected.

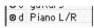

Figure 5.36 A hollow circle means only some members of a group are currently selected.

Figure 5.37 A circle with a dot inside it means all members of a group are currently selected, plus additional members outside of the group.

Figure 5.38 Enable a group by clicking its name in the Groups list.

Figure 5.39 Double-click to the left of a group name to rename it.

Using the Groups list

The Groups list (**Figure 5.34**) lets you manage groups in a session. The list displays the name of each group, a group ID (a letter from a to z), and symbols that indicate the group's selection status in the Mix or Edit window. Here's what the symbols mean:

◆ A filled-in circle (**Figure 5.35**) indicates that all members of the group are currently selected.

◆ A hollow circle (**Figure 5.36**) indicates that only some members of the group are currently selected.

◆ A circle with a dot inside it (**Figure 5.37**) indicates that all members of the group are currently selected, along with additional members outside of the group.

By default, every session has a group named All, which includes every track in the session. You cannot edit or delete the All group.

To enable a group:

◆ In the Groups list, click the name of the group that you want to enable. The group name is highlighted to indicate that it's enabled (**Figure 5.38**).

To disable a group:

◆ In the Groups list, click the name of the group that you want to disable.

To rename a group:

1. In the Groups list, double-click to the left of the group's name (**Figure 5.39**). The New Group dialog box appears.

2. Enter a new name for the group.

3. Click OK. The group is renamed in the Groups list.

GROUPING TRACKS

Using the Groups pop-up menu

The Groups pop-up menu (**Figure 5.40**) lets you create new groups, display groups by type (Edit, Mix, or Edit and Mix), suspend groups, change group members, and delete groups.

To change the members of a group:

1. Shift-click the tracks that you want to keep in the group.

2. Choose New Group from the Group pop-up menu (**Figure 5.41**).

   The New Group dialog box appears.

3. In the New Group dialog box, select the group ID that you want to update.

4. Click OK.

   The new group definition overwrites the original one.

To delete a group:

1. In the Groups list, select the name of the group that you want to delete.

2. Choose Delete Selected Groups from the Group pop-up menu.

   Be careful: You can't undo this deletion.

Figure 5.40 The Group pop-up menu.

Figure 5.41 Choose New Group from the Group pop-up menu.

GROUPING TRACKS

Figure 5.42 Deselect the Link Mix and Edit Group Enables checkbox.

— *Mix Group ID button*

Figure 5.43 The Mix Group ID button.

Figure 5.44 The Mix Group ID button shows the active Mix Group members.

Linking Mix and Edit groups

You can create three types of groups: Mix groups, Edit groups, and Mix and Edit groups. By default a Mix and Edit Group's enable functions are linked. This means that when you enable a group in the Mix window, it's also enabled in the Edit window.

But you may not always want Mix and Edit Groups linked. For example, you may want to keep tracks grouped in the Mix window to maintain relative fader levels, but ungroup them in the Edit window so you can edit a single track. For this reason, Pro Tools lets you unlink groups.

To unlink Mix and Edit groups:

1. Choose Setups > Preferences.

2. Click the Operation tab.

3. Deselect the Link Mix and Edit Group Enables checkbox (**Figure 5.42**).

4. Click Done.

✔ Tip

■ Click on a channel strip's Mix Group ID button (**Figure 5.43**) to view the active mix groups (**Figure 5.44**).

About Track Priority and Voice Assignments

Although Pro Tools LE hardware systems are limited to a maximum of 32 simultaneous playback voices (depending on the system), a Pro Tools 6 session can contain additional audio tracks beyond this fixed playback number. When a session contains more tracks than playback voices, Pro Tools assigns a playback priority for tracks according to their order in the Mix window, Edit window, or Show/Hide Tracks list.

Pro Tools LE automatically assigns voices to tracks (unlike TDM systems, which let you assign specific voices to tracks). Pro Tools LE systems do, however, let you turn a track's voice selection off (**Figure 5.45**). This is useful if you wish to free up voices for use with other tracks.

For more information on track priority and voice assignments, see the *Pro Tools Reference Guide*.

To increase a track's playback priority:

◆ In the Edit window, drag the Track Name button to a higher position. Tracks in a higher position of the Edit window have higher playback priority than tracks in a lower position.

   or

◆ In the Mix window, drag the Track Name button to the left. Tracks to the left of the Mix window have higher priority than tracks to the right.

   or

◆ In the Show/Hide Tracks list, drag the track to a higher position. Tracks in a higher position on the list have higher playback priority than tracks in lower positions.

Figure 5.45 To turn off automatic voice assignment, click on the Voice selector.

TRACK PRIORITY AND VOICE ASSIGNMENTS

Figure 5.46 Command-Control-click (Macintosh) or Control-Start-click (Windows) the Track Type Indicator to make a track inactive.

Making Tracks Inactive

Pro Tools 6 lets you make Audio, Auxiliary Input, and Master Fader tracks inactive. Making a track inactive deactivates all plug-ins, sends, voices, and automation; consequently, the track uses no CPU power. If you're running low on processing power, making unused tracks inactive can help improve system performance.

To make a track inactive:

◆ Command-Control-click (Macintosh) or Control-Start-click (Windows) the Track Type Indicator in the Mix Window (**Figure 5.46**).

The track becomes inactive and appears grayed out.

GETTING
READY TO RECORD

The instruments are plugged in, the microphones are turned on, and you're ready to record. Well, almost. There are just a few more critical steps to take before you press the Record button. This chapter will take you through them.

We'll start with a look at Pro Tools' record modes: Non-destructive, Destructive, Loop, and QuickPunch. You'll learn how to record-enable tracks, and how to set proper audio input and output levels.

Then we'll discuss how to monitor audio in Pro Tools. We'll cover monitor modes and show you some useful workarounds for minimizing monitor latency.

We'll finish with a look at Pro Tools' features for allocating hard drives and generating a click track for your session.

Setting Record Modes

Pro Tools has four record modes; each provides a different method of recording audio to hard disk.

Non-destructive Record: This is the default record mode. When you record on a track with existing audio regions, the regions are protected and both old and new audio files remain on your hard drive. The files are available as regions from the Audio Regions list.

In Non-destructive Record mode, you can select a record range within a track's playlist, or you can input a start and stop time in the Transport window.

Destructive Record: In this mode, recording over existing regions permanently replaces the original audio. Although this mode can help you save hard disk space, it's generally best to use Non-destructive Record mode, as it helps prevent you from accidentally erasing your recordings.

Loop Record: This mode lets you record multiple takes while the same section of audio repeats. It's helpful when you want to quickly record multiple takes of a part without losing spontaneity. Loop Record mode is non-destructive. For more information on Loop Recording, see *Chapter 7: Recording and Playing Back Audio.*

QuickPunch: This mode lets you punch in (initiate recording) and punch out (stop recording) on a record-enabled audio track at any time during playback. See *Chapter 7: Recording and Playing Back Audio.*

Figure 6.1 Choose a different record mode in the Operations menu.

Figure 6.2 The Record button displays the current record mode: a blank circle for Non-destructive...

Figure 6.3 D for Destructive...

Figure 6.4 A loop symbol for Loop Record...

Figure 6.5 ...and P for QuickPunch mode.

Figure 6.6 The Link Selections button in the Edit window.

To set a record mode:

◆ Pro Tools is automatically set to Non-destructive Record mode. To enable Destructive Record, Loop Record, or QuickPunch mode, select the desired mode from the Operations menu (**Figure 6.1**).

or

◆ Control-click (Macintosh) or right-click (Windows) the Record button in the Transport window to cycle among the four modes. The Record button displays a blank circle for Non-destructive, D for Destructive, a loop symbol for Loop Record, and P for QuickPunch mode (**Figures 6.2** through **6.5**).

✔ Tip

■ If you want to set a record range by selecting within a track's playlist, you must first link the Edit and Timeline selections. To do this, press the Link Selections button in the Edit window (**Figure 6.6**). For more information on linking Edit and Timeline selections, see *Chapter 11: Working with Regions*.

Record-Enabling Tracks

Before you can record an audio or MIDI track, you must first *record-enable* it. This opens the track to audio or MIDI input. You can then set appropriate levels and start recording.

A track must be record-enabled before recording can begin. You can record-enable individual tracks or multiple tracks simultaneously.

To record-enable an audio or MIDI track:

◆ In either the Mix or Edit window, click the track's Record-Enable button (**Figure 6.7**).

To record-enable all audio or MIDI tracks:

◆ Option-click (Macintosh) or Alt-click (Windows) the Record-Enable button on any audio or MIDI track.

To record-enable all selected tracks:

◆ Shift-Option-click (Macintosh) or Shift-Alt-click (Windows) the Record-Enable button on any selected track.

✔ Tips

■ To select multiple tracks, Shift-click their track names.

■ Record-enabling a track that belongs to a group does not record-enable other tracks in the group. To record-enable all tracks in a group: Click to the left of the group name in the Groups list. This selects the group. Then, Shift-Option-click (Macintosh) or Shift-Alt-click (Windows) the Record-Enable button on a selected track.

Figure 6.7 Press a track's Record-Enable button to prepare for recording.

RECORD-ENABLING TRACKS

☑ Latch Record Enable Buttons
☐ Latch Solo Buttons
☐ Link Mix And Edit Group Enables
☐ Link Record And Play Faders
☐ Use F11 Key for Wait For Note
☐ Automatically Copy Files on Import

Figure 6.8 The Latch Record-Enable Buttons checkbox in the Operation Preferences window.

Figure 6.9 To put a track in Record Safe mode, Command-click (Macintosh) or Control-click (Windows) the track's Record-Enable button.

- If the Latch Record-Enable Button checkbox (**Figure 6.8**) in the Operation Preferences window is selected, you can record-enable multiple tracks simultaneously.

  If you want to record-enable only one track at a time, deselect the Latch Record-Enable Button checkbox. Record-enabling a subsequent track will take a previously record-enabled track out of Record-Enable mode.

- Record Safe Mode protects tracks from being placed into Record-Enable mode. To put a track in Record Safe mode, Command-click (Macintosh) or Control-click (Windows) a track's Record-Enable button (**Figure 6.9**). To put all tracks in Record Safe mode, Command-Option-click (Macintosh) or Control-Alt-click (Windows) the Record-Enable button on any track.

Microphone Polarity Patterns

A microphone's polarity pattern refers to the directions from which it picks up sound. The most common polarity patterns are as follows (**Figure 6.10**):

Cardioid (or directional): Cardioid mics pick up sound only from in front of them.

Figure-8 (or bi-directional): Figure-8 mics pick up sound from both the front and back.

Omni-directional: Omni-directional mics capture sounds from all directions.

Figure 6.10 The three most common microphone polarity patterns are cardioid, figure-8, and omni-directional.

Microphone Types

Microphones have different sound properties and applications, depending on how they're constructed. The most common microphone types include:

Dynamic microphones: Dynamic mics (such as the Shure SM57 and SM58) can handle lots of volume, which makes them perfect for close-miking drums, amplifiers, and loud vocalists. They are also durable enough to survive most live settings. Dynamic mics tend to accentuate mid-range and can sometimes make tracks sound boxy. Still, they have many applications both live and in the studio. They are also the least expensive type of microphone.

Condenser microphones: Condenser mics are more sensitive and accurate than dynamic mics, and, as a result, are used frequently in recording studios. Condenser mics come with either large or small diaphragms. Large diaphragm mics tend to pick up more low end and have less self-noise. Small diaphragm condensers generally have an even frequency response and are particularly good at capturing higher-end sound, such as violin.

A condenser mic requires a small amount of voltage to function (between 9 and 48 volts). Thus, you'll need to plug it into a mixer or preamp with *phantom power*—a low-level electric current sent from the mic preamp to the condenser mic. Condenser mics come with either tube or solid-state electronics. Tube condensers tend to sound warmer, while solid-state condensers tend to be more transparent (they have less sound coloration). Condenser mics cost more than dynamic mics, but you can find some good models at reasonable prices.

Ribbon microphones: Ribbon mics are expensive and fragile, but they can produce a unique silky tone—the result of a slight roll-off that tends to occur in the high end. Ribbon mics were popular from the 1930s to the 1960s, but were pretty much replaced in the studio by condenser mics. In recent years, however, many musicians and producers have returned to them to capture their vintage tone.

Microphone Placement Techniques

Microphone placement has a major influence on the sound of a recording. The mic's location in the room, its distance from the source, and the room's size, shape, and reflectivity all affect the sound going to disk. Before placing mics, consider the sound you want. For instance, do you want to capture the pure instrument sound alone, or do you want to capture a blend of instrument and room sound? Experiment with the following microphone placement techniques until you find a sound you like. You may be surprised to discover a sound you didn't know was there.

Close (or spot) miking: Close miking involves placing the mic anywhere from two inches to two feet away from the audio source. This technique is useful for picking up the pure sound of an audio source with little or no room sound. But keep your ears open and check your levels—you don't want the mic too close to the source. If you're getting too many transient peaks (or clipping), pull the mic back and turn it a bit off-axis.

Distant miking: Distant miking involves placing the mic anywhere from two to five feet from an audio source. This technique lets you capture a blend of the source audio and the room sound. Distant miking is often used along with close miking to add varying amounts of depth to the raw sound.

Ambient (or room) miking: In ambient miking, the mic is placed far enough away from the audio source that it picks up more of the room's reflected sound than the instrument's direct sound. You can place the mic either close to the source but in the opposite direction, or across the room. Ambient miking is useful if you want to add spaciousness or a unique room sound to a track.

Stereo miking: Stereo miking involves using two mics to capture a stereo image of an audio source. The most common stereo miking approaches are:

- **X-Y (coincident) pairs:** X-Y pair miking involves placing two mics on right angles (along the x and y axes), with the diaphragms of each mic as close together as possible without touching.

- **Blumlein technique:** Blumlein technique uses two figure-8 pattern microphones positioned at right angles, with their diaphragms as close together as possible. The two mics are mounted on separate stands, one above the other. Because figure-8 pattern mics pick up sound from both front and back, the Blumlein technique can help capture more realistic stereo images.

- **Spaced pairs:** Spaced pair miking involves placing mics at a distance from the source and a distance from each other. This technique is useful for recording band setups or any larger group of players. If not spaced properly, spaced pairs can have phase problems. To avoid this, use the 3:1 rule: Place mics three times farther apart than they are from the sound source.

- **Stereo microphones:** Stereo microphones include two separate diaphragms in one mic. They also have two channels outputs, which let you record each channel to its own track. Stereo mics are a good alternative if you don't want to worry about potential phasing problems.

Setting Audio Input Levels

The mic pre-amps built into the Digi 002 (Mic/Line 1-4), and the Digi 001 and Mbox (Mic/Line 1-2) interfaces have gain knobs, which let you boost and cut audio input levels.

Digi 002 has 4 additional line-level inputs (analog inputs 5-8). These inputs cannot be adjusted inside Pro Tools. To get proper input levels for these inputs you need to adjust the level output at the audio source. Digi 001 has six additional line-level inputs (analog inputs 3-8). If you're using these, or the analog inputs of an Audiomedia III card, you'll have to adjust the output of your mixer (or other audio source) to achieve proper input levels. Digi 001 also lets you adjust input levels using six Gain Level faders found in the Playback Engine dialog box (**Figure 6.11**).

Set audio input levels to the loudest volume possible without *clipping* the signal. Ideally, a signal should top out in the yellow zone of a track's level meter. An audio signal that enters the red zone is too loud and should be reduced to prevent clipping and digital distortion.

At the same time, make sure the signal isn't too soft. If you have to boost it later, you may add unwanted noise to your track. For more information on clipping and distortion, see the *What is Clipping?* sidebar later in this chapter.

Figure 6.11 Input Gain level faders in the Digi 001's Playback Engine dialog box

SETTING AUDIO INPUT LEVELS

Figure 6.12 Ideally, your audio input levels should be in the yellow zone of the level meter.

Red (clipping)

Yellow (target level)

Green

To adjust the input level on the Digi 002 or Digi 002 Rack (Mic/Line inputs 1-4):

1. Connect an instrument or microphone to the input. (Apply phantom power to the mic by pressing the 48V switch on the Digi 002's back panel, if required.)

2. Create an audio track by choosing File > New Track (or Shift-Command-N/ Shift-Control-N).

3. Assign a track input (Mic/Line 1-4) using the Input selector.

4. Press the track's Record-Enable button.

   Play the instrument or audio source at the same volume you'll play it at when you record.

5. Adjust the input gain for the channel using the gain knob on the Digi 002's front panel.

To adjust the input level on the Digi 001 or Mbox (Mic/Line inputs 1-2):

1. Connect an instrument or microphone to the input. (Apply 48V phantom power to the mic, if required.)

2. Create an audio track by choosing File > New Track.

3. Assign a track input (Mic/Line 1 or 2) using the Input selector.

4. Press the track's Record-Enable button.

   Play the instrument or audio source at the same volume you'll play it at when you record.

5. Adjust the input gain for the channel using the gain knob on the front of the Digi 001 or Mbox.

   Increase or decrease the gain until you achieve the highest possible signal level without clipping (**Figure 6.12**). Ideally, the levels should top out in the yellow zone of the track's level meter.

SETTING AUDIO INPUT LEVELS

To adjust the input gain on the Digi 001 (Analog Inputs 3-8) and Audiomedia III:

1. Connect the instrument or audio source to the Digi 001 box or Audiomedia III card.

2. Choose Setups > Playback Engine (**Figure 6.13**).

3. Set the Gain Level fader to match the output level of the connected instrument or audio source.

   If you don't know the output level of the instrument, use the default gain level, and then fine-tune the input level as recommended on the next page.

Figure 6.13 Choose Setups > Playback Engine to adjust Gain Input level faders on Digi 001 systems.

To fine-tune the input level gain on the Digi 001 (Analog Inputs 3-8) and Audiomedia III:

1. Choose File > New Track.

2. Assign the appropriate track input using the Input selector.

3. Play the instrument at the same volume you'll play it at when you record.

4. Check the track level meters.

   Ideally, the levels should top out in the yellow zone of the track's level meter. If the levels are too high or too low, choose Setups > Playback Engine, then adjust the gain level of the appropriate input.

5. Click Done.

   Repeat, if necessary, until you achieve the maximum input level possible without clipping.

Figure 6.14 The 60-Hz high-pass filter in the Digi 001's Playback Engine dialog box.

✔ Tips

- The Digi 001's Playback Engine dialog box gives you a high-pass filter at 60 Hz on analog inputs 1-2. To enable this filter, choose Setups > Playback Engine, then click the Enable Mic/Line HP Filter checkbox (**Figure 6.14**).

- Pro Tools does not have a way to adjust gain for digital audio inputs. Adjust gain from the digital audio source, if possible.

For information on connecting external audio devices to your Pro Tools LE system, see *Appendix A: Connecting Your Studio.*

What Is Clipping?

Clipping is digital distortion that occurs when you record a signal at levels that overload your system's inputs. When a signal clips, it distorts, and the peaks of its waveform are literally clipped off.

Unlike the snarling but warm overtones of analog distortion produced by certain pieces of vintage gear such as tube amps and electric guitars, digital distortion sounds like a high-pitched buzzer—it has artistic applications, but it's bothersome to most people's ears.

Ideally, input levels should be as high as possible in the yellow zone of the level meter—without clipping the red. But don't trash an irreplaceable take because of a few errant spikes. Pro Tools offers some headroom between the level at which the meter indicates clipping and the level at which clipping actually occurs. The bottom line: Always listen to your takes carefully and trust your ears.

SETTING AUDIO INPUT LEVELS

["

Monitoring at Safe Levels

Hearing is priceless, and hearing loss is epidemic. Long-term exposure to loud sound can cause hearing loss and tinnitus (permanent ringing in the ears). So don't abuse your ears by sitting in front of cranked speakers for hours, or by falling asleep with your headphones blasting. Keep the monitors in check and take lots of breaks in the studio.

You don't need to crank the monitors to hear a mix accurately. In fact, the more you crank them, the more distorted the sound becomes—and the quicker your ears fatigue. Although it *is* important to listen at a level loud enough to hear all the elements in the mix, it's just as important to evaluate your mixes at low levels. As the volume drops, key elements may begin to fade or stick out.

The ideal level to monitor audio is around 80 dB. Anything over 85 dB is considered hazardous, and earplugs—not cheap drugstore models, but custom-molded *musician's earplugs*—are strongly recommended. (See **Table 6.1** for a list of common sounds and their decibel levels.)

Sounds may damage your hearing if:

◆ The noise hurts your ears.

◆ It makes your ears ring.

◆ You're slightly deaf for several hours after being exposed to the noise.

◆ You have to shout over background noise to make yourself heard.

Did you know?

◆ The longer you're exposed to a loud noise, the more damaging it may be.

◆ The closer you are to the source of intense noise, the more damaging it is.

◆ Stuffing cotton balls or wads of tissue paper into your ears is not adequate protection; it reduces noise by a mere 7 dB.

◆ Properly fitted musician's earplugs or ear muffs reduce noise by 15 to 30 dB.

Source: American Tinnitus Association

MONITORING AUDIO

Minimizing Monitor Latency

The lag time between audio entering and leaving your recording system is known as *latency*. Pro Tools LE systems are susceptible to latency because of the heavy processing load placed on the host computer's CPU.

You may experience latency during recording as a delay between when an audio signal is recorded and when it's heard back in the monitors. Latency is, of course, disconcerting to performers, causing time problems, and in rare cases, insanity. Either way, it can mess up your session.

Fortunately, Pro Tools provides effective workarounds for latency. There's a direct relationship between latency time and the Pro Tools LE hardware buffer size: The larger the buffer size, the larger the latency (**Table 6.2**). While you may want a larger buffer size to handle extra tracks or additional plug-ins, if you want to minimize latency, you'll need to set a smaller buffer size.

To set the hardware buffer size:

1. Choose Setups > Playback Engine.

2. Choose the number of samples for the hardware buffer from the Hardware Buffer Size pop-up menu (**Figure 6.17**).

3. Click OK.

Table 6.1

Decibel Levels of Common Sounds	
DECIBELS (DB)	FAINT
20	Ticking watch
30	Whisper, dripping faucet
40	Refrigerator
DECIBELS (DB)	MODERATE
50	Rainfall
60	Conversation
65	Washing machine
70	Restaurant
DECIBELS (DB)	VERY LOUD
80	Alarm clock
85	Busy street
90	Subway
105	Chain saw
110	Dance club
DECIBELS (DB)	EXTREMELY LOUD
120	Band practice, thunderclap
130	Jackhammer, rock concert
DECIBELS (DB)	PAINFUL
140	Gunshot, firecracker
150	Jet take-off

Source: American Tinnitus Association

Table 6.2

Hardware Buffer Size and Monitor Latency	
BUFFER SIZE	LATENCY (MS) AT 44.1/48KHZ (SAMPLE RATE) (SAMPLES)
128	2.9/2.7 (use for recording drums and other time-critical instruments)
256	5.8/5.3 (use for recording vocals and instruments with slower attacks)
512	11.6/10.7 (use when mixing with 24 tracks)
1024	23.2/21.3 (use for final mix-down or with many plug-ins)

Figure 6.17 Set the hardware buffer size in the Playback Engine dialog box.

Figure 6.18 Choose Low Latency Monitoring from the Operations menu.

Using low latency monitoring

Reducing the hardware buffer size will minimize latency, but it won't eliminate it. For this reason, Digi 002, Digi 001, and Audiomedia III systems can use the low latency monitoring option. This lets you monitor audio at a latency of only 3.0 milliseconds, which is the time it takes for a signal to pass through your system's D/A (digital to analog) and A/D (analog to digital) converters.

When using low latency monitoring, the following limitations apply:

- ◆ You can record only on a track with inputs set to an audio interface (not a bus).
- ◆ You can monitor only tracks assigned to outputs 1-2.
- ◆ All plug-ins and sends assigned to record-enabled tracks (routed to outputs 1-2) are automatically bypassed.
- ◆ Record-enabled tracks will not register on master fader level meters.
- ◆ When using the Bounce To Disk command, only audio tracks are included— Auxiliary inputs are ignored.

To use low latency monitoring:

1. Record-enable the audio track (or auxiliary input).

2. Assign each track to either output 1 or 2 using the Output selector.

3. Select Operations > Low Latency Monitoring (**Figure 6.18**).

For more information on Low Latency Monitoring, see the *Pro Tools Reference Guide*.

MINIMIZING MONITOR LATENCY

111

Allocating Hard Drives

To enhance system performance, Pro Tools lets you record audio tracks simultaneously to different hard drives. You can automatically distribute audio to drives using the Round Robin feature in the Disk Allocation dialog box.

To allocate audio hard drives:

1. Choose Setups > Disk Allocation.

2. In the Disk Allocation dialog box, assign a hard drive for each track by clicking in the Root Media Folder column and selecting a volume in the Disk Allocation pop-up menu (**Figure 6.19**).

   A new Session folder is created on each hard drive.

3. To automatically distribute new audio tracks among system hard drives, select the Use Round Robin Allocation for New Tracks checkbox (**Figure 6.20**).

4. To save new audio files to an existing folder (without creating another new Session folder), select the Custom Allocation Options checkbox, click the Change button, and choose the folder.

   To create subfolders in this folder, select the Create Subfolders for Audio, Video, and Fade Files checkbox.

5. Click OK.

Figure 6.19 Assign a hard drive to each track by clicking the Root Media Folder column in the Disk Allocation dialog box.

Figure 6.20 Select the Round Robin allocation checkbox to automatically distribute audio to multiple hard drives.

ALLOCATING HARD DRIVES

Figure 6.21 In the Workspace browser, set the Volume designator to Record, if you wish to record audio to your system volume.

✔ Tip

■ If you run out of space on an external hard drive, you can allocate recording to the system drive. Although Digidesign doesn't generally recommend doing this, it can be a lifesaver in an emergency. To allocate recording to the system drive, select the Round Robin Allocation option of the Disk Allocation dialog box and click OK. Next, open the Workspace browser and set the Volume Designator for your system volume to Record (**Figure 6.21**). This lets you record and playback audio from the volume.

For more information on Workspace volume designation, see *Chapter 9: Managing Audio Files with DigiBase* or the *DigiBase Guide, Version 6.0 for TDM of LE systems on Macintosh.*

Allocating Hard Drive Space

You can also allocate the amount of hard drive space used for recording on individual drives. By managing a drive's recording space, you can help keep it from slowing down as it fills up with audio files.

To allocate a portion of your hard drive for recording:

1. Choose Setups > Preferences.

2. Click the Operation tab.

3. Under the Open Ended Record Allocation option, select the Limit To checkbox and enter a number of minutes to allocate (**Figure 6.22**).

4. Click Done.

Figure 6.22 Use the Open Ended Record Allocation option to limit a disk's audio recording.

Figure 6.23 The Click plug-in window.

Figure 6.24 In the MIDI controls panel of the Transport Window, click on the Click button.

Figure 6.25 From the Click plug-in settings pop-up menu, select a click sound preset.

Recording Audio with the Click Plug-in

No matter how musically proficient you are, recording to a *click track* is a good idea. A click track provides an absolute time reference, which can help you produce takes with a steadier feel. It can also help you keep your tracks properly aligned later on when you're overdubbing, editing, and mixing.

Pro Tools 6 provides a MIDI-based click plug-in (**Figure 6.23**), which generates an audio click track during a session. You can set the click plug-in to a tempo and meter of your choice. Because the click plug-in receives its tempo and meter data from the current session, if your session contains tempo and meter changes, the click will follow those changes accordingly. The click plug-in lets you choose from several different preset click sounds.

To use the Click plug-in:

1. Enable the Click option by doing one of the following:

   Choose MIDI > Click.

   or

   In the MIDI controls panel of the Transport Window, click on the Click button so it becomes highlighted (**Figure 6.24**).

2. Create a mono Auxiliary input and insert the click plug-in.

3. From the Click plug-in settings pop-up menu, select a click sound preset (**Figure 6.25**).

continues on next page

4. Choose MIDI > Click Options.

   or

   Double-click the Click button or Countoff button in the Transport window (**Figure 6.26**).

   The Click/Countoff Options dialog box appears (**Figure 6.27**).

5. Select Click and Countoff options as desired.

6. Begin Playback. A click is generated according to the Click/Countoff option settings and the current tempo and meter of the session.

Figure 6.26 Double-click the Countoff button to open the Click/Countoff Options dialog box.

Figure 6.27 The Click/Countoff Options dialog box.

Figure 6.28 Tempo and Meter rulers in the Edit window.

Figure 6.29 Double-click the Meter button in the Transport window.

Figure 6.30 The Tempo/Meter Change window.

Figure 6.31 Set the manual tempo with the tempo slider, or with the Tap button.

Setting Click tempo and meter

The click plug-in follows the tempo and meter information displayed in the Tempo and Meter rulers at the top of the Edit window (**Figure 6.28**). When you open a new session, the click plug-in automatically defaults to a tempo of 120 beats per minute (BPM) and a meter of 4/4 (4 beats per measure). You can, however, set the default click tempo and meter of your session as desired.

To set the default tempo:

1. Choose Windows > Show Tempo/Meter.

   or

   Double-click the Meter button in the Transport window (**Figure 6.29**).

   The Tempo/Meter Change window appears (**Figure 6.30**).

2. From the Tempo/Meter Change pop-up menu, select Tempo Change.

3. Enter the desired BPM for the session.

4. Set Location to 1|1|000. This replaces the current default tempo with the new default tempo.

5. Set Resolution to the note value you want the tempo based on. Default note value is quarter note.

6. Click Apply to set the new tempo.

✔ Tip

- In Manual Tempo mode, Pro Tools ignores events in the Tempo Track ruler and instead plays back at the tempo displayed in the Transport window. You can set the manual tempo with the tempo slider, or with the Tab button (**Figure 6.31**).

RECORDING AUDIO WITH THE CLICK PLUG-IN

To set the default meter:

1. Choose Windows > Show Tempo/Meter.

   or

   Double-click the Meter button in the Transport window.

   The Tempo/Meter Change window appears.

2. From the Tempo/Meter change pop-up menu, select Tempo Change.

3. Enter the desired meter for the session.

4. Set Location to 1|1|000. This replaces the current default tempo with the new default tempo.

5. Set the Click note value to the desired number of clicks per measure. Default note value is quarter note.

6. Click Apply to set the new meter.

For additional information on tempo and meter see *Using Rulers, Chapter 10: Editing Basics*. For information on generating a click track from a MIDI device, see *Chapter 17: Recording MIDI*.

RECORDING AUDIO WITH THE CLICK PLUG-IN

RECORDING AND PLAYING BACK AUDIO

Now that you've configured a session and set audio input levels, it's time to lay down some tracks.

This chapter will show you the basics of recording and playing back audio in Pro Tools. We'll begin by discussing the Transport window—the control center for all recording and playback operations. You'll learn how to use various transport controls and features for punching, looping, and navigating tracks.

In addition, I'll show you how to record a single audio track, as well as how to record multiple audio tracks simultaneously. Then, we'll talk about overdubbing tracks using automated punch recording, loop recording, recording to playlists, and recording on the fly with QuickPunch.

Finally, we'll cover Pro Tools' playback features such as playback scrolling, loop playback, and scrubbing tracks to locate punches.

The Transport Window

Although the Transport window (**Figure 7.1**) features many of the basic controls you'll find on a CD player or tape deck, it also provides some advanced tools for punching, looping, and synching tracks.

The Transport window contains the following buttons:

Online: This button lets Pro Tools receive an external time code source for synchronization. Pressing the button puts Pro Tools online.

Return to Zero: This button locates to the session start point. Alternatively, you can press Return (Macintosh) or Enter (Windows).

Rewind: This button rewinds from the current play location.

Stop: This button stops playback or recording. Alternatively, you can press the spacebar.

Play: This button begins playback. If you're in *Record-Ready mode*, however, it begins recording from the timeline insertion point. (See tip later in this section.) Pressing the spacebar also works. For half-speed playback, press Shift-spacebar.

Fast Forward: This button fast-forwards from the timeline insertion point.

Go to End: This button locates to the end of the session. You can also press Option-Return (Macintosh) or Control-Enter (Windows).

Record: This button, which flashes when pressed, puts Pro Tools in Record-Ready mode. You can also press F12, Command-spacebar (Macintosh), or Control-spacebar (Windows).

Pre-Roll: This button specifies the amount of track that plays before a punch-in point. Click the button to enable pre-roll, and then enter a pre-roll value in the adjacent field.

Post-Roll: This button specifies the amount of track that plays after a punch-out point. Click the button to enable post-roll, and then enter a post-roll value in the adjacent field.

Transport Master: The Transport Master lets you drive (or *slave*) devices from the Pro Tools transport controls. Conversely, you can set Pro Tools to slave from the transport controls Transport Master, see the *Pro Tools Reference Guide.*

Figure 7.1 The Transport window.

The Transport window also contains these indicators:

Start: The Start indicator displays the start time of a record or play range. Enter a value in the field to set the start time.

End: The End indicator specifies the end point of a record or play range. Enter a value in the field to set the end time.

Length: The Length indicator displays the length of a record or play range. Enter a value in the field to set a new length.

✔ Tips

- You can play tracks at different speeds and in different directions by setting your keyboard's numeric keypad to Transport mode. To do this, choose Setups > Preferences. Click the Operation tab, and then select Transport from the Numeric Keypad options.

- To change the track playback speed, select a maximum of two tracks. Then, press Control (Macintosh) or Start (Windows), and a number key (0–9). The higher the number, the faster the playback speed.

- To change the playback direction, press either the Plus key to go forward or the Minus key to go backward. For more information on Numeric Keypad modes, see the *Pro Tools Reference Guide*.

- Record-Ready mode is not to be confused with the Record-Enable button. The former is a built-in safety mode, common to most recording devices, that protects your tracks from inadvertent erasures. The latter is a channel strip track control that opens a track to audio signal input.

THE TRANSPORT WINDOW

Viewing the Transport window

You can expand or contract the Transport window as needed. If you're tight on screen space, you can condense it to a simple control strip (**Figure 7.2**).

To open the Transport window:

◆ Choose Windows > Show Transport.

    You can expand the Transport window to include the following views (**Figure 7.3**):

    Counters: The Counters view includes the same Location indicator found in the Edit window. It displays the current play position in both Main and Sub Time Scales.

    Expanded: The Expanded view includes pre- and post-roll buttons, and start, end, length, and transport master indicators.

    MIDI Controls: The MIDI controls view includes Wait for Note, Click, Countoff, MIDI Merge, Tempo, Meter, and Conductor. For more information on MIDI Transport controls, see *Chapter 17: Recording MIDI.*

To see the Transport window's Expanded view:

◆ Choose Display > Transport Window Shows > Expanded (**Figure 7.4**).

To see the Transport window's Counters view:

◆ Choose Display > Transport Window Shows > Counters.

To see the Transport window's MIDI Controls view:

◆ Choose Display > Transport Window Shows > MIDI Controls.

Figure 7.2 Condensed view of the Transport window.

Transport control strip

Figure 7.3 Expanded view of the Transport window.

Expanded view   Counters view   MIDI view

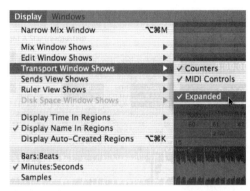

Figure 7.4 Choose Display > Transport Window Shows > Expanded to view the expanded Transport window.

THE TRANSPORT WINDOW

Figure 7.5 Click the Return to Zero button in the Transport window to return to the start of a track.

Figure 7.6 Click the Record button to put Pro Tools in Record-Ready mode.

Recording Audio Tracks

When you record audio into Pro Tools, it's saved on your hard disk as an audio file. Audio files are stored in the Audio Files folder inside the Session folder. In Pro Tools' default Non-destructive Record mode, audio files are protected from being accidentally overwritten or erased. For more information on audio files, see *Chapter 2: Software Basics* and *Chapter 8: File Management Basics.*

Pro Tools lets you record both mono and stereo audio tracks.

To record an audio track:

1. Choose File > New Track.

2. Create a new mono or stereo audio track.

   (For instructions on creating new audio tracks, see *Chapter 5: Working with Tracks.*)

3. Assign an input to the track.

   (For information on assigning track inputs and outputs, see *Chapter 5: Working with Tracks.*)

4. Record-enable the track.

5. Set the audio input level.

   Ideally, input levels should top out in the yellow zone of the level meter. If levels are consistently hitting the red zone, the signal is *clipping* and the level should be turned down. (For information on setting audio input levels, see *Chapter 6: Getting Ready to Record.*)

6. Click the Return to Zero button in the Transport window to ensure that you start recording from the beginning of the track (**Figure 7.5**).

7. Click Record in the Transport window (**Figure 7.6**).

continues on next page

RECORDING AUDIO TRACKS

8. Click Play in the Transport window or press the spacebar to begin recording (**Figure 7.7**).

9. Click Stop in the Transport window or press the spacebar to stop recording.

✔ Tips

■ To start recording, use these quick key commands: Press F12; press Command-spacebar (Macintosh) or Control-spacebar (Windows); or press 3 on the numeric keypad in Transport mode.

■ To cancel a take while recording, press Command-period (Macintosh) or Control-period (Windows). This removes the audio from your hard drive and deletes the region from the track's playlist.

■ To delete audio files from your hard drive, select the name of the audio file that you want to delete in the Audio Regions list of the Edit window (**Figure 7.8**). Choose Clear Selected from the Audio Regions List pop-up menu (**Figure 7.9**), and then select Delete from the Clear Audio window.

Figure 7.7 Click the Play button to start recording.

Figure 7.8 The Audio Regions list on the right side of the Edit window.

Figure 7.9 Use the Clear Selected command in the Audio Regions List pop-up menu to delete audio files from your hard drive.

Figure 7.10 Specify the number of audio tracks that you want to create in the New Track dialog box.

Figure 7.11 You can record-enable multiple tracks simultaneously. See Record-Enabling Tracks in *Chapter 6*.

What is Feedback?

A *feedback* loop is created when an active microphone picks up its own signal from a loudspeaker and amplifies that signal again in a self-perpetuating cycle.

Feedback can be piercing and shrill, but like distortion, it has creative applications. In particular, when electric guitars are overdriven, they can produce a pleasing blend of feedback and distortion that can be rich in harmonic content and texture.

In the studio, however, unplanned feedback can occur suddenly and really zap your ears. Avoid feedback by keeping live mics isolated from the monitors—in another room, if possible.

Recording multiple audio tracks

You can record multiple tracks of audio simultaneously. This is useful for live band situations or any time you have multiple audio sources.

To record multiple audio tracks simultaneously:

1. Choose File > New Track.

2. Specify the number of mono or stereo audio tracks you want, and then click Create (**Figure 7.10**).

3. Assign an input to each track.

4. Record-enable the tracks (**Figure 7.11**).

5. Set the audio input level.

6. Click Record in the Transport window.

7. Click Play in the Transport window or press the spacebar to begin recording.

8. Click Stop in the Transport window or press the spacebar to stop recording.

✔ Tips

- To append new material to the end of a track, press the Go to End button in the Transport window, and begin recording. The new audio is added to the end of the track.

  Note that in Non-destructive Record mode, appending new audio creates a new audio file and region. In Destructive Record mode, the new audio is added to the original audio file on the track.

- You may want to experiment with recording an instrument at half-speed. Reducing the speed can create some interesting sonic effects. To record and play back audio at half-speed, press Command-Shift-spacebar (Macintosh) or Control-Shift-spacebar (Windows).

Punch-Recording Audio

If you have a great take with only a glitch or two, try fixing it with *punch recording*. Punch recording means literally pressing or *punching* the Record buttons into and out of Record mode at precise track locations.

Pro Tool's Zoom and Selection tools let you make incredibly precise punches—automatically. The Edit window's viewing features let you quickly zoom in on waveforms to accurately identify errors (**Figure 7.12**), and select audio regions to punch.

Once you've selected a region to punch, Pro Tools does the punching for you—entering Record mode at the punch-in point, and leaving Record mode at the punch-out point. You can also set pre- and post-roll values to give the performer some lead-in time.

To punch-record audio:

1. Record-enable the track you want to punch.

2. Select Operation > Link Edit and Timeline Selection (**Figure 7.13**).

3. Select a range to punch (**Figure 7.14**).

4. Set pre- and post-roll times (**Figure 7.15**). Be sure to give the performer enough time to get in the groove of the track.

5. Click the Record button in the Transport window.

6. When you're ready to record, click Play. If pre-roll is enabled, the track plays back until the punch-in point, and then switches into Record mode. If post-roll is enabled, the track switches back out of Record mode at the punch-out point, and plays for the post-roll time.

   In Non-destructive Record mode, a new audio file is written to your hard drive and a new audio region appears in the Audio Regions list.

Figure 7.12 Use the Edit window's Zoom tools to zoom in to the sample level on waveforms.

Figure 7.13 Select Operation > Link Edit and Timeline Selection.

Figure 7.14 Use the Selector tool in the Edit window to select a range to punch.

Figure 7.15 Set a pre-roll time in the Transport window to give yourself some lead time before the punch.

PUNCH-RECORDING AUDIO

Figure 7.16 Select a record range in any Timebase ruler. The above ruler is minutes:seconds.

Figure 7.17 Drag the playback markers to select a record range.

Figure 7.18 The Memory Location dialog box lets you save and recall selections.

Figure 7.19 Use Destructive Record mode to permanently overwrite an audio file.

✔ Tips

■ You can set the start and end points of a record range for punch- and loop-recording in the following ways:

  ▲ Select a range in a track's playlist.

  ▲ Select a range in a Timebase ruler (**Figure 7.16**).

  ▲ Drag the playback markers in the ruler (**Figure 7.17**).

  ▲ Enter start and end times in the Transport window.

  ▲ Recall a memory location (**Figure 7.18**).

■ Use Destructive Record mode if you want to overwrite the region of the audio file that you're punching. Choose Operations > Destructive Record (**Figure 7.19**).

■ When punching, use Auto Input Monitoring in the Operations menu. This plays back the track until the punch-in point, when it switches to the audio input (so you can monitor what you're recording). At the punch-out point, it switches back to track playback.

Using QuickPunch

You can use QuickPunch mode to make on-the-fly punches. QuickPunch lets you punch up to 100 times during one playback.

To punch on the fly with QuickPunch:

1. Select Operations > QuickPunch (**Figure 7.20**).

   The letter P appears inside the Record button (**Figure 7.21**).

2. Set a QuickPunch crossfade length in the Editing Preferences window.

   Setting a crossfade length can help smooth the attack on punch-ins and punch-outs. (For instructions, see the next task.)

3. Record-enable the track you want to punch in on.

4. Locate a start point.

   Set pre- and post-roll times, if desired.

5. Start playback by clicking Play in the Transport window.

6. When you reach the punch-in point, click Record in the Transport window.

   or

   If you're using Digi 001 or Digi 002 systems with a connected footswitch, press the footswitch at the punch-in point.

7. To punch out, click the Record button (or press the footswitch) again.

Figure 7.20 Use QuickPunch Record mode to make on-the-fly punches.

Figure 7.21 In QuickPunch Record mode, the letter P appears inside the Record button.

QuickPunch Crossfade Length : [200] msec

Levels Of Undo : [16] Max : 16

Figure 7.22 Enter a value (in milliseconds) for the QuickPunch crossfade length.

To set the QuickPunch crossfade length:

1. Choose Setups > Preferences.

2. Click the Editing Preferences window tab.

3. Enter a value (in milliseconds) for the QuickPunch crossfade length (**Figure 7.22**).

✔ Tip

■ A 24-track session is limited to eight simultaneous tracks of QuickPunch. If you want to QuickPunch on more tracks, reduce the session's total tracks. For example, a 20-track session can record 10 tracks with QuickPunch; a 16-track session can record 12 tracks with QuickPunch. For more information on QuickPunch, see the *Pro Tools Reference Guide*.

USING QUICKPUNCH

Loop-Recording Audio

You can use Pro Tools' Loop Record mode to lay down successive non-destructive takes over the same section of a track. This is a good way to maintain inspiration and focus. For example, it can help a vocalist maintain concentration and stay in the flow of the music. Or, a guitar player may want to loop-record while developing a part. You can listen back later and select the best performance.

To loop-record audio:

1. Enable Loop Record Mode by selecting Operations > Loop Record (**Figure 7.23**). The Record button displays a loop symbol (**Figure 7.24**).

2. Record-enable the track.

3. Select a recording range in the track's playlist (**Figure 7.25**).

4. Set a pre-roll time, if desired.

5. Click Record in the Transport window.

6. When you're ready to record, click Play.

   When the start point is reached, Pro Tools begins recording. When the end point is reached, the track loops back to the start point and continues recording.

7. When you've finished recording, click Stop.

   The recorded takes appear in the Audio Regions list numbered sequentially. The most recently recorded take remains visible in the audio track.

Figure 7.23 Select Operations > Loop Record.

Figure 7.24 In Loop Record mode, the Record button displays a loop symbol.

Figure 7.25 Select a recording range in the track's playlist.

LOOP-RECORDING AUDIO

Figure 7.26 Select a take to audition by clicking on it with the Grabber tool.

Figure 7.27 In the Audio Regions list, Command-drag (Macintosh) or Control-drag (Windows) the take that you want to audition.

Auditioning Takes

Pro Tools provides some thoughtful ways to audition takes created with punch- and loop-recording. One easy way is to grab and drag individual takes from the Audio Regions list onto the track.

To audition takes using the Audio Regions list:

1. In the Edit window, select the current take by clicking on it with the Grabber tool (**Figure 7.26**).

2. Command-drag (Macintosh) or Control-drag (Windows) from the Audio Regions list the take you want to audition (**Figure 7.27**). The region replaces the previous take on the track, and snaps to the correct location.

3. Repeat the above steps as desired to audition other takes.

AUDITIONING TAKES

131

The Takes List pop-up menu

You can also audition multiple takes on a track with the Takes List pop-up menu. This menu lets you choose from a list of takes with the same *user time stamp*, which means they have matching start times.

For more information on the Takes List pop-up menu, see the *Pro Tools Reference Guide*.

Figure 7.28 The Takes List pop-up menu.

To audition takes using the Takes List pop-up menu:

1. Command-click (Macintosh) or Control-click (Windows) with the Selector tool at the precise beginning of the loop or punch range.

    or

    Select the track and Command-click (Macintosh) or Control-click (Windows) it.

    The Takes List pop-up menu appears with a list of takes with the same user time stamp (**Figure 7.28**).

2. Choose a region from the pop-up menu. The region replaces the previous take and snaps to the current location.

3. Repeat the above steps to audition other takes.

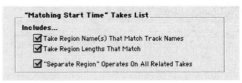

Figure 7.29 Use the "Matching Start Time" Takes List in the Editing Preferences window to determine which takes appear in the Takes List pop-up menu.

✔ Tip

- Use these Editing Preferences options to specify which takes are included in the Takes List pop-up menu (**Figure 7.29**):

    Take Region Name(s) That Match Track Names: When this option is selected, regions that share the same root name with the track appear in the Takes List pop-up menu.

    Take Region Lengths That Match: When this option is selected, takes matching the length of the current selection appear in the Takes List pop-up menu.

    "Separate Region" Operates on All Related Takes: When this option is selected, editing a region with the Separate Region command also affects all other takes with the same user time stamp.

AUDITIONING TAKES

Figure 7.30 Create new playlists for a track from the Playlist Selector pop-up menu.

Figure 7.31 Audition a playlist with the Playlist selector.

Recording to Playlists

Perhaps the best way to record multiple takes on a track is to record to playlists. All you do is create a new playlist, and then record. Use the Playlist selector to audition each playlist—each take—separately and identify the best one.

When you record to a new playlist, the audio file is written to disk and appears in the Audio Regions list. For more information on playlists, see *Chapter 2: Software Basics* and *Chapter 10: Editing Basics*.

To record to a new playlist for a track:

1. From the track's Playlist Selector pop-up menu, choose New (**Figure 7.30**).

   Enter a name for the new playlist and click OK.

2. Record-enable the track.

3. In the Transport window, click the Return to Zero button.

4. Click Record in the Transport window.

   When you're ready to record, click Play.

5. When you've finished recording, click Stop.

   A new audio region appears in the track's region playlist.

   To audition a take, choose its playlist with the Playlist selector (**Figure 7.31**).

Recording from a Digital Source

Pro Tools lets you record from digital sources, such as DAT or ADAT, depending on your system's digital hardware inputs. Digi 002 and Digi 001 users can choose from S/PDIF (RCA) inputs and ADAT optical inputs, while Mbox and Audiomedia III users are limited to S/PDIF (RCA) digital inputs.

For more information on connecting digital devices, see *Appendix A: Connecting Your Studio* and the *Pro Tools Reference Guide*.

To record from a DAT or ADAT into a Pro Tools session:

1. Connect the digital output of the DAT or ADAT recorder to the appropriate digital inputs of your interface.

2. Choose Setups > Hardware.
   The Hardware Setup dialog box appears.

3. Select the appropriate sample rate.

4. Select the appropriate sync mode (S/PDIF or Optical) and click OK (**Figure 7.32**).

5. Record-enable a track.
   Because this is a digital transfer, there's no need to set input levels.

6. Click Record in the Transport window.
   When you're ready to record, click Play.

7. Start playback on the DAT or ADAT recorder.

8. When you're finished recording, click Stop in the Transport window.
   Note: When you've finished recording from a digital source, return the sync mode to Internal. Failure to do so could result in record and playback errors.

Figure 7.32 Choose the appropriate sync mode in the Hardware Setup dialog box.

✔ Tip

■ The digital outputs of Pro Tools LE systems are active at all times. Thus, you can send digital audio to multiple external digital devices (such as an ADAT or DAT machine) simultaneously during mixdown.

Figure 7.33 The Link Selection button in the Edit window.

Playing Audio Tracks

Playback in Pro Tools is instantaneous: You can go immediately to any location in a recording without having to rewind or fast-forward. Just click anywhere in a track with the Selector tool to begin playback from that point.

There are two cursors in the Edit window: The *playback cursor* is a solid line that shows the current playback location, and the *edit cursor* is a flashing line that shows the current edit location. The latter appears when you click on a track with the Selector tool.

By default, the playback and edit cursors are linked. To unlink them for editing purposes, just use the Link Selection button (**Figure 7.33**) in the Edit window.

To begin playback from a track location:

1. Select Operation > Scrolling Options > No Auto Scrolling.

2. Select Operation > Link Edit and Timeline Selection.

   or

   Enable the Link Selection button.

3. With the Selector, click in the track at the location at which you want playback to start.

4. Click Play in the Transport window to start playback.

5. Click Stop in the Transport window to stop playback.

✔ Tip

■ To hear playback during fast forward and rewind, select the Audio During Fast Forward/Rewind checkbox in the Operation Preferences window. This will help you cue up a track location by ear.

Setting playback scrolling

Pro Tools offers the following options for scrolling the contents of the Edit window during playback and recording (**Figure 7.34**):

No Auto Scrolling: The Edit window does not scroll during or after playback. The playback cursor moves across the Edit window, indicating the playback location.

Scroll After Playback: The Edit window scrolls to the final playback location after playback has stopped. The playback cursor moves across the Edit window, indicating the playback location.

Page Scroll During Playback: The Edit window scrolls during playback. The playback cursor moves across the Edit window, indicating the playback location.

To choose a playback scrolling option:

◆ Choose Operations > Scroll Options > Select a Scrolling Option.

✔ Tip

■ You can set the edit cursor to appear at the precise location at which playback stops. To do so, select the Timeline Insertion Follows Playback checkbox in the Operation Preferences window. Then, select Operations > Link Edit and Timeline Selection.

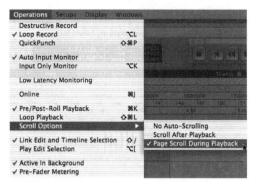

Figure 7.34 Select a Playback Scrolling option in the Operations menu.

Figure 7.35 Select Operations >
Loop Playback.

Figure 7.36 The Play button displays a loop symbol
when in Loop Playback mode.

Looping playback

Looping playback is a great way to create
drum loops or loops of any other sound.
Just select a playback range to loop, and
then fine-tune the range until the loop fits
the session. (Looping playback is also a useful, hands-free way to listen back to takes
while making coffee.)

To loop-playback a selection:

1. Select Operations > Link Edit and
   Timeline Selection.

2. With the Selector tool, choose the track
   range that you want to loop.

3. Select Operations > Loop Playback
   (**Figure 7.35**).

   The Play button displays a loop symbol
   (**Figure 7.36**).

4. Click the Play button.

   Playback begins from the start point and
   continues until the selection's end point,
   where it loops back to the start point
   and repeats.

5. Click Stop in the Transport window to
   stop playback.

✔ Tip

■ You can also enable Loop Playback by
   Control-clicking (Macintosh) or Right-
   clicking (Windows) the Play button in
   the Transport window. Or, with the
   numeric keypad set to Transport mode,
   press 4.

PLAYING AUDIO TRACKS

137

Locating the playback cursor

Pro Tools 6 provides a handy Playback Cursor Locator, which lets you quickly find the playback cursor when it moves off-screen. This feature is mainly relevant when Scrolling Options are set to No Auto-Scrolling.

If the playback cursor moves beyond the time visible in the Edit window, the Playback Cursor Locator appears at the right edge of the Main Timebase ruler. If the playback cursor is located before the time visible in the Edit window, the Playback Cursor Locator appears at the left edge of the Main Timebase ruler.

To locate the playback cursor:

◆ Click the Playback Cursor Locator in the Main Timebase ruler (**Figure 7.37**).

The moving playback cursor appears at its current time location in the center of the Edit window.

Figure 7.37 Click the Playback Cursor Locator to center the moving playback cursor at its current location in the Edit window.

Figure 7.38 The Scrubber tool in the Edit window.

Figure 7.39 Drag the Scrubber over the region of audio that you want to audition.

Figure 7.40 Drag the Scrubber between two adjacent tracks to audition both simultaneously.

Display	Operation	Editing	Automa

☐ Timeline Insertion Follows Playback
☑ Edit Insertion Follows Scrub/Shuttle
☐ Support Background Record Applications
☐ Sends Default To "-INF"
☐ Audio During Fast Forward/Rewind

Figure 7.41 To locate to the point where scrubbing stops, select the Edit Insertion Follows Scrub/Shuttle checkbox in the Operation preferences.

Scrubbing tracks

You can audition, or *scrub*, audio by running the Scrubber tool (**Figure 7.38**) back and forth over an audio region. Scrubbing is quite useful for locating punch or edit points that might be difficult to see in a waveform.

To scrub an audio track:

◆ Select and drag the Scrubber over the audio region that you want to audition (**Figure 7.39**).

The length and speed of audio played during scrubbing depends on the distance and speed at which you drag the Scrubber.

The resolution of the Scrubber is dependent on the zoom resolution of the track. Press Command (Macintosh) or Control (Windows) to scrub at finer resolutions.

To scrub two audio tracks simultaneously:

◆ Drag the Scrubber between two adjacent tracks (**Figure 7.40**).

or

◆ Scrub within a selection that contains multiple tracks.

(Only the first two tracks are scrubbed.)

✔ Tips

■ To scrub at fast speed, press Option (Macintosh) or Alt (Windows) while scrubbing.

■ To automatically locate to the point where scrubbing stops, select the Edit Insertion Follows Scrub/Shuttle checkbox in the Operation Preferences window (**Figure 7.41**).

PLAYING AUDIO TRACKS

Part III: Audio File Management

FILE MANAGEMENT BASICS

Pro Tools provides a number of smart file-management features that can help you work more efficiently and creatively. Mastering these tools for organizing, moving, and copying audio files will help you streamline your sessions and, most importantly, help you protect irreplaceable, one-of-a-kind sound recordings.

In Pro Tools 6, most file-management functions have been revamped to incorporate elements of DigiBase, a new database-like utility that uses a powerful file-indexing protocol to keep track of audio files and session-related files on your hard drives. This chapter will show you how to use many of these basic but important file-management features. You'll learn how to locate missing files, import audio, and convert audio file formats (when necessary). In addition, I'll explain how to import entire tracks from a session using the Import Session Data command. (We'll get more into the specifics of DigiBase in the next chapter.)

Next, I'll show you how to export audio files from a session; then we'll look at Pro Tools' features for saving hard drive space, including compacting and deleting audio files. I'll wrap things up with a brief but important discussion on why you should always back up your audio files.

Locating Audio Files

Each time you create a new audio file, Pro Tools tags it with a unique ID. This lets Pro Tools locate the file even if its name or location has changed. When you open a session, Pro Tools looks for all audio files belonging to that session. In Pro Tools 6, if any audio files (or other session-related files) are missing, Pro Tools launches a Missing Files warning.

The Missing Files warning indicates how many files are missing. It also gives you the option of manually finding and *relinking* missing files with their sessions (using the *Relink window*), or letting Pro Tools find and relink missing files automatically.

Pro Tools 6 also distinguishes between files found on volumes suitable for record and playback (*Performance volumes*) and files found on non-suitable volumes, such as CD-ROM or network servers (*Transfer volumes*). If Pro Tools determines that a file is located on a Transfer volume, a dialog appears prompting you to copy them to a suitable Performance volume.

For more information on the Relink window, Performance volumes, and Transfer volumes, see *Chapter 9: Managing Audio Files with DigiBase.*

Figure 8.1 The Missing Files warning.

To locate audio files:

1. Open a session.

   If any audio files are missing, the Missing Files warning appears (**Figure 8.1**).

2. Choose one of the following options:

   Automatically Find and Relink: Pro Tools searches all Performance volumes for matching files and automatically relinks matching files with the session.

   or

   Manually Find and Relink: The Relink window opens (**Figure 8.2**). In the Relink window you can search, compare, verify, and relink missing files.

   or

   Skip All: Ignores all missing audio files and fades. Missing files remain offline in the session.

   or

   Regenerate Missing Fades: Excludes fades from the relinking process and recalculates them instead.

For more information on relinking missing files, see *Chapter 9: Managing Audio Files with DigiBase.*

Figure 8.2 The Relink window lets you manually search, audition, and relink missing files.

To locate Transfer files:

1. Open a session.

   If any files are located on Transfer volumes unsuitable for playback, Pro Tools launches a warning.

2. Click Yes to open the Copy and Relink dialog box.

3. Specify a location for the copied files on a valid Performance volume.

4. Click OK.

✔ Tip

- A region whose parent audio file cannot be located is called an offline region. The name of an offline region appears italicized and dimmed in the Audio Regions list (**Figure 8.3**); it appears in blue italicized letters in track playlists. Offline regions can be edited like other regions, but they cannot be processed with Real Time AudioSuite (RTAS) plug-ins.

Figure 8.3 Offline regions appear italicized in the Audio Regions list.

LOCATING AUDIO FILES

Importing Audio

Pro Tools lets you import audio files and audio regions from other sessions or applications. You can use either the Import Audio to Track command in the File menu, or the Import Audio command in the Audio Regions List pop-up menu. Both commands launch the Import Audio dialog box, which lets you audition, convert, and import audio files and regions.

When you use the Import Audio to Track command, Pro Tools automatically creates a new audio track and places the imported audio on it. When you import audio via the Audio Regions list, the audio file name appears in the list. You can then drag it onto a new or existing track.

In Pro Tools 6, you can also import audio by dragging it directly from a DigiBase browser into the Edit window of the current session.

You can import audio files in the following formats:

◆ AIFF

◆ MP3

◆ SDI

◆ SDII

◆ Sound Resource (AIFL), Macintosh only

◆ WAV

◆ WMA (Windows Media), Windows only

Using the Import Audio dialog box

The Import Audio dialog box (**Figure 8.4**) includes the following options for handling imported audio files and regions:

Add: This option lets you add audio files that match the current session's sample rate and bit depth. Adding files does not require any additional hard drive space because the files are not copied; they remain in their existing location.

Audio files whose bit depths do not match the current session must be converted to the correct bit depths before they can be added to Pro Tools. The application *will* let you add audio files whose sample rates do not match the current session; however, they'll play at the wrong speed unless they're converted to the appropriate sample rate.

For more information on bit depth and sample rate, see *Chapter 4: Starting a New Session*.

Copy: This option creates a copy of the audio file and places it in the folder of your choice. The Copy option is useful for organizing and consolidating imported audio files in a new location.

Convert: If an audio file does not match the current session's sample rate, bit depth, and file type, the Import Audio dialog box displays a message prompting you to convert it (**Figure 8.5**). When you convert audio files, Pro Tools creates a new file with the correct attributes and places it in the folder of your choice.

Figure 8.4 The Import Audio dialog box.

Figure 8.5 If an imported audio file's attributes (such as sample rate, bit depth, and file type) do not match the current session, you are prompted to convert them in the Import Audio dialog box.

Figure 8.6 Choose File > Import Audio to Track.

Figure 8.7 The Import Audio command in the Audio Regions List pop-up menu.

Figure 8.8 The Show pop-up menu in the Import Audio dialog box.

To import audio files or regions into a session:

1. Choose File > Import Audio to Track (**Figure 8.6**).

   or

   Choose Import Audio from the Audio Regions List pop-up menu (**Figure 8.7**). The Import Audio dialog box appears.

2. At the top of the Import Audio dialog box, click on an audio file to display its properties and associated regions. Use the Show pop-up menu to choose which audio file types are displayed (**Figure 8.8**).

3. Press the Play button to audition selected files.

   Use the horizontal slider to navigate to any location in the audio file. Use the vertical slider to adjust volume.

4. To place a file or region in the Import list, select the file (Shift-click to select multiple files) and click Add or Convert (**Figure 8.9**).

   You can also click Add All or Convert All to import all files and regions in the current directory.

   continues on next page

Figure 8.9 Click Add or Convert to place a file in the Import list.

IMPORTING AUDIO

5. To remove a file or region from the Import list, select it and click Remove.

To remove all files or regions, click Remove All.

6. Click Done.

7. If you're copying or converting files, you'll be prompted to choose a location for the new audio files.

Choose a folder on a valid audio drive.

If you choose File > Import Audio to Track, the audio files and regions are converted (if applicable) and imported to individual audio tracks. They also appear as regions in the Audio Regions list.

or

If you choose Import Audio from the Audio Regions list, the files and regions appear as regions in the Audio Regions list (**Figure 8.10**). You can then drag them to new or existing tracks.

Figure 8.10 Imported audio files and regions appear in the Audio Regions list.

IMPORTING AUDIO

Figure 8.11 You can import selected audio files using drag and drop from a DigiBase browser.

To import audio using Drag and Drop from a DigiBase browser:

1. Select the audio files you wish to import in a DigiBase browser (**Figure 8.11**).

2. Do one of the following:

   Drag the files onto the Audio Regions list of the current session.

   The imported audio files appear in the Audio Regions list.

   or

   Drag the files onto an existing track in the Edit window of the current session.

   The imported audio files appear within the existing track at the desired location.

   or

   Drag the files onto any empty space in the Edit window (or Shift-drag the files anywhere in the Edit window) of the current session.

   The imported audio files appear in new tracks inside the Edit window.

For more information on using DigiBase to import audio, see *Chapter 9: Managing Audio Files with DigiBase.*

✔ Tip

■ To batch-load multiple audio files into a session: Open a Pro Tools session, and drag the audio files you want to import onto the Pro Tools icon (the bit depth, sample rate, and file type must match the current session). The batch-loaded audio files will appear in the open session's Audio Regions list. You can then drag them onto new or existing tracks.

IMPORTING AUDIO

151

Setting Sample Rate Conversion Quality

When you import audio files into Pro Tools, you may need to convert the sample rate to match the current session. Conversion quality settings include Low, Good, Better, Best, and Tweak Head. The higher the quality, the longer the length of the conversion process. (Tweak Head can take significantly longer than the other options.)

To set the sample rate conversion quality:

1. Choose Setups > Preferences.

2. Click the Editing tab.

3. From the Conversion Quality pop-up menu, select a sample rate conversion quality (**Figure 8.12**).

✔ Tips

■ Keep in mind that converting audio can degrade sound quality: While Good or Better conversion quality settings are generally adequate, consider using Best or Tweak Head settings whenever practical. This will help you maintain the highest-quality audio possible.

■ When using the Import Audio to Tracks command, interleaved (single-file) stereo files are automatically imported to stereo tracks. Split stereo files can also be imported to stereo tracks, but the split pair must be the same length, and they must be named "filename.L" and "filename.R." In Windows or in Mac/Windows compatibility mode, these files will have a three-letter file extension appended after the ".L" or ".R."

Figure 8.12 The Conversion Quality pop-up menu.

SETTING SAMPLE RATE CONVERSION QUALITY

Figure 8.13 The Import Session Data dialog box.

Figure 8.14 Audio Media Options offer alternatives for copying and consolidating audio files.

Importing Tracks

You can use the File Menu's Import Session Data command to import entire tracks from other sessions, including audio, MIDI, auxiliary input, and master fader tracks.

The Import Session Data dialog box lets you view the properties of the source session and select which tracks to import. It also gives you options for handling source media, placing imported tracks, and converting audio file type, sample rate, and bit depth to match the current session. (In Pro Tools TDM systems, the Import Session Data dialog also lets you import track attributes, such as channel strip settings, track views, and automation.)

The Import Session Data dialog box (**Figure 8.13**) provides the following features:

Source Properties: The Source Properties area displays information about the source session, including source session name, type, start time, bit depth, and sample rate.

Audio Media Options (**Figure 8.14**): These options provide alternatives for copying and consolidating imported audio files. They include:

◆ **Consolidate from Source Media:** This option consolidates audio by copying only currently used portions of audio files. It also lets you set a handle value. A handle is a preserved segment of the original audio file before and after each region. It can be useful for fine-tuning the boundaries of a region.

◆ **Copy from Source Media:** This option copies all audio files related to the imported tracks from the source media to a new location.

IMPORTING TRACKS

◆ **Refer to Source Media (Where Possible):** This option refers the current session to the existing audio files, thus avoiding audio file duplication and saving hard drive space.

If the source files don't reside on "playable" media (such as CD-ROM), or if the files require conversion, the files are copied.

◆ **Convert Audio Media to New Session Format:** This option copies and converts any files that do not match the current session's file format, bit depth, and sample rate.

Video Media Options (**Figure 8.15**): This lets you choose between copying video files to a new location or referring to them in their original location.

Timecode Mapping Options: These options provide alternatives for placing imported tracks in the current session. Options include:

◆ **Maintain Absolute Timecode Values:** This option places imported tracks at the same time location as in the source session.

◆ **Maintain Relative Timecode Values:** This option places imported tracks at the same time offset from the session start time as in the source session.

◆ **Map Start Timecode To:** This option lets you place imported tracks at a start time that you input in the Time Value field (**Figure 8.16**). Imported track start times are relative to start times in the source session.

◆ **Track Offset Options:** This option lets you specify a track offset in addition to any offset incurred with the Time Code Mapping options. Any imported audio is offset in the current session's timeline by the specified amount.

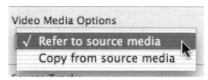

Figure 8.15 Video Media options offer alternatives for copying and consolidating video files.

Figure 8.16 The Map Start Timecode To option lets you input a start time for imported tracks.

Figure 8.17 Sample Rate Conversion options.

Sample Rate Conversion Options (Figure 8.17): These options let you convert the sample rate of imported audio files. If the source sample rate and the current session sample rate match, this area is dimmed. Sample Rate Conversion options include:

◆ **Source Sample Rate:** This option lets you choose a sample rate from which to begin the conversion process.

◆ **Destination Sample Rate:** The Destination Sample Rate always displays the sample rate of the current session.

◆ **Conversion Quality:** This option lets you change the quality of the sample-rate conversion process. At lower quality settings audio processing is faster; at higher settings audio processing is slower. For more information, see *Setting Sample Rate Conversion Quality,* earlier in this chapter.

Source Tracks: The Source Tracks area lets you select source tracks to import. Each source track has its own corresponding pop-up menu, which lists options for importing the track. The pop-up menus display the following items:

◆ **Do Not Import:** The source track is not imported.

◆ **Import as New Track:** The source track is imported to a new track. (On TDM systems, selected track attributes are imported as well.)

Import Tempo/Meter Map: This checkbox lets you import meter and tempo tracks from the source session.

IMPORTING TRACKS

To import tracks:

1. Open a session or create a new one.

2. Chose File > Import Session Data (**Figure 8.18**).

3. Select a session and click Open.

   or

   Drag the session file whose tracks you want to import from a DigiBase browser into the track playlist area in the current session's Edit window.

   The Import Session Data dialog box appears.

4. Select the tracks to import in the Source Tracks list (**Figure 8.19**).

   Shift-click to select multiple contiguous files. Command-click (Macintosh) or Alt-click (Windows) to select multiple non-contiguous files.

5. Choose the timecode mapping option for imported audio files.

6. If the sample rates of the current session and the source session do not match, choose the sample rate of the source session.

7. Choose options for imported audio and video media files (if applicable).

8. Select Import Tempo/Meter Map, if you want to import the configured Tempo and Meter rulers from the source session.

9. Click OK.

10. If you are copying or consolidating media, choose a location to place the media files.

✔ Tip

■ Imported tracks are made inactive if their source media is unavailable or if the current session's I/O Setup has configuration conflicts.

Figure 8.18 Choose File > Import Session Data.

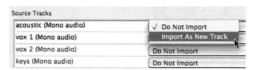

Figure 8.19 The Source Tracks list lets you select tracks to import.

Find...   ⇧⌘F
Display All   ⇧⌘D
Sorting   ▶

Import Audio...   ⇧⌘I

Select   ▶
Select All   ⇧⌘A

Clear Selected...   ⇧⌘B
Compact Selected...
Rename Selected...   ⇧⌘R
Auto Rename Selected...
Time Stamp Selected...   ⇧⌘M
Export Region Definitions... ⇧⌘Y
Export Selected As Files... ⇧⌘K
Recalculate Waveform Overviews

✓ Show File Names
  Show Disk Names
  Show Full Pathnames
✓ Select Parent Files in Project Browser

Figure 8.20 The Export Selected As Files command in the Audio Regions List pop-up menu.

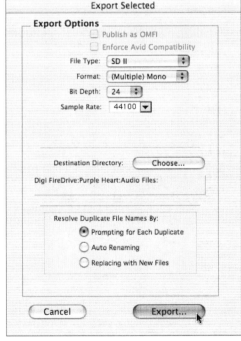

Figure 8.21 The Export Selected dialog box.

Exporting Audio

Pro Tools provides a variety of methods to export audio. The most straightforward way is to use the Export Selected As Files command in the Audio Regions List pop-up menu (**Figure 8.20**).

You can also export audio by bouncing or consolidating audio tracks. For information on the Bounce to Disk command, see *Chapter 16: Mixdown and Mastering*. For information on the Consolidate Selection command, consult the *Pro Tools Reference Guide*.

Exporting a region as a new audio file

The Export Selected As File command lets you export audio regions as new audio files. It also lets you convert the audio file type, bit depth, and sample rate. This command is helpful if you want to extract a region as a distinct new audio file for use with another session.

To export a region as a new audio file:

1. In the Audio Regions list, select the audio regions you want to export.

2. From the Audio Regions List pop-up menu, choose Export Selected As Files. The Export Selected dialog box appears (**Figure 8.21**).

continues on next page

EXPORTING AUDIO

157

3. In the Export Options area, set a file type, format (mono or stereo), bit resolution, and sample rate for the file you want to export (**Figure 8.22**).

4. Choose one of the following options for resolving duplicate file names (**Figure 8.23**):

▲ **Prompting for Each Duplicate:** If a file in the destination directory already has the name of the file you're trying to export, Pro Tools will prompt you to enter a new file name.

▲ **Auto Renaming:** This option automatically changes the name of a duplicate file by adding a number to its end (such as file-01).

▲ **Replacing with New Files:** This option replaces an existing audio file with a new audio file with the same name.

5. Click Export.

The new audio files are exported.

✔ Tip

■ If you want to re-use a region in another session, use the Export Region Definitions command in the Audio Regions List pop-up menu (**Figure 8.24**). This command lets you export region information that points to the original audio on disk—without creating a new audio file.

Figure 8.22 The Export Options area lets you set multiple parameters for exported files.

Figure 8.23 Select an option to resolve duplicate file names when exporting audio files.

Figure 8.24 Use the Export Region Definitions command in the Audio Regions List pop-up menu to export region definitions without creating a new audio file.

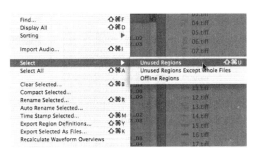

Figure 8.25 Select unused regions in a session by choosing Select > Unused Regions in the Audio Regions List pop-up menu.

Figure 8.26 The Clear Selected command lets you remove audio regions from a session or delete audio files from a hard disk.

```
                    Clear Audio
┌─────────────────────────────────────────────┐
│ This operation clears selected regions        │
│ from the audio region list.                    │
│                                                 │
│ Do you want to REMOVE the selected     ┌────────┐│
│ audio regions from this session?       │ Remove ││
│                                         └────────┘│
│                                                 │
│ Or remove and permanently DELETE the   ┌────────┐│
│ selected sound files from your disk?   │ Delete ││
│                                         └────────┘│
│                                         ┌────────┐│
│                                         │ Cancel ││
│                                         └────────┘│
└─────────────────────────────────────────────┘
```

Figure 8.27 The Clear Audio dialog box.

Compacting and Deleting Audio Files

A good way to free up valuable hard disk space is to compact or delete audio files. The Audio Regions List pop-up menu provides commands for both compacting and deleting unused or unwanted audio files.

Removing audio regions

The Compact Selected command helps you reduce the size of an audio file. It does this by permanently deleting unused portions of an audio file that are not referenced by any region definitions.

Before running the Compact Selected command, remove any unused regions from a session. This eliminates unwanted region references and ensures that the maximum amount of file compacting takes place.

To remove audio regions from a session:

1. In the Audio Regions List pop-up menu, Click Select > Unused Regions (**Figure 8.25**).

    The unused regions in the session are highlighted in the Audio Regions list.

2. Choose Clear Selected from the Audio Regions List pop-up menu (**Figure 8.26**). The Clear Audio dialog box appears (**Figure 8.27**).

3. Click Remove.

    Unused audio regions are removed from the session, although the audio files they reference remain intact on the hard drive. For more information on managing regions with the Audio Regions list, see *Chapter 10: Editing Basics.*

Compacting audio files

When you use the Compact Selected command, the Compact dialog box appears, which lets you *pad* regions (**Figure 8.28**). A pad is a small segment of audio before and after a region. It can be useful for creating fades or trimming region start and end times.

To compact an audio file:

1. Select the regions you want to compact in the Audio Regions list.

2. Choose Compact Selected from the Audio Regions List pop-up menu (**Figure 8.29**).
   The Compact dialog box appears.

3. Enter the amount of padding in milliseconds.

4. Click Compact.

✔ Tip

■ Keep in mind that the Compact Selected command is destructive: It permanently alters the original audio file and cannot be undone. Therefore, use the command only after you've finished editing and are certain that you don't need the audio data any longer.

Figure 8.28 The Compact dialog box.

Figure 8.29 Choose Compact Selected from the Audio Regions List pop-up menu.

Figure 8.30 Click Delete to permanently delete audio files from hard disk. Use this command with care!

Deleting audio files

The Clear Selected command lets you permanently delete entire audio files from your hard disk.

To delete audio files from your hard disk:

1. Select the audio files you wish to delete in the Audio Regions list.

2. Choose Clear Selected from the Audio Regions List pop-up menu.

   The Clear Audio dialog box appears.

3. Click Delete (**Figure 8.30**).

   The Clear Selected command is destructive and cannot be undone. Deleted files are permanently erased from the hard disk.

COMPACTING AND DELETING AUDIO FILES

Transferring Audio from CD (Macintosh Only)

Pro Tools lets you transfer audio tracks from a CD using the Import Audio From Other Movie command. This imports the track as a QuickTime movie, and then converts it to the session's file format.

To import a CD audio track:

1. Insert an audio CD into the CD-ROM drive.

2. Choose Movie > Import Audio From Other Movie (**Figure 8.31**).

3. Select the audio track to be imported, and click Open.

4. In the Track Import window, click OK (**Figure 8.32**).

5. Navigate to a destination for the imported audio, and click Choose.

    Pro Tools converts the CD audio track to the session's audio file format, bit depth, and sample rate, and saves it on your hard drive.

    The imported audio file appears in the Audio Regions list. From there you can drag the audio region to an existing track.

Figure 8.31 To import a CD audio track, choose Movie > Import Audio From Other Movie.

Figure 8.32 The Track Import window.

Figure 8.33 Use the Save Session Copy In dialog box to backup Session files and Audio files.

Backing Up Your Files

No chapter on file management would be complete without a discussion of backup. You only need to lose an irreplaceable recording once to appreciate the value of backing up your audio files. Get in the habit of backing up all new audio files—and session files—to a different hard drive *immediately* after a session.

To back up session files and audio files:

1. Choose File > Save Session Copy In.

   The Save Session Copy In dialog box appears (**Figure 8.33**).

2. Select All Audio Files in the Items to Copy area.

3. Create a folder named Backup, followed by the current date.

4. Click Save.

   or

1. On the desktop, navigate to the Pro Tools Session folder that you want to back up.

2. Copy the entire folder (including session files, and the Audio Files and Fade Files folders) to a different hard drive.

✔ Tip

■ The Save Session Copy In command is the only way to change the sample rate of an existing session.

MANAGING AUDIO FILES WITH DIGIBASE

DigiBase is a database-like file-management utility (new in Pro Tools 6) designed especially for managing Pro Tools files. DigiBase's comprehensive file-management tools and smartly designed user interfaces (or *browsers*) make performing file-management tasks quick, easy, and painless.

This chapter will show you how to use DigiBase to manage your audio files. We'll start with an overview of DigiBase, including how DigiBase's database works. Then we'll take a closer look at DigiBase *browsers*. You'll learn how to use browsers to view audio file information, and you'll learn how to perform file-management tasks, such as searching, copying, auditioning, and importing audio files.

We'll conclude with a look at DigiBase's other windows: I'll introduce you to DigiBase's Relink window, which helps you locate missing files; and DigiBase's Task window, which lets you regulate background file-processing tasks.

About DigiBase

DigiBase uses a file-indexing process to gather information about audio files and other session-related files. This file information, or *metadata,* includes basic file data (file name, file size, date created, etc.) and more complex data (audio file formats, waveforms, sample rate, bit depth, duration, etc.). DigiBase stores this metadata in database files on your system's *storage volumes* (hard drives).

Pro Tools uses stored file data to maintain *links* between audio files and their associated sessions. This data is also displayed in browsers, where you can perform file-management tasks (**Figure 9.1**).

For more information on browsers, see *About Browsers* later in this chapter, or see the *DigiBase Guide.* For more information on DigiBase's database features, see the *DigiBase Guide.*

DigiBase elements

DigiBase includes the following browsers and windows, or *elements*:

Workspace browser: The Workspace browser gives you access to all mounted storage volumes, as well as the folders and files they contain. It lets you search multiple volumes (and catalogs) and designate volume classifications (whether a drive is suitable for recording and playback of audio and video).

Figure 9.1 Typical DigiBase Project Browser displaying the contents of a Pro Tools session folder, including audio waveforms and other file information.

Volume browsers: Volume browsers let you manage files on local volumes and network volumes. Changes made using a Volume browser (such as copying, deleting, or moving files and folders) are mirrored on the actual volumes.

Project browsers: Project browsers display files associated with the current session. Project browsers give you tools for viewing, managing, auditioning, and spotting individual audio files.

Catalogs (TDM only): Catalog browsers let you organize files from multiple sources into libraries. Catalog browsers give you tools for searching and sorting audio files, and let you share files with other Pro Tools users.

Relink window: The Relink window gives you tools for locating missing files, and reestablishing links (*relinking*) between audio files and their associated sessions.

Task window: The Task window lets you regulate background file-processing tasks, such as copying, searching, indexing, and fade creation.

For more information on DigiBase elements, see the corresponding sections of this chapter, or see the *DigiBase Guide*.

For more information on Workspace browsers, Volume browsers, and Project browsers, see the following sections of this chapter, or see the *DigiBase Guide*. For more information on Catalogs (TDM only), see the *DigiBase Guide*.

Understanding data flow

To manage your files effectively, it's important to understand how data flows between DigiBase's various elements (**Figure 9.2**).

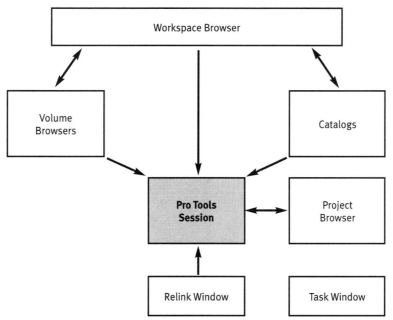

Figure 9.2 Diagram of data flow between DigiBase elements. Arrows indicate the direction of data flow.

About Browsers

Much like your computer's operating system, DigiBase browsers give you access to the contents (folders and files) of your storage volumes. Browsers display your volumes, folders, and files, as well as information about this content (stored in the associated database file), including detailed information about your audio files. You can use browsers to organize your storage volumes, audition audio files, open sessions, and perform file-management tasks, such as indexing, searching, moving, copying, deleting, and relinking audio files.

The Browser window

Although each browser type has different features, the basic design of the browser window remains the same (**Figure 9.3**).

Browser windows include the following features:

Title bar: The Title bar shows the browser type, and the name of its associated volume.

Toolbar: The Toolbar contains the Browser menu, Search icon, view presets, and browser navigation tools.

Items list: The Items list displays the contents of a volume, folder, or session.

Figure 9.3 The Browser window's basic design is the same for all types of browsers. The Workspace browser is shown.

ABOUT BROWSERS

Columns: Columns display metadata for volumes, folders, and files in the Items list. Columns can be resized, rearranged, and dragged between fixed and scrolling panes.

Search icon: The Search icon lets you search for files in volumes and folders.

View presets: View presets let you save up to five different browser layouts.

Sort toggle: The Sort toggle lets you shift the sort order between ascending and descending.

Browser menu: The Browser menu provides commands specific to each type of browser. For more information on the Browser menu, see *Browser menu commands*, later in this chapter.

Columns and metadata

The metadata gathered about items (volumes, folders, files), and stored in database files, is displayed in columns inside the browser window (**Figure 9.4**). Each column displays a specific data field pertaining to the item. Columns display the following data:

Status: This column displays the status of each item. A **T** icon is displayed for items on Transfer volumes (**Figure 9.5**). No icon is displayed for online or offline items.

File Name: This column displays the name of the file, folder, volume, catalog (TDM only), or session. This text field is editable in all browsers except catalogs.

A: This column designates volumes for audio as R (Record), P (Playback), or T (Transfer) (**Figure 9.6**).

Figure 9.4 Browser Columns display detailed information about your storage volumes (hard drives), session folders, and audio files.

Figure 9.5 The Status column displays the status of each item. A T indicates the item is on a Transfer volume, such as a CD-ROM.

Figure 9.6 The Audio and Video Designator columns let you designate storage volumes as R (Record), P (Playback), or T (Transfer).

V: This column designates volumes for video as R (Record), P (Playback), or T (Transfer).

Kind: This column indicates whether a file is a session files, audio file, or other. This field cannot be edited.

Date Created: This column displays the creation date of an item. This field cannot be edited.

Date Modified: This column displays the last date the item was modified. This field cannot be edited.

Capacity: This column displays the capacity of a volume. This field cannot be edited.

Free: This column displays the amount of unused space on a volume. This field cannot be edited.

Duration: This column displays the duration, in absolute time, of a file, regardless of time code format. This field cannot be edited.

Number of Channels: This column indicates if a file is mono or stereo. This field cannot be edited.

Sample Rate: This column displays an audio file's sample rate.

Bit Depth: This column displays an item's bit depth. This field cannot be edited.

Format: This column indicates the file format of an audio file, such as WAV, AIFF, or SDII. This field cannot be edited.

Waveform: This column displays an audio waveform of an audio file.

File Comment: This column displays any embedded comments associated with an audio file. (AIFF files not supported.)

Database Comment: This column displays any user comments stored with the database. Available in Project browser only.

Path: This column displays the directory path to the item.

UID: This column displays the unique ID for a Pro Tools file.

Clip Name: This column displays the name of the file, or the Avid clip name when the file is an OMF file.

Tape: When DigiTranslator is installed, this column displays the original Avid tape name if the file is an OMF file. If the file was originally recorded into a Pro Tools session, the original session name is displayed.

FPS: When DigiTranslator is installed, this column displays the frame rate if the file is an OMF file.

Original Timestamp: This column displays an audio files original timestamp.

User Timestamp: This column displays an audio files user timestamp if one exists.

Link Path: This column displays the path to the file used for relinking. Available in Relink window only.

Browser menu commands

The Browser menu provides a slightly different set of commands for each type of browser, as specified below. Browser menu commands include the following:

Update Database for Selected: This command updates the database for the currently selected volumes or folders.

Calculate Waveform: This command calculates waveform displays for selected audio files, or all files contained in a selected folder.

New Folder: This command creates a new folder on the current volume. In Volume browsers, a new folder is created on disk.

Reveal in Finder: This command opens the corresponding parent window in the Finder for the currently selected file.

Select Offline Files: This command selects all files currently offline.

Invert Selection: This command inverts (reverses) the current selection.

Copy and Relink: This command copies items currently selected in the Project browser to a chosen location, and relinks the session to the copies (instead of the originals). Use this to easily move files from a *Transfer* to a *Performance* volume. For more information on Transfer and Performance volumes, see *Using the Workspace Browser*, later in this chapter.

Relink Offline: This command opens the Relink window; available in Project Browsers only. For more information on the Relink Window, see *Using the Relink Window*, later in this chapter.

Relink Selected: This command opens the Relink window, with all selected files from the current browser displayed and selected as Files to Match; available in Project Browser only.

Duplicate Selected: This command creates duplicates of selected items in the same location.

Lock Selected: This commands locks all selected. Currently lock files remain locked. Locking a folder locks all files and sub-folders it contains.

Unmount: This command lets you unmount any online volume; available in the Workspace browser only.

Delete Selected: This command deletes any selected items. Deleted items are deleted from disk.

Viewing Browsers

Browser windows provide flexible features
for viewing the contents of your hard drives.
Using these features will help you find and
evaluate your session folders and audio files
more effectively.

Using fixed and scrolling panes

A browser's Items list consists of columns
that display information (such as file size,
creation date, and sample rate). The Items
list provides two panes for viewing these
columns: a fixed pane and a scrolling pane.

To show or hide the scrolling pane:

◆ Click the Show/Hide icon in the lower right
corner of the fixed pane (**Figure 9.7**).

Arranging columns

You can move columns in the Items list
between the fixed pane and scrolling pane.
(You may want to place frequently used
columns in the fixed pane and less frequently
used columns in the scrolling pane.) In
addition, you can resize and sort columns
as desired.

To move columns from the fixed pane to the scrolling pane:

◆ Click the column header and drag to the
desired pane (**Figure 9.8**).

To rearrange columns in a pane:

◆ Drag the column header to a new position.

To resize a column:

◆ Drag the column header boundary to the
desired width (**Figure 9.9**).

Figure 9.7 Click on the Show/Hide icon to show or
hide a browser window's scrolling pane.

Figure 9.8 To move a column between a browser's
fixed pane and scrolling pane, click and drag the
column header.

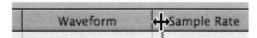

Figure 9.9 To resize a column, drag the column's
boundary to the desired width.

VIEWING BROWSERS

Figure 9.10 To sort items by column data, click the column header. The number 1 appears in the column header, indicating that column is the primary sort column.

Figure 9.11 To perform a secondary sort, Option-click (Macintosh) or Alt-click (Windows) the desired column. The number 2 appears in the column header, indicating that column is the secondary sort column.

Figure 9.12 To toggle a sort column between ascending and descending order, click the arrow at the top of the vertical scroll.

Figure 9.13 Browser windows include five view preset buttons, which let you store customized browser configurations.

Sorting items by columns

You can sort the contents of any column in ascending or descending order. This lets you view items (volumes, folders, and files) according to the data displayed in a column.

You can perform secondary sorts, as well, up to a maximum of four.

To sort items by columns:

◆ Click the column title header.

The number 1 appears in the column header (**Figure 9.10**).

To add a secondary sort:

◆ Option-click (Macintosh) or Alt-click (Windows) the column title for the secondary sort.

The number 2 appears in the column header (**Figure 9.11**).

To toggle a column sort order between ascending and descending:

◆ Click the Sort toggle arrow at the top of the vertical scroll bars (**Figure 9.12**).

Storing view presets

Browser windows provide five view presets (**Figure 9.13**), which let you save and recall customized browser configurations. You can save up to five preset views for each type of browser.

To store a view preset:

1. Open a browser.

2. Arrange columns and views as desired.

3. Command-click (Macintosh) or Control-click (Windows) one of the five view preset buttons.

VIEWING BROWSERS

173

Using Browsers

DigiBase includes the following three types of browsers: the Workspace browser, Volume browsers, and Project browsers.

The Workspace browser gives you access to all storage volumes attached to your system, although Volume browsers give you access to individual volumes only, and Project browsers give you access to the current session folder only. In effect, Volume browsers and Project browsers are subsets of the Workspace browser; you can launch Volume browsers and Project browsers by double-clicking the icon of a volume or session folder within the Workspace browser.

The Workspace browser

The Workspace browser (**Figure 9.14**) displays the contents of all storage volumes attached to your system, including all session folders, audio files, and non-Pro Tools files.

The Workspace browser gives you access to the contents of all session folders: From within the browser you can open session files, audition and import audio files, and manage all of your Pro Tools session-related files. You can also mount and unmount storage volumes within the browser; and you can designate storage volumes as Record and Playback, Playback Only, or Transfer.

In addition, and with its broad access to all volumes, the Workspace browser gives you the most comprehensive search capabilities available in Pro Tools. For more information on searches, see *Searching Items*, later in this chapter.

Figure 9.14 The Workspace browser displays the contents of all storage volumes attached to your system, including all session folders, audio files, and non-Pro Tools files.

Figure 9.15 To open the Workspace browser, choose Windows > Show Workspace.

Figure 9.16 To unmount a volume, choose Unmount from the Browser menu.

To open the Workspace browser:

1. Launch Pro Tools.

2. Choose Windows > Show Workspace (**Figure 9.15**).

   or

   Press Option-; (semi-colon) (Macintosh) or Alt-; (Windows).

   The Workspace browser appears.

Mounting and unmounting volumes

The Workspace browser lets you mount and unmount volumes while Pro Tools is launched.

To unmount a volume from within the Workspace browser:

1. Select a volume in the Workspace browser.

2. Choose Unmount from the Browser menu (**Figure 9.16**).

   The Workspace browser closes the database file for the selected volume and removes it from the Workspace browser, and then unmounts the disk from the computer. Removable volumes (such as a CD-ROM) are ejected.

USING BROWSERS

Designating audio and video volumes

The Workspace browser provides audio and video designator columns, which let you classify whether storage volumes are *Performance volumes* (suitable for Record and Playback or Playback only) or *Transfer volumes* (suitable for storage only).

The audio and video volume designator columns provide the following volume designator options:

R (Record): R designates that a volume can record and play audio and video files.

P (Playback): P designates that a volume can play audio and video already on it, but cannot have new files recorded to it.

T (Transfer): T designates that a volume can be used for storing, transferring, or auditioning files, but cannot be used for recording or playback (such as CD-ROMs).

To designate an audio or video volume:

1. Open the Workspace browser.

2. Click in the desired Audio or Video Designator column (**Figure 9.17**).

3. From the Designator pop-up menu, choose the desired designation for the volume (R, P, or T) (**Figure 9.18**).

Figure 9.17 The Audio and Video Designator columns in the Workspace browser.

Figure 9.18 To designate an Audio or Video volume, choose R (Record), P (Playback), or T (Transfer) from the Designator pop-up menu.

Figure 9.19 To open a session from within a browser, double-click on the session file icon.

Figure 9.20 To open a Volume browser, double-click on the desired volume's icon in the Workspace browser.

✔ **Tip**

■ Use the Workspace browser as the start point and end point for working in Pro Tools. This will help you become familiar with the file-management environment, and it will help you remember to back up your audio files

To start, launch Pro Tools from the application icon. Open the Workspace browser, then open your session files by double-clicking on the session file icon inside the browser window (**Figure 9.19**). To end, close the session without quitting Pro Tools by pressing Shift-Command-W (Macintosh) or Shift-Control-W (Windows), and then back up your audio files and other session files from inside the Workspace browser.

Volume browsers

Volume browsers give you access to the contents of individual mounted hard drives, network storage, and CD-ROMs. You can use Volume browsers to manage, audition, and import individual items in the volume. You can also use a Volume browser to update the database for a volume.

To open a Volume browser:

◆ Double-click a volume or folder in the Workspace browser (**Figure 9.20**).

   or

◆ Click the Expand/Collapse icon next to the item. This displays the contents of the volume or folder within the current browser.

Project browsers

Project browsers (**Figure 9.21**) give you access to all files related to the current session, regardless of what volume they reside on. Project browsers are useful for quickly viewing and auditioning audio files in the current session. Project browsers also provide a Copy and Relink command, which is useful for relinking Transfer files.

The Project browser displays the following:

Audio Files Folder: This folder contains all audio files referenced by the session.

Fade Files Folder: This folder contains all fade files referenced by the session.

Render Sources Folder: This folder contains all files that have been imported into the session, but are still being converted, copied, or processed.

Video Files Folder: This folder contains all video files referenced by the session.

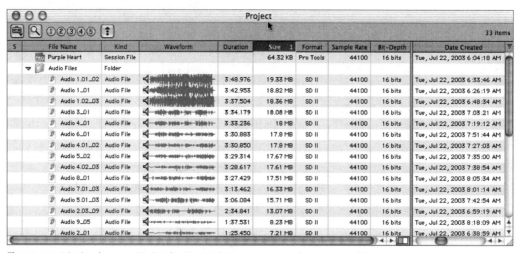

Figure 9.21 A Project browser. Project browsers give you access to the contents of the current session.

USING BROWSERS

Figure 9.22 To Open a Project browser for the current session, choose Windows > Show Project Browser.

Figure 9.23 The Copy and Relink command in a Project browser's Browser menu.

To open a Project browser:

1. Launch Pro Tools and open a session.

2. Choose Windows > Show Project Browser (**Figure 9.22**).

   or

   Press Option-O.

   The Project browser opens.

Copying and relinking files

The Copy and Relink command lets you copy files and relink the session to the copies rather than to the originals. This is useful for copying files from Transfer volumes to Performance volumes.

To copy files to a new location and relink to the copies:

1. In the Project browser, select the files you want to copy and relink.

2. Choose Copy and Relink from the Browser menu (**Figure 9.23**).

   The selected files are copied to the chosen location and relinked in the background.

For information on auditioning files, see *Waveforms and Auditioning*, later in this chapter, or see the *DigiBase Guide*.

Indexing

DigiBase uses an indexing process to extract metadata from files. It then stores that data in the associated database file, and displays it in the columns of a browser. When you open a browser, Pro Tools automatically indexes the contents of each folder. You can manually index the entire contents of a volume or folder using the Update Database command in the Browser menu.

Figure 9.24 To index a volume, folder, or audio file, from the Browser menu, select Update Database for Selected.

To manually index the contents of a volume or folder:

1. Select the volume, folder, or item in the Items list.

2. From the Browser menu, choose Update Database for Selected (**Figure 9.24**).

   The database for the entire contents of the selected volume or folder is updated.

For more information on indexing, see the *DigiBase Guide*.

INDEXING

Searching Items

DigiBase browsers include a powerful search tool. The Workspace browser gives you the broadest search capability, letting you access the content of all volumes attached to your system. All other browsers let you search the contents of that individual browser only.

When you perform a search, you can filter the contents of your volumes according to a number of *search criteria*, including file name (text), date and time, or time code; or you can select a search criterion from the Kind pop-up menu.

Search results are displayed in the Search Results pane, which appears below the Items list when you click the Search icon.

For more information on searching items, see the *DigiBase Guide*.

To search the current browser:

1. Click the Search icon.

The Search Results pane appears (**Figure 9.25**).

continues on next page

Figure 9.25 The Search Results pane (lower).

SEARCHING ITEMS

2. Enter text in the File Name field, or enter a date, or select search criteria from the Kind pop-up menu (**Figure 9.26**).

3. Click the Search button (**Figure 9.27**) or press Return (Macintosh) or Enter (Windows).

The search begins (indicated by the Search button becoming a Stop button). Results of the search are displayed Search Results pane (**Figure 9.28**).

Figure 9.26 The Kind pop-up menu lets you select additional search criteria.

Figure 9.27 Click the Search button to begin a search.

Figure 9.28 Search results appear in the Search Results pane.

Figure 9.29 Click the Stop button to stop an active search.

Figure 9.30 Click the Reset button to reset your search settings.

To stop a search:

◆ During a search, click the Stop button (**Figure 9.29**).

The search is stopped. Search results already found are displayed.

To reset your search settings:

◆ Click the Reset button (**Figure 9.30**).

All search fields are cleared and the main browser view (all items) returns.

To close the search pane:

◆ Click the Search icon to toggle the search pane closed/open.

The search is stopped. The Search pane is closed and the window returns to the main Browser view.

For more information on searching items, see the *DigiBase Guide*.

SEARCHING ITEMS

Waveforms and Auditioning

DigiBase lets you audition audio files by clicking directly on the audio file's waveform inside a DigiBase browser. When you open a session, DigiBase automatically calculates waveforms for each audio file in that session. DigiBase also calculates waveforms when you import audio into a session (**Figure 9.31**).

Calculating waveforms

When browsing in DigiBase, you may encounter audio files (in folders other than the current session) that do not yet have waveforms calculated. In this case, a gray bar appears in the waveform column (**Figure 9.32**). These files have not yet been indexed by Pro Tools, and thus do not have waveforms calculated. In order to audition these files, you can, however, direct Pro Tools to calculate waveforms as follows:

To calculate waveforms in a browser:

1. Select online audio files, or folders, in a browser.

2. Choose Calculate Waveform from the Browser menu (**Figure 9.33**).

   The audio file's waveform appears in the Waveforms column.

Figure 9.31 Audio file waveforms displayed in a browser.

Figure 9.32 If an audio file's waveform has not been calculated, a gray bar appears in the browser's Waveform column.

Figure 9.33 To calculate a selected audio file's waveform, choose Calculate Waveform from the Browser menu.

Figure 9.34 To audition an audio file, click and hold the Speaker icon.

Figure 9.35 To audition an audio file from a specific point, click and hold on the audio file's waveform at the desired location.

Auditioning audio files

You can audition audio files inside any browser. Auditioning is useful for identifying and evaluating audio files before importing, copying, or deleting them.

To audition an audio file:

1. Select an audio file in the browser's Items list.

2. Press the spacebar.

   or

   Click and hold the Speaker icon (to the left of the waveform display) (**Figure 9.34**).

To audition from a specific point within an audio file:

◆ Click and hold on the audio file's wave-form display at the desired location (**Figure 9.35**).

To loop audition an audio file:

1. Select an audio file in the browser's Items list.

2. Press Option-Spacebar.

   or

   Option-click (Macintosh) or Alt-Click (Windows) in the waveform.

Moving, Copying, Duplicating, and Deleting Items

DigiBase follows the same protocol for moving, copying, duplicating, and deleting items as your computer's operating system. For example, moving an item from one volume to another volume copies the file, and Pro Tools warns you if an item is about to be overwritten.

To move items:

◆ Select one or more items and drag them to a new location.

Moving an item to a new location on the same volume moves the item. Moving an item to a different volume copies the item.

To copy and move items:

◆ Select one or more items and Option-drag (Macintosh) or Alt-drag (Windows) them to a new location.

To duplicate one or more items:

1. Select one or more items.

2. Press Command-D (Macintosh) or Control-D (Windows).

   or

   Choose Duplicate Selected from the Browser menu (**Figure 9.36**).

Figure 9.36 To duplicate selected items, choose Duplicate Selected from the Browser menu.

New Folder
Calculate Waveform
Update Database for Selected

Invert Selection
Reveal in Finder

Duplicate Selected
Lock Selected
Unlock Selected
Delete Selected

Figure 9.37 To delete selected items, choose Delete Selected from the Browser menu.

To delete one or more items:

1. Select one or more items.

2. Press Delete.

   or

   Choose Delete Selected from the Browser menu (**Figure 9.37**).

   Pro Tools asks you to confirm that you want to permanently delete selected files from disk.

3. Click Delete.

   The files are deleted from disk.

To delete locked files:

1. Select one or more locked files.

2. Press Command-Delete (Macintosh) or Control-Delete (Windows).

   The locked files are deleted from disk.

MOVING/COPYING/DUPLICATING/DELETING ITEMS

Importing Audio Files Using Drag and Drop

DigiBase lets you import audio files by dragging and dropping them from a browser into the current session. You can drag and drop audio into the Audio Regions list or into existing or new tracks. You can also spot audio at a desired location in a track.

If an imported audio file does not match the sample rate, bit depth, or file format of the current session, Pro Tools automatically converts the file to match the session upon import. For more information on file conversion, see *Chapter 8: File Management Basics*.

To import audio files into the Audio Regions list:

1. Select the audio files in a browser.

2. Drag the files onto the Audio Regions list of the current session (**Figure 9.38**).

   The imported audio files appear in the Audio Regions list.

To import audio files into an existing track:

1. Select the audio files in a browser.

2. Drag the files onto an existing track in the Edit window of the current session.

   The imported audio files appear within the existing track at the desired location.

To import audio files into new tracks:

1. Select the audio files in a browser.

2. Drag the files onto any empty space in the Edit window.

   or

   Shift-drag the files anywhere in the Edit window.

   The imported audio files appear in new tracks inside the Edit window.

Figure 9.38 To import audio files into the Audio Regions list, drag and drop the files you want to import directly into the Audio Regions list.

Figure 9.39 Select Spot mode in the Edit Modes section of the Edit window.

Figure 9.40 The Spot Dialog box lets you select an exact location to place imported audio files.

Figure 9.41 To import and spot an audio file using its waveform, Command-click (Macintosh) or Control-click (Windows) at the approximate location you want the audio spotted. Drop the waveform into a track.

To import and spot audio into a track:

1. Enable Spot Mode (**Figure 9.39**).

2. Select an audio file in a browser.

3. Drag and drop the items into a Track playlist.
   The Spot Dialog box appears (**Figure 9.40**).

4. Enter the time location where you want to spot the item.

5. Click OK.
   The imported audio file appears in the track at the desired time location.

To import and spot an audio file using its waveform:

1. Command-click (Macintosh) or Control-click (Windows) in the audio file's waveform display at the approximate time location you want to spot the audio in the track (**Figure 9.41**).

2. While pressing Command-click or Control-click, drag and drop the waveform onto an existing audio track.
   The imported audio file appears in the track at the desired time location.

For more information on importing audio files, see *Chapter 8: File Management Basics.* For more information on importing items with drag and drop in DigiBase, see the *DigiBase Guide.*

IMPORTING AUDIO FILES USING DRAG AND DROP

189

Relinking Audio Files

When you open a session, Pro Tools attempts to locate all files linked to that session. When missing files or Transfer files (files on drives unsuitable for record and playback) are detected, Pro Tools prompts you to relink the files.

Relinking Transfer files

When a Transfer file is detected, a dialog box appears, prompting you to copy the Transfer file to a Performance volume (suitable for record and playback).

To relink Transfer files:

◆ In the Transfer files dialog, click Yes.

Files are copied to the selected Performance volume. The copies are then relinked to the session.

Relinking missing files

When a missing file is detected, Pro Tools launches the Missing Files dialog box (**Figure 9.42**). The Missing Files dialog box gives you the following options:

Skip All: The Skip All option ignores all missing audio files and fades. Missing files remain offline in the session.

Automatically Find and Relink: The Automatically Find and Relink option searches all performance volumes and automatically relinks matching files with the session. Note: This option automatically commits relinked files without asking for verification.

Manually Find and Relink: The Manually Find and Relink option opens the Relink window, where you can search, compare, verify, and relink missing files.

Regenerate Missing Fades: The Regenerate Missing Fade option excludes fades from the relinking process and recalculates them instead.

Figure 9.42 The Missing Files dialog box.

The Relink window

The Relink window (**Figure 9.43**) lets you search, compare, verify, and relink missing files. The Relink window includes the following:

Menu and Toolbar: This includes the Relink menu, view presets, and relinking buttons.

Areas to Search: This selects volumes on which to search for missing items.

Files to Relink: This lists missing files.

Candidates: This lists files that match the "relinking criteria" for a missing file. The link icon next to the candidate can be toggled to link (or unlink) the candidate to the selected missing file.

Figure 9.43 The Relink window.

To open the Relink window:

1. From the Missing Files dialog box, select Manually Find and Relink.

or

In an open session, Choose Windows > Show Project Browser.

2. Choose Relink Offline from the Browser menu (**Figure 9.44**).

The Relink window appears.

Configuring areas to search

You can configure searches in the Relink window by selecting specific volumes and folders in the Areas to Search (**Figure 9.45**) pane. When you perform a search, only those volumes and folders selected are searched. Configuring the Areas to Search pane will help make your searches more accurate and less time-consuming.

To configure the Areas to Search pane:

◆ In the Areas to Search pane, click the Search column next to each volume or folder you want included in the search (**Figure 9.46**).

Figure 9.44 To open the Relink window from inside a browser, in the Browser menu, select Relink Offline.

Figure 9.45 The Areas to Search pane of the Relink window.

Figure 9.46 In the Areas to Search pane, check the box next to the volumes and/or folders you want included in the search.

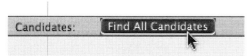

Figure 9.47 In the Select Files to Relink pane, select a single file.

Figure 9.48 The Find All Candidates button in the Relink window.

Figure 9.49 The Candidates list displays all candidate files matching search criteria for relinking.

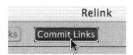

Figure 9.50 Click the Link toggle next to the candidate file you want to relink.

Figure 9.51 The Commit Links button.

Relinking single and multiple missing files

The Relink window lets you relink missing files individually or in batches. When you relink files individually, you use the Find All Candidates button, which displays all candidate files. You can then select the best-suited file to relink.

Relinking multiple files in batches is handy if you need to relink numerous missing files in short order. When you relink files in batches, you use the Find Links button, which displays a link icon, indicating Pro Tools has found the best-suited candidate. You can then view that candidate file and commit the link. (Or, if you need further confirmation before committing a relink, you can view all candidates for an individual file, and select the best-suited candidate yourself.)

To relink a single missing file:

1. Configure the Areas to Search pane.

2. Select one item in the Files to Relink list (**Figure 9.47**).

3. Click Find All Candidates (**Figure 9.48**). Pro Tools searches the selected volumes and folders and displays all files with matching File Name and/or Unique ID in the Candidates list (**Figure 9.49**). (Link icons indicate if a file is already linked.)

4. Click the Link toggle next to the candidate you want to relink (**Figure 9.50**).

5. Click Commit Links (**Figure 9.51**). (Note: Committed links cannot be undone).

   or

   Repeat for additional missing files, leaving the Commit process until later.

RELINKING AUDIO FILES

To relink multiple missing files:

1. Configure the Areas to Search pane.

2. Select one of more items in the Files to Relink list.

3. Click Find Links (**Figure 9.52**).

   The Linking Options dialog appears (**Figure 9.53**).

4. Select the desired Linking options.

5. Click OK.

   Pro Tools searches the selected volumes and folders. A link icon appears next to each file in the Files to Relink list as Pro Tools identifies a suitable candidate for the link.

6. In the Files to Relink list, click on an individual file to view the candidate file.

7. Press Commit Links.

   or

   Press Find All Candidates to view all candidate files, and select the best-suited candidate.

Committing links

Relinking cannot be undone. When using the Relink window to relink missing files, you must press the Commit Link button in order to finalize the relink. Once you have committed a relink, the old link is lost, and the relink cannot be undone.

To commit links:

1. Use the Relink window to find a relinking candidate.

2. Press Commit Link.

   The candidate file is relinked to the session.

Figure 9.52 Click the Find Links button to search for multiple files to relink.

Figure 9.53 The Link Options dialog box.

RELINKING AUDIO FILES

Managing Background Processing with the Task Window

Pro Tools performs most file-management tasks (such as copying, indexing, and relinking) in the background, letting you record, edit, and mix without interruption. Background processing can, however, especially on slower computers, divert CPU power and impact a session.

To help you optimize CPU resources, the Task window (**Figure 9.54**) lets you monitor, pause, and cancel background processing. The Task window is also useful for checking the status of a task, and for stopping unwanted tasks from being performed.

The Task window

The Task window includes the following features:

Active Tasks Pane: The Active Tasks pane (upper) shows the tasks that are in progress or in queue to start. When a task is completed it disappears from the queue. Incomplete tasks are moved to the Paused Tasks pane.

Paused Tasks Pane: The Paused Tasks pane (lower) displays paused tasks. Tasks listed in this pane must be moved to the Active Tasks pane for processing to proceed.

Task Window menu: The Task Window menu provides commands for Task window operation.

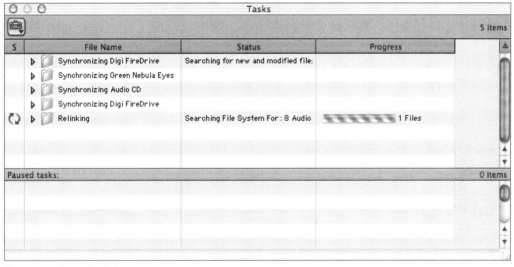

Figure 9.54 The Task window.

Columns: Columns display the following data:

◆ **Item Name:** This column indicates the name of the audio file or other affected item.

◆ **Status:** This column indicates the action being taken.

◆ **Progress:** This column indicates the progress of the task.

◆ **Progress Indicator:** This column indicates that the task is in process.

◆ **Quantification:** This column shows the percentage of progress of the current task.

◆ **Warning Message:** If a task does not complete successfully, this column displays a warning symbol and a message describing the problem.

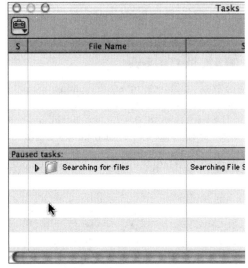

Figure 9.55 To pause a task, drag the task from the Active Tasks pane to the Paused Tasks pane.

To open the task window:

◆ Choose Windows > Show Task Window. The Task window opens.

To toggle between maximized and minimized views:

◆ Click the green View Toggle icon in the top of the Task window.

Pausing and canceling tasks

The Task window lets you pause, resume, and cancel tasks, as follows:

To pause a task:

◆ Drag the appropriate task from the Active Tasks pane to the Paused Tasks pane (**Figure 9.55**).
The Task moves to the top of the Paused Tasks pane.

Figure 9.56 To pause all tasks, select Pause All from the Task window menu.

Figure 9.57 To Resume all paused tasks, select Resume All from the Task menu.

Figure 9.58 To cancel selected tasks, select Cancel Selected from the Task menu.

To pause all tasks:

◆ Choose Pause All from the Task window menu (**Figure 9.56**).

To resume a task:

◆ Drag a task from the Paused Tasks pane to the Active Tasks pane.

The task returns to its previous position in the queue.

To resume all paused tasks:

◆ Select Resume All from the Task window menu (**Figure 9.57**).

All tasks in the Paused Tasks pane (except failed tasks) are moved to the Active Tasks pane.

To cancel a task:

1. Select any task in either pane of the Task window.

2. Select Cancel Selected in the Task menu (**Figure 9.58**).

   or

   Press Delete.

   The task is canceled and removed from the Task window.

To cancel all tasks:

1. Select any task in either pane of the Task window.

2. Press Command-A (Macintosh) Control-A (Windows) to select all tasks in that pane.

3. Press Delete.

   All tasks are removed from the Task window. (This command cannot be undone.)

For more information on the Task window, see the *DigiBase Guide*.

BACKGROUND PROCESSING WITH THE TASK WINDOW

Part IV:
Editing Audio

10

EDITING BASICS

Using a visual interface to edit audio is perhaps the most powerful feature of hard-disk recording: You can use your eyes and ears to manipulate visual representations of audio with remarkable speed and precision. Pro Tools provides many tools for working in this visual environment. With a little practice, you'll be able to transform raw audio material into streamlined final mixes.

This chapter introduces you to the basics of editing audio in Pro Tools. We'll start off with some concepts such as non-destructive editing and playback editing. Next, we'll talk about regions, and I'll show you several tools for viewing and handling them.

We'll also get into playlist editing, a feature that lets you create multiple arrangements of audio regions on a single track. And we'll look at how Edit modes influence the movement of regions in a session. Lastly, we'll discuss the Edit window's rulers and the useful memory location feature.

Editing Audio in Pro Tools

Audio editing tasks in Pro Tools are performed in the Edit window. The Edit window provides versatile tools for viewing, auditioning, selecting, and assembling audio. For a detailed description of the Edit window, see *Chapter 3: The Mix and Edit Windows.*

What is non-destructive editing?

Editing in Pro Tools is *non-destructive.* This means that when you edit audio, the original audio file saved on disk is not altered. Instead, you perform edits on audio *regions*, which are visual representations of audio files. Regions can be whole audio files or segments of audio files, and are usually displayed during editing as audio waveforms.

Certain Pro Tools commands—such as those that delete or compact audio files—are *destructive*: They permanently alter the parent audio file on disk. Pro Tools generally warns you before completing a destructive command.

What is playback editing?

You can perform many editing tasks while Pro Tools is in playback mode. This makes the editing process highly interactive and can help increase your editing speed and productivity. You can perform the following tasks during playback:

◆ Capture, separate, or trim regions

◆ Place, spot, or rearrange regions

◆ Add fades or crossfades to audio regions

◆ Nudge audio regions

◆ Audition playlists

◆ Adjust automation data

◆ Process audio with AudioSuite plug-ins

Some editing commands (such as those for setting audio inputs, outputs, and sends) cannot be performed during playback.

Figure 10.1 A whole-file audio region.

Figure 10.2 A region representing a segment of an audio file.

acoustic guitar
acst.gtr.1-01-00
acst.gtr.1-01-01

Figure 10.3 Whole-file audio regions are represented in bold in the Audio Regions list.

Understanding Regions

An audio region is a visual representation of a parent audio file stored on disk. A region can represent a whole audio file (**Figure 10.1**) or a segment of an audio file (**Figure 10.2**). When track view is set to Waveform, regions are displayed as audio waveforms. There is no limit to the number of regions you can have in a track playlist.

When you edit audio, you're editing the regions that represent the audio, not the actual audio file. The original audio file is protected and remains unchanged on your hard disk. Regions can be edited, copied, looped, and arranged in any number of ways to create new parts, sections, or song structures.

Region types

Pro Tools has various types of regions, including:

Whole-File Audio Regions: These are created when you record or import audio, consolidate existing regions, or process audio non-destructively with an AudioSuite plug-in. Whole-file audio regions represent the entire audio file on hard disk, and are displayed in bold letters in the Audio Regions list (**Figure 10.3**).

When you record audio into Pro Tools, it appears initially as a whole-file audio region. When you select segments of a whole-file audio region, you create new regions that reference only the selected portion of the parent audio file.

User-Defined Regions: These regions are created when you perform certain tasks, such as recording, capturing, separating, or consolidating audio regions. They are also created when you trim a whole-file audio region or rename an existing region.

Auto-Created Regions: These are automatically created when you edit regions or punch-record over existing regions. You can turn auto-created regions into user-defined regions by renaming them.

Offline Regions: These are regions whose parent audio file cannot be located when you launch a session. Offline regions appear italicized and dimmed in the Audio Regions list (**Figure 10.4**) and as light-blue regions with italicized names in a track's playlist. You can edit offline regions, but you cannot process them with AudioSuite plug-ins.

Stereo Regions: These are displayed as single regions in the Audio Regions list. Click on the triangle next to the stereo file name to see its individual mono channels (**Figure 10.5**).

Figure 10.4 Offline regions are italicized and dimmed in the Audio Regions list.

Figure 10.5 A stereo region displaying its associated mono regions.

Figure 10.6 A Waveform track view.

Figure 10.7 Volume track view. Use the Pencil tool to drag the breakpoints on the line graph.

Figure 10.8 The Track View pop-up menu.

Viewing Regions

The Edit window provides several features for viewing regions and their attributes.

Setting the track view

The track view determines which type of region data is displayed in a track's playlist. You can select from Waveform, Volume, Pan, Mute, and Blocks. You can also view automated plug-in parameters. In most cases, you'll perform edits using Waveform view (**Figure 10.6**).

When track view is set to Volume, Pan, or Mute, a line graph representing the data appears against a dimmed waveform view. These line graphs include *breakpoints,* which you can edit by dragging with the Pencil tool (**Figure 10.7**).

When track view is set to Blocks, audio regions are displayed as empty blocks bearing the region's name. Blocks view is less CPU-intensive and can help accelerate screen redraws during playback scrolling.

To set the track view:

1. Click the Track View selector.

   The Track View pop-up menu appears (**Figure 10.8**).

2. Choose a track view from the pop-up menu.

✔ Tip

- To toggle between Waveform and Volume track views, click in the track you want to toggle. (If you want to toggle multiple tracks, Shift-click on the additional tracks.) Then press Control-minus (Macintosh) or Start-minus (Windows) on the keyboard.

VIEWING REGIONS

Setting the track height

You can display tracks in the Edit window at six different heights: Mini, Small, Medium, Large, Jumbo, and Extreme. Large track heights are useful for precise editing; smaller track heights help conserve screen space.

You can select a default Zoom Toggle Track Height as well, which lets you zoom back and forth between the current track height and a default track height.

To set the track height:

1. Click the arrow next to the Track View selector (**Figure 10.9**).

    or

    Click in the area to the right of the track controls (**Figure 10.10**).

    The Track Height pop-up menu appears.

2. Select a track height from the pop-up menu (**Figure 10.11**).

Zoom toggling track height

Pro Tools 6 lets you increase zoom level and track height with a single keystroke. This is useful for making edit selections, examining glitches, or for any other task that requires quickly zooming in and out. You can set the default zoom toggle track height in the Display preferences.

To use Zoom Toggle:

1. Make a selection on one or more tracks.

2. Press Control-E (Macintosh) or Start-E (Windows).

    or

    With Commands Focus enabled, press E.

    The selection is zoomed in at the default zoom toggle track height.

Figure 10.9 Press the arrow button to open the Track Height pop-up menu.

Figure 10.10 Click to the right of the track controls to open the Track Height pop-up menu.

Figure 10.11 The Track Height pop-up menu.

Figure 10.12 The expanded track display lets you view data separately on both tracks of a stereo pair.

Figure 10.13 Choose Expanded Track Display from the Track Height pop-up menu.

Figure 10.14 Region names are displayed in the upper left corner.

Figure 10.15 To display the region name, choose Display > Display Name In Regions.

To set the default Zoom Toggle Track Height:

1. Choose Setups > Preferences.

2. Click on the Display Preferences tab.

3. Select a default track height from the Zoom Toggle Track Height selector.

✔ Tip

■ Pro Tools provides an expanded track display, which lets you view volume, mute, and pan data separately for each channel of a stereo pair (**Figure 10.12**). To turn on expanded track display for a stereo track, select Expanded Track Display in the Track Height pop-up menu (**Figure 10.13**).

Displaying region names and time locations

Region names and time locations are displayed in the upper left corner of each region (**Figure 10.14**). Pro Tools lets you turn these displays on and off to prevent interference with waveform editing.

To display region names:

◆ Choose Display > Display Name In Regions (**Figure 10.15**).

To display region time locations:

1. Choose Display > Display Time In Regions.

2. Select one of the following time location display options (**Figure 10.16**):

   None: This option disables the display of region times.

   Current Time: This option displays the start and end times of regions.

   Original Time Stamp: This option displays each region's original time stamp (the time location of the region when it was first created).

   User Time Stamp: This option displays each region's user time stamp. The user time stamp is identical to the original time stamp by default, but you can redefine it using the Time Stamp Selected command.

Zooming

The Edit window gives you several tools for quickly zooming in and out on audio regions. These tools include Horizontal and Vertical Zoom buttons, the Zoomer tool, and zoom preset buttons. Learning these zooming tricks will help make editing fast and painless.

To zoom in and out horizontally on all tracks:

◆ To zoom in, click the right Horizontal Zoom button (**Figure 10.17**). To zoom out, click the left Horizontal Zoom button.

   or

◆ To zoom in, press Command-] (Macintosh) or Control-] (Windows). To zoom out, press Command-[(Macintosh) or Control-[(Windows).

Figure 10.16 To display region time locations, choose Display > Display Time In Regions.

Left Horizontal Zoom button (zooms out)   *Right Horizontal Zoom button (zooms in)*

Figure 10.17 Horizontal Zoom buttons.

VIEWING REGIONS

Left Vertical Zoom button (zooms in) — Right Vertical Zoom button (zooms out)

Figure 10.18 Vertical Zoom buttons.

Figure 10.19 The Zoomer tool.

Figure 10.20 To zoom in horizontally, drag the Zoomer in any track.

Figure 10.21 To zoom in vertically and horizontally: Press Command (Macintosh) or Control (Windows) while dragging the Zoomer in any track.

Figure 10.22 To store a zoom preset: Command-click (Macintosh) or Control-click (Windows) on a zoom preset button.

Zoom preset buttons

To zoom in and out vertically on all tracks:

◆ To zoom in, click the top Vertical Zoom button. To zoom out, click the bottom Vertical Zoom button (**Figure 10.18**).

or

◆ To zoom in, press Command-Option-] (Macintosh) or Control-Alt-] (Windows). To zoom out, press Command-Option-[(Macintosh) or Control-Alt-[(Windows).

To zoom around a specific track point:

1. Select the Zoomer tool (**Figure 10.19**).

2. Click once on the desired point within the track.

   All tracks are zoomed in one level and centered around the point.

3. To zoom out one level, Option-click (Macintosh) or Alt-click (Windows) with the Zoomer tool.

To zoom into a specific track area:

1. Select the Zoomer tool.

2. To zoom horizontally, drag with the Zoomer tool in the track's playlist (**Figure 10.20**).

   or

   To zoom horizontally and vertically, press Command (Macintosh) or Control (Windows) while dragging in the track's playlist (**Figure 10.21**).

To store a zoom preset:

1. Navigate to a zoom level that you want to store.

2. Command-click (Macintosh) or Control-click (Windows) one of the five zoom preset buttons (**Figure 10.22**).

   The preset button flashes to indicate the zoom is being stored, and then remains highlighted.

VIEWING REGIONS

209

To recall a zoom preset:

◆ Click a zoom preset button.

or

◆ While pressing Control (Macintosh) or Start (Windows), press the zoom preset number on the keyboard.

✔ Tips

■ To zoom in on a selection, press Option-F (Macintosh) or Alt-F (Windows).

■ To zoom so that all regions are visible in the Edit window, do one of the following:

▲ Double-click the Zoomer tool in the toolbar.

▲ Press Option-A (Macintosh) or Alt-A (Windows).

▲ Press the F5 key twice.

■ To toggle between zoomed-in and zoomed-out views of a track selection, press Control-E (Macintosh) or Start-E (Windows). The selection is zoomed in to fill the Edit window, and tracks containing the selection are set to Large view (**Figure 10.23**).

Figure 10.23 To toggle between zoomed-in and zoomed-out views of a track selection: Press Control-E (Macintosh) or Start-E (Windows).

Figure 10.24 Choose Duplicate from the Playlist Selector pop-up menu.

Figure 10.25 Enter a name for the duplicated playlist.

Figure 10.26 To create a new playlist, choose New from the Playlist Selector pop-up menu.

Working with Playlists

An *edit playlist* is a snapshot of a track's current arrangement of regions. Pro Tools lets you create multiple edit playlists on each track, and switch quickly between them using the Playlist selector. This gives you the flexibility to experiment with different region-editing ideas. An edit playlist can contain a single region or multiple regions.

When you create a new track, its playlist is empty until you record or import audio onto it, or drag a region to it from the Audio Regions list. It's a good practice to work off a duplicate of a track's original playlist: This preserves the track's region arrangement and frees you to try new edits.

To duplicate a track's current playlist:

1. Click the track's Playlist selector.

2. Choose Duplicate from the pop-up menu (**Figure 10.24**).

3. Enter a name for the duplicated playlist (**Figure 10.25**).

4. Click OK.

   The duplicated playlist appears and the track's name is changed to the name of the new playlist.

   You can also create a new playlist, then record or drag regions to it.

To create a new playlist:

1. Click the track's Playlist selector.

2. Choose New from the pop-up menu (**Figure 10.26**).

3. Enter a name for the new playlist menu.

4. Click OK.

   An empty playlist appears in the track.

To assign a playlist:

1. Click the track's Playlist selector.

2. Choose an existing playlist from the pop-up menu (**Figure 10.27**).

   The selected playlist appears in the track and the track's name is updated to that of the selected playlist.

To delete a track's current playlist:

1. Click the track's Playlist selector.

2. Choose Delete Unused from the pop-up menu.

3. Select the playlist you want to delete (**Figure 10.28**).

4. Click OK.

   The selected playlist is deleted. Caution: You cannot undo this action.

✔ Tips

- You can rename a playlist by renaming the track to which it is assigned: Double-click the track's name, enter a new name, and click OK.

- Each track also has a single automation playlist for each automated track control (such as volume, mute, and pan). For more information on automation playlists, see *Chapter 15: Automating a Mix*.

Figure 10.27 Choose a playlist from the pop-up menu.

Figure 10.28 The Delete Unused Playlists dialog box.

Figure 10.29 The Audio Regions list.

Figure 10.30 The Audio Regions list pop-up menu.

Using the Audio Regions List

When you record, import, or create a new audio region during editing, it appears in the Audio Regions list (**Figure 10.29**). This list lets you manage the flow of audio regions in and out of a session. Whole-file audio regions are displayed in bold, and stereo regions can be expanded to view individual channels. You can drag regions from the list directly onto any audio track.

The Audio Regions list pop-up menu (**Figure 10.30**) provides options for displaying, sorting, finding, and selecting audio regions. You can also use the list to import, export, compact, and delete audio files on disk. For information on managing audio files, see *Part III: Audio File Management.*

Displaying audio file info

The Audio Regions list lets you display
information about a region's parent audio
file. You can display the parent audio file's
name, the disk name on which it resides, or
the file's full pathname.

To display audio file info:

1. Click on the Audio Regions List
   pop-up menu.

2. Choose any of the following
   (**Figure 10.31**):

   ▲ Show File Names

   ▲ Show Disk Names

   ▲ Show Full Pathnames

   The Audio Regions list displays the
   chosen information for parent audio
   files (**Figure 10.32**).

✔ Tip

■ In Pro Tools 6, Project browsers (and
  other DigiBase browsers) display detailed
  audio file data, including sample rate,
  bit depth, file format, date created, date
  modified, and time stamp. You can also
  audition audio files and import them
  using drag and drop directly into the current session. Choose Windows > Show
  Project Browser. For more information
  on DigiBase browsers, see *Chapter 9:
  Managing Audio Files with DigiBase*.

Figure 10.31 Choose an option from the Audio
Regions list pop-up menu to display information
about a region's parent audio file.

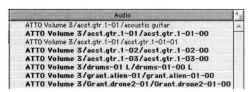

Figure 10.32 The Audio Regions list displaying parent
audio file disk names.

Figure 10.33 The Audio Regions list lets you select options for sorting audio regions.

Figure 10.34 Choose Find, then type a region name to display it in the Audio Regions list.

Figure 10.35 When displaying regions with the Find command, a small diamond appears at the top of the Audio Regions list.

Sorting regions

The Audio Regions list provides options for sorting audio regions. These options can help you manage regions, which can become quite numerous during a session. You can sort audio regions by name, length, time stamp, start time, and end time.

You can also sort regions by their parent audio file attributes, including creation date, disk name, and track format (stereo or mono).

To sort regions:

1. Click on the Audio Regions List pop-up menu.

2. Choose Sorting.

3. Select a sorting parameter (**Figure 10.33**). Audio regions are displayed in order according to the sorting parameter.

✔ Tip

■ To reverse the order of the displayed regions repeat Steps 1 and 2 above, then select Ascending or Descending from the pop-up menu.

Finding regions

The Audio Regions list provides a Find command, which displays regions that match a word or phrase.

To find regions:

1. Click on the Audio Regions List pop-up menu.

2. Choose Find (**Figure 10.34**).

3. Type the region name or portion of the region name you want to find.

4. Click OK.

   All regions matching the specified name appear in the Audio Regions list. A small diamond at the top of the list indicates the found regions (**Figure 10.35**).

Selecting in the Audio Regions list

You can select single or multiple regions in the Audio Regions list and drag them to tracks.

To select a single region:

◆ Click on the region name that you want to select in the Audio Regions list.

The selected region is highlighted and can be dragged to a track.

To select multiple regions:

◆ Shift-click on each region that you want to select (**Figure 10.36**).

or

1. Move the cursor to the left of the region names until the Marquee cursor appears (**Figure 10.37**).

2. Command-click to the left of each region that you want to select.

The selected regions are highlighted and can be dragged to tracks.

To select a range of regions:

1. Move the cursor to the left of the region names until the Marquee appears.

2. Drag the Marquee over the regions you want to select (**Figure 10.38**).

or

Shift-click to the left of the first and last regions that you want to select.

All regions in the selected range are highlighted and can be dragged to tracks.

Figure 10.36 To select multiple regions, Shift-click on their names in the Audio Regions list.

Figure 10.37 Move the cursor to the left of the regions to enable the Marquee cursor.

Figure 10.38 Drag the Marquee in the Audio Regions list to select multiple regions.

Figure 10.39 To select unused regions in a session: Choose Select > Unused Regions in the Audio Regions List pop-up menu.

Figure 10.40 You can select regions by clicking the a-z button, and then typing the first few letters of the region's name.

Figure 10.41 To remove regions from the Audio Regions list: Choose Clear Selected from the Audio Regions List pop-up menu.

Figure 10.42 The Clear Audio dialog box.

To select unused regions:

1. Click on the Audio Regions List pop-up menu.

2. Choose Select > Unused Regions (**Figure 10.39**).

   All unused audio regions are highlighted and can be dragged to tracks or cleared from the Audio Regions list.

✔ Tip

■ You can also select audio regions using the keyboard. To do this, click on the a-z button in the upper right of the Audio Regions List pop-up menu (**Figure 10.40**), and then type the first few letters of the region name. The region name is high-lighted and can be dragged to a track.

Clearing audio regions

You can remove unwanted audio regions from the Audio Regions list using the pop-up menu. Periodically clearing unused regions will help you keep the Audio Regions list manageable.

To clear unused audio regions:

1. Click on the Audio Regions List pop-up menu.

2. Choose Select > Unused Regions.

   All unused regions are highlighted.

3. Choose Clear Selected from the Audio Regions List pop-up menu (**Figure 10.41**). The Clear Audio dialog box appears.

4. Click Remove (**Figure 10.42**).

   All unused regions are removed from the Audio Regions list.

✔ Tips

■ The parent audio files of a removed audio region remain untouched on disk.

■ Caution: You cannot undo the Remove command.

217

Using Multiple Undo

In Pro Tools 6.1 and later, the Edit menu's Undo command lets you undo up to 32 previous sequential operations. (Pro Tools 6.0 and earlier lets you undo a maximum of 16 operations.) Undo lets you quickly return to earlier editing configurations. After an operation is undone, you can use the Redo command to return to a later editing configuration.

Certain Pro Tools commands will clear the undo queue, such as those for deleting a track or playlist, or for clearing a region from the Audio Regions list. Pro Tools will warn you before it clears the undo queue.

To undo the last operation:

◆ Choose Edit > Undo (**Figure 10.43**).
or
◆ Press Command-Z (Macintosh) or Control-Z (Windows).

To redo the last undone operation:

◆ Choose Edit > Redo (**Figure 10.44**).
or
◆ Press Shift-Command-Z (Macintosh) or Shift-Control-Z (Windows).

✔ Tip

■ If you're low on RAM, reducing the levels of undo can help save memory. Choose Setups > Preferences, and click the Editing tab. In the Levels of Undo field, enter a value between 1 and 32 (Pro Tools 6.1 and later); 1 and 16 (Pro Tools 6.0 and earlier) (**Figure 10.45**). Click Done.

Figure 10.43 To undo the last operation, choose Edit > Undo.

Figure 10.44 Choose Edit > Redo to recall the last undone operation.

Figure 10.45 Choose Setups > Preferences > Editing, then input up to 32 levels of undo (Pro Tools 6.1 and later) or 16 levels of undo (Pro Tools 6.0 and earlier.

Figure 10.46 The Edit mode buttons in the upper left corner of the Edit window.

Figure 10.47 The Spot dialog box.

Setting Edit Modes

Pro Tools has four Edit modes: Shuffle, Spot, Slip, and Grid. These modes control how regions are moved and placed in the Edit window. Using the appropriate Edit mode for a task can help make editing faster and more efficient.

To set the Edit mode:

◆ Select one of the four Edit mode buttons in the upper left corner of the Edit window (**Figure 10.46**).

Edit modes affect the movement and placement of regions as follows:

Shuffle: In Shuffle mode, adjacent audio regions automatically snap together. This is useful for removing a segment from a continuous piece of audio—such as removing a section from a song. When a new region is created or placed on a track, it automatically snaps to the region to its left.

In Shuffle mode, you can rearrange the order of regions on a track, but regions can't overlap. When you change a region's start or end time, the other regions on the track are moved accordingly.

Spot: Spot mode lets you move a selected region to an exact time location. When you select a region in Spot mode, the Spot dialog box appears (**Figure 10.47**). You can then enter a precise start time for the selected region.

Spot mode is useful for precision tasks such as synchronization: You can enter SMPTE frame locations (TDM only) or another time format, capture an incoming timecode address, or use a region's time stamp as a reference point.

Slip: Slip mode lets you move regions freely in a track with few constraints. Unlike Shuffle mode, Slip mode lets you overlap regions or separate regions with space (silence).

In Slip mode, you can use edit tools—the Trimmer, Selector, Grabber, and Pencil—without time restrictions. This freedom makes Slip mode ideal for use in most editing situations.

Grid: Grid mode lets you snap selected regions to a user-defined time grid. This mode is useful for placing regions cleanly on the beat. It's also good for making precise Edit and Timeline selections.

In Pro Tool 6, there are two types of Grid mode:

▲ **Absolute Grid Mode:** Absolute Grid mode snaps a selection cleanly to the grid.

▲ **Relative Grid Mode:** Available only in Pro Tools 6 and later, Relative Grid mode moves selections by the current grid unit. Relative mode is useful when working with regions that fall between boundaries.

To set the grid size, choose a time in the Grid Value pop-up menu (**Figure 10.48**).

To display grid lines in the Edit window, choose Setups > Preferences. Click the Display tab. Select "Draw Grids for Edit Window." You can also toggle the display of grid lines on and off by clicking on any Timebase ruler (**Figure 10.49**).

For more information on using Edit modes, see *Chapter 11: Working with Regions*.

Figure 10.48 The Grid Value pop-up menu.

Figure 10.49 Toggle the display of grid lines on and off by clicking on any Timebase ruler.

✔ Tips

■ To switch between Grid mode and Slip mode while dragging a region: Press Command (Macintosh) or Control (Windows).

■ The Grid Value pop-up menu contains an option for Regions/Markers. This lets you snap a region to other region locations (start, end, and sync points), markers, and track selections.

Conductor rulers

Timebase rulers

Figure 10.50 The Edit window's Timebase and Conductor rulers.

Figure 10.51 The Tempo and Meter rulers.

Using Rulers

Pro Tools provides two types of track rulers: Timebase and Conductor. These rulers appear directly above the track playlists, along the top of the Edit window (**Figure 10.50**).

Timebase rulers provide a timing reference for track material. You can also use them to make _Edit selections_ of track material or _Timeline selections_ of record and play ranges. When you make a selection in a Timebase ruler, all tracks in the Edit window are selected.

Pro Tools LE displays the following Timebase rulers:

◆ Bars:Beats

◆ Minutes:Seconds

◆ Samples

Conductor rulers indicate important track locations within a session. Pro Tools provides the following Conductor rulers:

◆ Tempo

◆ Meter

◆ Markers

The Tempo and Meter rulers indicate locations where tempo or meter (time signature) changes occur (**Figure 10.51**). You can use these rulers to map out a session's tempo and meter fluctuations. This is useful for aligning track material with a fixed time reference such as bars and beats.

The Marker ruler displays user-defined memory locations.

USING RULERS

To display all rulers:

◆ Choose Display > Ruler View Shows > All (**Figure 10.52**).

or

1. Click the Ruler Options pop-up menu to the right of the Ruler names.

2. Choose All (**Figure 10.53**).

   All Timebase and Conductor rulers appear along the top of the Edit window.

To display the Minutes:Seconds ruler (or any other specific ruler):

◆ Choose Display > Ruler View Shows > Minutes:Seconds (or any other ruler you want to display).

To remove a ruler from the display:

◆ Option-click the ruler's name to the left of the ruler display (**Figure 10.54**).

or

1. Click the Ruler Options pop-up menu.

2. Deselect the ruler you want to hide.

To display only the Main Time Scale in the ruler:

◆ Choose Display > Ruler View Shows > None.

or

1. Click the Ruler Options pop-up menu.

2. Choose None.

   For information on the Main Time Scale, see *Chapter 3: The Mix and Edit Windows.*

✔ Tip

■ You can change the order of the ruler display by clicking and dragging on the name of any ruler.

Figure 10.52 Choose Display > Ruler View Shows to display Timebase rulers.

Figure 10.53 The Ruler Options pop-up menu.

Figure 10.54 Option-click a ruler's name to remove it from the ruler display.

USING RULERS

Figure 10.55 The New Memory Location dialog box.

◇Marker 1

Figure 10.56 A Marker memory location in the Markers ruler.

◇Marker 2   ▭Marker 3

Figure 10.57 Memory locations referenced to Bars:Beats appear as yellow chevrons in the Markers ruler. Those that are referenced to Absolute appear as yellow diamonds.

Using Memory Locations

Pro Tools lets you set *memory locations*, which store information about specific edit points and selected track ranges. Memory locations are useful for recalling important locations in a session and quickly navigating to them.

You can recall memory locations by clicking on them in the Memory Locations window (see *Recalling Memory Locations*, later in this chapter).

Setting memory locations

When you set a memory location, the New Memory Location dialog box appears (**Figure 10.55**). This lets you set time properties and general properties for each memory location.

Time properties determine whether a memory location represents a specific edit point or a selected range. You can choose the following time properties in the New Memory Locations dialog box:

Marker: This property recalls a specific time location in a session. When you create a *Marker memory location*, a yellow marker appears in the Markers ruler (**Figure 10.56**).

You can choose a timeline reference for each memory location using the Reference selector in the New Memory Locations dialog box. Memory locations referenced to Bars:Beats appear as yellow chevrons in the Markers ruler, while those referenced to Absolute appear as yellow diamonds (**Figure 10.57**).

Selection: This property recalls a selected track range. Create a *Selection memory location* if you want to return to a selected record or play range.

None: This property recalls no time information. Memory locations created without a time property are called *General Properties memory locations.*

The New Memory Locations dialog box also lets you save the following general properties with each memory location:

Zoom Settings: This recalls horizontal and vertical zoom values for audio and MIDI tracks. Zoom settings are useful for quickly moving between zoomed-in and zoomed-out track views.

Pre-/Post-Roll Times: This recalls pre- and post-roll times. You can use this in conjunction with a Selection memory location to recall the pre- or post-roll values of a selected track range.

Track Show/Hide: This recalls which tracks are hidden in a session. You can use this to recall different groups of tracks during editing or mixing.

Track Heights: This recalls all of the session's current track heights. This is useful in conjunction with zoom settings for quickly switching between different track views.

Group Enables: This recalls which Edit and Mix groups are enabled. Use this option if you want to recall a particular group for editing or mixing.

To create a Marker memory location:

1. Configure any settings you want to save along with the Marker memory location (such as zoom settings, pre-/post-roll times, Show/Hide tracks, track heights, or Edit and Mix Group enables).

2. Select Operations > Link Edit and Timeline Selection. (This makes all selections apply to both Timebase rulers and track playlists.)

3. Select Display > Ruler View Shows > Markers (**Figure 10.58**).

Figure 10.58 Select Display > Ruler View Shows > Markers to display the Markers ruler.

USING MEMORY LOCATIONS

Figure 10.59 Click the Marker Well button to the left of the Marker ruler to create a Marker memory location at the current track location.

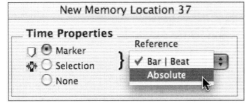

Figure 10.60 Click on the Reference pop-up menu to choose a time reference (Bars:Beats or Absolute) for a new memory location.

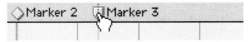

Figure 10.61 Click and drag a marker to move its location in the Markers ruler.

4. Click with the Selector tool at the desired location in any track or ruler.

5. Click the Marker Well button to the left of the Marker ruler (**Figure 10.59**).

   or

   Press Enter on the numeric keypad.

   or

   Control-click (Macintosh) or Start-click (Windows) in the Markers ruler at the desired location.

   The New Memory Location dialog box appears.

6. Select the Marker option.

7. Click on the Reference selector and select Bars:Beats or Absolute (**Figure 10.60**).

8. Enter a name for the new marker and select any general properties you want to save with the marker.

9. Click OK.

   A marker appears at the designated location in the Markers ruler and in the Memory Location window.

✔ Tip

■ To move a marker to a new location: Click and drag it to the new location in the Markers ruler (**Figure 10.61**).

   or

   Click with the Selector in the Markers ruler (or any Timebase ruler or track). In the Memory Location window or in the Markers ruler, Control-click (Macintosh) or right-click (Windows) on the Marker memory location you want to redefine. Enter a new name for the marker. Click OK.

USING MEMORY LOCATIONS

To create a Selection memory location:

1. Configure any settings you want to save with the Marker memory location (such as zoom settings, pre-/post-roll times, Show/Hide tracks, track heights, or Edit and Mix Group enables).

2. Select Operations > Link Edit and Timeline Selection. (This makes all selections apply to both Timebase rulers and track playlists.)

3. Select a range of material in one or more tracks.

4. Press Enter on the numeric keypad.
   or
   Choose Add Memory Location from the Memory Location pop-up menu at the top of the Memory Location window (**Figure 10.62**). (Click on Name to open the pop-up menu.)
   The New Memory Location dialog box appears.

5. Choose the Selection option.

6. Click on the Reference selector and select Bars:Beats or Absolute.

7. Enter a name for the new memory location and select any general properties you want to save with it.

8. Click OK.
   The Selection memory location is created and appears in the Memory Locations window.

✔ Tip

■ To change a selection stored with a memory location: Select a range of material in one or more tracks. In the Memory Location window, Control-click (Macintosh) or right-click (Window) on the memory location you want to redefine. Enter a name for the memory location and click OK.

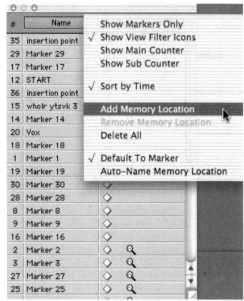

Figure 10.62 Click Name to open the Memory Location window's pop-up menu.

Figure 10.63 Select Default to Marker in the Memory Location window pop-up menu to create a memory location on the fly.

To create a General Properties location:

1. Configure any settings you want to save with the Marker memory location (such as zoom settings, pre-/post-roll times, Show/Hide tracks, track heights, or Edit and Mix Group enables).

2. Press Enter on the numeric keypad.
   The New Memory Location dialog box appears.

3. Select None.

4. Enter a name and select any general properties you want to save with it.

5. Click OK.
   The General Properties memory location is created and appears in the Memory Locations window.

✔ Tip

■ To redefine general properties stored with a memory location: Make the changes you want to the session's configuration. In the Memory Location window, Control-click (Macintosh) or right-click (Windows) on the memory location that you want to redefine; or Control-click (Macintosh) or right-Click (Windows) on the marker in the Marker ruler. Select the general properties you want to save in the New Memory Location dialog box and click OK.

To create a memory location on the fly:

1. Select Default to Marker in the Memory Location window pop-up menu (**Figure 10.63**).

2. Select Auto-Name Memory Location in the Memory Location window pop-up menu.

continues on next page

USING MEMORY LOCATIONS

3. Click Play in the Transport window.

4. Press Enter at the desired location.

A marker is automatically created and appears in the Markers ruler.

Note that the New Memory dialog box does not appear when creating memory locations on the fly.

✔ Tips

■ To rename a memory location: Double-click on it in the Memory Locations window or double-click the marker in the Markers ruler. Enter a new name in the New Memory Location dialog box, and click OK.

■ To change a memory location's time properties: Double-click on it in the Memory Locations window or double-click the marker in the Markers ruler. Select Marker, Selection, or None, and then click OK.

Recalling memory locations

You can recall memory locations by clicking on them in the Memory Locations window (**Figure 10.64**). You can also recall them from the numeric keypad.

The Memory Locations window pop-up menu (**Figure 10.65**) provides options for viewing, sorting, creating, and deleting memory locations. The menu has the following options:

Show Markers Only: This displays only Marker memory locations in the Memory Locations window.

Show View Filter Icons: This extends the Memory Locations window to include an icon-based view filter, which lets you show or hide memory locations based on their properties (**Figure 10.66**). To show or hide memory locations containing a specific property, click on the appropriate icon.

Figure 10.64 To recall a memory location, click on its name in the Memory Locations window.

Figure 10.65 The Memory Locations window's pop-up menu.

Figure 10.66 View filter icons in the Memory Locations window.

USING MEMORY LOCATIONS

Figure 10.67 The Main and Sub Counters display the location of Marker memory locations and the start times of Selection memory locations.

Figure 10.68 Click the top of each Main and Sub Counter column to select a Main and Sub Time Scale.

Show Main and Show Sub Counter: These options extend the Memory Locations window to include columns displaying the location of Marker memory locations, and the start times for Selection memory locations (**Figure 10.67**). Click at the top of each column for a pop-up menu that lets you change the Main and Sub Time Scale (**Figure 10.68**).

Sort by Time: This option sorts markers by their order in the timeline, followed by Selection memory locations and General Properties memory locations, which are listed in the order in which they were created.

Add Memory Location: This command creates a new memory location.

Remove Memory Location: This command removes the currently selected memory location in the Memory Location window.

Delete All: This command deletes all memory locations from the session.

Default to Marker: This option causes all new memory locations to default to Marker memory locations.

Auto-Name Memory Location: This command lets you create a memory location without launching the Memory Locations dialog box. When the Default to Marker option is selected, a Marker memory location is automatically created.

To recall a memory location:

1. Choose Windows > Show Memory Locations (**Figure 10.69**).

The Memory Location window appears.

2. Click on the memory location you want to recall.

or

With the Numeric Keypad Mode set to Classic, press the memory location number on the keypad followed by the period key.

or

With the Numeric Keypad Mode set to Transport, press the period key, the memory location number, and the period key again.

or

Click on a Marker memory location in the Markers ruler.

In all the above cases, the playback cursor locates to the chosen memory location and any general properties stored with it are recalled.

✔ Tips

■ To delete a marker from the Markers ruler: Option-click (Macintosh) or Alt-click (Windows) on the marker you want to delete.

■ To delete a memory location: In the Memory Locations window, Option-click (Macintosh) or Alt-click (Windows) on the memory location.

or

In the Memory Location window, select the memory location and choose Delete Memory from the pop-up menu.

Figure 10.69 To open the Memory Locations window, choose Windows > Show Memory Locations.

WORKING WITH REGIONS

When you edit audio in Pro Tools, you don't alter the original audio files saved on disk. Rather, you edit *regions* (usually displayed as waveforms) that represent the original audio files. Working with regions non-destructively makes it easy to clean up a track's rough spots, experiment with different arrangements, and generate new musical ideas.

This chapter covers the fundamentals of regions. You'll learn how to make region selections and select waveforms, and how to create new regions from larger ones. Next, I'll introduce various methods of sliding regions within tracks and between tracks; and I'll show you how to place regions, align regions, and trim regions, too.

We'll conclude with a look at ways to manage regions, including renaming regions, hiding regions, and removing regions from your session.

About Selections

Selections in Pro Tools are classified in two ways: *Edit selections* and *Timeline selections*. An Edit selection refers to the actual audio region and/or track space that becomes highlighted when you make a selection (**Figure 11.1**). Edit selections can include a single region or multiple regions, and can include the space before, after, and between regions. You can make Edit selections on single tracks or across multiple tracks.

When you make a Timeline selection, you select a range of time in any Timebase ruler (**Figure 11.2**). Timeline selections automatically apply across all tracks in a session.

Timeline selections are indicated in the ruler by blue arrows called *Playback markers* (**Figure 11.3**). Playback markers turn red during recording. *Pre-* and *post-roll flags* accompany Playback markers. These indicate the current pre- and post-roll times and turn green when the Pre- or Post-Roll buttons in the Transport window are enabled.

Figure 11.1 An Edit selection. Edit selections apply only to the selected track. Shift-click on additional tracks to extend the Edit selection.

Figure 11.2 A Timeline selection. Timeline selections automatically apply across all tracks.

Figure 11.3 Playback markers with pre- and post-roll flags in the Min:Secs ruler.

Edit markers

Figure 11.4 Edit markers, which indicate an Edit selection, appear when Edit and Timeline selections are unlinked.

   Figure 11.5 The Link Selection button.

Unlinking Edit and Timeline selections

Edit and Timeline selections are linked by default. This means that when you select inside a track, the corresponding range of timeline is also selected.

You may, however, want to unlink Edit and Timeline selections to perform certain editing tasks. For instance, if you're working with video, you may want to retain a Timeline selection of video while you search for sounds to accompany it elsewhere in the session. Once you've found the desired sound, you can return to the current Timeline selection and apply the sound to the video.

When Edit and Timeline selections are unlinked, Edit selections are displayed in the ruler as *Edit markers*, which appear as black brackets (**Figure 11.4**).

To unlink Edit and Timeline selections:

◆ Deselect Operations > Link Edit and Timeline Selection.

   or

◆ Click the Link Selection button in the upper left area of the Edit window (**Figure 11.5**).

   The Link Selection button is highlighted, and the Link Edit and Timeline Selection function is disabled.

Selecting Regions

The Selector tool in the Edit window lets you select portions of audio regions within individual tracks. Using the proper technique to select regions is key to making smooth, noise-free edits.

Editing waveforms

When you select a portion of an audio region in Waveform view, make sure that your selection does not begin or end at a point of high waveform amplitude. This can introduce audible clicks and pops at the boundaries of a newly created region. Instead, make sure your selections begin and end as close as possible to a *zero crossing*. A zero crossing is a point where the waveform crosses its center line, and the waveform's amplitude is zero (**Figure 11.6**).

In addition, try to begin your selections immediately before a volume peak, and end them immediately before another volume peak (**Figure 11.7**). Selecting at zero crossings and before volume peaks—both points of low volume—will help ensure that your edits flow seamlessly and are free of clicks and pops.

To select a portion of a region:

◆ Click and drag the Selector tool over the portion of the region you want to select (**Figure 11.8**).
   The selected portion is highlighted.

To select an entire region:

◆ Click the region with the Grabber.
   or
◆ Double-click the region with the Selector.

Figure 11.6 An Edit selection that begins and ends at a zero crossing.

Figure 11.7 An Edit selection that begins before one volume peak and ends before another volume peak.

Figure 11.8 Click and drag the Selector over a portion of a region to make an Edit selection.

Figure 11.9 A selection including two regions and the time range between them.

Figure 11.10
Click All in the Edit Groups list to group all tracks in a session.

To select two regions and the time range between them:

1. Click with the Grabber on the first region.

2. Shift-click the second region.

   Both regions and the time range between them (including any other regions) are highlighted (**Figure 11.9**).

To select an entire track:

1. Click in the track with the Selector.

2. Choose Edit > Select All.

   or

   Triple-click in the track with the Selector.

To select all regions in all tracks:

1. Select All in the Edit Groups list (**Figure 11.10**).

2. Click in any track with the Selector.

3. Choose Edit > Select All.

   or

   Triple-click with the Selector in any track.

To make a selection on the fly:

1. Use the Selector to click in the track before the start location of the range you want to select.

2. Click Play in the Transport window.

3. When playback reaches the start location, press the Down Arrow key.

4. When playback reaches the end location, press the Up Arrow key.

   The selected range is highlighted.

5. Click Stop.

SELECTING REGIONS

Changing a Selection's Length

You can make an existing selection longer or shorter by pressing the Shift key while clicking or dragging (or by dragging the Playback markers in the ruler).

To change the length of a selection:

◆ Shift-click or Shift-drag with the Selector to the left or right of the existing selection.

   or

◆ In the ruler, drag the Playback markers for a selection's start or end point (**Figure 11.11**).

Figure 11.11 Drag the Playback markers in the ruler to move a selection's start or end point.

Figure 11.12 The Nudge Value field.

Before nudge

After nudge

Figure 11.13 To nudge a selection forward or backward, hold down the Shift key, and press the Plus or Minus key on the numeric keypad.

Before nudging selection end point

After nudging selection end point

Figure 11.14 To nudge a selection's end point, hold down Command-Shift (Macintosh) or Control-Shift (Windows), and press the Plus or Minus key on the numeric keypad.

Nudging Selections

Nudging is useful for fine-tuning the boundaries of a region selection. You can nudge a selection by the current Nudge value. You can also nudge the start and end points for a selection by the current Nudge value.

To nudge a selection range:

1. Make a selection with the Selector.

2. Enter a Nudge value in the Nudge Value field, located in the upper right area of the Edit window (**Figure 11.12**).

3. Hold down the Shift key, and press the Plus or Minus key on the numeric keypad.

   The selected range moves by the Nudge value (**Figure 11.13**).

To nudge a selection's start point:

1. Make a selection with the Selector.

2. Enter a Nudge value in the Nudge Value field, located in the upper right area of the Edit window.

3. Hold down Option-Shift (Macintosh) or Alt-Shift (Windows), and press the Plus or Minus key on the numeric keypad.

   The selection's start point moves by the Nudge value.

To nudge a selection's end point:

1. Make a selection with the Selector.

2. Enter a Nudge value in the Nudge Value field, located in the upper right area of the Edit window.

3. Hold down Command-Shift (Macintosh) or Control-Shift (Windows), and press the Plus or Minus key on the numeric keypad.

   The selection's end point moves by the Nudge value (**Figure 11.14**).

NUDGING SELECTIONS

Extending a Selection

You can extend a selection in three ways: to region start and end points, to include an adjacent region, or to markers and memory locations.

To extend a selection to a region's start point:

1. Select a portion of a region with the Selector.

2. Press Shift-Option-Tab (Macintosh) or Shift-Start-Tab (Windows).

   The selection extends to the region's start point.

To extend a selection to a region's end point:

1. Select a portion of a region with the Selector.

2. Press Shift-Tab.

   The selection extends to the region's end point (**Figure 11.15**).

To extend a selection to include an adjacent region:

1. Select a region with the Grabber.

2. Press Shift-Control-Tab (Macintosh) or Shift-Start-Tab (Windows).

   The selection extends to include the next region (**Figure 11.16**).

   or

   Press Shift-Control-Option-Tab (Macintosh) or Shift-Start-Alt-Tab (Windows).

   The selection extends to the previous region.

Figure 11.15 To extend a selection to a region's end point, select a portion of the region and press Shift-Tab.

Figure 11.16 To extend a selection to include the next region: Select a region with the Grabber, and then press Shift-Control-Tab (Macintosh) or Shift-Start-Tab (Windows).

Figure 11.17 To extend a selection to a marker, Shift-click the marker in the Markers ruler.

To extend a selection to a marker or memory location:

1. Make a selection with the Selector or Grabber.

2. Shift-click a marker in the Markers ruler (**Figure 11.17**).

   or

   Shift-click a memory location in the Memory Locations window.

   The selection is extended from the original insertion point to the marker or memory location.

✔ Tip

■ If a long selection doesn't fit in the Edit window, press the Left Arrow key to jump to the beginning of the selection, or the Right Arrow key to jump to the end of it.

EXTENDING A SELECTION

Using Selection Indicators

The selection indicators at the top of the Edit window let you make precise edit selections. They use the time format of the session's Main Time Scale.

Figure 11.18 The selection indicator in the Transport window.

To make a selection using the selection indicators:

1. Click in the track you want to select.

2. Enter a value for the selection start point in the selection indicator's Start field (**Figure 11.18**).

3. Enter a value for the selection end point in the selection indicator's End field.

4. Press Enter.

   The selected range of track is highlighted.

USING SELECTION INDICATORS

Figure 11.19
The Tab to Transients button.

Transient peak

Figure 11.20 Press the Tab button to locate the cursor to the next transient.

Figure 11.21 The Smart tool in the Edit window.

Tabbing to Transients

The Tab to Transients button automatically locates the cursor to the next *transient peak* in an audio waveform. A transient is a sound, such as a drum hit, a piano note, or a guitar strum, that occurs for a brief time period. The transient peak is the instance of strongest attack in the transient. For example, a snare drum hit consists of a strong initial attack—a transient peak—followed by a period of decay.

Tabbing to transients is quite handy for locating the precise start and end point of audio regions.

To set the start and end points of a selection using Tab to Transients:

1. Click the Tab to Transients button to enable it (**Figure 11.19**).

2. Click in the audio track before the material you want to select.

3. Press the Tab key repeatedly until the cursor locates to the transient at the start of the selection (**Figure 11.20**). If necessary, press Option-Tab (Macintosh) or Control-Tab (Windows) to return the cursor to the previous transient peak.

4. Press Shift-Tab until the cursor locates to the end of the selection. If necessary, press Shift-Option-Tab (Macintosh) or Shift-Control-Tab (Windows) to move the selection end point to the previous transient.

✔ Tip

■ Use the Edit window's Smart tool (**Figure 11.21**) whenever possible during editing. It lets you quickly access the Selector, Grabber, and Trimmer tools, and create fades, all from within a region. The Smart tool is very intuitive and will save you time and reduce fatigue in your mousing hand.

Making Timeline Selections

When you make a Timeline selection, you select a range of time in a Timebase ruler. The current Timeline selection (as indicated by the Playback markers) always determines the range for playback and recording.

When Edit and Timeline selections are linked, edit selections are mirrored in the timeline. When Edit and Timeline selections are unlinked, however, you can make Timeline selections that are distinct from Edit selections.

To make a Timeline selection:

◆ Drag with the Selector in any Timebase ruler (**Figure 11.22**).

All tracks in the session are highlighted within the selected range.

or

1. Place the cursor over the first Playback marker (Down arrow).
The Grabber appears (**Figure 11.23**).

2. Drag the first Playback marker to set the desired start point.

3. Drag the second Playback marker (Up arrow) to set the desired end point (**Figure 11.24**).

All tracks in the session are highlighted within the selected range.

To move a Timeline selection in the ruler:

◆ Hold down Option (Macintosh) or Alt (Windows), and drag either Playback marker to the left or right.

The Timeline selection slides backward or forward along the timeline while the selection's length is maintained.

Figure 11.22 A Timeline selection. To make a Timeline selection, drag with the Selector in any Timebase ruler.

Figure 11.23 The Grabber appears when you place the cursor over any Playback marker.

Figure 11.24 Drag the second Playback marker to make a Timeline selection.

Figure 11.25 To capture a new region, choose Edit > Capture Region.

Creating New Regions

Pro Tools provides several commands for creating new regions from selected portions of regions. When you create a new region, it's displayed in the track's playlist and in the Audio Regions list.

Capturing regions

The Capture Region command lets you define a selection as a new region and automatically adds it to the Audio Regions list. You can then drag the new region from the list to any track.

To capture a new region:

1. Select the portion of the existing region you want to capture.

2. Choose Edit > Capture Region (**Figure 11.25**).

3. Enter a name for the new region and click OK.

   The new region appears in the Audio Regions list. The selected portion of region remains selected.

✔ Tips

■ To set Pro Tools to automatically name new regions: Select a newly created region in the Audio Regions list. In the pop-up menu, choose Auto Rename Selected (**Figure 11.26**). Enter the desired auto-name parameters in the Auto Rename dialog box.

■ To add Conductor tracks to a Timeline selection, press Option (Macintosh) or Alt (Windows) while dragging in a Timebase ruler with the Selector.

Figure 11.26 Choose Auto Rename Selected in the Audio Regions List pop-up menu.

CREATING NEW REGIONS

Separating regions

The Separate Region command lets you define
a selection as a new region and separate it
from adjacent audio data. You can separate
Edit selections made within a single region,
across adjacent regions in the same track,
or across multiple tracks. If no selection is
made, the region is split at the edit cursor's
insertion point.

To separate a region:

1. Select the portion of the existing region
   you want to separate.

   or

   Click with the Selector at the point
   where you want to split the region.

2. Choose Edit > Separate Region
   (**Figure 11.27**).

3. Enter a name for the new region and
   click OK.

   A new, separate region is created and
   appears in the Audio Regions list. New
   regions with new start and end times are
   created on either side of the separated
   region (**Figure 11.28**).

To separate a region using the Separation Grabber:

1. With the Selector, select the region you
   want to separate.

2. Choose the Separation Grabber from the
   Grabber pop-up menu (**Figure 11.29**).

3. Drag the separated region to the desired
   location on any track (**Figure 11.30**).

   A new, separate region is created and
   appears at the desired location. New
   regions with new start and end times
   are automatically created on either side
   of the separated region.

Figure 11.27 To separate a region, choose Edit > Separate Region.

Figure 11.28 New regions with new start and end times are created on either side of a separated region.

Figure 11.29 Choose the Separation Grabber from the Grabber pop-up menu.

Figure 11.30 You can drag a separated region to a new location on any track.

CREATING NEW REGIONS

Original region (unchanged)

Separated region

Figure 11.31 To separate a region without altering the original region, choose the Separation Grabber. Then, while pressing Option (Macintosh) or Alt (Windows), drag the selection to a new location on any track.

Figure 11.32 To restore separated regions, choose Edit > Heal Separation.

To separate a selection without altering the original region:

1. Select the region you want to separate.

2. Choose the Separation Grabber from the Grabber pop-up menu.

3. Hold down Option (Macintosh) or Alt (Windows), and drag the selection to the desired location on any track.

   A new, separate region is created and placed at the desired location. The original region remains intact (**Figure 11.31**).

✔ Tip

■ You can restore a separated region with the Heal Separation command: Select part of the first region, the entire separation between the regions, and part of the second region. Choose Edit > Heal Separation (**Figure 11.32**). (Regions must remain adjacent, with start and end points unchanged, for the Heal Separation command to work.)

CREATING NEW REGIONS

245

Placing Regions in Tracks

Once you've created a new region, you can place it in a track by dragging it within the same track, dragging it from another track, or dragging it from the Audio Regions list. The exact placement of a region in a track is affected by the current Edit mode (**Figure 11.33**) as follows:

Figure 11.33 The Edit mode buttons.

Figure 11.34 You can place regions on tracks by dragging them from the Audio Regions list.

Shuffle Mode: In this mode, adjacent regions automatically snap together and cannot overlap. When you place a new region at the start point of an existing region, the existing region is pushed to the right and snaps to the end of the new region.

Spot Mode: In this mode, you can move a region to an exact time location on a track. Spotting is useful when working with film and video, or whenever you need to move a region to a precise time location. When you place a new region while in Spot mode, the Spot dialog box prompts you to enter a time location.

Grid Mode: In this mode, the dragged region snaps to the nearest Grid boundary. You can choose a Grid value in the Grid Value pop-up menu in the upper right of the Edit window.

Slip Mode: In this mode, you can move and place regions anywhere in a track. Slip mode is useful for moving regions quickly within and between tracks.

For more information on Edit modes, see *Sliding Regions,* later in this chapter; or see *Chapter 10: Editing Basics.*

To place a region in a track:

1. Select a region in the Audio Regions list.

2. Drag the selected region to the desired track location (**Figure 11.34**).

   The region is placed in the track at the desired location, as determined by the current Edit mode.

PLACING REGIONS IN TRACKS

Figure 11.35 To place the start of a region in the same track at the edit insertion point, Control-click (Macintosh) or Start-click (Windows) with the Grabber.

Figure 11.36 To place the end of a region in the same track at the edit insertion point, Command-Contol-click (Macintosh) or Control-Start-click (Windows).

To place the start of a region at the edit insertion point:

1. Use the Selector to click in the track at the desired insertion point.

2. Hold down Control (Macintosh) or Start (Windows), and drag the region from either a track or from the Audio Regions list to the destination track.

   or

   If the region is already in the track, Control-click (Macintosh) or Start-click (Windows) the region with the Grabber.

   The region appears in the track with its start at the edit insertion point (**Figure 11.35**).

To place the end of a region at the edit insertion point:

1. Use the Selector to click in the track at the desired time location.

2. Hold down Command-Control (Macintosh) or Control-Start (Windows), and drag the region from either another track or from the Audio Regions list to the destination track.

   or

   If the region is already in the track, Command-Control-click (Macintosh) or Control-Start-click (Windows) the region with the Grabber.

   The region appears in the track with its end at the edit insertion point (**Figure 11.36**).

PLACING REGIONS IN TRACKS

Sliding Regions

You can slide regions (or groups of regions) within a track or between tracks using the Edit window's Grabber tool. Sliding is a useful and intuitive way to move audio regions: You can slide regions into rough arrangements quickly by eye; or you can move them to precise time locations.

Pro Tools offers a number of sliding methods, which depend on the current Edit mode.

Slipping regions

In Slip mode, you can move regions freely with the Grabber tool within a track or between tracks. You can slip a region between other regions, or you can slip a region so that it overlaps or completely covers another region.

To slip regions:

1. In the Edit window, set the Edit mode to Slip (**Figure 11.37**).

2. Click on the Grabber tool (**Figure 11.38**).

3. With the Grabber, click and drag the region you want to slip.

   The region moves freely to any location on any track.

Figure 11.37 Click on Slip to set the Edit mode.

Figure 11.38 The Grabber tool in the Edit window.

Figure 11.39 Set the Edit mode to Shuffle.

Region start point

Region shuffled to right

Figure 11.40 Click and drag a region to the start point of another region. The dragged region snaps to the start point of the other region. The other region is shuffled to the right and snaps to the end point of the dragged region.

Space between regions

Slide region between two regions

Figure 11.41 Click and drag a region between two other regions.

Space between regions retained

Region shuffled to right

Figure 11.42 The dragged region snaps to the end of the existing region on the left. The region to the right is displaced to the right by the length of the dragged region. The space between the two regions is retained.

Shuffling regions

In Shuffle mode, adjacent regions automatically snap together and cannot overlap. When you place a new region at the start point of an existing region, the existing region is pushed to the right and snaps to the end of the new region.

To shuffle regions:

1. In the Edit window, set the Edit mode to Shuffle (**Figure 11.39**).

2. With the Grabber tool, click and drag a region to the start point of another region.

   The dragged region appears at the existing region's start point. The existing region is shuffled to the right and snaps to the end of the newly placed region (**Figure 11.40**).

   or

   With the Grabber tool, click and drag a region between two existing regions (**Figure 11.41**).

   The dragged region snaps to the end of the existing region on the left. Any regions to the right are displaced to the right by the length of the newly placed region (**Figure 11.42**).

SLIDING REGIONS

Spotting regions

In Spot mode, you can place regions at exact time locations in a track. Spotting is useful for accurately placing regions dragged from the Audio Regions list. It's also useful for fixing timing problems between tracks of music; and for accurately synchronizing dialog or sound effects during video post-production.

To spot a region:

1. In the Edit window, set the Edit mode to Spot (**Figure 11.43**).

2. Drag a region from the Audio Regions list to an existing track.

   or

   Click a region already in a track with the Grabber tool.

   The Spot dialog box appears (**Figure 11.44**).

3. In the Spot dialog, select the desired time format from the Time Scale pop-up menu (**Figure 11.45**).

4. Click in the field for Start, Sync Point, or End and type in a new time location.

   or

   Click the Up arrow next to Original Time Stamp or User Time Stamp to enter those values into the currently selected field (**Figure 11.46**). For more information on time stamps, see *Chapter 10: Editing Basics,* or see the *Pro Tools Reference Guide.*

   The region is moved to the new location specified for its start or sync point. (If a region does not have a Sync point defined, the Sync Point field in the Spot dialog functions the same as the Start field.)

Figure 11.43 Click on Spot to set the Edit mode.

Figure 11.44 The Spot dialog box.

Figure 11.45 Select a time format from the Time Scale pop-up menu.

Figure 11.46 Click the Up arrow next to the Original Time Stamp or User Time Stamp to enter those values in the currently selected field.

Figure 11.47 The Grid Value pop-up menu.

Figure 11.48 Click on the Grid mode button, then choose Absolute or Relative from the pop-up menu.

Figure 11.49 In Absolute Grid mode, regions snap to grid boundaries only.

Figure 11.50 In Relative Grid mode, regions move by the amount of the current Grid value from their current location.

Using Grid Modes

In Grid mode, a dragged region snaps to the nearest Grid boundary. You can choose a Grid value in the Grid Value pop-up menu, to the right of the Grid Value indicator (**Figure 11.47**).

Pro Tools 6 provides two different Grid modes, as follows:

Absolute Grid mode: In Absolute Grid mode, moving any region snaps the region to the nearest Grid boundary.

Relative Grid mode: In Relative Grid mode, you can move regions by the amount of the current Grid value, retaining the region's relative position.

To select Absolute or Relative Grid mode:

◆ In the Edit window, Click on Grid mode and choose Absolute or Relative from the pop-up menu (**Figure 11.48**).

To place or move a region while in Grid mode:

1. In the Edit window, select a Grid value from the Grid value pop-up menu.

2. Drag a region from the Audio Regions list to an existing track.

   or

   With the Grabber, drag an existing region within a track to a new location.

   In Absolute Grid mode, the region snaps to the nearest Grid boundary (**Figure 11.49**). In Relative Grid mode, the region moves by the amount of the current Grid value (**Figure 11.50**).

   For more information on Grid mode, see *Chapter 10: Editing Basics,* or see the *Pro Tools Reference Guide.*

SLIDING REGIONS

Aligning Regions

You can align a region to the start, end, or sync point of another region on a different track. This is useful for bringing regions on different tracks into alignment for playback.

To align the start points of regions on different tracks:

1. Use the Grabber to select the region you want to align to (**Figure 11.51**).

2. Control-click (Macintosh) or Start-click (Windows) with the Grabber on the region you want to align.

   or

   Control-drag (Macintosh) or Start-drag (Windows) a region from the Audio Regions list to another track.

   The start point of the second region aligns to the start point of the first region (**Figure 11.52**).

Region start point

insertion point

Region start point

Figure 11.51 To align the start point of regions on different tracks: Click with the Grabber on the region you want to align to. Control-click (Macintosh) or Start-click (Windows) on the region you want to align.

Region start point

insertion point

Region start point

Figure 11.52 The start point of the second region aligns to the start point of the first region.

Region start point

Region end point

Figure 11.53 To align the end point of a region to the start point of a region on another track: Click with the Grabber on the region you want to align to. Command-Control-click (Macintosh) or Control-Start-click (Windows) on the region you want to move.

Region start point

Region end point

Figure 11.54 The end point of the second region aligns to the start point of the first region.

To align the end point of a region to the start point of another region on a different track:

1. Use the Grabber to select the region you want to align to (**Figure 11.53**).

2. Command-Control-click (Macintosh) or Control-Start-click (Windows) with the Grabber on the region you want to move.

   or

   Command-Control-drag (Macintosh) or Control-Start-drag (Windows) a region from the Audio Regions list to another track.

   The end point of the second region aligns to the start point of the first region (**Figure 11.54**).

ALIGNING REGIONS

253

Identifying Sync Points

When you identify a region sync point, you define a specific point within a region. You can then align the sync point with an exact time location in a session.

Sync points are particularly useful in film and video work, where sound effects must occur at an exact moment. For instance, a video of a car crash might call for a sound effect consisting of a screech and a crash. By placing a sync point at the peak volume of the crash, you can easily spot the sound effect to the precise instant of the crash.

To create a sync point in a region:

1. Click with the Selector on the location at which you want to place the sync point.

2. Choose Edit > Identify Sync Point (**Figure 11.55**).

   An arrow appears in the region indicating the sync point's location (**Figure 11.56**).

Figure 11.55 To identify a region sync point, choose Edit > Identify Sync Point.

—— *Region sync point*

Figure 11.56 An arrow appears in the region at the sync point.

Figure 11.57 A region with its sync point at the edit insertion point.

— Region start point
— Region sync point

Figure 11.58 The sync point of one region aligned to the start point of another region on a different track.

To place the sync point of a region at the edit insertion point:

1. Click with the Selector in the track to define an edit insertion point.

2. Hold down Shift-Control (Macintosh) or Shift-Start (Windows), and drag the region from either the Audio Regions list or from another track to the destination track.

   or

   If the region is already in the track, Shift-Control-click (Macintosh) or Shift-Start-click (Windows) on the region with the Grabber.

   The region appears in the track with its sync point at the edit insertion point (**Figure 11.57**).

To align the sync point of a region to the start point of another region on a different track:

1. Click with the Grabber to select the region you want to align to.

2. Shift-Control-click (Macintosh) or Shift-Start-click (Windows) with the Grabber on the region you want to move.

   or

   Shift-Control-drag (Macintosh) or Shift-Start-drag (Windows) a region from the Audio Regions list to another track.

   The sync point of the second region aligns to the start point of the first region (**Figure 11.58**).

Trimming Regions

Trimming is a quick way to condense or expand regions. Pro Tools gives you a number of trimming options, including a versatile Trimmer tool and a set of Trim commands.

Using the Trimmer tool

In Pro Tool 6, the Edit window's Trimmer tool includes the following modes:

Standard Trimmer: The Standard Trimmer tool lets you move region boundaries, without moving the region. This is useful for hiding unwanted audio segments; or for revealing currently hidden audio segments. The Standard Trimmer lets you shorten regions or lengthen them up to the full length of the original audio file on disk.

Time Trimmer: The Time Trimmer lets you compress or expand audio regions. Unlike the Standard Trimmer, which lets you change region boundaries only, the Time Trimmer stretches or shrinks the actual audio currently displayed within a region. The Time Trimmer processes the audio with the Time Compression/Expansion (AudioSuite) plug-in, which creates a new file.

The Time Trimmer is useful for correcting audio segments that are too short or too long. It's also useful for matching the length of audio segments on separate tracks. For example, when you record harmonies or multiple vocal tracks, out-of-sync phrasing is common. With the Time Trimmer, you can compress or expand a region to match the phrasing of the other vocal parts.

A word of caution: The Time Trimmer can alter the sonic character of an audio region—as always, trust your ears. For more information on trimming regions, see the *Pro Tools Reference Guide*.

Figure 11.59 The Trimmer tool.

Figure 11.60 Drag with the Trimmer to shorten or lengthen a region.

Figure 11.61 Click on the Trimmer tool and choose the Time Trimmer from the pop-up menu. The Time Trimmer is labeled "TCE" for Time Compression/Expansion.

Figure 11.62 Move the cursor near the start or end of a region until the Time Trimmer cursor appears.

Figure 11.63 To compress or expand a region's time length, click and drag the Time Trimmer to the left or right of the region.

To trim a region with the Standard Trimmer tool:

1. Click on the Trimmer in the Edit window (**Figure 11.59**).

2. Move the cursor near the start or end of the region until the Trim cursor appears.

3. Drag the Trimmer to the left or right to shorten or lengthen the region, respectively (**Figure 11.60**).

   The region boundaries move, and the region is shortened or lengthened by the desired amount. If you're trimming a stereo region, both channels are trimmed.

To compress or expand a region with the Time Trimmer:

1. Select the Time Trimmer in the Edit window (**Figure 11.61**).

2. Move the cursor near the start or end of the region until the Time Trimmer cursor appears (**Figure 11.62**).

3. Click and Drag the Time Trimmer to the left or right to compress or expand the region, respectively (**Figure 11.63**).

   The Time Compression/Expansion (AudioSuite) plug-in processes the audio, and the region is compressed or expanded by the desired amount. A new audio file is created, which appears in the Audio Regions list.

✔ Tips

- In Grid mode, the Time Trimmer lets you compress or expand regions by precise grid increments. In Spot mode, the Time Trimmer lets you compress or expand regions to a specified time location.

- To reverse the direction of the Trim cursor, press Option (Macintosh) or Alt (Windows).

TRIMMING REGIONS

257

Using the Trim command

The Edit window's Trim command offers the following options for trimming selections:

Trim to Selection: This removes all audio in a region except the selected portion. It's useful if you want to create a new region and clear the remaining unused part of the region from a track.

Trim Start to Insertion: This removes all audio in a region from the start point to the edit insertion point. It's useful for quickly clearing audio at the beginning of a take.

Trim End to Insertion: This removes all audio in a region from the end point to the edit insertion point. It's useful for quickly clearing audio at the end of a take.

To trim a selection:

1. Select a portion of a region.

2. Choose Edit > Trim > To Selection (**Figure 11.64**).

   The selected portion of region becomes a new region, while the unselected portion is removed from the track (**Figure 11.65**).

Figure 11.64 To trim a selection, choose Edit > Trim > To Selection.

Figure 11.65 The selected portion of the region becomes a new region, and the unselected portion is removed from the track.

Figure 11.66 To Trim a region from the start point to the edit insertion point, choose Edit > Trim > Start To Insertion

Figure 11.67 The edit insertion point becomes the region's new start point.

Figure 11.68 To trim a region from the end point to the insertion point, choose Edit > Trim > End To Insertion.

To trim a region from the start point to the insertion point:

1. Click in the track with the Selector to designate an edit insertion point.

2. Choose Edit > Trim > Start To Insertion (**Figure 11.66**).

   The edit insertion point becomes the region's new start point (**Figure 11.67**).

To trim a region from the end point to the insertion point:

1. Click in the track with the Selector to designate an edit insertion point.

2. Choose Edit > Trim > End To Insertion (**Figure 11.68**).

   The edit insertion point becomes the region's new end point.

✔ Tips

- You can trim the start and end point of a region by nudging: First, define a Nudge value in the upper right of the Edit window. Then, use the Grabber to select the region you want to trim.

- To trim a region's start point, hold down Option (Macintosh) or Alt (Windows), and press Plus or Minus on the numeric keypad. To trim a region's end point, hold down Command (Macintosh) or Control (Windows), and press Plus or Minus on the numeric keypad.

TRIMMING REGIONS

Nudging Regions

You can nudge selected regions by precise increments using the numeric keypad's Plus and Minus keys. Nudging is very helpful for fine-tuning the placement of a region.

To set the Nudge value:

1. In the Nudge Value pop-up menu, choose a time scale for the Nudge value (**Figure 11.69**).

2. Select a Nudge value from the pop-up menu.

   or

   Type a number into the Nudge Value field (**Figure 11.70**).

Figure 11.69 The Nudge Value pop-up menu.

Figure 11.70 The Nudge Value field.

To nudge a region:

1. Set the Nudge value, following the instructions above.

2. Select the region you want to nudge using the Grabber or Selector.

3. Press the Plus key on the numeric keypad to move the selection forward by the Nudge value. Press the Minus key to move the selection back by the Nudge value.

Before

After

Figure 11.71 While Pressing Control (Macintosh) or Start (Windows), press Plus or Minus on the numeric keypad to nudge the contents of a selected region without changing its start or end points.

Nudging a region's contents

You can nudge a region's contents without changing its start or end point. This is useful if a region is placed at the correct location (such as a precise time location), but the material within the region is situated too early or late.

To nudge a region's contents without changing its start or end points:

1. Set the Nudge value, following the instructions on the previous page.

2. With the Grabber, select the region whose contents you want to nudge.

3. Hold down Control (Macintosh) or Start (Windows), and press Plus or Minus on the numeric keypad to move the audio waveform by the Nudge value.

   The region's contents are moved by the Nudge value. The region's start and end times remain unchanged (**Figure 11.71**).

NUDGING REGIONS

Using Edit Commands

You can use these standard Edit menu commands to manipulate audio regions in Pro Tools:

Copy: The Copy command duplicates the selected region and places it on the Clipboard.

Cut: The Cut command places a selection on the Clipboard and removes it from a track.

Paste: The Paste command places a cut or copied region from the Clipboard onto a track at the edit insertion point. Pasted regions will overwrite pre-existing audio regions on the track.

Clear: The Clear command removes a region from a track without placing it on the Clipboard.

When you cut or copy a selection, the current track view determines what is placed on the Clipboard. For example, in Waveform view, cutting or copying a selected region places any volume, pan, mute, send, or plug-in automation on the Clipboard, along with audio region data.

If a track displays automation data (such as in Volume, Mute, or Pan view), cutting or copying places only the automation data on the Clipboard. For more information on editing automation, see *Chapter 15: Automating a Mix.*

To cut or copy a selected region:

1. Set the track view for the tracks you want to edit (**Figure 11.72**).

2. Select the audio material you want to cut or copy.

Figure 11.72 Click the Track View selector to set the track view.

Edit AudioSuite MIDI Movie

Figure 11.73 To place a copy of a selection on the Clipboard, choose Edit > Copy.

Figure 11.74 To place a selection on the Clipboard and remove it from the track, choose Edit > Cut.

3. Choose Edit > Copy to place the selection on the Clipboard without removing it from the track (**Figure 11.73**).

or

Choose Edit > Cut to place the selection on the Clipboard and remove it from the track (**Figure 11.74**).

If the selected region was cut or copied, the selection appears as a new region in the Audio Regions list. If the selected region was cut, new regions are automatically created on either side of the selection (**Figure 11.75**).

Figure 11.75 New regions are automatically created on either side of cut regions.

USING EDIT COMMANDS

263

To paste a selected region:

1. Click in the track with the Selector to set an edit insertion point.

   Press Tab to move the insertion point to the end of a region. Press Option-Tab (Macintosh) or Control-Tab (Windows) to move the insertion point to the start of a region.

   or

   Select a region with the Grabber or Selector.

2. Choose Copy > Paste (**Figure 11.76**).

   The cut or copied selection appears in the track at the edit insertion point.

To clear a selected region:

1. Set the track view for the tracks you want to edit.

2. Select the audio material you want to clear.

   or

   Use the Grabber to select one or more regions.

3. Choose Edit > Clear (**Figure 11.77**).

   The selected region is removed from the track. If a portion of a region was cleared, new regions are automatically created on either side of the selection.

✔ Tips

- You can quickly slide a copy of a region to another location by pressing Option (Macintosh) or Alt (Windows) while dragging the region (**Figure 11.78**). The original region remains unchanged.

- You can retain the timeline location of a dragged region by pressing Control (Macintosh) or Start (Windows) while dragging the region.

Figure 11.76 To place a region from the Clipboard onto a track at the edit insertion point, choose Copy > Paste.

Figure 11.77 To remove a selected region from a track, choose Edit > Clear.

Figure 11.78 To slide a copy of a region from one location to another without changing the original region, press Option (Macintosh) or Alt (Windows) while dragging the region.

Figure 11.79 The Event Edit area at the top of the Edit window.

Figure 11.80
To duplicate a region, choose Edit > Duplicate.

Duplicating and Repeating Regions

The Duplicate command copies a selected region and places the copy at the end of the region. Duplicating is useful for quickly making back-to-back copies of a region. For example, you may want to duplicate a measure or two of drums to create a drum loop. Duplicate is similar to the Copy and Paste commands, only faster and more convenient.

The Repeat command is similar to Duplicate, except the Repeat dialog box prompts you to specify the exact number of copies to create.

To duplicate a selected region:

1. With the Selector, select the region you want to duplicate.

   or

   Click in the track and enter the start and end points for the selection in the Event Edit area (**Figure 11.79**).

2. Choose Edit > Duplicate (**Figure 11.80**).

   The selected region is placed immediately after the selection's end point (**Figure 11.81**).

Figure 11.81 A duplicated region is placed immediately after the selection's end point.

To repeat a selected region:

1. With the Selector, select the region you want to repeat.

   or

   Click in the track and enter the start and end points for the selection in the Event Edit area.

2. Choose Edit > Repeat (**Figure 11.82**). The Repeat dialog box appears (**Figure 11.83**).

3. Enter the number of times you want to repeat the selected region.

4. Click OK.

   The selected region is placed immediately after the selection's end point and duplicated the specified number of times.

Figure 11.82 To repeat a region, choose Edit > Repeat.

Figure 11.83 The Repeat dialog box.

DUPLICATING AND REPEATING REGIONS

Figure 11.84 To shift a selected region, choose Edit > Shift.

Figure 11.85 The Shift dialog box.

Shifting Regions

The Shift Command lets you move a selected region backward or forward in a track by a specified amount. Shifting is useful for moving regions by precise distances in a track.

To shift a selected region:

1. With the Selector or Grabber, select the region you want to shift.

2. Choose Edit > Shift (**Figure 11.84**).
   The Shift dialog box appears
   (**Figure 11.85**).

3. Click the Earlier or Later radio button.

4. Type a value in one of the Timebase fields to specify the amount by which the selection will be shifted.

5. Click OK.
   The selected region is shifted backward or forward in time by the specified amount.

Quantizing Regions

The Quantize Regions command aligns
the start points (or sync points) of selected
audio and MIDI regions to the nearest grid
boundary. Quantizing is useful for adjusting
the rhythmic timing of regions in a session.
You can simultaneously quantize selected
regions on multiple tracks. Keep in mind,
however, that a region cannot be quantized
unless the entire region is selected.

To quantize regions:

1. Define a Grid value in the upper right of
the Edit window.

2. Select the regions you want to quantize.

3. Chose Edit > Quantize Regions
(**Figure 11.86**).

Figure 11.86
To quantize regions,
choose Edit > Quantize
Regions.

Figure 11.87 To lock or unlock regions, choose Edit > Lock/Unlock Region.

Figure 11.88 A locked region displays a small lock icon.

Locking Regions

Locking a region anchors it to its current location. This is a good way to ensure that carefully spotted regions are not accidentally moved in a session.

To lock a region:

1. With the Grabber, select the regions you want to lock.

2. Choose Edit > Lock/Unlock Region (**Figure 11.87**).

   A small lock icon appears in the region, indicating that it has been locked (**Figure 11.88**).

Muting/Unmuting Regions

The Mute/Unmute Region command lets you mute playback of a selected region. You can mute regions simultaneously on multiple tracks. Muted regions appear dimmed in track playlists.

To mute regions:

1. With the Grabber, select the regions you want to mute.

2. Choose Edit > Mute/Unmute Region (**Figure 11.89**).

   The selected regions are muted and dimmed in the track playlist (**Figure 11.90**). Selected regions that were previously muted become unmuted.

Figure 11.89 To mute or unmute regions, choose Edit > Mute/Unmute Region.

Figure 11.90 Muted regions are dimmed in the track playlist.

MUTING/UNMUTING REGIONS

Figure 11.91 The Rename Selected dialog box.

Managing Regions

Anytime you cut, separate, or otherwise break an audio region into two or more segments, Pro Tools *auto-creates* new regions from the remaining segments. As a result, the number of regions in a session can multiply like rabbits. This multitude of regions tends to crowd the Audio Regions list, and make it difficult to find the regions you want.

Fortunately, Pro Tools provides the following features to help you manage regions; and to help you keep the number of regions in a session to a minimum.

Renaming regions

Renaming regions with more descriptive or memorable names can make them easier to identify. Pro Tools lets you rename regions by double-clicking on them with the Grabbers tool; or by selecting a region, then choosing the Rename Selected command in the Audio Region list's pop-up menu.

To rename a region using the Grabber tool:

1. In the Edit window, select the Grabber tool.

2. With the Grabber, double-click on the region you want to rename.

   The Rename Selected Regions dialog box appears (**Figure 11.91**).

3. Enter the new name of the region. If you selected a whole audio file, specify whether to rename just the region, or both the region and the audio file on disk.

4. Click OK.

   The region is renamed.

MANAGING REGIONS

To rename one or more regions in the Audio Regions list:

1. Select Display > Display Auto-Created Regions (**Figure 11.92**).

   This displays all auto-created regions in the Audio Regions list.

2. In the Audio Regions list, select one or more region to rename.

   or

   With the Editing preference for "Regions List Selection Follows Track Selection" enabled, select a region in a track.

3. Choose Rename Selected from the Regions list pop-up menu (**Figure 11.93**).

   The Rename Selected dialog box appears.

4. In the Rename Selected dialog box, enter a new name for the region. If you selected a whole audio file, specify whether to rename just the region, or both the region and the audio file on disk.

5. Click OK.

   The selected region is renamed. If renaming more than one region, the Rename Selected dialog box prompts you for each successive region.

Figure 11.92 Select Display > Auto-Created Regions.

Figure 11.93 To Rename a region, choose Rename Selected in the Audio Regions list pop-up menu.

Figure 11.94 To set auto-name parameters, choose Auto Rename Selected in the Audio Regions list pop-up menu.

Figure 11.95 The Rename Selected Regions dialog box.

Setting auto-name parameters

When new regions are auto-created during editing, Pro Tools also *auto-names* these new regions. By default, Pro Tools names these new regions numerically in sequential order. This can lead to a lengthy Audio Regions list full of numbered regions that are difficult to identify.

To help you better differentiate regions (and avoid a mind-boggling list of numbered regions), Pro Tools lets you create a naming scheme for auto-created regions.

To set auto-name parameters for a region:

1. Select a region in the Audio Regions list.

2. Choose Auto Rename Selected from the Audio Regions list pop-up menu (**Figure 11.94**).

   The Rename Selected Regions dialog box appears (**Figure 11.95**).

3. In the Rename Selected Regions dialog, enter the text you want used when naming new regions created from the selected region. You can input the following auto-name parameters:

   Name: This parameter determines the root name for the auto-created region.

   Number: This parameter sets the start number for the sequentially numbered new regions.

   Zeros: This parameter determines the number of zeros that occur before the auto numbers.

   Suffix: This parameter specifies the text to be appended to the end of the name, following the auto-numbering.

4. Click OK.

   Regions created from the selected region will be auto-named according to the set parameters.

MANAGING REGIONS

Hiding auto-created regions

Pro Tools lets you hide auto-created regions in the Audio Regions list, while *user-defined* regions continue to be displayed. This can help you keep the Audio Regions list down to a manageable length.

To hide auto-created regions:

◆ Deselect Display > Display Auto-Created Regions (**Figure 11.96**).

Auto-created regions are removed from the Audio Regions list. User-defined regions remain visible in the Audio Regions list. User-defined regions include the following:

▲ Whole-file audio regions

▲ Regions created during recording

▲ Imported regions

▲ Renamed regions

▲ Regions created during AudioSuite plug-in processing

▲ New regions created with Capture Regions and Separate Region commands.

▲ Regions created by trimming whole-file audio regions.

Figure 11.96 To hide auto-created regions in the Audio Regions list, deselect Display > Display Auto-Created Regions.

MANAGING REGIONS

Figure 11.97 To select unused regions: In the Audio Regions list pop-up menu, choose Select > Unused Regions.

Figure 11.98 To remove unused regions, choose Clear Selected from the Audio Regions list pop-up menu.

Figure 11.99 The Clear Audio dialog box.

Removing unused regions

Removing unused regions, when possible, can help you keep the number of regions in your session from getting out of hand. You can locate and remove unused regions in a session with the Clear Selected command.

To find and remove unused regions:

1. In the Audio Regions list pop-up menu, under Select, choose one of the following (**Figure 11.97**):
   ▲ Unused regions
   ▲ Unused Regions Except Whole Files
   ▲ Offline Regions
   The desired unused regions are selected.

2. Choose Clear Selected from the Audio Regions pop-up menu (**Figure 11.98**). The Clear Audio dialog box appears (**Figure 11.99**).

3. Click Remove.
   The unused regions are removed from the session.
   or
   If you're clearing a whole-file audio region and you want to permanently remove the audio file from your hard drive, click Delete.
   The unused whole-file audio region is removed from the session and permanently deleted from your hard drive.
   For more information on managing regions, see *Chapter 12: Advanced Editing*, or see the *Pro Tools Reference Guide* and the *DigiBase Guide*.

MANAGING REGIONS

275

12

ADVANCED EDITING

Now that you've mastered the basics of editing in Pro Tools, it's time to learn a few advanced editing features. The features covered in this chapter are easy to learn. With a bit of practice, they'll help you produce even smoother and more pristine-sounding audio.

We'll begin with an in-depth look at fades and crossfades. You'll learn when to use them, and how to create them in Pro Tools. We'll also look at the Batch Fade feature, which lets you apply multiple fades or cross-fades across several regions simultaneously.

Next, we'll explore repairing audio waveforms. I'll show you how to quickly locate problematic glitches in your audio waveforms, and how to easily re-shape the waveform with the Pencil tool to eradicate the unwanted noise.

Lastly, we'll explore silence—that is, Pro Tools' Strip Silence feature, which removes portions of audio files that fall below a user-defined volume threshold. We'll sign off with the Insert Silence feature, which lets you add silence to a selected audio region.

Creating Fades and Crossfades

Pro Tools lets you add *fades* and *crossfades* to audio regions. A fade is a volume curve that controls the rate of increase (*fade-in*) or decrease (*fade-out*) of a region's volume. Fade-ins are placed at the start of regions; fade-outs are placed at the end (**Figure 12.1**).

Fades let you smooth the entrance and exit of audio during a mix. You can use fades on final mixes (such as a fade-out at the end of a song). Or, you can use fades to blend individual elements into a mix. For example, you may want to embellish a song chorus with a sample or instrumental part. Fades can help you smoothly incorporate these sounds.

A crossfade is an overlapping fade-out and fade-in placed between two adjoining audio regions (**Figure 12.2**). Crossfades let you smooth transitions between separate audio regions on a track. You can use crossfades to reduce noise (such as clicks and pops), or to reduce distracting changes in sound character that can occur between regions during playback.

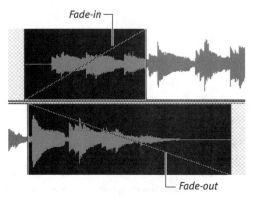

Figure 12.1 A standard fade-in and fade-out.

Figure 12.2 A crossfade is an overlapping fade-out and fade-in placed between two adjoining audio regions.

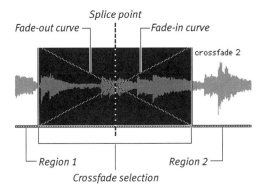

Figure 12.3 A centered crossfade.

Figure 12.4 A pre-crossfade. The selection range extends just up to the beginning of Region 2.

Figure 12.5 A post-crossfade. The selection range begins just after the end of Region 1.

You can assign different volume curves to the fade-out and fade-in portion of a cross-fade. The type of volume curve you assign determines the crossfade's character. Crossfade types include:

Centered: Centered crossfades extend across both sides of the splice point—the location where two cross-faded regions join (**Figure 12.3**). In a centered crossfade, the first region must contain audio material beyond its end point, and the second region must contain audio material before its start point.

Pre-Crossfade: Pre-crossfades are created before the splice point (**Figure 12.4**). This maintains the volume at the very beginning of the second region, which is useful if you want to preserve a strong attack at the beginning of the region.

Post-Crossfade: Post-crossfades are created after the splice point (**Figure 12.5**). They're useful if you want to maintain the volume of the first region until its end.

About the Fades dialog box

The Fades dialog box (**Figure 12.6**) lets you select, view, audition, and edit fade volume curves. It includes the following buttons:

Audition: This button lets you preview a fade or crossfade.

View First Track: If a fade includes multiple tracks, this button lets you view the first pair of adjacent tracks.

View Second Track: If a fade includes multiple tracks, this button lets you view the second pair of adjacent tracks.

View Both Tracks: This button displays the waveforms of the first two adjacent tracks in a multi-track fade.

Figure 12.6 The Fades dialog box.

Figure 12.7 The Fade Curves Only button in the Fades dialog box displays the fade curves without showing the audio waveforms.

Figure 12.8 The Fade Curves and Separate Waveforms button displays fade curves and separate views of the fade-in and fade-out waveforms.

Figure 12.9 The Fade Curves and Superimposed Waveforms button displays the fade curves along with superimposed views of the fade-in and fade-out waveforms.

Fade Curves Only: This button displays the fade curves without showing the audio waveforms (**Figure 12.7**).

Fade Curves and Separate Waveforms: This button displays fade curves along with separate views of the fade-in and fade-out waveforms (**Figure 12.8**).

Fade Curves and Superimposed Waveforms: This button displays fade curves along with superimposed views of the fade-in and fade-out waveforms (**Figure 12.9**).

Fade Curves and Summed Waveform: This button displays the fade curves along with a single waveform representing the summation of the cross-faded audio.

Zoom In: This button zooms in on the audio waveform.

Zoom Out: This button zooms out on the audio waveform.

The Fades dialog box provides the following fade-in and fade-out curve shapes:

Standard: This is an all-purpose fade curve. You can adjust its shape by dragging it (**Figure 12.10**).

S-Curve: The S-shaped fade curve inverts at the start and end to make fade-ins faster and fade-outs slower (**Figure 12.11**). You can adjust its shape by dragging it.

Preset Curves: The Preset Curves pop-up menu (**Figure 12.12**) lets you choose from seven curves. You can adjust preset curves by dragging their endpoints (**Figure 12.13**).

Figure 12.10 The Standard fade curve.

Figure 12.11 The S-shaped fade curve. Drag on the curve to adjust its shape.

Figure 12.12 The Preset Curves pop-up menu.

Figure 12.13 You can adjust preset curves used as crossfades by dragging their endpoints.

Figure 12.14 You can link fade-in and fade-out parameters in the Fades dialog box.

Figure 12.15 Click the Use Dither check box in the Fades dialog box to add dither to a fade.

Linking curves can help smooth the transition between fade-ins and fade-outs of a crossfade. When fades are linked, adjusting one fade curve automatically adjusts the other. The Fades dialog box offers the following options for linking fade-in and fade-out curves (**Figure 12.14**):

Equal Power: The Equal Power option is useful when cross-fading between audio regions that are out of phase or differ in sound character. It can also help prevent volume drop-outs that can occur with an Equal Gain crossfade. Option-click (Macintosh) or Alt-click (Windows) on the fade curve to reset it to its default shape.

Equal Gain: The Equal Gain option is useful when cross-fading between audio regions that are in phase or have similar or identical sound character (such as a drum loop). It can also help prevent the clipping that can occur when using an Equal Power crossfade. Option-click (Macintosh) or Alt-click (Windows) on the fade curve to reset it to its default shape.

None: This option disables linking between the fade-out and fade-in curves. This lets you adjust the curves separately and create custom crossfade shapes. To adjust the fade-in curve, press Option (Macintosh) or Alt (Windows) while dragging the curve. To adjust the fade-out curve, press Command (Macintosh) or Control (Windows) while dragging the curve.

The Fades dialog box also provides a Use Dither option (**Figure 12.15**), which lets you add *dither* to fades. Dither is a form of randomly generated noise that helps smooth out fade-ins or fade-outs from silence. Dither can also help smooth crossfades between low-level audio regions.

For more information on fades, see the *Pro Tools Reference Guide*.

CREATING FADES AND CROSSFADES

To create a fade-in:

1. With the Selector, select the beginning of the region you want to fade in. The selection must extend to the exact beginning of the region or a blank area prior to the region in the track (**Figure 12.16**).

2. Choose Edit > Fades > Create Fades (**Figure 12.17**).
   The Fades dialog box appears.

3. Choose an In Shape.

4. Click the Audition button to play the fade. If desired, adjust the curve by dragging it in the Fades dialog box (**Figure 12.18**).

5. Select a Link option.

6. Click OK.
   Pro Tools calculates the fade-in and writes it to disk. The chosen fade curve appears in the region (**Figure 12.19**).

Figure 12.16 A fade-in selection. The selection must extend to the exact beginning of the region or a blank area prior to the region in the track.

Figure 12.17 To create a fade-in or fade-out, choose Edit > Fades > Create Fades.

Figure 12.18
You can adjust a fade curve by dragging it.

Figure 12.19 Pro Tools calculates the selected fade curve and it appears in the region.

Figure 12.20 Fade files are stored in the Fade Files folder inside the Session folder.

Figure 12.21 A crossfade selection between two regions.

To create a fade-out:

1. Select the end of the region you want to fade out. The selection must extend to the exact end of the region or a blank area after the region in the track.

2. Choose Edit > Fades > Create Fades. The Fades dialog box appears.

3. Choose an Out Shape.

4. Click the Audition button to play the fade. If desired, adjust the curve by dragging it in the Fades dialog box.

5. Select a Link option.

6. Click OK.
   Pro Tools calculates the fade-out and writes it to disk (**Figure 12.20**). The chosen fade curve appears in the region.

To create a crossfade between two regions:

1. With the Selector, click and drag from where you want the crossfade to begin (in the first region) to where you want it to end (in the second region) (**Figure 12.21**).

2. Choose Edit > Fades > Create Fades.

3. Use the view buttons to adjust the view of the crossfade.

4. Choose an Out Shape and an In Shape.

5. Select a Link option.

6. Audition the crossfade.

7. Click OK.
   Pro Tools calculates the crossfade and writes it to disk. The crossfade appears between the two selected regions.

CREATING FADES AND CROSSFADES

To create a pre- or post-crossfade:

1. Click with the Selector in the track you want to cross-fade.

2. Press Tab to move forward to the next region boundary.

   or

   Press Option-Tab (Macintosh) or Control-Tab (Windows) to move back to the previous region boundary.

3. Shift-drag or press Shift-Tab to extend a selection forward to the next region boundary (**Figure 12.22**).

   or

   Press Option-Shift-Tab (Macintosh) or Control-Shift-Tab (Windows) to extend the selection back to the previous region boundary (**Figure 12.23**).

4. Choose Edit > Fades > Create Fades.

5. Choose an In Shape and Out Shape for the crossfade.

6. Audition the crossfade.

   Adjust the fade-in and fade-out curves, if desired, by dragging them in the Fades dialog box.

7. Click OK.

   A pre- or post-crossfade appears between the selected regions.

Figure 12.22 Shift-drag or press Shift-Tab to extend a selection forward to the next region boundary.

Figure 12.23 Press Option-Shift-Tab (Macintosh) or Control-Shift-Tab (Windows) to extend the selection back to the previous region boundary.

Figure 12.24 To remove a crossfade, choose Edit > Fades > Delete Fades.

Trimmer

crossfade 2

Figure 12.25 To trim a crossfade, drag the Trimmer at the start or end of a crossfade.

To remove a crossfade:

1. Select the area of the track containing the crossfade you want to delete.

2. Choose Edit > Fades > Delete Fades (**Figure 12.24**).

   or

1. Select the crossfade with the Grabber or Selector.

2. Press Delete (Macintosh) or Backspace (Windows).

   The crossfade is removed and the regions are returned to their previous state.

To trim a crossfade:

1. Select the crossfade with the Grabber or Selector.

2. Drag the Trimmer at the start or end of the crossfade to lengthen or shorten it (**Figure 12.25**).

   The crossfade is recalculated and a new crossfade appears.

✔ Tips

- When making selections for crossfades that occur on the border of two regions, use the Tab key to move the cursor to the exact beginning or end of a region.

- Disabling the Use Dither function when editing fades and crossfades can help speed previews and fade re-calculations.

CREATING FADES AND CROSSFADES

Creating Fades and Crossfades in Batches

Pro Tools lets you create multiple fades and crossfades simultaneously. Creating fades and crossfades in batches lets you quickly smooth transitions between multiple regions.

To create batch fades you must first make a selection across multiple regions, and then run the Create Fades command. This launches the Batch Fades dialog box (**Figure 12.26**), which provides options for creating multiple fades and crossfades.

To create crossfades between multiple regions at once:

1. Click and drag with the Selector from the first region you want to cross-fade to the last region you want to cross-fade (**Figure 12.27**).

2. Choose Edit > Fades > Create Fades. The Batch Fades dialog box appears.

3. Select a Batch Operation.

4. Select a crossfade type (pre-splice, centered, or post-splice).

5. Enter a crossfade length in milliseconds.

6. Click OK.
   Fades and crossfades appear in the selected regions (**Figure 12.28**).

✔ Tip

■ To smooth region transitions for an entire audio track, select Create New Fades and Create New Fade-Ins and -Outs from the Operation area of the Batch Fades dialog box. This creates a fade-in at the start of the first selected region, crossfades between subsequent regions, and a fade-out at the end of the last region.

Figure 12.26 The Batch Fades dialog box.

Figure 12.27 A multiple region selection.

Figure 12.28 Multiple crossfades created with the Batch Fades dialog box.

CREATING FADES AND CROSSFADES IN BATCHES

Figure 12.29 The Waveform view zoomed in to the sample level.

Figure 12.30 To repair a waveform, drag the Pencil tool over the area of the waveform you want to reshape.

Figure 12.31 The Duplicate AudioSuite plug-in lets you quickly back up a region's underlying audio file.

Repairing Waveforms with the Pencil Tool

Pro Tools lets you make destructive edits to waveform data using the Edit window's Pencil tool. This is useful for repairing pops, clicks, or other sharp volume spikes in a waveform. The Pencil's waveform repair feature only functions when the waveform is zoomed-in to the sample level.

To edit an audio waveform with the Pencil tool:

1. Use the Zoomer or Vertical Zoom buttons to zoom in to the sample level where the waveform appears as a thin line (**Figure 12.29**).

2. Using the Pencil tool, drag over the area of the waveform you want to reshape (**Figure 12.30**).

✔ Tips

■ Limit your edits to small problem areas, and be careful not to over-edit. Too much re-shaping can alter the sound or add noise.

■ Repairing waveforms with the Pencil tool is destructive: It permanently alters the underlying audio file. Always back up an audio region before repairing it. To do this, select the region you want to repair, and then choose AudioSuite > Duplicate. In the Duplicate plug-in window, select Playlist and Use In Playlist (**Figure 12.31**), and click the Process button. The AudioSuite plug-in creates a duplicate audio file. The duplicate replaces the region on the track and the suffix .DUPL is added to the region name.

■ When working with the Pencil tool, use Zoom Preset buttons or memory locations to quickly recall a sample-level zoom setting. For information on zoom presets and memory locations, see *Chapter 10: Editing Basics.*

Stripping Silence from Regions

The Strip Silence command removes portions of audio regions that fall below a user-defined volume threshold. This process divides audio regions into separate regions.

Stripping silence is useful for quickly breaking larger audio regions into smaller, more manageable regions. For example, stripping silence from a sound effect makes it easier to locate it to a specific point. It's also useful for condensing regions in preparation for compacting audio. For information on compacting audio, see *Chapter 8: File Management Basics*.

About the Strip Silence window

The four sliders in the Strip Silence window (**Figure 12.32**) let you determine how Pro Tools defines silence in audio regions.

Strip Threshold: This slider determines the volume threshold below which audio is considered silence (-48 dB to 0).

Minimum Strip Duration: This slider sets a minimum time period (0 to 1,000 ms) below which audio is considered silence.

Region Start Pad: This slider sets a time value that is added to the start of new regions. Use this to preserve audio that falls below the volume threshold.

Region End Pad: This slider sets a time value that is added to the end of new regions.

Figure 12.32 The Strip Silence window.

Figure 12.33 The Rename Selected Regions dialog box.

Figure 12.34 To show the Strip Silence window, choose Windows > Show Strip Silence.

Figure 12.35 Adjust the sliders for Strip Threshold and Minimum Strip Duration until the strip rectangles appear in the selection.

Figure 12.36 Strip Silence removes the selected audio from the track and creates new regions in the Audio Regions list.

The Strip Silence window includes a Rename button, which, when pressed, launches the Rename Selected Regions dialog box (**Figure 12.33**). Here, you can set the following parameters for automatically naming regions created with the Strip Silence command:

Name: The Name field lets you enter a base name for all regions created with Strip Silence.

Number: The Number field lets you enter a start number for sequential auto numbering.

Zeros: The Zeros field lets you enter the number of zeros that will precede the auto-numbers.

Suffix: The Suffix field lets you append text to the end of the name (after the auto-numbering).

To strip silence from an audio selection:

1. Select one or more regions (Shift-click to select multiple tracks).

2. Choose Windows > Show Strip Silence (**Figure 12.34**).

   The Strip Silence window appears.

3. Press the Rename button to establish a naming scheme for regions created with Strip Silence.

4. Adjust the Strip Threshold and Minimum Strip Duration sliders until rectangles appear, which indicate areas of silence (**Figure 12.35**).

5. Adjust the Region Start Pad and Region End Pad sliders to fine-tune the Strip Silence region selections.

6. Press the Strip button.

   The selection is removed from the track (**Figure 12.36**). New regions are created and appear in the Audio Regions list.

✔ Tip

■ Use the Undo command or Heal Separation command to restore stripped silence.

STRIPPING SILENCE FROM REGIONS

Inserting Silence

The Insert Silence command lets you add silence to an audio region selection. The command is affected by the current Edit mode as follows:

Slip Mode: In Slip mode, if a selected track is displaying audio data, the selected range is cleared of the audio data, as well as all underlying automation data on all selected tracks.

If a selected track is displaying automation data (such as volume, mute, or pan), then silence is inserted into the automation type visible on each track. Press Control (Macintosh) or Start (Windows) while choosing the Insert Silence command to insert silence on all automation playlists for all selected tracks.

Shuffle Mode: If a selected track is displaying audio data in Shuffle mode, silence is inserted into the selected range and existing audio regions are shuffled. If a selected track is displaying automation data, only the visible automation type is cleared, and a blank gap appears. Regions are not shuffled.

Grid Mode: In Grid mode, inserting silence clears all audio and automation data within a selected range.

To insert silence into a track:

1. Select the portion of a region in which you want to insert silence (**Figure 12.37**).

2. Choose Edit > Insert Silence (**Figure 12.38**).

   Silence is inserted into the selected audio range. In Slip mode, all audio data and automation data is cleared from the selected range (**Figure 12.39**). In Shuffle mode, silence is inserted in the selected range, and existing audio regions are shuffled.

Figure 12.37 Select the segment of the region in which you want to insert silence.

Figure 12.38 To insert silence, choose Edit > Insert Silence.

Figure 12.39 In Slip mode, inserting silence clears all audio data and automation data from the selected range.

Part V:
Mixing Audio

MIXING BASICS

Mixing is a process of slowly building and shaping multiple tracks of audio into a balanced and coherent presentation. There are no absolute rules in mixing—following your own ears and tastes is essential. There are, however, a few important basics that you need to know if you want to turn a rough mix into an exciting sound production.

This chapter starts with an in-depth look at creating stereo mixes. I'll describe how stereo imaging is used to simulate a three-dimensional acoustic space, and explain how panning, equalization, and spatial effects can create the perception of width, height, and depth in a stereo mix.

I'll also discuss how audio signal flows through individual channel strips, as well as how to assign track inputs and outputs. Next, I'll cover inserts: how they operate, how signal flows through them, and the basics of mono and stereo plug-ins. Then I'll show you how to assign sends, and how to use send and track Output windows.

Last up, we'll cover the useful trick of creating submixes, which can help conserve track space and system resources.

Creating Stereo Mixes

A stereo mix refers to mixing multiple tracks of audio down to two channels (a left channel and a right channel). Stereo mixes are designed for listening over two speakers (a left speaker and a right speaker).

When we create a stereo mix, we're actually constructing a simulation or "image" of a three-dimensional acoustic space. To construct this *stereo image*, we use various techniques to trick our binaural (two-ear) auditory system into perceiving sound in the three dimensions of width, depth, and height. These techniques include left/right panning, *spatial effects* (reverb, delay, chorus, and flange), and EQ shaping (**Figure 13.1**).

The process of creating a stereo image begins during recording: The size, shape, and reflectivity of the recording space all contribute to the character of the sound. Various miking techniques, such as close miking, distant miking, ambient miking, and stereo miking, let you capture the three-dimensional character of the recording space. For more information on miking techniques, see the Chapter 6 sidebar, *Microphone Placement Techniques*.

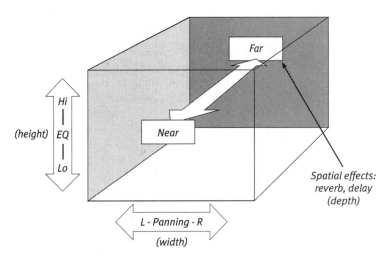

Figure 13.1 A stereo image is a simulation of a three-dimensional acoustic space: Left/right panning simulates width, EQ shaping simulates height, and spatial effects simulate depth.

Creating width

When we create a stereo mix, we use left/right panning to spread tracks out across the stereo image. This *separation* lets us hear tracks with more clarity, and introduces the perception of width in the stereo image (**Figure 13.2**). Panning tracks tastefully is key to making mixes sound balanced and spacious.

Left/right panning gives sound a location within the stereo image as a result of the *precedence effect*. The precedence effect describes how we locate sounds in a three-dimensional space: Whichever of your ears first hears a sound perceives it as significantly louder than your other ear does. Our binaural auditory system uses this difference in perceived loudness to automatically triangulate the location of the sound source.

Panning a track to the left or right changes the proportional level of the track in each speaker. Due to the precedence effect, we can create the illusion that a sound is coming from any point between the left and right speakers. When the level of a track is equal in both speakers, we perceive it as coming from straight ahead.

Figure 13.2 Left/right panning lets you simulate the acoustic spread of a band on stage. The perception of width is created by panning elements from left to right.

CREATING STEREO MIXES

Creating depth

When a sound occurs within an acoustic space, we hear both *direct sound* and *reflected sound*. Direct sound emanates from the sound source and travels unimpeded to the listener. Reflected sound bounces off surfaces such as floors, ceilings, and walls; thus, it takes longer to reach the listener (**Figure 13.3**). The time delay between direct sound and reflected sound, combined with their relative volumes, lets us perceive depth (front to back) within an acoustic space.

In stereo mixing, we use spatial effects to simulate the characteristics of acoustic spaces. Most reverbs provide pre-set room shapes with adjustable parameters (including room size, reverb decay time, and number of reflections), so you can define the character of the acoustic space.

We then mix the direct sound (*uneffected signal*) with the reflected sound (*effected signal*) to place the sound at the desired depth within the stereo image. For example, a sound placed in a large hall with many reflections (high *diffusion*), slow reverb decay, and no direct sound mixed in will sound distant. The same sound placed in a small room with few reflections, quick reverb decay, and lots of direct sound mixed in will sound "in your face."

For more information on spatial effects, see *Chapter 14: Adding Effects to a Mix.*

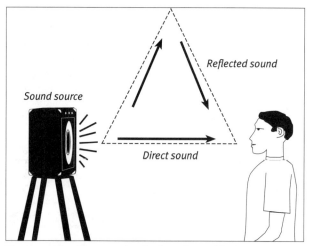

Figure 13.3 The direct sound and reflected sound from an audio source reach the ear at different times. This time delay creates the perception of depth.

Creating height

Humans hear sounds in a frequency spectrum between 20Hz and 20kHz. In audio production, this spectrum is generally broken down into four frequency bands: low (20Hz–200Hz), low-middle (200Hz–1kHz), high-middle (1kHz–5kHz), and high (5kHz–20kHz). Every instrument occupies a different range in this spectrum (**Figure 13.4**). Low-pitched instruments such as bass and tuba tend toward the lower end of the spectrum, while higher-pitched instruments such as flute and piccolo tend toward the higher end.

When we talk about creating height in a stereo mix, we're referring to using equalization, or *EQ*, to open up spaces within these frequency ranges to enhance the clarity and separation of sounds within the stereo image.

Most instruments have fundamental frequencies within the low-mid range. Making small decreases (or *cuts*) or increases (or *boosts*) in this frequency range can dramatically alter the character of an instrument's sound. Higher-pitched instruments have more frequencies in the high-mids. Boosting these frequencies can help enhance clarity, brightness, and definition.

Keep in mind that most instruments also generate harmonics up into the highs. Boosting these high harmonics can add sparkle and brilliance to a track.

For more information on EQ, see *Chapter 14: Adding Effects to a Mix*.

Figure 13.4 Frequency ranges of common instruments.

About mono compatibility

Many people still listen to music over car radios that have only one speaker. So, before you call the mix a wrap, listen to it for mono compatibility. If you notice a decrease in clarity, or if lower frequencies seem unstable, you may have some *phase cancellation* in the stereo mix. Phase cancellation occurs when sound waves overlap in such a way that they cancel each other out. This can cause frequencies to lose clarity or drop out entirely.

If you hear phase cancellation, try reversing the phase on any stereo-pair microphones. It's not uncommon for improperly placed stereo microphones to introduce phasing problems. Several Pro Tools plug-ins provide phase invert buttons, including the DigiRack EQ and delay plug-ins (**Figure 13.5**). Also, double check any stereo effects in the mix— some stereo effects processors can introduce out-of-phase signals.

Phase Invert button

Figure 13.5 The Phase Invert button on the DigiRack EQ plug-in.

The Mixing Process

Most producers and engineers follow the general mixing process outlined below. Remember, there's no absolute order to these steps. Mixing is a fluid process: Through repeated listening and tweaking, you'll gradually approach an ideal blend of audio elements.

Finish recording: Before you start mixing, make sure you've got all your ideas recorded. Then, give yourself some time—however much you need—to gain some perspective on the tracks before you begin mixing. You might realize that you forgot to record a bass part, or that the track really needs a background vocal to bring it all together. You can always record a take during mixing should the inspiration hit you, but don't start mixing with tired ears—you won't be able to hear accurately and your mixes may suffer.

Choose tracks: Choose the best takes for your final mix. Arrange them in the Mix window in as ergonomic a fashion as possible.

Clean up tracks: Remove any unwanted regions from the tracks. Then listen to each track individually and erase any distracting noises such as glitches, bad punches, chair creaks, and voices. Perform any additional editing tasks you desire.

Prepare tracks: Assign track outputs to the main mix. Create master faders and auxiliary inputs as needed. Create submixes and mix groups. Set all track faders as close to unity level (0 dB) as possible.

Create a rough balance: Set initial track volumes and pan placements.

Apply effects: Add internal DSP plug-in effects or external hardware effects. Begin with sparing amounts of EQ, subtracting frequencies, when possible, to clear space for sounds. Then add *dynamic effects* (such as compressors, limiters, gates, or expanders) to smooth out spiking volumes or minimize background noise. Finally, add spatial effects to add depth to the mix. For additional information see *Chapter 14: Adding Effects to a Mix.*

Check gain staging: Check levels on each gain stage in your system. Optimize levels on all inserts, sends, inputs, and outputs. Avoid clipping audio signals. For more information on gain staging, see *Chapter 4: Starting a New Session.*

Set the final balance: Adjust the final volume levels and pan settings. Practice any mix moves on faders, mutes, solos, and plug-in controls that you want to automate.

Record automation: Record mix moves on faders, sends, mutes, solos, and plug-in controls. If necessary, do multiple passes—Pro Tools saves the automation and you can add to it later.

Bounce the mixes to hard disk: Bounce the mix to disk using Pro Tool's Bounce feature. Convert audio file type, sample rate, or bit depth, if necessary.

Check the mix: Copy the mix to CD or DAT tape. Listen to it on a variety of systems, including a shelf-size system, a car stereo, and a home stereo—the more, the better. Make sure the mix retains the same overall balance of audio elements across all systems. Repeat as many of the above steps as many times as needed.

CREATING STEREO MIXES

Monitoring a Mix

Many factors influence the way we hear a mix, including the type of speakers, the acoustics of the room, and the playback volume. Although a mix may sound great on your studio monitors, the same mix can sound dramatically different on another system.

Knowing the performance specifications of your speakers, as well as the acoustics of the mixing space, can help you avoid introducing compensation errors into the mix. For example, knowing that the room tends to exaggerate bass will keep you from removing too much bass from the mix.

To make sure your mixes sound good on as many systems as possible, do the following:

Use alternate speakers: Listen to the mix on different size speakers: small, medium, and large. Make sure you can hear all the elements of the mix clearly over each type of speaker.

Use reference CDs: Play some CDs that you know well over the monitor system as a sonic reference point. This gives you something to compare your mixes to, and can help you identify the acoustic tendencies of your monitors and mixing room.

Use consistent levels: Monitor your mixes at consistent levels—ideally, between 70 and 90 decibels. Monitoring at overly loud levels will quickly fatigue your ears (especially in the mid-range). This can lead to mid-range heavy mixes that lack spaciousness and clarity.

Listen on alternate systems: Burn a CD of the mix and listen to it on as many systems as possible—from boomboxes to home stereos to the best audiophile components you can find. Also, try listening to the mix in both large and small spaces, and play it on a car stereo while driving to see if the low-end is audible over the engine hum. Listening on a range of systems will give you excellent perspective on the mix and alert you to any consistent problems that need fixing.

Understanding Audio Signal Flow

Audio signal flow refers to the path that audio takes through the Pro Tools mixer. Generally, this path is fixed, moving from top to bottom through audio track, auxiliary input, and master fader channel strips.

Don't confuse audio signal flow with I/O Setup—they're related but not identical. Audio signal flow refers to the path audio takes within channel strips, while I/O Setup determines the specific channel assignments for inputs, outputs, inserts, and buses. For more information on I/O Setup, see *Chapter 2: Software Basics,* and *Chapter 4: Starting a New Session.*

About audio tracks and auxiliary inputs

Audio tracks and auxiliary inputs have the same top-to-bottom audio signal flow: Audio travels first to any inserts, then to sends and faders, and lastly to the outputs. The main difference between audio tracks and auxiliary inputs is the audio input source: Audio tracks receive input from external audio sources, or from audio files playing back on disk (**Figure 13.6**). Auxiliary inputs receive audio signal from internal buses or external hardware sources (**Figure 13.7**).

Figure 13.6 Audio signal flow through an audio track channel strip.

Figure 13.7 Audio signal flow through an auxiliary input channel strip.

Audio tracks and auxiliary inputs are designed for different mixing tasks. Audio tracks let you control the playback parameters (such as mute, solo, pan, volume level, and automation) of individual audio files as they play back from disk.

Auxiliary inputs are designed for creating *submixes*. A submix is created when you bus an audio signal from multiple audio tracks to a single auxiliary input. For instance, you can create a stereo submix of drums and bass by busing their tracks to an auxiliary input. This lets you control the entire rhythm section using one fader. Or, you can use an auxiliary input to create a *send-and-return* submix, also called an *effects loop*, which lets you add an effect to multiple tracks of audio simultaneously. For more information on submixes, see *Creating Submixes* later in this chapter. For more information on effects loops, see *Chapter 14: Adding Effects to a Mix.*

For additional information on audio tracks and auxiliary inputs, see *Chapter 3: The Mix and Edit Windows.*

About master faders

Master faders control the main volume levels of outputs and bus paths. You can use master faders for many purposes, such as to control the main mix output, submix levels, send levels, or bus levels, or to apply effects to a main mix.

Master fader inserts are always *post-fader* (unlike the inserts for audio tracks and auxiliary inputs, which are always *pre-fader*). This means the Main Mix fader always comes before the Inserts section (**Figure 13.8**). Thus, you can insert an effect (such as dither or an aural exciter) on the final main mix output. But use effects on the main outputs cautiously. Adding compression to a main mix is not a good idea—this is better left until mastering. Compressing the main outputs

Input source: Input determined by output assignment

Volume fader

Insert (post-fader)

Output

Main mix output

Figure 13.8 Audio signal flow through a master fader.

Figure 13.9 To create a new master fader, select File > New Track. Select Master Fader from the pop-up menu.

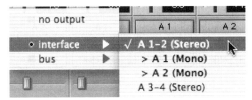

Figure 13.10 Set the outputs of each track in the mix to the main mix outputs (typically 1-2).

Figure 13.11 Set the output of the master fader to the main mix output (typically 1-2).

can reduce the openness of a mix and limit a mastering engineer's options for enhancing the final output. For more information on compression and other effects, see *Chapter 14: Adding Effects to a Mix.*

For more information on master faders, see *Chapter 3: The Mix and Edit Windows.*

To use a master fader as a master volume control for the main mix:

1. Select File > New Track.

   The New Track dialog box appears.

2. Select Mono or Stereo from the pop-up menu.

3. Select Master Fader from the pop-up menu (**Figure 13.9**).

4. Enter the number of master faders and click Create.

5. Set the outputs of all audio tracks in the session to the main mix outputs (typically 1-2) (**Figure 13.10**).

6. Set the panning position of each track.

7. Set the output of the master fader to the main mix output (**Figure 13.11**).

✔ Tip

■ In Pro Tools 6, you can make Audio Tracks, Auxiliary Inputs, and Master Faders inactive. Making these tracks inactive can help you conserve your system's overall mixer and DSP resources. For more information on making tracks inactive, see *Chapter 5: Working with Tracks.* Or, see the *Pro Tools Reference Guide.*

UNDERSTANDING AUDIO SIGNAL FLOW

Assigning Inputs and Outputs

Audio tracks and auxiliary inputs have *Input selectors* and *Output selectors* that let you route audio to and from their respective channel strips.

Input selectors let you assign audio input from external sources (via the Pro Tools interface) or from internal buses. Output selectors let you route audio output to external destinations (via the Pro Tools interface) or to internal buses.

Master faders, on the other hand, have only Output selectors, which let you route audio output to the main mix or to internal buses.

For more information on assigning inputs and outputs, see *Chapter 5: Working with Tracks.*

To assign inputs to audio tracks or auxiliary inputs:

◆ In the Mix or Edit window, click the track Input selector and choose from the available audio interface channels and buses (**Figure 13.12**).

Select No Input to remove all the input assignments on that track.

To assign outputs to an audio track or auxiliary input:

◆ In the Mix or Edit window, click the track Output selector and choose from the available audio interface channels and buses (**Figure 13.13**).

Select No Output to remove all the output assignments on that track.

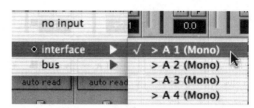

Figure 13.12 Click the track Input selector and choose from the available audio interface channels and buses.

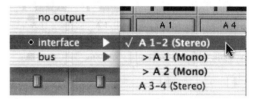

Figure 13.13 Click the track Output selector and choose from the available audio interface channels and buses.

ASSIGNING INPUTS AND OUTPUTS

Figure 13.14 Click the master fader Output selector and choose from the available audio interface channels and buses.

To assign outputs to a master fader:

◆ In the Mix or Edit window, click the master fader Output selector and choose from the available audio interface channels and buses (**Figure 13.14**).

✔ Tip

■ In Pro Tools 6, you can make output paths inactive. Making a track output inactive silences output, while maintaining all automation and playlist data. Pre-fader sends continue to feed audio signal to their assigned destination. This can help you conserve your system's overall mixer resources, while maintaining your track configuration and effects output.

To make an output inactive/active: Command-Control-click (Macintosh) or Control-Start-click (Windows) on the desired output. Or, uncheck/check the inactive/active box for the desired output in the I/O Setup window.

For more information on making outputs inactive, see the *Pro Tools Reference Guide*. For information on making tracks inactive, see *Chapter 5: Working with Tracks*. Or, see the *Pro Tools Reference Guide*.

ASSIGNING INPUTS AND OUTPUTS

About Inserts

Pro Tools provides five insert slots on each audio track, auxiliary input, and master fader channel strip. Inserts can be either *hardware inserts* or *software plug-in inserts*.

In terms of audio signal flow, audio travels through the inserts section of a channel strip sequentially from top to bottom (**Figure 13.15**). Therefore, a plug-in inserted in a higher position will deliver an effected audio signal to a plug-in inserted in a lower position. For example, if you insert a reverb below a delay, the audio signal entering the reverb will already have delay on it. You can change the order of inserts by dragging them up or down (**Figure 13.16**).

Figure 13.15 Audio flows through the Inserts section of a channel strip sequentially from top to bottom.

Figure 13.16 You can change the order of inserts by dragging them up or down.

When you insert a stereo plug-in on a mono channel strip, all subsequent mono plug-ins convert to their stereo equivalents, and the mono channel strip becomes a stereo channel strip (**Figure 13.17**). This lets Pro Tools quickly accommodate stereo effects during a mix. For more information on using inserts, see *Chapter 14: Adding Effects to a Mix*. For information on viewing inserts, see *Chapter 3: The Mix and Edit Windows*.

Mono plug-in

Stereo plug-in

Mono plug-in becomes stereo plug-in

Mono track

Mono track becomes stereo track

Before   *After*

Figure 13.17 When you insert a stereo plug-in on a mono track, all subsequent mono plug-ins convert to their stereo equivalents, and the mono track becomes a stereo track.

Assigning Sends

Pro Tools provides up to five mono or stereo sends on each audio track and auxiliary input (**Figure 13.18**). Sends let you route audio to internal buses or external outputs: You can send audio via internal buses to auxiliary inputs to create submixes or to add plug-in effects. Or, you can send audio via external outputs to a headphone mix, or to external hardware effects. Sends always receive audio after it passes through the Inserts section of a channel strip.

You can set a send to either Pre- or Post-Fader mode (**Figure 13.19**). When a send is in Pre-Fader mode, audio signal first passes through the send, and then goes to the fader. In Post-Fader mode, the signal first passes through the fader, and then travels to the send. Post-fader sends are frequently used for effects processing; pre-fader sends are used for headphone and monitor mixes.

You can control send parameters (including level, pan, mute, pre-, and post-fader) through a send Output window, or by using individual send controls that appear within the Sends view. For more information on viewing sends, see *Chapter 3: The Mix and Edit Windows*. For more information on using sends, see *Chapter 14: Adding Effects to a Mix*.

To assign a send to a track:

1. Click on a Send button and choose an output or bus path (**Figure 13.20**).

2. Set the output level of the send in the individual send control or in a send Output window.

To open a send Output window:

◆ Click a Send button.

A send Output window appears (**Figure 13.21**).

Figure 13.18 Pro Tools gives you up to five mono or stereo sends on each audio track and auxiliary input.

Pre/Post-Fader button

Figure 13.19 Post-fader sends are frequently used for effects processing; pre-fader sends are used for headphone and monitor mixes.

no send		√ Bus 1–2 (Stereo)
		> Bus 2 (Mono)
interface	▶	> Bus 1 (Mono)
○ bus	▶	**Bus 3–4 (Stereo)**
		> Bus 3 (Mono)
		> Bus 4 (Mono)
		Bus 5–6 (Stereo)

Figure 13.20 To assign a send to a track, click a Send button and choose an output or bus path.

Figure 13.21 A stereo send Output window.

Figure 13.22 To open individual send controls, select Display > Sends View Shows. Select any send (Send A through Send E).

Figure 13.23 An individual send control.

— *Bus path*

Figure 13.24 To display send level meters for individual send controls, Select Setups > Preferences, click the Display tab, and select Show Meters in Sends View.

Figure 13.25 Naming bus paths in the I/O Setup can help you keep track of bus assignments.

To open individual send controls:

1. Select Display > Sends View Shows.

2. Select any send (Send A through Send E) (**Figure 13.22**).

   Send controls appear for the chosen send (**Figure 13.23**).

To display send level meters for individual send controls:

1. Choose Setups > Preferences.

2. Click the Display tab.

3. Select Show Meters in Sends View (**Figure 13.24**).

4. Click OK.

✔ Tips

■ If you're using a slower computer, try hiding send level meters to improve screen redraw times. Also, making a send inactive releases its processing resources and helps improve system performance.

■ To quickly set the send output level to zero, Option-click (Macintosh) or Alt-click (Windows) the Send fader.

■ To set the default level for new sends to 0 dB (unity gain), choose Setups > Preferences > Operations. Uncheck Sends Default to "-INF."

■ Naming bus paths in the I/O Setup can help you keep track of send assignments (**Figure 13.25**). For more information on I/O Setup, see *Chapter 4: Starting a New Session*.

ASSIGNING SENDS

311

Using Output Windows

Pro Tools provides dedicated Output windows for tracks and sends. Output windows look just like channel strips, but are larger and can hover independently over the Mix and Edit windows. This lets you easily access the output controls of the track or send during editing or mixing.

Track Output windows provide Track Volume faders, Pan sliders, Mute and Solo buttons, and automation controls (**Figure 13.26**). Send Output windows provide Send Volume faders, Pan sliders, Mute and Solo buttons, and automation controls (**Figure 13.27**).

Figure 13.26 A stereo audio track Output window.

Figure 13.27 A stereo send Output window.

Figure 13.28 The expanded meter view in the stereo send Output window lets you view path level meters.

Meters View box

Track meters

Path meters

Path Meter selector

Output Window button

Figure 13.29 To open a track Output window, click the Output window button.

All Output windows have these additional controls:

Track Selector: The Track selector lets you choose any audio track, auxiliary input, or master fader in the session.

Output Selector: The Output selector lets you access any existing outputs.

Send Selector: The Send selector lets you access any existing sends on the track.

Path Selector: The Path selector lets you assign the Output path for the current track or send.

Panner Linking Button: The Panner Linking button lets you link and unlink the left and right pan knobs of stereo Output windows.

Target Button: The Target button lets you keep the current Output window open when you open a new Output window. Clicking the target changes it from red to gray, and anchors it to its current location and output assignment.

Automation Safe: The Automation Safe button places the track in Safe mode and prevents existing automation from being overwritten.

Meter View Box: The Meter View box opens an expanded Output window that includes path level meters (**Figure 13.28**).

To open a track Output window:

◆ Click the Output Window button of an audio track, auxiliary input, or master fader channel strip (**Figure 13.29**).

The track Output window appears.

To open a sends Output window:

◆ When the Sends view is showing assignments, click on the send (**Figure 13.30**).
or

◆ When the individual send controls are showing, click on the send Output selector button.

A sends Output window appears.

Figure 13.30 To open a send Output window, click the send itself.

Linking stereo pans

Stereo Output windows provide a Panner Linking button that lets you move left and right pan knobs simultaneously. When linked, left and right pan knobs move in the same direction in unison.

Pro Tools also provides Inverse Panner Linking, which lets you move the pans in mirror opposite directions.

To enable Panner Linking:

◆ Click the Panner Linking button (**Figure 13.31**).

The Panner Linking button becomes highlighted. The stereo pans now move together in unison.

To enable Inverse Panner Linking:

1. Click the Panner Linking button.

2. Click the Inverse Panner Linking button (**Figure 13.32**).

The Inverse Panner Linking button becomes highlighted. The stereo pans now move in mirror opposite directions.

✔ Tips

■ To open multiple track or sends Output windows, Shift-click any Output button or send assignment.

■ To keep an Output window open, press the red Target button (**Figure 13.33**). The Output window remains open when other output windows are opened.

Figure 13.31 The Panner Linking button. Click this button to move stereo pans in unison.

—*Inverse Panner Linking button*

Figure 13.32 The Inverse Panner Linking button. Click this button to move stereo pans in mirror opposite directions.

Figure 13.33 The Target button.

Creating Submixes

When you create a *submix*, multiple tracks of audio are merged into a single track. Submixing is useful if you're running low on tracks and you want to free up additional track space. Submixes also let you control groups of instruments from a single set of track controls. For instance, creating a stereo submix of multiple drum tracks lets you control the entire drum section from a single stereo fader.

When you create a submix, audio is routed from either sends or track outputs to available buses. The audio is then received by audio tracks or auxiliary inputs whose track inputs are assigned to the same bus. To merge source tracks into a single destination track, you must record the combined signals to a new audio track.

When creating a *stereo* submix make sure the sound quality, relative levels, and stereo panning are how you want them to be in the final mix. It's a good idea to save the original audio files in case you decide later that you don't like the submix—this way you can import the original files and start over.

You can also create submixes to add effects to multiple audio tracks simultaneously. This is called an effects loop. When you create an effects loop, you *send* the audio (on a bus) to an auxiliary input. The signal is then routed through any effects inserted on the auxiliary input. The auxiliary input then *returns* the effected signal to the main mix. For more information on creating effects loops, see *Chapter 14: Adding Effects to a Mix*. For more information on creating submixes, see the *Pro Tools Reference Guide*.

To create a submix of multiple audio tracks to a single audio track:

1. Choose File > New Track.

2. Create a stereo audio track.

   A new stereo audio track appears. This is the destination audio track for the submix.

3. Assign a send or track output to a bus path for each source track you want in the submix (**Figure 13.34**).

4. Assign the destination track inputs to the same bus path assigned to the source tracks (**Figure 13.35**).

5. Assign the outputs of the destination audio track to the main mix (**Figure 13.36**).

6. Record-enable the destination audio track.

7. Using either the sends output controls (for sends) or track controls (for track outputs), adjust the relative volumes and stereo panning of the source tracks. (To accurately monitor the submix when using sends, make sure the source track's outputs are set to the main mix outputs.)

8. In the Transport window, press Record-Play to record the submix to the destination stereo audio track.

9. Listen to the submix.

   Make any necessary volume or panning adjustments to the source track's output controls. Repeat as many times as necessary.

Figure 13.34 When creating a submix, assign send or track outputs to a bus path for each track you want in the submix.

Figure 13.35 Assign the inputs of the destination track to the same bus path assigned to the source tracks.

Figure 13.36 Assign the outputs of the destination audio track to the main mix.

CREATING SUBMIXES

✔ Tips

■ If you've used up all available tracks in a session, you can still free up tracks by bouncing a submix to disk. Bouncing to disk does not require any additional tracks. You can bounce as many or as few tracks as you want, including the entire final mix (with effects and automation). For more information on bouncing to disk, see *Chapter 16: Mixdown and Mastering.*

■ An advantage of using sends instead of track outputs to bus audio is that each send has separate output controls. This lets you adjust volume, pan, and mute for each track without changing the track control settings on the actual audio track.

■ If you have open tracks (and don't need to merge tracks into a submix for effects processing or any other reason), consider creating mix groups. Mix groups let you control the parameters (such as volume, solos, mutes, send levels, and automation) for all grouped tracks from a single set of track controls. For more information on mix groups, see *Chapter 5: Working with Tracks.*

ADDING
EFFECTS TO A MIX

Adding effects can help you transform a flat and lifeless rough mix into a spacious and exciting sound production. Effects let you shape a mix in many ways: You can balance track levels with compression or open up frequency ranges with equalization (EQ). You can even place tracks inside spacious sonic landscapes with reverb and delay.

Pro Tools lets you use both internal software plug-ins and external hardware effects. Third-party vendors offer numerous RTAS plug-ins, many of which use the same algorithms as their hardware ancestors. And if you have a roomful of vintage gear that you're aching to use, it's a snap to patch in external hardware.

Think of this chapter as a primer on effects. We'll cover plug-in and external hardware effects, and I'll introduce you to three useful types of effects: EQ, dynamic effects, and spatial effects. With a little practice you'll be sending your mixes into new dimensions... literally.

What Is a DSP Plug-in?

A DSP (digital signal processing) plug-in is
software that lets you add effects such as
reverb, compression, and EQ to audio signals
within the Pro Tools environment. Pro Tools
LE supports the following DSP plug-ins:

Real-Time AudioSuite (RTAS):
RTAS plug-ins use your computer's CPU to
process audio non-destructively in real-time
(**Figure 14.1**). The plug-ins don't change
the original audio file saved on disk; effects
are applied only during playback or when
bouncing to disk. You can, however, monitor
effects on audio tracks while recording. Pro
Tools LE ships with Digidesign's DigiRack
RTAS plug-ins.

Using large numbers of RTAS plug-ins can
tax CPU resources and hamper the performance of other Pro Tools features such as track
count, edit density, graphics, and automation.
Keeping an eye on the System Usage window
(**Figure 14.2**) can help you manage CPU
resources and get the most out of RTAS
plug-ins.

AudioSuite: Pro Tools ships with a diverse
set of non-real-time AudioSuite plug-ins.
These process audio directly to disk, creating
a new audio file that includes the effect.

Figure 14.1 The DigiRack RTAS one-band EQ plug-in.

Figure 14.2 The System Usage window can help you
manage CPU resources.

Line insert

Figure 14.3 A compressor plug-in used as a line insert. A line insert applies its effect only to the track on which it's inserted.

About Plug-ins as Inserts

Pro Tools lets you use up to five real-time DSP plug-ins as inserts on each track. You can use these inserts in two ways:

Line Inserts (single tracks): You can use plug-ins as *line inserts* on individual audio tracks, auxiliary inputs, and master faders (**Figure 14.3**). A line insert applies its effect only to the track on which it's inserted. For example, you can add compression to a lead vocal by simply inserting a compressor on the lead vocal track. Inserts on audio tracks and auxiliary inputs are always pre-fader. Inserts on master faders are always post-fader.

What Is DSP?

In Pro Tools, DSP refers to the manipulation or processing of digital audio. DSP occurs during many Pro Tools tasks, from simple volume changes to complex effects processing.

DSP is measured in terms of how much processing power a Pro Tools system has. In Pro Tools LE systems, all DSP tasks are handled by the host computer's CPU. The system's total DSP power thus depends on the processing power of the host computer. (Pro Tools TDM systems have dedicated sound cards with embedded DSP chips. This gives TDM systems a big DSP boost.)

Pro Tools lets you insert up to five real-time DSP plug-in effects on each audio track. Pro Tools LE ships with Digidesign's DigiRack RTAS plug-ins, which include one- and four-band parametric EQ, dynamic effects, and delay effects.

You may also want to add a reverb plug-in, such as Digidesign's D-Verb (sold separately), to your effects toolkit. In addition, there are a wide variety of third-party DSP plug-ins available, including reverbs, compressors, equalizers, pitch shifters, and mic and amp simulators. For a list of third-party DSP plug-ins, see *www.digidesign.com* or *www.digidevelopers.com*.

Effects Loop (multiple tracks): You can use a plug-in in a send-and-return submix, known as an *effects loop* (**Figure 14.4**). An effects loop lets you add an effect to multiple tracks simultaneously. To create an effects loop, you insert a plug-in on an auxiliary input, and then bus as many tracks as you want to the auxiliary input for simultaneous processing. The auxiliary input then *returns* the processed audio to the main mix outputs. Because effects loops process multiple tracks simultaneously, they can help you conserve CPU resources. For more information on effect loops, see *Creating Effects Loops* later in this chapter.

Understanding plug-in formats

Pro Tools lets you use the following plug-in formats:

Mono Plug-ins: Mono plug-ins are designed for use on mono tracks. They have mono (one-channel) outputs.

Mono/Stereo Plug-ins: Mono/stereo plug-ins are designed for use on mono tracks; however, they have stereo (two-channel) outputs. When a mono/stereo plug-in is inserted on a track, all subsequent inserts (and the track itself) become stereo.

Multi-Channel (Stereo) Plug-ins: Multi-channel plug-ins are designed for use on stereo or larger multi-channel tracks. In Pro Tools LE, all multi-channel plug-ins are stereo.

Multi-Mono Plug-ins: Multi-mono plug-ins are designed for use on stereo or larger multi-channel tracks when a multi-channel version of the plug-in is not available. Parameters for all channels are linked by default. You can, however, unlink parameters using the Master Link button. Unlinking parameters lets you control the parameters for each channel separately.

Insert (DSP effects plug-in)

Effects sends

Input bus from effects sends

Effects return (to main mix)

Figure 14.4 An effects loop. Each track's effects sends bus audio to the auxiliary input. The auxiliary input's volume fader acts as the effects return. For an example of an effects loop, see Figure 14.28.

Figure 14.5 The Inserts view displays all currently inserted plug-ins.

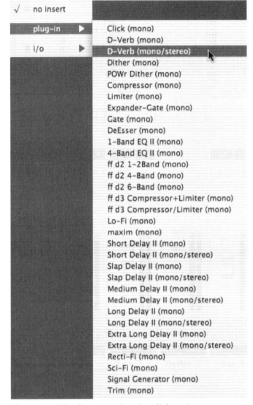

Figure 14.6 To choose a plug-in, click an Insert selector and choose the desired plug-in.

Inserting Plug-ins on Tracks

In order to use an RTAS plug-in in Pro Tools, you must first insert it on a track. You can do this in the Inserts view of either the Mix or Edit window. Both windows display all currently inserted plug-ins (**Figure 14.5**).

To insert a plug-in on a track:

1. Choose Display > Mix Window Shows > Inserts View.

2. Click an Insert selector on the track and choose the desired plug-in (**Figure 14.6**). The plug-in appears.

Inserting plug-ins during playback

In Pro Tools 6, you can insert plug-ins during playback, with the following restrictions:

◆ Plug-ins cannot be inserted or removed during recording.

◆ Plug-ins that change a tracks format cannot be inserted or removed during playback. (For instance, when you insert a stereo plug-in on a mono track, the track automatically becomes a stereo track.)

◆ Plug-ins that contain automation cannot be removed during playback.

◆ Plug-in automation cannot be enabled during playback.

◆ Side-chain inputs cannot be created during playback.

Moving and duplicating inserts

You can move or duplicate already inserted plug-ins by dragging them to open insert slots on the same track or on another track. When you move or duplicate inserts, they retain their original settings and automation.

Figure 14.7 You can move inserts by dragging them between slots in the Inserts view.

To move an insert:

◆ Drag the insert to the desired location (**Figure 14.7**).

The moved insert appears in the new location.

Figure 14.8 When a line insert is lit, the corresponding plug-in window is open.

To duplicate an insert:

◆ Option-drag (Macintosh) or Alt-drag (Windows) the insert to the desired location.

A copy of the insert appears in the new location.

For more information on inserts, see *Chapter 13: Mixing Basics* and *Chapter 3: The Mix and Edit Windows*.

✔ Tip

■ A lighted Insert button in the Inserts view indicates that the corresponding plug-in window is open (**Figure 14.8**).

Using Plug-in Windows

When you click on an insert, a window for the assigned plug-in appears. This window lets you adjust the parameters of the corresponding DSP plug-in.

By default, Pro Tools displays one plug-in window at a time, but for convenience, you can display multiple plug-in windows. You can also open and adjust parameters on individual channels of multi-mono plug-ins.

Plug-in windows share the following parameters (**Figure 14.9**):

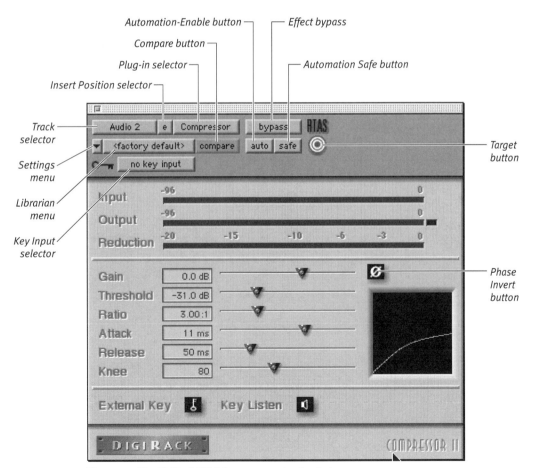

Figure 14.9 The DigiRack RTAS Compressor plug-in window.

Key Input Selector: The Key Input selector lets you select audio on a particular input or bus and route it to the plug-in. This menu only appears on plug-ins that feature side-chain processing.

Librarian Menu: The Librarian menu lets you recall settings files saved in the plug-in's root settings folder or in the current session's Settings folder.

Settings Menu: The Settings menu lets you copy, paste, save, and import plug-in settings.

Track Selector: The Track selector lets you choose any non-MIDI track in the session.

Insert Position Selector: The Insert Position selector lets you choose any insert on the current track.

Plug-in Selector: The Plug-in selector lets you choose any real-time plug-in from the DAE Plug-ins folder.

Compare Button: The Compare button toggles between the original saved plug-in setting and the current plug-in setting.

Effect Bypass: The Effect Bypass disables the currently displayed plug-in. This lets you hear the track with and without the plug-in.

Automation-Enable Button: This feature lets you enable automation recording for individual plug-in parameters.

Automation Safe Button: The Automation Safe button protects plug-in automation from being overwritten.

Link-Enable Buttons: The Link-Enable buttons let you link channels of a multi-mono plug-in. Each square represents a channel. (The Master Link button must be disabled to use the Link-Enable buttons.)

Channel Selector: The Channel selector lets you access specific channels within a multi-channel track. This feature appears on multi-mono plug-ins only. Shift-click the Channel selector to open a separate plug-in window for each channel.

Master Link Button: The Master Link button links the parameter controls on all channels of a multi-mono plug-in. This lets you adjust multiple channels simultaneously.

Target Button: The Target button lets you select a plug-in as the target for any keyboard commands.

Phase Invert Button: The Phase Invert button lets you invert the phase polarity of the input signal.

Figure 14.10 To open a plug-in window, click the insert in the Inserts view.

Figure 14.11 The red Target button.

Figure 14.12 To select a different plug-in on the same track, click the Plug-in selector and choose a plug-in from the pop-up menu.

To open a plug-in window:

◆ Click on an insert (**Figure 14.10**).
The selected plug-in window appears.

To open multiple plug-in windows:

◆ Click the red Target button on each plug-in window that you want to remain open (**Figure 14.11**).
The Target button becomes grayed out and the window remains open when other plug-in windows open.

or

◆ Shift-click the Insert button of the desired plug-in.
The selected plug-in window opens, and any open plug-in windows remain open.

To select a different plug-in on the same track:

◆ Click the Plug-in selector and choose a plug-in from the pop-up menu (**Figure 14.12**).
The window for the new plug-in appears.

USING PLUG-IN WINDOWS

327

To select a plug-in on a different track:

◆ Click the Track selector and choose a track from the pop-up menu (**Figure 14.13**).

To open plug-in windows for each channel of a multi-mono plug-in:

1. Option-click (Macintosh) or Alt-click (Windows) the Channel selector in the plug-in window of the desired plug-in (**Figure 14.14**).

2. Select the desired channel.

   The plug-in window of the desired channel appears.

Figure 14.13 To select a plug-in on a different track, click the Track selector and choose a track from the pop-up menu.

Figure 14.14 To open plug-in windows for left and right channels of a multi-mono plug-in, Option-click (Macintosh) or Alt-click (Windows) the Channel selector.

Insert (blue)

Figure 14.15 When a plug-in is in Bypass mode, the Insert selector appears blue.

Insert (purple)

Figure 14.16 If one channel (left or right) of a multi-mono plug-in is bypassed, the insert appears purple.

Bypassing Plug-ins

Pro Tools lets you bypass a plug-in by clicking its Effect Bypass button. Bypassing a plug-in lets you compare the effected signal with the original dry signal. This is different from using the Compare button, which lets you compare the original saved effect settings with the current plug-in setting configuration.

To bypass a plug-in:

◆ Click the plug-in window's Bypass button.

   or

◆ Command-click (Macintosh) or Control-click (Windows) the plug-in's Insert button.

✔ Tip

■ The Inserts view in both the Mix and Edit windows displays the bypass status of all inserted plug-ins: In Pro Tools 6, when a plug-in is in Bypass mode, the Insert appears blue (**Figure 14.15**). If one channel (left or right) of an unlinked multi-mono plug-in is bypassed, the Insert appears purple (**Figure 14.16**).

Adjusting Plug-in Parameters

One nice thing about real-time plug-ins is that you can adjust them in real-time—in other words, you can make changes to their parameters during playback. You can edit a plug-in's parameters by dragging its slider or by typing values into its value field.

For instructions on adjusting individual RTAS plug-ins, see the *DigiRack Plug-ins Guide*, or consult the documentation that came with your third-party plug-in.

To adjust a plug-in parameter:

1. Begin audio playback so you can hear parameter changes in real time.

2. Adjust the parameters of the plug-in to achieve the desired effect.

To fine-tune plug-in parameter settings:

◆ Command-drag (Macintosh) or Control-drag (Windows) on the desired parameter control.

ADJUSTING PLUG-IN PARAMETERS

Figure 14.17 Use the keyboard to input values directly into the value field of any plug-in parameter.

To return a control to its default value:

◆ Option-click (Macintosh) or Alt-click (Windows) on the desired parameter control.

✔ Tips

■ If you have multiple plug-in windows open, click the Target button of the plug-in window that you want to make active.

■ You can use the computer keyboard to make the following edits:

Click in the value field of the parameter that you want to edit. Enter the desired value (**Figure 14.17**).

In fields that support values in kilohertz, typing "k" after a number value will multiply the value by 1000. For example, for 4000, enter 4k.

To increase a value, press the Up arrow on your keyboard. To decrease a value, press the Down arrow.

To move downward through the different parameter fields, press the Tab key. To move up, press Shift-Tab.

What Is EQ?

Equalization (EQ) refers to *cutting* or *boosting* the volume level of specific frequencies of an audio signal. EQ is used to open up frequency ranges, and thus enhance the clarity, spaciousness, and blending of sounds in a mix.

Every instrument occupies its own frequency range (**Figure 14.18**). When you record multiple tracks of audio, the frequency ranges of various instruments overlap, often creating a unique blend of sound. But overlapping frequencies can also interfere with each other and produce frequency build-ups that make a mix sound unbalanced, cloudy, and flat.

Figure 14.18 The frequency ranges of some familiar instruments. All instruments have high harmonics that contribute to the character of a sound.

This is where EQ enters. EQ lets you adjust the volume level of specific audio frequencies. Using EQ, you can turn down the volume of interfering frequencies and open up spaces for the main frequencies of instruments in the mix. This *EQ carving* enhances the clarity, spaciousness, and perceived height of the stereo image. For more information on stereo images, see *Chapter 13: Mixing Basics*.

EQ effects are most frequently used as line inserts on individual tracks. When you apply EQ to a track, it's a good idea to begin by gently cutting (or *subtracting*) frequencies on other tracks that may be interfering with the track you want to bring out. Subtracting EQ opens up space for the desired frequency range without adding new frequencies and boosting the overall mix volume.

You can then (sparingly) boost the frequency range of the track you want to bring out. For example, if you're mixing bass and kick drum, you may want to cut the kick and boost the bass at 100Hz, and also boost the kick and cut the bass at 60Hz. This will bring out each instrument's primary frequency ranges and add definition to both the kick and bass.

Remember, you don't want to "box" sounds into narrow frequency ranges by cutting off all their highs and lows. The interplay of harmonics and blending of frequency ranges gives a mix much of its unique character.

For more information on EQ, see the *Plug-ins Guide* that comes with your system.

WHAT IS EQ?

Using EQ

Pro Tools' DigiRack plug-ins provide both one-band and four-band *parametric* EQs. A parametric EQ lets you choose the specific range of frequencies that you want to change. When you use a parametric EQ, you dial in a specific frequency, and then set the range around that frequency. This range is referred to as *Q*. The Q represents the number of octaves that the applied EQ affects. You can usually adjust Q to affect frequencies between one-half and two octaves wide.

The DigiRack one-band EQ (**Figure 14.19**) lets you apply a single EQ filter to an audio signal. The DigiRack four-band EQ (**Figure 14.20**) lets you apply up to four different EQ filters simultaneously. DigiRack EQ plug-ins include the following EQ filters:

Hi Pass/Low Pass: Pass filters are useful for eliminating unwanted high- or low-frequency ranges. A hi-pass filter lets high frequencies pass through, but cuts off low frequencies. A low-pass filter lets low frequencies pass through, but cuts off high frequencies.

Hi Shelf/Low Shelf: Shelf filters let you cut or boost both high- and low-frequency ranges. A hi-shelf filter lets you cut or boost frequencies above a chosen target frequency. A low-shelf filter lets you cut or boost frequencies below a chosen target frequency.

Peak: Peak filters let you cut or boost frequencies around a selected frequency. The Peak filter's Q button lets you set the frequency range that the Peak filter affects.

Figure 14.19 The DigiRack one-band EQ plug-in lets you apply a single EQ filter to an audio signal.

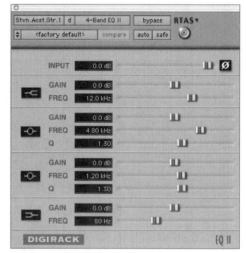

Figure 14.20 The DigiRack four-band EQ plug-in lets you apply up to four different EQ filters simultaneously.

USING EQ

Figure 14.21 The DigiRack RTAS Compressor plug-in.

Using Dynamic Effects

Dynamic effects such as compressors, limiters, gates, and expanders let you control the *dynamic range* of an audio signal. The dynamic range is the difference between the softest and the loudest volume produced by a sound source. Controlling the dynamic range lets you smooth out performances that have erratic spikes in volume. It also lets you eliminate unwanted background noise.

Pro Tool's DigiRack RTAS plug-ins include the following dynamic effects:

Compressor: The Compressor plug-in (**Figure 14.21**) lets you reduce the dynamic range of signals that exceed a specified volume threshold. This lets you reduce extreme volume peaks on tracks that are prone to erratic levels (such as vocals and bass). For example, you can use compression to smooth out a vocal track that has both overly loud and overly soft moments. Once the extreme volume peaks are tempered, you can then turn up the volume of the track. This helps even out the volume of the vocal track, and, in some cases, adds more presence and punch to a track.

The DigiRack RTAS Compressor plug-in has the following adjustable parameters:

◆ **Threshold:** The threshold is the level at which compression kicks in.

◆ **Ratio:** Ratio is the amount that a signal's volume is decreased (relative to the signal's original volume).

◆ **Attack:** Attack refers to the speed at which the compressor reacts to a loud signal.

◆ **Release:** The release is the speed at which the compressor lets go of the compression.

◆ **Knee:** The knee refers to the rate at which the compressor reaches full compression once the threshold has been exceeded.

Limiter: The Limiter plug-in (**Figure 14.22**) is a compressor that removes (rather than reduces) all signal exceeding the specified volume threshold. Limiters eliminate extreme volume spikes and thus prevent clipping. Because they eliminate loud volume peaks, limiters, like compressors, let you turn up the overall volume of a track. The DigiRack RTAS Limiter plug-in has the same adjustable parameters as the DigiRack RTAS Compressor plug-in.

Gate: The Gate plug-in (**Figure 14.23**) lets audio signals above a selected volume threshold pass through, while signals below the threshold are attenuated (decreased) by a specified amount. Gates (or noise gates) are the opposite of limiters: Rather than limit how loud a sound can get, they limit how soft a sound can get. Gates are useful for removing unwanted background noise on tracks. When recording drums, for instance, gates are often applied to each drum track to eliminate extraneous low-level noise coming from other drum mics. This not only helps make drum tracks less noisy, but can also increase their punch.

Figure 14.22 The DigiRack RTAS Limiter plug-in.

Figure 14.23 The DigiRack RTAS Gate plug-in.

USING DYNAMIC EFFECTS

Figure 14.24 The DigiRack RTAS Expander plug-in.

The DigiRack RTAS Gate plug-in has the following parameters:

◆ **Threshold:** Threshold refers to the volume level below which the gate closes and attenuates the signal.

◆ **Attack:** Attack refers to the speed at which the gate reacts to a signal below the threshold.

◆ **Range:** Range is the amount (in decibels) that the gate attenuates the signal. For example, a range of 50dB decreases any signal below the threshold by 50dB.

◆ **Decay:** Decay determines the rate at which the gate closes after the signal reaches the threshold.

◆ **Hold:** Hold refers to the length of time that the gate stays open after the signal falls below the threshold. When the hold time is reached, the gate slams shut. This can sometimes produce a chopped-off sound.

Expander: The Expander plug-in (**Figure 14.24**) attenuates any signal falling below a specified volume threshold by a user-defined ratio. Compared to a gate, which reduces sounds below a set threshold by a specified amount, an expander's ratio changes the signal gradually. This makes the resulting signal sound more natural. Expanders are useful when you want to subtly reduce noise from a track, rather than completely filter it out. For example, when dealing with a singer's breaths, you may want to use an expander rather than a gate. The expander will reduce the volume of the breath gradually, creating a more natural breathing sound than a gate, which would chop off the breath entirely.

The DigiRack RTAS Expander plug-in has the same parameters as the Gate plug-in.

Using Key Inputs for Side-Chain Processing

Many RTAS plug-ins let you set up *side-chain processing*. Side-chain processing occurs when an effect on a track is triggered by audio from a different track. The audio source used to trigger the effect is called the *key input*. In Pro Tools you can use any bus or input as the key input.

Side chains and key inputs are typically used with dynamic effects such as compressors and noise gates (although you can no doubt find many other creative uses for them). For example, a kick drum can be used as the key input to trigger gating on a bass guitar.

To use a key input for side-chain processing:

1. From the Key Input menu, choose the input or bus carrying the audio that you want to trigger the plug-in (**Figure 14.25**).

2. Click External Key to activate side-chain processing (**Figure 14.26**).

3. Click Key Listen to audition the key input audio source (**Figure 14.27**).

4. Begin playback.

   The plug-in uses the key input to trigger its effect. Adjust plug-in parameters, if necessary, to achieve the desired effect.

✔ Tip

- Certain plug-ins feature key input filters (such as hi- and low-pass filters), which let you define specific frequency ranges as key inputs to trigger the plug-in effect. This is useful for filtering instruments so that only specific high frequencies (such as a hi hat) or low frequencies (such as a kick drum) trigger the effect. For more information on key input filters, see the *Digidesign Plug-ins Guide*.

Figure 14.25 To activate a plug-in from a side-chain, click the Key Input selector and choose a bus or input.

Figure 14.26 The External Key button activates side-chain processing.

Figure 14.27 The Key Listen button lets you audition the key input audio source.

USING KEY INPUTS FOR SIDE-CHAIN PROCESSING

Creating Effects Loops

Pro Tools lets you create send-and-return submixes, known as *effects loops* (**Figure 14.28**). Effects loops are used to process multiple tracks of audio simultaneously through a single effect. For example, you might route several band tracks (such as drums, vocals, piano, and guitars) through a reverb to create the impression that a song is being played live inside a large hall. Effects loops can also help save DSP resources by minimizing the number of plug-ins used in a session.

When you create an effects loop, you bus audio from multiple tracks to an auxiliary input. (This is called an *effects send*.) A plug-in or hardware effect inserted on the auxiliary input then adds the desired effect to the signal. You then return the output of the auxiliary input to the main mix. (This is called an *effects return*.)

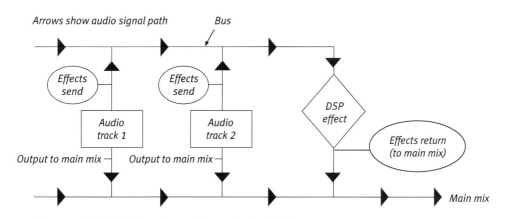

Figure 14.28 An effects loop. Arrows show audio signal path.

To create an effects loop:

1. Create an effects send: Assign a send on each source track to a mono or stereo bus path (**Figure 14.29**).

2. Assign each track's main output to the main mix outputs.

3. Choose File > New Track.

   The New Track dialog box appears.

4. Choose Auxiliary Input (stereo or mono), and click Create.

5. Insert a real-time plug-in or external hardware effect on the auxiliary input (**Figure 14.30**).

6. Set the plug-in or external effect to 100% Wet, and configure any other parameters as needed.

7. Click the Input selector of the auxiliary input and assign it to the same bus path as the source tracks.

8. Click the Output selector of the auxiliary input and choose the main mix outputs (**Figure 14.31**).

   This turns the auxiliary input into an effects return.

9. Adjust the level of the auxiliary input to balance the effects return in the mix.

Figure 14.29 Create an effects send by assigning audio tracks to buses.

Figure 14.30 On the destination auxiliary input, insert the real-time effect that you want to use in the effects loop.

Figure 14.31 Create an effects return by assigning the outputs of the auxiliary input to the main mix outputs. Use the effects return to mix varying amounts of the treated signal into the mix.

Simulating Space

When you yell across the Grand Canyon, your voice bounces (or *echoes*) back to you … back to you. The time it takes for your voice to return is the *delay time*. The delay time tells us how big a space is. For example, because it takes a long time for your voice to return from across the Grand Canyon, we know the space is pretty big.

In mixing, we use delay times to create the illusion of depth in the stereo image. The longer it takes for a delayed signal to *repeat*, the larger the perceived space.

For more information on stereo imaging, see *Chapter 13: Mixing Basics*.

CREATING EFFECTS LOOPS

Using Delay Effects

Delay effects let you add depth and dimension to sounds in a mix. All delay effects are created the same way—by repeating sounds at various delay times. But small changes in delay time can produce very different-sounding delay effects (**Figure 14.32**).

Many delay effects such as doubling, slapback, and echo simply repeat a signal at a specified delay time. Shorter delay times are useful for thickening sounds; longer delay times help reinforce rhythms, or create the perception of large spaces.

Some delay effects such as phase shifting, flanging, and chorus use short delay times together with *modulation*. Modulation occurs when the delay time is changed over time. When you add modulation to a delayed signal, slight pitch variations occur. These modulating delays can produce pretty far-out effects—from disembodied voices in desolate windscapes to shimmering choral effects.

Of course, take care not to over-saturate the mix with delay and reverb—a little takes you pretty far. Sometimes, spaces are best defined by what's not there. Like everything else in mixing (and recording), there are no absolutes with adding delay. As always, it's important to follow your ears.

DigiRack RTAS Mod Delay II plug-ins let you create the following delay effects:

Doubling: Doubling uses a single delay repeat at delay times between 30 and 80ms. Repeats with delay times less than 50ms are not discernable as discrete echoes; instead, they're perceived as additional voices or instruments. Doubling can help make a track sound thicker.

Slapback: Slapback usually consists of one or two repeats at delay times between 75 and 120ms. Slapback is good for creating punchy vocal tracks or reinforcing the beat or tempo of a song.

Echo: Echo refers to one or more discretely audible repeats of the original source sound. Repeated signals with delay times longer than 50ms are usually audible as discrete signals. Echoes produced by medium and long delay times (120–1000ms or more) are useful for simulating large spaces. For example, adding a long delay to a guitar lead can make it sound like it's in a huge, cavernous space.

Figure 14.32 Delay times (in milliseconds) of common delay effects.

Phase Shifting: Phase shifting uses very short delay times (1–3ms) and modulation. Mixing the delayed signal with its original non-delayed source signal produces a slightly out-of-phase effect with a subtle yet distinctive "whooshing" sound.

Flanging: Flanging uses short delay times (1–20ms) and modulation. This produces a more dramatic "whoosh" than phase shifting, which makes it good for creating frightening voices and otherworldly sound effects.

Chorus: Chorus uses short delay times (20–40ms) and modulation. By modulating repeated signals at these times and mixing them with the source signal, you can create the perception of multiple instruments and voices.

The DigiRack RTAS Mod Delay II plug-ins (**Figure 14.33**) include the following user-adjustable parameters:

Delay: Delay lets you set the delay time of the effect.

Feedback: Feedback controls the number of delay repeats. The higher the feedback level, the greater the number of delay repeats.

Depth: Depth lets you adjust the amount of modulation applied to the delayed signal.

Rate: Rate lets you adjust the speed of the modulation applied to the delayed signal.

Figure 14.33 The DigiRack RTAS Mod Delay II plug-in.

What Is Reverb?

Reverb is a natural property of any enclosed room that occurs when sound waves bounce off walls, ceilings, and floors. You've probably experienced reverb, even if you're not familiar with the term—it's what makes singing in the shower sound so good. Reverb effects let you simulate acoustic spaces of all sizes, shapes, and reflectivity.

Reverb has three basic sound components (**Figure 14.34**):

Direct Sound: Direct sound is what you hear when sound waves travel unimpeded from the source to your ears. Direct sound cues you to the location of the sound source in a three-dimensional space.

Early Reflections: Early reflections are the first reflected sound waves to reach your ears after bouncing off the primary surfaces in a given room. Early reflections cue you to the size and shape of a room.

Reverberations: Reverberations are the final reflected sound waves to reach your ears. They consist of multiple sound reflections traveling from surface to surface within the confines of a room. The delay times of these reflected sound waves are so close together that you hear them as one long, decaying signal.

Direct sound   Early reflections   Reverberation

Figure 14.34 The three basic sound components of reverb.

Using Reverb

When you apply reverb to a sound, you're essentially bouncing that sound off the walls, floors, and ceilings of a simulated room. Adjusting reverb parameters (such as room size, decay, pre-delay, diffusion, and density) lets you create the illusion that a sound is inside of a space of almost any size or shape. For instance, if you want to place a pipe organ sound into a cathedral space, you'd run the organ through a reverb with long decay times and long pre-delay times. Then, by returning more of the reverb signal than the original signal to the main mix, you can create the distant vastness of a cathedral.

You can also combine delays and reverbs to create even more spacious sounds. For example, by adding short delay (doubling) to a background vocal, and then sending the delayed signal into a big reverb, you can create the illusion of a choir in a large hall.

In addition to its preset room algorithms such as halls, churches, plates, and rooms, Pro Tool's RTAS D-Verb reverb plug-in (sold separately) has the following user-adjustable parameters (**Figure 14.35**):

Size: The Size button lets you choose from three room sizes: small, medium, and large.

Decay: Decay is the length of time that the reverb lasts. Use longer decay times to simulate larger rooms.

Pre-delay: Pre-delay determines the amount of time between the beginning of an audio signal and the beginning of its reverberations. It lets you add definition to the source sound by separating it from its reverb.

Figure 14.35 Digidesign's D-Verb reverb plug-in.

Diffusion: Diffusion determines the rate of increase of sound reflections in the room. You can use diffusion to adjust the perceived reflectivity of a room. Higher diffusion simulates a more reflective room; lower diffusion simulates a less reflective room.

Hi Frequency Cut: The Hi Frequency Cut filter lets you control the decay of high-frequency components in the reverb. Use it with the Low Pass filter to shape the overall high-frequency contour of the reverb.

Low Pass: The Low Pass filter controls the volume of high frequencies in the reverb. The Low Pass filter attenuates by 6dB all sounds above a user-defined frequency.

Many third-party reverb plug-ins include these additional adjustable parameters:

Room Size: In addition to preset room sizes, many reverbs let you adjust the actual room size in meters or feet. This gives you more control over the size of a reverb space.

Density: Density refers to the level of early sound reflections that a room produces. Because early reflections reach your ear before the main body of reverb, density can cue you to the size of the space. The higher the density setting, the larger the apparent space.

USING REVERB

Using External Hardware Effects

You can use external hardware effects such as reverbs or delays as in-line inserts or as send-and-return effects loops. To use external hardware, you must map the insert's inputs and outputs to audio interface channels in the I/O Setup dialog box. You must also connect the external hardware device to the corresponding inputs and outputs of the audio interface.

For more information on I/O Setups, see *Chapter 4: Starting a New Session.* For information on connecting external hardware devices, see *Appendix A: Connecting Your Studio* or the *Pro Tools Reference Guide.*

To define hardware inserts:

1. Choose Setups > I/O Setup.

   The I/O Setup dialog box appears (**Figure 14.36**).

2. Click Inserts.

3. Select an Insert path (**Figure 14.37**).
   or
   Click New Path to create a new insert path.

4. Set the insert to the correct format (mono or stereo).

5. Map inserts in the Channel Grid as needed.

Figure 14.36 The I/O Setup dialog box.

Figure 14.37 To define hardware inserts, select an insert path in the I/O Setup dialog box.

USING EXTERNAL HARDWARE EFFECTS

Figure 14.38 To assign a hardware insert to a track, choose an insert from the track Insert selector.

To assign a hardware insert to a track:

◆ Select an insert from the track Insert selector (**Figure 14.38**).

✔ Tip

■ To save DSP resources, make external hardware inserts inactive. Inactive inserts retain their routing assignments but do not let signal pass through.

To make an insert inactive: Command-Control-click (Macintosh) or Control-Start-click (Windows) on the insert you want to make inactive. Inactive inserts appear shaded and italicized.

Making inserts inactive can also work as a mute or bypass for hardware inserts that don't have their own Bypass button.

For more information on Active and Inactive modes, see *Chapter 20: Optimizing Performance*.

USING EXTERNAL HARDWARE EFFECTS

Using AudioSuite Plug-ins

Unlike RTAS (and TDM) plug-ins, AudioSuite plug-ins do not process audio in real-time. Instead, they process audio directly to disk, creating a new audio file that includes the effected signal.

When using an AudioSuite plug-in, you must first select the audio region that you want to process. Keep in mind that delay or reverb effects will add additional material at the end of the selected audio region (a delay repeat or a reverb decay, respectively). For this reason, it's important to make the selection longer than the source audio. If there isn't enough room to write the effect into the audio file, the effect will be unceremoniously chopped off.

For more details on AudioSuite plug-ins, see the *Digidesign Plug-ins Guide* that came with your system.

To process audio with an AudioSuite plug-in:

1. Select the regions that you want to process.

2. Choose the desired AudioSuite plug-in from the AudioSuite menu (**Figure 14.39**).

3. Click the Preview button to audition the effect (**Figure 14.40**).

4. Adjust the plug-in parameters to achieve the desired effect.

5. Click the Process button.

   The selected audio is processed. Pro Tools appends an acronym to the region's name, indicating the AudioSuite process that has been applied. The new audio file then appears in the session.

Figure 14.39 The AudioSuite plug-in menu.

Figure 14.40 To audition an AudioSuite plug-in, click the Preview button.

USING AUDIOSUITE PLUG-INS

✔ Tips

■ To configure the plug-in for destructive processing, choose Create Individual files from the File Mode pop-up menu. This will overwrite and permanently modify the original source audio files.

■ To configure the plug-in for non-destructive processing, choose Create Individual Files from the File Mode pop-up menu. This will create new audio files that have been processed with the AudioSuite plug-in and leave the original source audio files untouched.

■ To process the selected region only in the track in which it appears, choose Playlist from the Selection Reference pop-up menu.

■ To process and update every occurrence of the selected region throughout the session, enable the Use In Playlist button (and also choose Region List from the Selection Reference pop-up menu).

■ For additional AudioSuite processed-file handling options, see the *Digidesign Plug-ins Guide* that came with your system.

USING AUDIOSUITE PLUG-INS

Improving RTAS Plug-in Performance

You can improve the performance of RTAS plug-ins by increasing Pro Tools' hardware buffer size and CPU usage limit. This will dedicate more processing power to RTAS plug-ins and other host processor tasks.

For more information on improving system performance, see *Chapter 20: Optimizing Performance* or the *Pro Tools Reference Guide*.

To improve RTAS plug-in performance:

1. Choose Setups > Playback Engine.

2. From the H/W Buffer Size pop-up menu, select the desired hardware buffer size.

3. From the CPU Usage Limit pop-up menu, select the percentage of CPU power you want to dedicate to RTAS plug-ins and host processor tasks (**Figure 14.41**).

Figure 14.41 To improve RTAS plug-in performance, choose Setups > Hardware. Increase the CPU usage limit to dedicate more processing power to RTAS plug-ins.

15

AUTOMATING A MIX

Not long ago engineers, producers, and band members alike engaged in a Twister-like ritual known as "performing" the final mix on the board. Pulling off such a mix was no easy feat: For instance, if one person failed to turn up a guitar or vocal on the mixing board, the entire mix had to be scrubbed—and performed again from scratch. Needless to say, more than a few good mixes (and tempers) were lost in this process.

Thankfully, computer automation has made this arduous mix choreography a thing of the past. Pro Tools automation remembers your mix moves and plays them back exactly as you performed them. This can save you a huge amount of time. You can build mixes in logical stages, and, if you make a mistake, a simple tweak fixes it—no more redoing mixes from scratch.

This chapter will show you how to use Pro Tools automation. You'll learn how to write an automation pass, and how to edit and view automation data. We'll also discuss how to thin unneeded automation data—a trick that enhances both automation and CPU performance.

About Automation Modes

Each channel strip in the Pro Tools Mix and Edit windows provides an Automation Mode selector (**Figure 15.1**), which lets you choose how track automation is written and played back. Choose from the following automation modes:

Auto Off: Auto Off turns off automation for all automation parameters.

Auto Read: Auto Read mode plays back automation that was previously written for a track.

Auto Write: Auto Write mode writes automation data during playback. It erases any pre-existing automation data on the track. After you record automation data in Auto Write mode, Pro Tools automatically switches to Auto Touch mode (see below). This prevents you from accidentally overwriting automation data on further playback.

Auto Touch: Auto Touch mode writes automation data only when you click on an automation parameter with the mouse. When you release the mouse, automation writing stops and the parameter returns to its previously automated position.

Auto Latch: Auto Latch mode is similar to Auto Touch mode: It writes automation only when you click on an automation parameter with the mouse. Auto Latch, however, continues to write automation until you stop playback. This mode is particularly useful for automating pan controls and plug-ins, since it doesn't revert to its previous position when you release a control.

Figure 15.1 The Automation Mode selector lets you choose how track automation is written and played back.

Figure 15.2 The Automation Enable window.

Figure 15.3 To open the Automation Enable window, choose Windows > Show Automation Enable.

Figure 15.4 To suspend automation writing on all tracks, click the Auto Suspend button in the Automation Enable window.

Enabling Automation

The Automation Enable window (**Figure 15.2**) lets you enable (or suspend) automation writing for the following automation parameters:

◆ Volume

◆ Pan

◆ Mute

◆ Send Level

◆ Send Pan

◆ Send Mute

◆ Plug-in parameters

To enable automation writing on all tracks:

1. Choose Windows > Show Automation Enable (**Figure 15.3**).

   The Automation Enable window appears.

2. Select the automation parameters that you want to automate.

To suspend automation writing on all tracks:

1. Choose Windows > Show Automation Enable.

2. To suspend automation writing on all tracks, click the Auto Suspend button (**Figure 15.4**).

   or

   To suspend automation writing of a specific parameter on all tracks, click the button for that parameter.

ENABLING AUTOMATION

353

To suspend automation writing and playback on individual tracks:

1. In the Edit window, set the Track View selector to show the automation parameter that you want to suspend.

2. To suspend automation writing and play-back for the displayed parameter, Command-click (Macintosh) or Control-click (Windows) on the name of the displayed parameter in the Track View selector (**Figure 15.5**).

   or

   To suspend writing and playback of an automation parameter on all tracks, Command-Option-click (Macintosh) or Control-Alt-click (Windows) on the name of the automation parameter in the Track View selector.

Figure 15.5 Command-click (Macintosh) or Control-click (Windows) the name of the displayed parameter in the Track View selector to suspend automation writing and playback.

Figure 15.6 Enable the track parameters that you want to automate in the Automation Enable window.

Figure 15.7 Select an automation mode for each track that you want to automate.

Writing Automation

Pro Tools lets you write automation in real time by simply moving the controls for the desired parameter during playback. As you move the controls, Pro Tools records (or writes) these moves. This is called an *automation pass*.

To write automation on a track:

1. Choose Windows > Automation Enable.

2. Enable the track parameters that you want to automate (**Figure 15.6**).

3. Select an automation mode for each track that you want to automate (**Figure 15.7**).

   For the initial automation pass, select Auto Write.

4. Click Play to begin writing automation. Move the controls that you want to automate.

5. When you've finished writing automation, click Stop.

WRITING AUTOMATION

After the first automation pass, you can write additional automation to the track without erasing the previous pass. To do so, set the automation mode to Auto Touch or Auto Latch.

Figure 15.8 Make a selection or place the cursor in the location where you want to write automation.

To write additional automation to a previous automation pass:

1. Link the Edit and Timeline selections.

2. In the Edit window, make a selection or place the cursor in the location where you want to write automation (**Figure 15.8**).

Figure 15.9 To write additional automation to a previous automation pass, select Auto Touch or Auto Latch mode.

3. Select Auto Touch or Auto Latch mode (**Figure 15.9**) on the tracks that you want to automate.

4. Click Play and begin writing automation. Move the controls that you want to automate.

5. When you've finished writing automation, click Stop.

Figure 15.10 The Pencil tool in the Edit window.

✔ Tip

■ You can use the Pencil tool (**Figure 15.10**) to draw automation directly into an automation playlist. The Pencil tool provides five shapes: Free Hand, Line, Triangle, Square, and Random (**Figure 15.11**). Experiment with them and see which one works for you. For more information on drawing automation, see the *Pro Tools Reference Guide*.

Figure 15.11 The Pencil tool's five shapes.

WRITING AUTOMATION

Figure 15.12 To view an automation parameter, click the Track View selector and choose from the pop-up menu.

Figure 15.13 The Volume track view displays the Volume automation playlist as an editable line graph.

Viewing Automation

Pro Tools creates a separate *automation playlist* for each automation parameter that you write. Unlike track playlists, which can display multiple region configurations, an automation playlist displays only a single automation line graph for each parameter. The Track View selector lets you view automation playlists.

To show automation data:

◆ Click the Track View selector and choose the automation playlist that you want to view (**Figure 15.12**).

The selected automation playlist appears in the track. The automation playlist displays an editable line graph representing the value of the automation parameter against time. Waveforms are displayed behind the line graph and appear lighter in color (**Figure 15.13**).

✔ Tip

■ To toggle between Waveform and Volume views, select the track that you want to toggle, and then press Control-Minus (Macintosh) or Start-Minus (Windows).

Automating Sends

Pro Tools lets you write automation for send volume, send mute, and send pan (for stereo and multi-channel sends only). This lets you precisely control effects levels and placement during a mixdown.

To write send volume, mute, or pan automation:

1. Choose Windows > Automation Enable.

2. Enable the send automation parameters that you want to automate (**Figure 15.14**).

3. Choose Auto Write as the automation mode for the initial pass.

4. Display an individual send control, or display a send Output window.

5. Click Play and begin writing automation. Move the send controls that you want to automate.

6. When you've finished writing automation, click Stop.

✔ Tip

- You can apply send volume and send mute automation to all members of a group. For more information, see *Appendix B: Setting Preferences.*

Figure 15.14 Select the send parameters that you want to automate from the Automation Enable window.

AUTOMATING SENDS

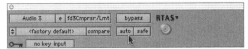

Figure 15.15 To enable plug-in automation, click the Automation-Enable button in the plug-in window.

Figure 15.16 The Plug-in Automation dialog box lets you select plug-in parameters to automate.

Figure 15.17 The Automation Safe button protects plug-in automation from being overwritten.

Automating Plug-ins

Pro Tools lets you write automation for most plug-in parameters. First, however, you must enable the parameters that you want to automate using the Plug-in Automation dialog box.

To enable plug-in automation:

1. Open the window of the plug-in that you want to automate.

2. Click the Automation-Enable button (**Figure 15.15**).

   The Plug-in Automation dialog box appears (**Figure 15.16**).

3. Select the parameters to automate.

4. Click Add.

5. Click OK.

To write plug-in automation:

1. Make sure the desired parameter is automation-enabled.

2. Choose an automation mode on the track in which the plug-in is inserted.

   For an initial pass, choose Auto Write.

3. Click Play to begin writing automation. Move the controls that you want to automate.

4. When you've finished writing plug-in automation, click Stop.

Once you've written plug-in automation, use the Automation Safe button to protect it from being overwritten.

To place plug-in automation in Safe mode:

1. Open the window for the plug-in.

2. Select the Automation Safe button (**Figure 15.17**).

Editing Automation

Pro Tools displays automation data as a line graph with editable breakpoints. You can graphically edit automation data by moving these breakpoints within a track's automation playlist. Dragging breakpoints up or down increases or decreases their value, respectively, while dragging them to the left or right makes the automation event occur earlier or later on the timeline.

Pro Tools also lets you cut, copy, and paste automation data.

Graphically editing automation breakpoints

To graphically edit automation breakpoints, display the automation parameter that you want to edit by choosing it from the Track View selector. Then, do one of the following:

To create a breakpoint:

◆ Click with the Grabber (or the Pencil) on the automation playlist's line graph (**Figure 15.18**).

A new breakpoint appears on the line graph.

To move a breakpoint:

◆ Click an existing point on the line graph with the Grabber and drag it to a new position (**Figure 15.19**).

To move several breakpoints at once:

1. Select a range in the automation playlist that contains the breakpoints that you want to move (**Figure 15.20**).

2. Press the Plus key to nudge the breakpoints to the right (later in the timeline) or the Minus key to nudge them to the left (earlier in the timeline). The breakpoints move by the current nudge value.

Figure 15.18 To create a breakpoint, click with the Grabber (or the Pencil) on the automation playlist's line graph.

Figure 15.19 To move a breakpoint, click an existing point on the line graph and drag it to a new position.

Figure 15.20 Select a range in the automation playlist that contains the breakpoints that you want to move.

Figure 15.21 Click in the region with the Trimmer and drag breakpoints up or down to increase or decrease their value.

Figure 15.22 A selected range of automation data.

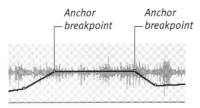

Anchor   Anchor
─ breakpoint   ─ breakpoint

Figure 15.23 After the selected automation is cut, anchor breakpoints are inserted at the beginning and end of the cut region.

Figure 15.24 When a cut (or copied) selection is pasted, the anchor breakpoints are also pasted.

To change all breakpoint values in a region:

◆ Click in the region with the Trimmer and drag the breakpoints up to increase their value, or down to decrease their value (**Figure 15.21**).

Cutting, copying, and pasting automation

You can also use traditional cut, copy, and paste commands to edit automation data.

When you cut a selected range of automation data (**Figure 15.22**), Pro Tools adds anchor breakpoints to the data's beginning and end points. This preserves the value and slope of the breakpoints on the line graph inside the cut selection. It also preserves a portion of the slope of the line graph before and after the cut region (**Figure 15.23**). When you paste the cut selection, the anchor breakpoints are also pasted (**Figure 15.24**).

Copying automation data does not affect the selected region. When you paste a copied selection, however, anchor breakpoints are also pasted.

Deleting automation

To delete automation data, display the automation parameter that you want to edit by selecting it from the Track View selector. Then, do one of the following:

To delete a single breakpoint:

◆ With the Grabber or Pencil tool, Option-click (Macintosh) or Alt-click (Windows) the breakpoint.

To delete several breakpoints:

1. Use the Selector to select a range that contains the breakpoints (**Figure 15.25**).

2. Press Delete (Macintosh) or Backspace (Windows).

   All breakpoints within the selected range are erased (**Figure 15.26**).

Figure 15.25
Select the portion of automation data that you want to delete.

To delete all automation data of the displayed parameter:

1. Click with the Selector in the track and choose Edit > Select All.

2. Press Delete (Macintosh) or Backspace (Windows).

Figure 15.26
The automation line graph after the selected automation has been deleted. Deleting automation does not create anchor breakpoints.

To delete all automation data in all automation playlists on a track:

1. Use the Selector to select a range of data to be removed.

2. Press Control-Delete (Macintosh) or Control-Backspace (Windows).

   Pro Tools removes all automation data within the selected range on each of the track's automation playlists.

✔ Tips

■ In Waveform view, cutting or copying a section of an audio track's waveform will also cut or copy any automation data associated with it.

■ On auxiliary inputs or master faders, only displayed automation data is cut or copied. To cut or copy all automation data on these track types, press Control while cutting or copying.

■ Don't confuse cutting automation data with deleting it. When you delete a selected range of automation, all automation data is removed and no anchor breakpoints are created. This can alter the shape of the automation line graph.

EDITING AUTOMATION

Figure 15.27 The Smooth and Thin Data After Pass option in the Automation Preferences window.

Figure 15.28 Select the amount of automation thinning from the Degree of Thinning option in the Automation Preferences window.

Thinning Automation

Pro Tools lets you reduce, or *thin*, the density of automation data written during an automation pass. This helps clear memory allocated to automation, which can enhance automation-writing efficiency and improve CPU performance.

Pro Tools provides two ways to thin automation data: The Smooth and Thin Data After Pass option in the Automation Preferences window and the Thin Automation command.

When the Smooth and Thin Data After Pass option is selected (**Figure 15.27**), Pro Tools automatically thins the automation breakpoint data after each automation pass. You can also select the amount of thinning from the Degree of Thinning option in the Automation Preferences window, including None (no thinning), Little, Some, More, and Most (maximum thinning) (**Figure 15.28**). For additional automation preferences, see *Appendix B: Setting Preferences*.

The Thin Automation command lets you selectively thin areas in a track where automation data is too dense.

To use the Thin Automation command:

1. In the Edit window, click the Track View selector to display the automation parameter that you want to thin.

2. With the Selector, highlight the automation data that you want to thin.

3. Choose Edit > Thin Automation to thin the selected automation.

   The selected automation data is thinned by the amount set in the Degree of Thinning option in the Automation Preferences window.

THINNING AUTOMATION

MIXDOWN AND MASTERING

16

Now that you've built and shaped your mix to your liking (and, hopefully the liking of others), just one mixing step remains: *final mixdown.* This is where you combine all tracks, edits, effects, and automation events into a final two-track stereo master.

There are two basic ways to save a final mixdown in Pro Tools: You can output the main stereo mix to a two-track digital or analog recording machine such as a DAT or 1/4-inch tape machine. Or, you can *bounce* the final mix directly to hard disk, where it's saved as a new audio file.

This chapter will show you how to perform a final mixdown using the latter method. I'll cover the correct method for bouncing, as well as how to configure bounce output options according to your needs. I've also thrown in a brief discussion of mastering, which will help you understand how individual mixes are processed to create a sonically consistent final album.

Bouncing to Disk

Pro Tools' Bounce to Disk command lets you mix down multiple tracks of audio (along with all DSP effects and automation events) directly to a stereo mix on your hard disk. In the process, a brand new file is created, which you can save to the location of your choice.

Bouncing to disk is a fast and efficient way to generate a final mix. Should you later decide that you don't like the mix, no big deal—just make the desired adjustments to the mix and bounce it to disk again...as many times as you like.

When you bounce to disk, Pro Tools plays the mix back in real time so you can hear it as it's being bounced. You can't, however, make any adjustments at this point.

Bounced mixes include the following:

Audible tracks: All audible tracks are included in the bounce, including soloed tracks or regions. Muted tracks are not included.

Automation: All read-enabled automation is played back and incorporated into the bounced mix.

Inserts and sends: All active inserts (including real-time plug-ins and hardware inserts) and sends are applied to the bounced mix.

Selection or track length: If you make a selection in a track, only the selected area will be bounced to disk. If no selection is made, the bounce will be the length of the longest audible track in the session.

Figure 16.1 If you want to include a track's automation in the bounced mix, set the track's automation mode to Read.

Figure 16.2 Assign the output of each track that you want to include in the bounce to the main mix outputs.

Time stamp information: Bounced material is automatically time-stamped so you can drag it to the same track location as in the original material.

Delay compensation: DAE compensates for any bus delays due to a bounce. This means that if you import a bounced file back into a session and place it directly in time against the source mix, it will be phase-accurate with the original source mix.

To bounce a final mix to disk:

1. Finalize all output levels and mix automation.

2. If you want to include a track's automation in the bounced mix, set the track's automation mode to Read (**Figure 16.1**).

3. Make sure that all of the tracks you want to include in the bounce are audible (not muted or inactive).

4. Assign the output of each track that you want to include in the bounce to the main mix outputs (**Figure 16.2**).

5. Do one of the following:
   To bounce a portion of a file: Link Edit and Timeline selections. Select the portion of the file that you want to include in the bounce.

   or

   To bounce the entire session: Don't make any selections. Press Return (Macintosh) or Enter (Windows) to go to the beginning of the session. The bounce will be the length of the longest audible track in the session.

continues on next page

BOUNCING TO DISK

6. Select File > Bounce to Disk (**Figure 16.3**).

The Bounce to Disk dialog box appears (**Figure 16.4**).

7. Choose a Bounce Source option to set the audio source for the bounced mix (**Figure 16.5**).

8. Configure other Bounce options as needed.

For detailed information on Bounce options, see *Setting Bounce Options* later in this chapter.

9. Click Bounce.

10. Select a destination for the new audio file, enter a name, and click Save.

Pro Tools bounces the mix in real time, and performs Bounce option processing tasks.

Figure 16.3 Select File > Bounce to Disk.

Figure 16.4 The Bounce to Disk dialog box.

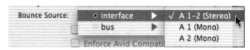

Figure 16.5 The Bounce Source option lets you choose the audio source for the bounced mix.

Figure 16.6 The File Type option lets you select a file type for the bounced mix.

Figure 16.7 The Format option lets you select the number of channels that a bounced file has.

Setting Bounce Options

The Bounce to Disk command provides several options for converting and processing bounced tracks:

Bounce Source: The Bounce Source option lets you choose the main output or bus path that supplies the audio source for the mix. All currently active paths (as defined in the I/O Setup) are available as the Bounce Source.

File Type: The File Type option (**Figure 16.6**) lets you select a file type for the bounced mix. Choose from the following:

- ◆ SDII (Sound Designer II)

- ◆ BWF (.WAV) (Broadcast .WAV Format)

- ◆ AIFF (Audio Interchange File Format)

- ◆ MP3 (MPEG-1 Layer 3)

- ◆ QuickTime (Macintosh only)

- ◆ RealAudio (Macintosh only)

- ◆ SND Resource (Macintosh only)

- ◆ Windows Media (.asf, .wma, or .wmv file extensions) (Windows only)

Format: The Format option (**Figure 16.7**) lets you select the number of channels that a bounced file has. Choose from these file formats:

- ◆ **Mono (summed):** This format combines mix elements to create a single mono disk file.

- ◆ **Multiple Mono:** This format creates the same number of mono files as the source path. For example, if the source is stereo, Multiple Mono creates two mono files appended with ".L" (left) and ".R" (right) suffixes.

- ◆ **Stereo Interleaved:** This format creates a single interleaved file containing all of the bounced mix elements.

Resolution (or bit depth): The Resolution option (**Figure 16.8**) lets you choose the bit depth of the bounced file. You can convert a bounced file to these resolution settings:

◆ **8-bit:** Some multimedia applications and dialogue-only recordings still use 8-bit resolution. Use this setting only if high-quality audio is not required.

◆ **16-bit:** This is the standard resolution for audio CDs.

◆ **24-bit:** Use this setting when you want to maintain the highest possible sound quality. The setting is also good for archiving master stereo mixdowns for future use.

Sample Rate: You can convert bounced files to several sample rates. Generally, the higher the sample rate, the better the audio quality. There may be times, however, when smaller file size takes precedence over audio quality.

You can convert bounced files to the following sample rates (**Figure 16.9**):

◆ 44.1kHz

◆ 48kHz

◆ 88.2kHz

◆ 96kHz

◆ 176.4kHz

◆ 192kHz

◆ Custom sample rate

◆ Pull Up and Pull-down sample rates

Figure 16.8 The Resolution option lets you choose the bit depth of the bounced file.

Figure 16.9 Choose a sample rate for the bounced mix.

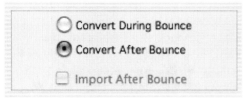

Figure 16.10 Choose from five conversion quality settings.

Figure 16.11 Select Convert After Bounce for more plug-in automation accuracy. Select Convert During Bounce for faster conversion, but less accuracy.

To set sample rate conversion quality:

◆ Choose Setups > Preferences. In the Editing preferences window, select from the Conversion Quality pop-up menu (**Figure 16.10**). Generally, the higher the conversion quality, the longer it takes for Pro Tools to convert the sample rate. Choose from five conversion quality settings: Low (fastest), Good, Better, Best, and Tweak Head (slowest).

Convert During or After Bounce: Pro Tools can process bounce options either during or after the bounce. Select Convert After Bounce (**Figure 16.11**) for the highest level of plug-in automation accuracy. Select Convert During Bounce for faster conversion, but less accuracy.

Import After Bounce: The Import After Bounce option automatically imports a newly bounced file into the current session's Audio Regions list. This option applies only when you're using the Bounce to Disk command to create submixes for use within the current session.

Mastering Basics

Mastering is the point at which you prepare your mixes for duplication. It's also when you stop thinking about individual mixes and start thinking about how your mixes sound as a group.

Mastering usually involves optimizing dynamics and tonal balance, as well as matching the volume levels of all of your songs. Thus, EQ, compression, limiting, and other effects processing are frequently applied during this step.

If you're mastering mixes for an album release, I strongly recommend hiring a professional mastering engineer. A good mastering engineer has the ears, the experience, the right gear, and perhaps most important, the perspective (usually in short supply at the end of a recording process) to make your mixes sound good together. You'll be amazed how much better your mixes can sound after being professionally mastered.

Some of the basic steps involved in mastering include:

Song Sequencing: Placing your songs in a sequence that flows is crucial to the listening experience. Think of a sequence theatrically, as if you're taking listeners on a sort of musical odyssey. Be aware of how different rhythms, lyrics, textures, and fade-ins and fade-outs affect the mood. Begin with tracks that draw listeners in. Then, take them through different moods and emotions, as you move toward a musical and thematic climax.

Equalization: EQ is often used in mastering to help balance frequencies within the aural-spectrum. Most good mixes are mastered with relatively flat EQ across the frequency spectrum, with some roll-off at the very top and bottom. Listen carefully to the tonal balance of your songs. If you hear any frequencies that sound too loud or soft, you may want to try gently cutting or boosting them. Keep in mind, however, that if a particular instrument is too loud, you can't individually EQ it without affecting the entire mix. Thus, you may need to return to the mixing stage to correct it.

Compression and Limiting: Dynamic effects, such as compression and limiting, are sometimes used in mastering to reduce transient volume peaks and boost a track's overall volume. Be careful not to overuse these effects: A touch of compression or limiting gives a track a nice volume boost while retaining clarity and dynamic range. But too much compression or limiting diminishes dynamic range and contrast, making a mix sound thin, dull, and flat. If you want to bring out individual instruments in a mix, consider using a multi-band compressor, which compress only specific frequency ranges. For more information on dynamic effects, see *Chapter 14: Adding Effects to a Mix*.

Balancing Levels: After you EQ and optimize the dynamics of each song, make sure the relative volume levels of your mixes are similar. This will keep listeners from having to make repeated trips to the volume knob. To balance levels, simply listen to your tracks and compare their volumes. If you hear any noticeable differences, just turn their levels up or down until they're roughly the same.

Dither and Noise Shaping: Dither is a form of random noise that helps minimize *quantization distortion* in digital recordings. Quantization distortion is noise that occurs as a result of errors introduced when sampling low-level audio signals, or when digital audio is converted from higher to lower bit depths (such as when converting 24-bit audio to 16-bit for CD mastering). The DigiRack Dither plug-in uses *noise shaping* to further reduce noise. Noise shaping uses digital filters to move noise from audible frequencies to less-audible frequencies. To use dither in Pro Tools, insert the Dither plug-in on the main mix's master fader.

MASTERING BASICS

Part VI:
MIDI Sequencing

RECORDING MIDI

Before Pro Tools 5, working with MIDI in Pro Tools simply did not happen. If a project demanded basic sequencing, a keyboard workstation or external hardware sequencer might get the job done. For more advanced integrated audio and MIDI, however, you had only one option: Buy and learn a second complex program that used Pro Tools hardware—all for the sole purpose of recording and editing MIDI tracks with audio tracks.

Fortunately, Pro Tools 5 changed that by integrating a solid sequencer into the familiar Pro Tools interface. With the release of version 6, Pro Tools has made a quantum leap towards becoming a full-featured MIDI sequencing interface.

This chapter will help you learn how to record MIDI into Pro Tools. I'll show you how to set up MIDI interfaces and devices so Pro Tools can use them, and how to select inputs and outputs for MIDI tracks. Next, you'll learn how to record single and multiple MIDI tracks into Pro Tools, and how to punch-record MIDI. We'll also cover two types of loop-recording, as well as how to import and export MIDI files to interface with other programs.

What Is MIDI?

The MIDI (Musical Instrument Digital Interface) communication protocol was originally designed to allow synthesizers created by different manufacturers to communicate with each other. MIDI became the glue that held together multiple keyboard and sound module setups. From very early in the computer music era, it also served as the protocol between computers and keyboards. Today, MIDI is most commonly used to record and play parts performed on a keyboard to trigger sounds in a synthesizer.

You can also use MIDI to:

◆ Send time code for synchronization

◆ Send Beat Clock information so all synthesizers receive the same tempo

◆ Modify parameters in synthesizers, samplers, and effects via controller information

◆ Send program and patch change commands to recall sounds and settings in external boxes.

MIDI terms

MIDI Channels: Each MIDI cable is capable of sending and receiving data on up to 16 channels. Each channel is generally reserved for a different instrument sound. For example, channel 10 is often reserved for drum sounds.

MIDI Interface: A hardware device that connects to a computer to send and receive MIDI. These can be simple devices that connect to a serial port and have 16 channels of MIDI send and receive, or complex devices that move hundreds of channels of MIDI to and from a computer. Many newer MIDI interfaces use USB connections, which provide self-powering (no AC connection required) and faster data transfer.

Controller: Any device that's used to send MIDI without necessarily making a sound on its own. A wind controller, for example, mimics the playing technique of a reed instrument, but is connected via MIDI to control the sounds of another MIDI sound generator. As another example, a keyboard controller can be used to program drum sounds in a sampler.

Sampler: A sound generator that takes individual sounds, or *samples*, and plays them back when triggered by a MIDI note. Many samplers can be used both to mimic real instruments, such as a piano, and to radically modify sounds in creative ways. Samplers are often used to trigger loops, as well.

Synthesizer: An electronic instrument used to make sounds. There are many different kinds of synthesizers and different methods for synthesizing sounds, including analog, sample playback, wave-table, granular, physical modeling, and virtual analog synthesis.

MIDI keyboard: A device with piano- or organ-style keys that sends MIDI information when played. Keyboards will often include onboard sounds in a synthesizer or sampler. In such cases, they can be used to play back the internal sounds as a synthesizer, or as a MIDI controller for other instruments.

Sound module: A MIDI synthesizer without a keyboard. A module can include any of the capabilities of a synthesizer, but must be triggered by an external MIDI device to make sounds.

Sequencer: A recorder that records MIDI instead of audio. Sequencers can be hardware devices or computer programs that are used to record, edit, and play back MIDI data. Sequencers can work with not only MIDI notes, but controller and SYSEX (system exclusive) data as well.

Keyboard workstation: A keyboard that includes an onboard synthesizer, sequencer, and effects, and often, a sampler. Originally conceived as "one-stop shopping" for full audio production, keyboard workstations are more often used today as hot-rod controllers and for onstage performance.

WHAT IS MIDI?

The Difference Between MIDI and Audio

A prominent audio engineer once told me with pride that he hadn't held a MIDI cable in his hand in five years because he was only interested in "real music." While plenty of music is made without MIDI or synthesizers, each year sees more MIDI in all stages of production. Most dance, hip-hop, and techno music begins with a sequencer and MIDI. And as production techniques from those styles like sampling and looping work their way into pop and rock productions, MIDI and sequencing are along for the ride. Finally, nearly all digital effects units have deep MIDI implementation, giving MIDI-savvy musicians new creative control—regardless of the kind of music they make.

MIDI offers several powerful advantages over audio. First, MIDI is a tempo-based protocol. Unlike an audio file, a MIDI note is not recorded at a specific moment in time; rather, it's recorded at a particular tempo and meter position (such as bar 34, beat 3, tick 117). This means that if you change the tempo of a project, the tempo of the MIDI tracks will automatically change as well.

MIDI tracks are also much more pitch- and sound-independent than audio tracks. An audio file of a bass track, for example, will always play back exactly as it was recorded. A MIDI track, however, is an event that the computer plays back at a certain time and place, according to your instructions, such as, "at bar 35, beat 1, send a C# out of port 3." With a few mouse clicks, you can make that C# play back a completely different sound on a different synthesizer. Or, you can transpose the note, or copy it to a different track so it plays back two different sounds at the same time. This flexibility is part of the charm of MIDI: Because it's so easy to make changes, you can quickly try out different ideas.

MIDI Input Device/
Channel selector

MIDI Output Device/
Channel selector

MIDI volume as
numeric value

MIDI pan as
numeric value

Automation Mode
selector

Default Program button

Record-Enable button

Mute button

Solo button

Pan slider

Volume fader

Track name

Figure 17.1 An audio track channel strip (left) and
MIDI track channel strip (right) in the Mix window.

MIDI in Pro Tools

Although MIDI and audio are quite different, working with MIDI in Pro Tools feels
much like working with audio in Pro Tools.
If you understand Pro Tools' audio features,
you'll find the MIDI functions to be intuitive.

Like audio tracks, MIDI tracks are displayed
in the Mix and Edit windows as channel
strips (**Figure 17.1**). Although both channel
strips have a number of similar controls, such
as solo, pan, and mute, MIDI track channel
strips do have some differences. For example,
MIDI tracks have no audio to send or bus, so
their channel strips don't have controls for
audio interface sends, RTAS plug-ins, or audio
buses. Instead, MIDI track channel strips
include controls for selecting MIDI inputs
and outputs.

The Edit window displays MIDI tracks horizontally, with notes running from left to right, sort of like a player piano roll (**Figure 17.2**). The buttons to the left of the MIDI track (**Figure 17.3**) serve many of the same functions as their audio track counterparts, such as the ability to resize, solo, mute, and name tracks.

MIDI notes

Figure 17.2 The Edit window displays audio tracks (top) and MIDI tracks (bottom) horizontally.

Track name
Record-Enable button
Automation Mode selector
Solo button
Mute button
Default Program button
Track Height selectoraa

Figure 17.3 The MIDI Track Size pop-up menu works much like its audio track counterpart.

MIDI IN PRO TOOLS

Figure 17.4 The MIDI Event list editor.

You can also view and edit MIDI data in the MIDI Event list. The MIDI Event list lets you make precise, numeric-based edits on all MIDI tracks data. In the MIDI Event list you can trigger notes by selecting them, and you can enter notes and other MIDI controller data using the MIDI Event list's Insert pop-up menu.

To open the Event List editor:

◆ From the Windows menu select MIDI event list, or press Option-= (equals sign). The MIDI Event List window opens (**Figure 17.4**).

OMS and MIDI Setup

Macintosh users who want to use MIDI in Pro Tools will have to install OMS (Open Music System). Developed by the now-defunct software pioneer Opcode, OMS is a utility that properly identifies and routes MIDI devices. OMS 2.3.8 comes with your Pro Tools LE installation CD (**Figure 17.5**). Install the software according to the OMS instructions.

Windows users needn't worry about OMS: Pro Tools on Windows uses system-level MIDI services, so no additional software is needed. Although different Windows versions require you to install and configure MIDI devices in slightly different ways, in general, you configure them in the Device Manager in the System control panel and in the Sounds or Multimedia control panels.

How OMS works

OMS creates a snapshot of all connected MIDI interfaces and devices in your studio. This snapshot, called an OMS Studio Setup, lets all MIDI applications use the same devices with meaningful names (**Figure 17.6**). When using OMS, for example, every application that works with MIDI, including Pro Tools, will know that an ASR-10 sampler is on port 4 of the MIDI interface, and will name it as such.

Follow the OMS documentation to create a Studio Setup. If you have problems with OMS or need to access the active Studio Setup, you can open the OMS utility from Pro Tools' Setups menu (**Figure 17.7**).

OMS works well—particularly considering its age—but many MIDI problems can be traced to OMS issues. Be sure to read the OMS documentation; it can save you some serious head-scratching. Also, OMS will refuse to start MIDI services if AppleTalk is turned on. If you don't want to have to turn AppleTalk off every time you start an OMS application, permanently disable it in the Chooser.

Figure 17.5 The OMS installer can be found on the Pro Tools CD.

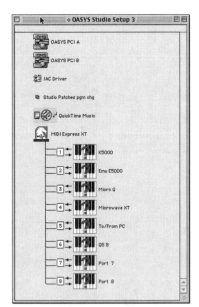

Figure 17.6 An OMS Studio Setup with all MIDI devices installed.

Figure 17.7 Use the Setups menu to open your OMS Studio Setup from within Pro Tools.

Figure 17.8 The Core MIDI Setup window for Mac OS X.

Figure 17.9 The MIDI device window for Core MIDI Setup using Mac OS X.

Figure 17.10 MIDI device configuration for Core MIDI.

MIDI Setup in Mac OS X

Mac OS X includes Apple's new Audio setup utility called Audio MIDI Setup (AMS), which automatically finds and configures your audio and MIDI devices (**Figure 17.8**). AMS replaces the notoriously difficult OMS (Open Music System).

Most MIDI interfaces connect directly to the Mac through USB ports, and the interfaces do not require external power because the USB port supplies the power. That means that simply plugging the device in will tell the Mac that it is connected and the Audio MID setup will find it.

To setup a MIDI device on Mac OS X:

◆ Navigate to Applications > Utilities > Audio MIDI Setup and launch the AMS utility.

Upon launch of the application, your Mac will search both the USB and FireWire ports, and if the drivers are installed properly, they will show up in both the Audio Devices page and the MIDI Devices page (**Figure 17.9**).

Once you have gotten your device into the Audio MIDI setup, you may leave the app and begin recording MIDI into Pro Tools (**Figure 17.10**).

MIDI SETUP IN MAC OS X

385

Selecting MIDI Inputs

In order to record MIDI into Pro Tools, you must first enable your MIDI devices for input, and then select a particular channel on the device for recording.

To enable MIDI inputs for use with Pro Tools:

1. Select MIDI > Input Devices.

   The MIDI Input Device panel opens.

2. Select the checkbox next to each input that you want to use, and click OK (**Figure 17.11**).

   The devices that you checked are now available for recording MIDI into Pro Tools.

Once you enable a MIDI input, you must select an input source for each track that you will record.

To choose a MIDI input for a track:

1. In the Mix window, click the MIDI Input Device/Channel selector on the MIDI track channel strip.

   The MIDI Input pop-up menu opens (**Figure 17.12**). You can use it to browse to any channel of any input in your OMS or Core MIDI studio.

2. Choose an input from the pop-up menu.

   The device becomes the input for the selected track.

Figure 17.11 In this window, four of the OMS devices are active as inputs.

Figure 17.12 The MIDI Input menu lets you select an individual channel for input.

SELECTING MIDI INPUTS

✔ Tips

- Pro Tools has a unique MIDI setting called All. While many MIDI studios have a large number of MIDI devices that can send and receive on any of 16 channels, often only one device will really ever send MIDI. This device, called a master controller, is usually a keyboard or synthesizer that's used to play back all of the other MIDI equipment in the studio. Selecting All as the input is often the easiest way to select your master controller when no other devices are sending MIDI.

- Depending on how you want to route MIDI data in your studio, you might want to use the MIDI Thru command, which echoes all incoming MIDI data back to the same device and channel from which it came. This is often an easier way to set up MIDI, since parts will automatically trigger on the correct device and channel. MIDI Thru often works best with simple MIDI setups.

- If you use MIDI Thru, turn the local setting on your synthesizer to Off. This will keep you from hearing the same note twice—once when you press a key on your synthesizer, and again when that same MIDI note is echoed by Pro Tools with MIDI Thru.

SELECTING MIDI INPUTS

Sending MIDI out of Pro Tools

Sending MIDI out of Pro Tools is similar to sending audio out of Pro Tools.

To send MIDI from Pro Tools to a MIDI device:

1. In the Mix window, click the MIDI Input Device/Channel selector on the MIDI track channel strip.

   The MIDI Output pop-up menu displays the available outputs (**Figure 17.13**).

2. Choose the output to which you want to send MIDI information.

   The device becomes the output for the selected track.

✔ Tips

- If you send MIDI from Pro Tools to another device, and the device sends it back to Pro Tools, a MIDI feedback loop can result—and it can sound nearly as awful as audio feedback. There are a number of ways to fix feedback loops, but this is one situation where you shouldn't use the All input setting mentioned earlier. If you're getting MIDI feedback loops, look carefully at things like MIDI Thru, local settings on your synthesizers, and general MIDI routing. Usually you'll be able to find where the loop originated and fix it by changing input, output, or thru settings.

- Most sequencers assume that when a MIDI channel is active, it should be routing MIDI in and out of the program. Pro Tools, however, treats MIDI more like audio than most sequencers do: In order for a MIDI input to send to an output in Pro Tools, you must click the Record-Enable button in either the MIDI track channel strip or in the Edit window's Track menu (**Figure 17.14**). Think of it like Record monitoring, but for MIDI.

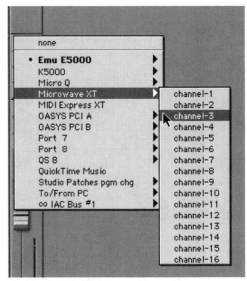

Figure 17.13 The MIDI Output Selector pop-up menu lets you select where MIDI is sent out of Pro Tools.

Figure 17.14 Click the Record-Enable button in either the MIDI track channel strip (left) or the Edit window's Track menu (right) to route MIDI.

Figure 17.15 Create a new MIDI track.

Recording MIDI

After all of this configuring and clicking and meandering about in Pro Tools, we can finally record a MIDI track.

To record a single MIDI track:

1. If you don't have a MIDI track in your session, select File > New Track, or Shift-Command-N.

   The New Track dialog box appears.

2. Select MIDI Track from the pop-up menu (**Figure 17.15**).

3. Enter the number of tracks and click Create.

4. As described earlier, select a MIDI channel input in the Mix window to record, and select the device and output; then click the Record-Enable button.

5. Click the Record and Play buttons in the Transport window (just as if you were recording an audio track).

   Play your MIDI controller, synthesizer, or other MIDI data-generating equipment (**Figure 17.16**).

6. When you're finished recording, click Stop.

Figure 17.16 The MIDI track ready for recording.

✔ Tips

- As you can see in **Figure 17.17**, I played a drum pattern with eighth-note hi hats and a simple kick-and-snare pattern. We'll cover how to fix my bad notes later, but for now, notice that MIDI notes appear on the screen as they're recorded, in real time. And although you can't see this in a black-and-white book, MIDI tracks, like audio tracks, are color-coded, which makes it easy to quickly locate specific tracks.

- If you wind up with a MIDI feedback loop, a stuck note in a synthesizer or sampler, or some other MIDI disaster, pressing Stop won't always fix the problem. Instead, use the All Notes Off command in the MIDI menu (**Figure 17.18**). It sends a command to all MIDI devices to immediately silence them.

Figure 17.17 The newly recorded MIDI drum track is located below the Transport window.

Figure 17.18 Don't panic! The All Notes command should make your gear stop squawking.

Recording Multiple MIDI Tracks

While MIDI tracks are recorded individually more often than audio tracks are, sometimes it's necessary to track multiple MIDI tracks simultaneously—for instance, when you're recording more than one musician, when you're transferring parts from one sequencer to another, or when a keyboard is split so that it plays back on different channels on different parts of the keyboard.

Let's use the latter scenario as an example: The bottom two octaves of a keyboard are playing a bass sound on MIDI channel 1, while the right hand plays a keyboard sound on the top octaves transmitting on MIDI channel 2.

Monitoring MIDI instruments without a mixer

You can monitor a MIDI instrument by connecting its audio output directly into the Digi 002, Digi 002 Rack, or Digi 001's line-level inputs.

To monitor the audio output of your MIDI device in Pro Tools:

1. Choose File > New Track.

2. From the File menu, choose New Track and create a mono or stereo auxiliary input.

3. Click the input selector of the auxiliary track, and choose the input to which your MIDI device is connected.

4. Adjust the input level with the volume fader.

5. To record the incoming signal, re-assign the output of the auxiliary channel to a bus and create an audio track whose input is assigned to the same bus.

To record two MIDI tracks simultaneously:

1. Create two new MIDI tracks as described earlier.

2. Set the inputs to different MIDI channels.

   In this example, the first track records MIDI channel 1 of the controller, and the second track records MIDI channel 2 of the controller (**Figure 17.19**).

3. Send each input channel to a different output.

   In this case, send the first track to channel 2 of the Microwave XT, and send the second track to channel 1 of the OASYS card (**Figure 17.20**).

4. Record-enable both tracks.

   To record-enable multiple MIDI tracks, hold down the Shift key while clicking all of the channels you want to record.

5. In the Transport window, click the Return to Zero button, and then press Record and Play.

6. When you're finished recording, press Stop.

✔ Tips

■ Splitting inputs to their own tracks is also useful for keeping controller, MIDI automation, or other MIDI information on its own track. It's just easier to follow that way.

■ You can also record one input to two tracks. Why would you want to do this? Each track can trigger different sounds from the same notes, by routing them to different synthesizers or different patches on the same synthesizer. For example, a single MIDI track can trigger an electric piano sound while also playing a string sound.

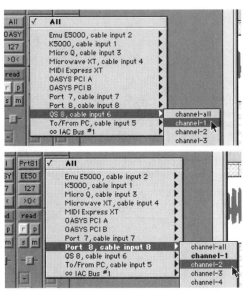

Figure 17.19 Select a different input for each MIDI track.

Figure 17.20 Set the MIDI outputs to play different sounds.

RECORDING MULTIPLE MIDI TRACKS

MIDI Merge button —

Figure 17.21 The MIDI Merge button is located on the right side of the Transport window.

Figure 17.22 Be sure to uncheck Destructive Record mode when you punch-record MIDI.

Punch-Recording MIDI

Punch-recording MIDI is similar to punch-recording audio. When punching MIDI, however, you use the MIDI Merge feature to determine how new MIDI data is recorded. You can turn this feature on and off through the MIDI Merge button, located in the Transport window (**Figure 17.21**).

How MIDI Merge works

When MIDI Merge is on, incoming MIDI data is *added* to the existing MIDI on the file. The existing recorded data remains unchanged. When MIDI Merge is off, incoming MIDI data *overwrites* the file.

MIDI Merge is useful, for example, if you have a drum pattern that you like and want to record another kick drum in some places. On the other hand, turning MIDI Merge off is helpful if you have a drum track that you like overall, but you want to redo a bar or two.

To punch-record MIDI:

1. Make sure Pro Tools is in Non-destructive Record mode (**Figure 17.22**).

   Although it doesn't affect MIDI, using Non-destructive Record mode will prevent you from inadvertently messing up an audio track.

2. Create a new MIDI track, if necessary, and record-enable it.

   If you want to punch-record an existing track, record-enable that track.

continues on next page

PUNCH-RECORDING MIDI

393

3. With the Selection tool, select the section of the track where you want to record (**Figure 17.23**).

4. Set the MIDI Merge button to either On or Off.

5. Set the pre-roll amount in the Transport window and turn pre-roll on. Do the same for post-roll, if you want (**Figure 17.24**).

6. Click Record and then Play in the Transport window.

Figure 17.23 Select the part of the MIDI track that you want to punch-record.

✔ Tips

■ To punch-record multiple MIDI tracks simultaneously, select all the tracks you want to punch and record-enable all of them. (The MIDI Merge setting applies to all punched tracks.) Remember to set the track inputs correctly.

■ Because MIDI is a tempo-based protocol, it's almost always best to work with it in Grid mode. Whether you're selecting, editing, moving, or recording MIDI tracks, stay in Grid mode unless there's a good reason to do otherwise.

Figure 17.24 All set to punch. The track is record-enabled, four bars are selected, MIDI Merge is on, and pre- and post-roll are set to two bars.

Figure 17.25 The selected bars will be loop-recorded. Note that record-enable is active.

Figure 17.26 To build a MIDI part by looping, activate Loop Playback in the Operations menu.

Loop-Recording MIDI

Pro Tools offers two distinct modes for loop-recording MIDI. The first, called Loop Playback, lets you add individual parts or notes to a looped section, building a full MIDI part over many passes. This method is most commonly used to program drum parts. On the first pass, you record the kick drum; on the next pass, the snare; then the closed hi-hats; and finally, the open hi-hats on select beats. Looping in real time is an intuitive and creative way to program drum loops.

The second loop-recording mode, called Loop Record, is more akin to the way Pro Tools is used to record audio in Loop mode. In Loop Record mode, the same section is looped, and each performance becomes its own MIDI region. This is generally used to work out parts or try new things. Because there's no need to start and stop the recording process, the creative juices can keep flowing, and you can the retrieve the serendipitous events later. We'll cover both methods.

To build a part in Loop Playback mode:

1. Create a new MIDI track, or select an existing track in your session.

2. In the Mix window, select the bars to be looped with the Selection tool (**Figure 17.25**).

3. Record-enable the track either in the MIDI track channel strip or the Edit window, and select the MIDI input and output.

4. If you want to hear a lead in, set the pre-roll amount in the Transport window. Click the Pre-Roll button to activate it.

5. Select Operations > Loop Playback to activate loop playback (**Figure 17.26**).

continues on next page

6. Click the MIDI Merge button to activate it (**Figure 17.27**).

Each looped pass will add notes to the selected part in the MIDI track.

7. Click Record and then Play in the Transport window.

You can now add new MIDI notes and other data with each pass.

8. When you're finished recording, click Stop.

To record multiple MIDI takes in Loop Record mode:

1. Create a new MIDI track or select an existing track in your session.

2. Select a section for the looped takes with the Selection tool.

3. Record-enable the track, and select inputs and outputs.

4. Turn pre-roll on and set the pre-roll amount in the Transport window, if you want.

5. Select Operations > Loop Record to activate loop recording (**Figure 17.28**).

The Record button displays the Loop indicator (**Figure 17.29**).

Figure 17.27 The Transport window is set for loop-recording: MIDI Merge is on, the Play button displays the Loop Playback indicator, and pre-roll is set.

Figure 17.28 Activate Loop Record in the Operations menu.

Figure 17.29 The Transport window set for loop recording.

Figure 17.30 Each piano take is now in the MIDI Regions list. Take 6 has been dragged to the playlist and is selected.

6. Click Record and Play to begin tracking.

Each pass creates a new numbered region in the MIDI Regions list (**Figure 17.30**). The MIDI Regions list works much like the Audio Regions list, but with MIDI sections instead. (We'll cover the MIDI Regions list more in *Chapter 18: Editing MIDI*.)

✔ Tips

■ You can move, edit, copy, or paste into the session any MIDI regions created by loop-recording. It edits like audio, but it's MIDI. It is very helpful to do this in the Edit window with your track view set to Regions. In Regions view, you can cut and copy regions aligned to your Grid (Grid mode), which is easier to manage than in the Notes view.

■ Because new MIDI regions are created with each loop in Loop Record mode, it's impossible to merge MIDI data; therefore, MIDI Merge is disabled in Loop Record mode.

■ Pro Tools lets you create a click track for recording. To set up a metronome click that will send out a MIDI note to a device, select MIDI > Click Options, and enter your settings in the Click/Countoff Options dialog box. This method is cumbersome, however, as it requires you to turn on a sound module, use a channel on that module for the click, and deal with latencies and audio routing. A much easier option is to sample a click, and copy it as an audio track in Grid mode. An even better and more musical option is to find a drum loop with the proper groove for the track, and use that in place of a click. In Pro Tools 6.1 on Mac OS X, the click is built right into the program. It will generate its own sound (selectable from a list of pre-configured sounds) and will play at your tempo.

Sysex Data and Pro Tools

Many MIDI parameters are defined in the MIDI protocol itself. Volume, for instance, is always on controller 7. Although this standardization can be helpful for various tasks, vendors can define MIDI events and messages that work only with their MIDI devices. This specialized MIDI data is called system exclusive, or *sysex*, data.

Sysex has all manner of uses for those willing to deal with it. One of the more common uses is to do a sysex dump, in which a MIDI device sends all of its current settings as sysex data. After it's recorded into a sequencer, the sysex can be played back to the device to reset it to the correct state for the Pro Tools session.

To record sysex into Pro Tools:

1. Create a new MIDI track or select the track in which you want to record the sysex data.

2. Select the correct input in the Mix window for the device that will be sending sysex data.

3. Record-enable the track.

4. Select MIDI > Input Filter (**Figure 17.31**). The MIDI Input Filter dialog box appears.

5. By default, Pro Tools allows sysex to record. Confirm that sysex is not being filtered in the dialog box, and then click OK to close it (**Figure 17.32**).

6. Click the Return to Zero button in the Transport window.

   Sysex is almost always used to set up a MIDI device. Sysex data should be at the beginning of a track.

Figure 17.31 Select MIDI > Input Filter.

Figure 17.32 Confirm that sysex will not be filtered out and can be recorded.

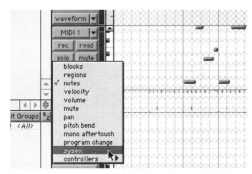

Figure 17.33 Setting a track to view sysex data is the only way to confirm that everything was recorded properly.

7. Click Record and then Play to begin recording.

8. Initiate a sysex dump on the MIDI device.

9. Click Stop when the device is finished sending MIDI.

✔ Tips

- Sysex data does not automatically display in the track where it's recorded. Click the Track View pop-up menu and select sysex to see the data on the track (**Figure 17.33**).

- Every MIDI device has a different way of initiating a sysex dump. Many have a Vulcan Death Grip kind of thing where three buttons on different parts of the device have to be pushed at the same time. Many devices also have a command on their Global or MIDI menu. Check your device's manual.

- Part of the beauty of sysex is that it gets around the need for saving presets or writing down parameters for an effect or a synthesizer. You can take your project to a different studio with the same gear, drench the studio with sysex, and voila! The devices in the studio are now set up just like your home studio was when the sysex was recorded.

- That said, sysex data can be extremely dense, and not all MIDI devices and interfaces deal with it very well. If, after a few tries, sysex isn't recording correctly, you may need to resort to pencil and paper for parameter settings.

SYSEX DATA AND PRO TOOLS

399

Working with MIDI Files

At some time, you may need to work with another sequencer—perhaps to transfer a part written in a different program or on a keyboard workstation into Pro Tools. Or, you might need to move Pro Tools MIDI tracks into a live situation, or export MIDI from a Pro Tools session into another program.

To do this, you need to use a Standard MIDI File (SMF). There are two kinds of SMFs: Type 0 and Type 1. Type 0 SMFs include an entire project's MIDI tracks in a single file. These files are generally "exploded" to individual tracks when they're imported to another application. Type 1 SMFs save a project's individual MIDI tracks as discrete files.

Type 0 SMFs are by far the more popular way to move MIDI files around, but Type 1 files can be more efficient in some cases. For example, in a very dense MIDI session, importing a Type 0 file can create dozens of new MIDI tracks when all you need is a bass line. Some hardware sequencers work better with one SMF than the other. In general, use Type 0 files.

To import a MIDI file to a session:

1. Select File > Import MIDI to Track (**Figure 17.34**).

   A standard dialog box opens.

2. Navigate to the file that you want to import.

3. Click the appropriate radio button to use either the tempo from the file you're about to import, or the tempo of the current Pro Tools session (**Figure 17.35**).

4. Click Open.

Figure 17.34 Select File > Import MIDI to Track.

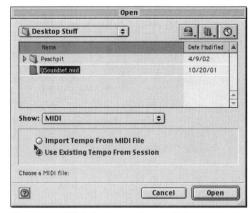

Figure 17.35 Click the appropriate radio button.

Figure 17.36 Choose whether to add MIDI from the imported file, or to replace all MIDI with the imported tracks. Be careful with this one!

Figure 17.37 You can add a MIDI file to the MIDI Regions list without creating a new track.

5. Pro Tools asks if you want to discard the session's existing MIDI tracks and regions and use only the new imported MIDI tracks, or if you want to keep the existing MIDI tracks and regions and add the new MIDI file to the session (**Figure 17.36**).

Choose your preference.

6. Pro Tools imports the MIDI file.

If the file includes multiple tracks in a Type 0 SMF, each track will get its own MIDI track in the session. These will concurrently appear in the MIDI bin in the bottom right of the EDIT window.

7. Select the proper playback device and channel for each track in the Mix window.

✔ Tips

■ In some situations, you will not want to create new tracks for each track in a SMF 0. For example, if you've created 32 drum patterns on a MIDI drum machine and want to try a few of them out, you can import a file directly to the MIDI Regions list without making a new track (**Figure 17.37**). After you import the file, you can drag the individual regions to tracks and edit them like any other MIDI region.

■ As you import an SMF, it may require a little more effort to get it to play right. If you import an SMF with 16 instrument tracks, you will need to reassign each track to the proper MIDI device and the proper patch (sound). It is a good idea to name the track with the sound and device/ channel in the exporting program.

WORKING WITH MIDI FILES

To export MIDI from Pro Tools:

1. Select File > Export MIDI (**Figure 17.38**). A standard dialog box opens.

2. Name the file and navigate to the folder where you want to save it.

3. Select an SMF file option by clicking one of the radio buttons (**Figure 17.39**):

   Select 0 if you want to export the file as an SMF Type 0 file.

   or

   Select 1 if you want to export the file as a group of SMF Type 1 files.

4. Click Save.

✔ Tip

■ It is a good idea to name the track with the sound and device/channel in the exporting program. That way, the importing program will know how to assign the MIDI channel and sound.

Figure 17.38 Select File > Export MIDI.

Figure 17.39 Choose which type of SMF to export.

WORKING WITH MIDI FILES

18

EDITING MIDI

Version 6 of Pro Tools, with its native use of Mac OS X, takes MIDI editing to a new level. If you're new to MIDI sequencing, Pro Tools MIDI may be all you'll ever need. If you're an experienced sequencing geek accustomed to another application, you'll find Pro Tools is rapidly evolving into a full-featured MIDI sequencing tool. Some welcome new features in Pro Tools 6 include: more MIDI tracks (up to 256); a groove quantize feature, which incorporates groove quantization models from Cubase, Logic, and Akai MPC; and the fun new Feel Injector templates.

In this chapter, we'll learn to edit MIDI both to correct mistakes made with previously recorded MIDI tracks, and to enter new tracks from scratch. I'll show you how to enter MIDI data manually and transform it directly in the Edit window. We'll also explore how the MIDI Operations tools can automatically edit MIDI data. Finally, we'll look at the MIDI Event list, which offers the deepest level of MIDI control in Pro Tools.

MIDI Regions

When you edit audio in Pro Tools, you must often create regions or move regions within a session. Editing MIDI also requires the use of regions. You can string MIDI regions together to form a playlist, just as you can when working with audio.

MIDI regions are displayed in the MIDI Regions list (**Figure 18.1**), which works very much like the Audio Regions list. You can use this list to add regions to a session, as well as move and rename them.

To add a MIDI region to a MIDI track:

1. In the MIDI Regions list, select the region you want to add to the session.

2. Hold down the mouse and drag the region to the track where you want to play it (**Figure 18.2**).

Figure 18.1 The MIDI Regions list is located below the Audio Regions list.

Figure 18.2 Click and drag a region from the MIDI Regions list to a MIDI track.

Figure 18.3 The MIDI region after it has been placed on the track.

Figure 18.4 Clicking the arrow in the Grid Value field opens a pop-up menu, where you can set the Grid value.

3. Release the mouse once you've positioned it.

The region is now visible and will play back at this location (**Figure 18.3**).

✔ Tip

■ Many MIDI editing processes, including simple ones like moving regions, are most easily done in Grid mode. The Grid value, which determines the meter or time division to which edits will snap, affects how these editing processes behave. The Grid value is displayed in the upper right corner of the Edit window (**Figure 18.4**). Most Grid editing for MIDI is best done in Bars & Beats mode so as to coincide with the musical performance.

Views for Editing MIDI

Pro Tools gives you many ways to view MIDI data. We'll cover a number of them in this chapter, but two views—the Regions view and the Notes view—merit special attention, as they do much more than just change the way a track looks.

Use the Track View pop-up menu in the Edit window (**Figure 18.5**) to select how you want to view a MIDI track.

Regions view

In Regions view, the MIDI region displays notes on a white background (**Figure 18.6**). You can't edit single notes in Regions view; instead, regions can be moved as a whole. Edits also automatically move MIDI data like MIDI controllers, sysex, and program changes. Use Regions view to move chunks of notes and data—to copy a bar or group of bars to another place in a session, for example.

The starting point of a MIDI note is important in Regions view. If a note starts *before* the region starts, it will not be included in cut, copy, and paste edits. This is true even if the note extends into the region. If a note starts in a region and extends *outside* of it, it will be included in cut, copy, and paste edits.

Figure 18.5 The Track View pop-up menu for a MIDI track. The Track view determines what's displayed in a MIDI track in the Edit window.

Figure 18.6 A MIDI track in Regions view.

Figure 18.7 The same MIDI track in Notes view.

Notes view

The MIDI track shown in Figure 18.6 looks a bit different in Notes view (**Figure 18.7**). Here, you can add individual notes with the Pencil tool or move them with the Grabber tool. Notes view also lets you edit a group of notes or single notes for duration and timing.

Notes view is best for detailed editing of notes or other MIDI data. Use it to do things like delete a bad note in a performance, copy just the snare part of a track to another measure, or draw a filter cutoff curve for a synthesizer patch.

For more information on MIDI Track views, consult the *Pro Tools Reference Guide, Chapter 15: Editing Basics.*

MIDI Playlists

Pro Tools derives a significant part of its audio editing power from the concept of a playlist. Quite sensibly, Pro Tools' MIDI implementation borrows extensively from this tool to manage MIDI parts and session arrangements.

Prior to version 6.0, MIDI data was always edited in Destructive mode. Now original performances can always be restored until you feel confident that your edits are final. Then the new Flatten Performance command lets you lock the current state of selected MIDI notes.

Figure 18.8 Select Duplicate from the Playlist Selector pop-up menu.

To work on a copy of a playlist:

1. Click the Playlist selector to open its pop-up menu.

2. From the pop-up menu, select Duplicate (**Figure 18.8**).

   A dialog box opens.

3. Enter a name for the new playlist and click OK (**Figure 18.9**).

   The new playlist is automatically chosen in the track's Playlist selector (**Figure 18.10**).

You can do more with playlists than create copies of MIDI regions. All of the great things that you can do with audio playlists—such as try out different edits and arrangements and automation on a track—can also be done with MIDI playlists.

Pro Tools 6.0's MIDI implementation now features a new Restore Performance function, which lets you return to an original MIDI-based performance at any time. Working in this non-destructive manner, you can experiment unhindered with the assurance that you can always recover from adjustments made during the course of your project. Of course, if you've settled on changes, the Flatten Performance feature solidifies your edits and gives you a new, permanent basis from which to proceed. Once flattened, a MIDI performance can no longer be restored to its original state.

Figure 18.9 Enter a name for the new MIDI playlist.

Figure 18.10 The new playlist is automatically chosen in the Playlist selector.

Figure 18.11 The Pencil tool has five modes, as seen in this pop-up menu.

Figure 18.12 Clicking on a track with the Pencil tool adds a note at that location.

Figure 18.13 The new note is added, and the Pencil tool becomes the Grabber.

Figure 18.14 Clicking on the same location with the Pencil tool but with a different Grid value will enter a note of a different length.

Entering and Deleting MIDI Notes Manually

Now that we've made a copy of our MIDI data, we can begin editing our MIDI track.

MIDI notes are usually recorded into Pro Tools via an instrument. If you miss or botch a note, however, it's often easier to manually enter the missed note or delete the mistake than it is to replay it on an instrument.

To enter a MIDI note manually:

1. If you're not in Notes view, select Notes from the Track View selector, as previously explained.

2. Click the Pencil Tool pop-up menu, and select Free Hand (**Figure 18.11**).

3. If necessary, zoom in to find the location on the track where you want to enter the note.

4. With the Pencil tool, click the note that you want to add (**Figure 18.12**).

   Pro Tools adds a new note at that location (**Figure 18.13**).

✔ Tips

■ In Version 6.0 the Pencil tool allows you to trim both MIDI notes and controller data. The Pencil tool has a Custom Note Duration command, which lets you define the note duration for inserting notes manually.

■ The Grid value determines the location and duration of a manually entered MIDI note. The above example uses a Grid value of a quarter note; clicking on the track adds a quarter note at that location. If you set the Grid value to a sixteenth note, the Pencil tool will add a sixteenth note instead (**Figure 18.14**).

■ The Pencil tool's various modes enter notes differently. Consult the Pro Tools Reference Guide for more information.

To delete a MIDI note manually:

1. Be sure you're in Notes view.

2. Select the Grabber tool.

3. To delete a single note, click on it with the Grabber tool (**Figure 18.15**).

   or

   To delete multiple notes, drag the Grabber over an area of the track to select all the notes in that area (**Figure 18.16**).

4. The selected notes are displayed in reverse: Instead of appearing as a solid color, they are white with a colored outline (**Figure 18.17**).

5. Press the Delete or Backspace key to remove the selected notes.

Figure 18.15 Use the Grabber tool to select a single MIDI note.

Figure 18.16 The Grabber tool drags over a group of MIDI notes.

Figure 18.17 The selected notes are now outlines, while the unselected notes are still solid.

Figure 18.18 The Grabber tool is positioned to copy three notes. Clicking on any note copies all selected notes.

Figure 18.19 The copied notes (left) are selected after the edit is completed.

Editing MIDI Notes Manually

You can use the Grabber tool to manually move, copy, and transpose MIDI notes. This is an easy way to fix minor timing problems or to copy notes to other parts of a session.

To copy MIDI notes manually:

1. If you're not in Notes view, select Notes from the Track View selector.

2. Using the Grabber tool, click and drag to select the notes to be copied.

3. Position the Grabber tool over any of the selected notes (**Figure 18.18**).

4. While pressing Shift-Option (Macintosh) or Shift-Ctrl (Windows), click and drag the MIDI notes to the new desired location.

   The Shift key keeps MIDI notes from changing pitch when you move them (more on this soon). The Option or Ctrl key copies the notes.

5. Release the mouse when you've moved the notes where you wish.

   The notes are copied and selected (**Figure 18.19**).

✔ Tips

■ The above example is in Slip mode. If the example was done in Grid mode with a half-note Grid value, the copied notes would snap to the nearest half note.

■ To move notes without transposing them, press Shift while clicking and dragging them to the new desired location.

Editing MIDI Velocity

MIDI supports a wide variety of performance parameters. In addition to pitch and note duration, MIDI can transmit information like breath control for wind instruments; *aftertouch*, which simulates how much pressure is applied to a key after it's struck; and whether a keyboard's sustain pedal is pressed.

Another common MIDI parameter is *note velocity*. Although velocity can be used to modulate a wide range of parameters in a synthesizer, it's most often used as a volume control for individual notes. Editing velocity is a good example of how MIDI parameters other than pitch and duration work in Pro Tools.

To edit MIDI velocity for a note:

1. Click the Track View selector.

    From its pop-up menu, choose velocity (**Figure 18.20**).

2. Pro Tools displays the velocity of each note as a stalk. A diamond atop each stalk does double duty: It represents the velocity value for that note, and acts as a handle that you can click and drag to edit the value (**Figure 18.21**).

3. Using the Grabber tool, click the diamond atop any of the velocity stalks.

    The stalk is selected and the diamond turns blue (**Figure 18.22**).

Figure 18.20 Choose velocity from the MIDI Track View Selector pop-up menu.

Figure 18.21 One measure of notes and velocity stalks. Taller stalks mean higher velocity, so the notes with the tallest stalks were struck the hardest.

Figure 18.22 Using the Grabber tool, click the diamond atop the velocity stalk.

Figure 18.23 The same stalk after its velocity has been reduced with the Grabber tool.

Figure 18.24 Select the Line tool from the Pencil Tool pop-up menu.

4. Drag the stalk to the desired velocity level and release it (**Figure 18.23**).

✔ Tip

■ To edit multiple velocity stalks simultaneously, select a group of MIDI notes with the Grabber tool. All of the notes' velocity stalks will be selected. Clicking and dragging any individual stalk will modify all of them.

Editing velocity with the Pencil tool

When working with audio, the Pencil tool lets you perform extremely precise, sample-level edits. The Pencil tool is also useful for performing many types of automated MIDI edits, including velocity edits.

Let's use the Pencil tool to draw velocity for multiple notes—in this case, a volume swell.

To edit MIDI velocity with the Pencil tool:

1. Click the Track View selector.

   Select Velocity for the track you want to edit.

2. Velocity stalks appear for each note.

3. Click and hold the Pencil Tool selector to view the pop-up menu.

   Select the Line tool from the pop-up menu (**Figure 18.24**).

continues on next page

4. On the MIDI track showing the velocity stalks, click a low velocity, and then drag to a higher velocity later in the track (**Figure 18.25**).

5. Release the mouse at the point where you want the velocity to reach its highest point.

✔ Tips

- In Pro Tools 6, you can use the Trimmer Tool to trim MIDI note duration on MIDI tracks set to Velocity view.

- The Pencil Line tool is probably most often used to draw a velocity swell for a sixteenth-note snare fill in a dance tune. You can also use it to fade sounds in and out, or to gently modify the volume of part of a drum track.

- Other tools also work well with velocity. For example, the Free Hand mode makes it easy to draw the velocity curve in **Figure 18.26**.

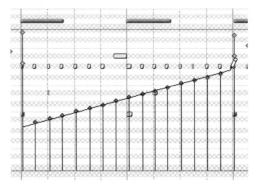

Figure 18.25 Use the Pencil tool in Line mode to draw velocity for multiple notes.

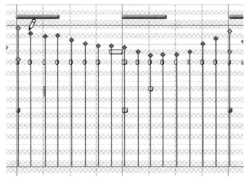

Figure 18.26 The Pencil tool in Free Hand mode lets you draws a softer velocity curve.

Figure 18.27 Select the Mod Wheel for editing in the Track View selector.

Figure 18.28 Use the Pencil tool in Free Hand mode to custom-draw controller curves.

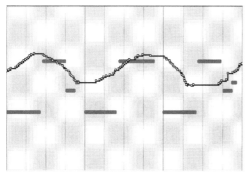

Figure 18.29 Pro Tools creates breakpoints for the curve drawn with the Pencil tool.

Editing MIDI Controller Data

MIDI's designers were smart enough to realize that synthesizers would use more than one kind of data to make sounds. Many parameters were predefined as MIDI Continuous Controllers (CCs), and nearly all devices adhere to the MIDI specification for defining controllers. For example, the Mod Wheel on a keyboard sends CC 1.

Pro Tools records CC information along with MIDI notes. Once CC data is on a MIDI track, you can edit it with the same tools used to edit velocity. In addition, you can enter completely new CC data with the Pencil tool.

In this example, we'll enter a curve for CC 1 on a keyboard part. One use for this would be if CC 1 on the synthesizer were set to change the cutoff point of a filter, or the feedback on a delay.

To edit CC data with the Pencil tool:

1. Click the Track View selector, and select Controllers > Mod Wheel (1) (**Figure 18.27**).

2. Click and hold the Pencil tool to open the pop-up menu.

3. Select the Free Hand tool (**Figure 18.28**).

4. Click and draw on the track to enter the CC data.

   The closer you draw to the top of the track, the higher the CC value will be.

5. When you've finished, Pro Tools creates *breakpoints* for the curve that you've just drawn (**Figure 18.29**). Breakpoints mark changes in MIDI data, and can be grabbed for further editing.

The Pencil tool's other modes makes drawing certain common shapes much easier.

To edit MIDI with other Pencil modes:

1. Click the Track View selector and select CC 1, as explained previously.

2. In the Pencil Tool pop-up menu, select a different mode.

   For this example, select the Triangle mode.

3. Click on the track at the point where you want the center of the controller data to be.

4. Drag to horizontally define the number of bars and beats where you want to enter the CC data (**Figure 18.30**).

   In this case, click on the left-most corner of the track and drag to the right.

5. Drag vertically to increase or decrease the degree of change that the Triangle tool creates (**Figure 18.31**).

6. Release the mouse when the CC data appears as you want it to be.

   Pro Tools draws the correct breakpoints (**Figure 18.32**).

Figure 18.30 Drag with the Pencil tool in Triangle mode.

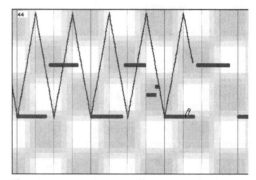

Figure 18.31 Dragging vertically increases the depth of the triangle.

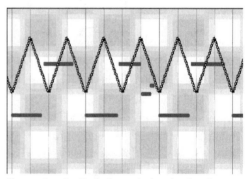

Figure 18.32 Pro Tools draws the breakpoint after you click and drag in Triangle mode.

✔ Tips

- The Grid value is very important for entering CC data with the Pencil tool and its various modes. The Triangle and Square tools, for example, change the density of their shape according to the Grid value.

- Since there's a Square and a Saw tool, MIDI geeks may wonder where the Sine tool is. There isn't one—you'll have to draw carefully with the Free Hand tool or enter data with something like the Mod Wheel on a keyboard.

- To get more mileage out of your MIDI-aware digital effects box, learn its MIDI parameters and modulate them with CC messages. You can vary sounds from subtle to dramatic by creating controller data with the Pencil tool in Square and Triangle wave mode, and having that data modulate parameters like delay feedback, filter frequencies, EQ settings, and reverb. In Grid mode, you can even use these tools to automatically create tempo-synchronized modulations.

- These examples only scratch the surface of what you can do with CC editing. Consult the Pro Tools Reference Guide for more information.

Using Pro Tools
MIDI Operations

Most of the editing we've done so far has been fairly simple manual additions, deletions, or modifications to MIDI data. Pro Tools can also automatically perform more complex edits on MIDI data via *MIDI operations*. These functions, located in the MIDI Operations menu, modify data offline. In other words, after you select a group of MIDI notes (or an entire track), Pro Tools modifies parameters such as timing, note length, and pitch for the entire group. In Pro Tools 6, MIDI operations, Tempo, and Meter dialog windows can float over other windows, which helps make MIDI recording and editing faster and more efficient.

One powerful feature which MIDI enthusiasts and professional alike have been clamoring for allows for MIDI Time Stamping (MTS) support. MTS provides sample-accurate MIDI with Pro Tools-compatible software synths and samplers, eliminating the possibility of compromised sync and drift issues. Also, you can take advantage of up to sub-millisecond-accurate MIDI with Digidesign's MIDI I/O and other supported MTS-capable interfaces. This guarantees that your MIDI performance matches its play back down to the millisecond.

Covering all the ways you can use MIDI operations is beyond the scope of this book, but some basic rules apply. We'll use a common MIDI operation called *quantizing* to show how MIDI operations work in Pro Tools. Quantizing is the process of automatically changing the timing of a group of MIDI notes. You can use it to either tighten up the timing of sloppy playing, or to add a certain rhythmic feel to notes that were not played as desired.

Figure 18.33 The hi hat notes selected on an eighth-note grid. Note that the kick and snare notes are not selected and will not be quantized.

Figure 18.34 The MIDI Operations dialog box with Quantize selected.

Figure 18.35 Clicking the eighth note will snap the selected notes to an eighth-note grid.

To quantize MIDI in Pro Tools:

1. Select the notes that you want to quantize.

   In this example, we'll tighten up the timing of the hi hats in the drum part we recorded in Chapter 16. By zooming in closely and setting the Grid value to eighth notes, we can see that the hi hats vary quite a bit. Use the Grabber tool to select only the hi hat (**Figure 18.33**).

2. Select MIDI > Quantize.

   The MIDI Operations dialog box opens; Quantize is already selected (**Figure 18.34**).

3. For this example, we'll accept most of the default Quantize parameters (**Figure 18.35**):

   Leave Attacks checked, because we want to quantize according to the start of the notes.

   Leave "Don't change durations" checked. This will keep the note length as is.

   Click the eighth note to set quantizing on an eighth-note grid.

   continues on next page

USING PRO TOOLS MIDI OPERATIONS

4. Click the Apply button.

Pro Tools moves the selected notes to the nearest eighth note (**Figure 18.36**).

MIDI Operations use the same methods to transpose, shorten, lengthen, split, and select MIDI notes. See the *Pro Tools Reference Guide, Chapter 24: MIDI Operations* for more information about editing MIDI with the Operations menu.

✔ Tips

- Quantizing affects only the selected notes; other notes on the track remain unchanged. This is helpful for changing the timing on only one part of a drum track.

- Quantizing can make a part sound extremely exact and robotic. Sometimes this is the desired effect, but if it's not, you can modify both the degree to which a note is quantized and the rules that are used to select notes for quantizing. See the Pro Tools Reference Guide for more information.

- Pro Tools 6 allows numerous different Goove Quantize models (**Figure 18.37**). This allows any performance to be modeled after rhythm templates that have been created by other programs, such as Logic Audio or Cubase or after the MPC drum machine patterns.

- Another new option unique to Pro Tools is Digidesign's Feel Injector templates. These various groove quantizers ad feel to shuffle, swing, and straight quantization, making for much less robotic-like quantizations of your performance.

Figure 18.36 The hi hat notes have all been moved to fall exactly on an eighth note, but the kick and snare remain unchanged.

Figure 18.37 The Groove Quantize options in the MIDI menu.

Figure 18.38 With the Grabber tool, select the first note in the bar.

Windows

Show Mix	⌘=
Hide Edit	⌘W
Show MIDI Event List	⌃=
Show Tempo/Meter	
Show MIDI Operations	
Show MIDI Track Offsets	
1–9 on numeric keypad only	
Show Transport	⌘1
Show Session Setup	⌘2
Show Big Counter	⌘3
Show Automation Enable	⌘4
Show Memory Locations	⌘5
Show Movie Window	⌘9
Show Strip Silence	⌘U
Show System Usage	
Show Disk Space	

Figure 18.39 Select Windows > Show MIDI Event List.

MIDI Event List			
MIDI 2 ▾	Options ▾	Insert ▾	300 Events
start	event		length/info
20| 4| 484	♩ Eb2 114 69		0| 0| 171
→ 20| 4| 492	♩ G#2 124 68		0| 0| 132
21| 1| 027	♩ B1 98 69		0| 0| 189
21| 1| 037	♩ G#2 127 69		0| 0| 133
21| 1| 493	♩ G#2 103 70		0| 0| 104
21| 2| 001	♩ Eb2 122 81		0| 0| 143
21| 2| 014	♩ G#2 127 72		0| 0| 122
21| 2| 472	♩ G#2 116 62		0| 0| 114
21| 2| 948	♩ G#2 112 56		0| 0| 103
21| 3| 454	♩ G#2 119 68		0| 0| 138
21| 3| 917	♩ B1 98 76		0| 0| 176

Figure 18.40 The selected note is highlighted in the MIDI Event list; the arrow indicates the cursor's location.

The MIDI Event List

The MIDI Event list displays every last bit of MIDI data for a selected region or track, letting you view and edit nearly any MIDI event in a session. Although it may not be the easiest or most intuitive MIDI feature, it can't be beat for precision and control.

For our example, let's insert a program change message at a particular point in a song to change the drum loop from mono under the verse to stereo for the chorus. Our sampler is set so that patch 10 has a kit mixed to mono, while patch 11 is the same kit mixed to stereo. You can use the Event list to change the patch in the sampler at precisely the right time.

To send a patch change with the MIDI Event list:

1. In the Track View selector for the MIDI track, select Notes view.

2. Find the location in the track where you want to send the patch change.

   For this example, send the change at bar 21, beat 1.

3. With the Grabber tool, select the first note in this bar (**Figure 18.38**).

4. Select Windows > Show MIDI Event List (**Figure 18.39**).

   The MIDI Event List window opens. The selected note is highlighted, and an arrow next to the nearest MIDI event indicates the cursor position (**Figure 18.40**).

continues on next page

5. In the Insert menu, select Program Change (**Figure 18.41**).

This creates the MIDI event at the top of the MIDI Event list, but Pro Tools does not put the event in the list (**Figure 18.42**). We still need to change a few parameters.

6. First, we want our program change to occur a bit before the first note of the chorus.

Double-click the last three numbers of the bars:beats number and change it to 000 (**Figure 18.43**).

7. Click on the value under the length/ info column, where the value is entered as None.

The Patch window opens.

Figure 18.41 Use the Insert menu to create a new program change event.

Figure 18.42 The new MIDI event is at the top of the Event List window, where you can edit it.

Figure 18.43 Change the timing of the event to 21|1|000.

Figure 18.44 Select patch 11 to be sent as the program change.

Figure 18.45 The event is edited for the proper time and patch, and is ready to be entered in the Event list.

Figure 18.46 The new MIDI event is added to the MIDI Event list.

8. Select patch 11 (**Figure 18.44**).

9. Click Done to close the Patch window.

    This changes the event so that at 21|1|000, Pro Tools will send the patch change 11 to the selected device for this track (**Figure 18.45**).

10. Press the Return key.

    The new MIDI event is added to the MIDI Event list (**Figure 18.46**).

You can use the MIDI Event list for much more than program changes. For more information, see the *Pro Tools Reference Guide, Chapter 25: MIDI Event List*.

THE MIDI EVENT LIST

Virtual MIDI Inputs

Pro Tools 6 offers four virtual MIDI inputs that let you receive MIDI data from other supported applications (such as Ableton Live or Propellorhead Reason). These new inputs, called Pro Tools Inputs, can receive data such as MIDI Time Code and MIDI Machine Control and eliminates the need to use third-party applications such as Re-fuse or Re-wire.

To record MIDI using Pro Tools Inputs:

1. Enable Pro Tools Inputs (1-4) from the MIDI > Input Devices menu.

2. Create a new MIDI track, record-enable it, and select one of the Pro Tools inputs (1-4) in the Track Input selector (**Figure 18.47**).

3. In the other MIDI application, select one of the Pro Tools inputs (1-4) for the MIDI output.

Figure 18.47 The Pro Tools Inputs on a MIDI track routes the output of other applications' virtual MIDI devices through Pro Tools.

Part VII:
Getting the Most
from Pro Tools

PRO TOOLS
FOR DIGITAL VIDEO

Pro Tools has become the digital audio workstation of choice for most film and television sound editors working today worldwide.

Just as Pro Tools has led the way to high-end, low-cost audio production, we've seen an explosive growth of desktop video production. The tools for broadcast quality video production have become available to anyone with a $500 video camera, a fast computer, and a big hard drive. Meanwhile, major Hollywood releases are being shot on digital video cameras and edited on Avid, Adobe, or Apple (and other) software on PCs and Macs. There is a corresponding growth in the need for soundtracks for all these video projects.

The field of sound for video draws on all aspects of sound technique. Soundtracks today feature the human voice and naturalistic use of sound effects to create realism, as well as music and theatrical sound designed to underscore character, drama, pacing, and emotion.

In this chapter we'll give you a quick tour of the basics of setting up and using Pro Tools to edit and mix sound for video using a video deck or QuickTime digital video. We hope you'll find the information here helps you get started on your first soundtrack, and that some of the tips save you time and headaches on the way.

Preparing to Edit Sound for Video

Since you'll be working with at least one other piece of technology—the picture editing system—and usually at least one other person—the picture editor—it's critical to coordinate your technical setup and your work approach with them in mind.

The picture editor edits sound along with the visuals, and often will incorporate location dialog recordings, voice over, music, and sound effects in her work. Typically the principal goal in this phase of post production is to tell the story well with final decisions made for all the picture edits in the show. Sound editing decisions made by the picture editor form the basic structure of the soundtrack may represent a huge amount of work by the editor. Nevertheless, because of the relatively unsophisticated audio editing tools available to the picture editor (this is changing!), and, more importantly, because the focus must be on the visual composition of the program, audio decisions tend to be rough and ready. Smoothing dialog transitions, tweaking music edits, and selecting sound effects are a lower priority for the picture editor than deciding which takes (picture and sound) go in what order and at what lengths. This leaves a huge amount of work for the sound editor(s).

The technical process of working on the sound for video begins at the location. Location sound recordists work with a wide range of analog and digital tape and disk recorders. Or they may record the sound directly to the videotape. The technical specifications of the location recordings typically determine the sample rate and bit depth for your work in Pro Tools.

To obtain the best quality sound from your location recordings, you'll want to make a direct digital transfer from DAT (or other digital sources) into Pro Tools. Analog audio should be recorded into Pro Tools at the highest possible sample rate and bit depth. If the picture editor has taken care to digitize the location sound in the best possible way, then getting the audio via the OMF or AAF interchange formats (discussed later in this chapter) is the obvious answer.

Preparing to Edit Sound for Video: Fundamental Technical Questions

Will you be working with an external videotape player or internal (digital) video?

This basic setup question will determine the type of equipment investment you make.

If you have access to a professional video deck with jog/shuttle wheel, fast and accurate locating, and a separate time-code track, working with a video deck can be a good experience. This approach also requires a time code-to-MIDI time code converter and some form of reference video and digital clock. We discuss the sync to videotape approach in the first section of this chapter after this introduction.

Digitized video in your digital audio workstation (DAW) is the most efficient way to achieve consistent, rapid, and accurate sync between Pro Tools and your picture. Working with digital video files requires a method of obtaining a digitized picture, and either a second computer monitor, or a digital video-to-analog video converter and a television (or video monitor). The random access method of editing to QuickTime picture is discussed in the second section of this chapter.

How will you get the picture editor's sound into Pro Tools?

The third section of this chapter explores some ways you can match the audio in Pro Tools to the audio in the picture editor's video workstation (also known as a non-linear editing system, or NLE).

Use OMF (or AAF) whenever possible to get the sound from your picture editor. This assumes that the picture editor took the time to digitize the audio correctly. You will also need access to DigiTranslator (part of DV Toolkit).

If the sound in the NLE is good but OMF/AAF isn't an option, the edited sound from the NLE can be recorded or imported directly into Pro Tools and then further edited and embellished. When this option is used, it is important to maintain the full quality of the audio by using a digital transfer, highest quality analog transfer, or export/import as a full-quality rendered audio file or QuickTime export. There can be as many exported tracks as required.

Picture system sound quality can be compromised, usually by inferior interim stages (analog video) between the audio master and the picture editing system, or by bad analog transfer between the audio master and the NLE. When this happens, it is best to re-digitize and re-sync all the audio from the original recordings.

When going back to the original production sound, you can re-sync the audio by hand or by region by region, or you can use a third-party EDL auto-conform program such as Titan 3. In order to make use of the auto-conforming features of Titan, you'll need to get the time code from the recording into Pro Tools while you digitize the audio. So you'll need a third-party time code-to-MIDI time code converter. You'll also need an EDL from the picture editor, which may be hard to provide if the use of an EDL wasn't planned from the beginning of the post.

continues on next page

Preparing to Edit Sound for Video:
Fundamental Technical Questions *continued*

Remember, the results of manually re-syncing are at least as good as the other methods, and may be required in some cases. While it is extremely tedious and generally to be avoided, the techniques for accomplishing this are useful even when working with OMF or auto-conforming.

How was the original production sound recorded?

Check the quality of the original audio from the location and compare it to the audio you are given by the picture editor. If there is a perceptible difference, you may need to go back to the original recordings for best results.

Always load the location sound into Pro Tools in the best possible way. For digital recordings this means going into Pro Tools digitally, so you'll want to set your session up to match the settings used by the location recordist. Music and sound effects can be matched, too, or converted to the same specs.

If the recordings are analog, play back on a properly maintained machine, perhaps the same deck used to record on (or an equivalent device). Since you can't choose a bad sample rate or bit depth in Pro Tools, set your session up for compatibility with music and FX.

What are the specifications for the final product (deliverable tracks)?

Will you be delivering mono, stereo, discrete surround, or matrixed Dolby surround? Will the track be broadcast, played in a movie theater, on videotape, or on a DVD? Each of these options has different dynamic range, frequency response, and number of channels. You need to be aware of the delivery requirements of your format.

When multiple delivery options are to be used, work to the highest, most demanding spec, and mix down to the other versions after completing the main mix master.

Choosing a Sample Rate and Bit Depth for Your New Project

You need to select a sample rate and bit depth to work with your production sound. If you are working with OMF, your session's sample rate and bit depth will come from the picture editor's exported production sound.

When you load the digital audio that you recorded on location into Pro Tools, the session sample rate and bit depth must match the sample rate and bit depth of the recording. Recordings that do not match the session's parameters must be converted when imported into Pro Tools. For more information on importing and converting audio, see *Chapter 8: File Management Basics.*

If the location recordings are analog, you can select the session parameters that are most convenient for your project.

For more information on choosing sample rate and bit depth in a new session, see *Chapter 4: Starting a New Session.*

Synchronization Basics: Position and Clock Concepts

There are two basic requirements for separate devices to play in sync and stay in sync indefinitely: they need to start in the same place and run at the same speed.

One device, the master, starts to play and sends out a time code signal with its position. Another device, the slave, listens for time code from the master and locates to the position indicated, catching up to the master, then playing.

Once the devices are playing, they will stay in sync if they play at exactly the same speed. This can be ensured by using a common clock reference for both devices.

Getting time code and clock from a video or audiotape deck into Pro Tools LE requires some additional equipment, which is described later.

The *Pro Tools Reference Guide* has a very good discussion of synchronization concepts in Chapter 34.

Head and tail leaders

Always use head and tail video countdown leaders with sync beeps for easy sync checking. Since you can't add these onto the picture after you receive it you'll need to insist that the picture editor provide them for you. The key thing is that there is a visible and audible one-frame-long synchronous event just before the start of the program and again just after the end of the program.

Any number of sync-related problems are solved by having these sync marks. Most obviously it allows unambiguous lining up of the head beep to the picture mark to sync up the picture and track. After synching the head, tail sync can be quickly checked. If there is a sync drift problem, measuring the distance between the tail sync mark and the tail beep can give valuable clues as to the cause.

The standard head countdown leader visually counts down for eight seconds. The first frame is labeled 8. The numbers 8 through 2 are visible at each full second mark, and there is a one-frame-long beep at the 2 mark. The last two seconds are black leader. The first frame of picture comes at exactly eight seconds from the start, or two seconds after the sync beep.

The tail leader is effectively the reverse of the head leader. Exactly two seconds after the last frame of picture there is a tail sync mark on the picture and a corresponding one-frame beep on the track.

Film-specific sound and pull down issues

The slight speed varying necessary when transferring between film and video is an annoying and initially confusing concept for editors to learn. If you don't have to deal with it, you're better off. Here's how to know if you need to know.

If you are working on sound for a film shot at 24 frames per second and then transferred to NTSC video, which runs at 29.97 frames per second (fps), a speed adjustment called a *pull down* was made in the process.

A neat 4 to 5 ratio exists between the 24 film frames in a second and the 30 video frames in just over a second. Sadly, NTSC video runs at 29.97 fps, so to enable the film frames to line up with the video frames, the film must be slowed down by .1% (one tenth of one per cent).

This adds complications for the sound editor since the sound, which was recorded in real time, must be slowed .1% to stay in sync with the film after it's been pulled down for transfer to video. All Pro Tools systems require an external clock source to pull down the audio playback speed. The Session Setup window *does not* change the playback speed of the sound.

DV Toolkit for Pro Tools LE

DV Toolkit is an optional add-on bundle of tools for Pro Tools LE that can help with several video- and film-specific tasks. The following are two crucial capabilities it adds to Pro Tools LE:

◆ DV Toolkit unlocks time code and feet/frames counting capability to the ruler and the other measuring tools of Pro Tools.

◆ Audio and video pull up/down adjustments become available to Pro Tools LE users.

Included with these nearly essential functions for sound for video and film are three very useful tools for audio post work:

◆ DigiTranslator is required for reliable and flexible opening of exported OMF or AAF files from Avid, Apple, and most other NLEs. It also allows for OMF/AAF export from Pro Tools to many other systems.

◆ The DINR BNR AudioSuite plug-in is useful for reducing broadband noise and hiss from some location recordings and analog audiotapes. (DINR is an acronym for Digidesign Intelligent Noise Reduction, and BNR stands for Broadband Noise Reduction.)

◆ VocALign is another AudioSuite plug-in. Its unique function is to adjust the sync of one recording to precisely match another. VocALign was designed to quickly match ADR recordings to the original location dialog. It also has other applications in music and sound design.

CHOOSING A SAMPLE RATE AND BIT DEPTH

Using Time Code or Feet.Frames Counter and Ruler (DV Toolkit Only)

Installing DV Toolkit adds two more counter modes and Timebase rulers to Pro Tools LE:

- Time Code

- Feet.Frames

These counter modes can be used for location indicators, in the Event Edit area, and for grid and nudge increments (**Figure 19.1**).

Like the standard Minutes:Seconds and Samples rulers, both of these new rulers count from the Session Start and share other general ruler properties. For more information on rulers, see *Chapter 10: Editing Basics*.

The Time Code ruler counts from the Session Start time set in the Session Setup window.

The Feet.Frames ruler counts from 0 at the Session Start time.

Since video frames are uniquely identified by a time code value, referring to video requires a time code counter. Time code numbers have four character fields: hours, minutes, seconds, and frames.

Figure 19.1 The top of the Edit Window shows the two post-production-related options unlocked by DV Toolkit for rulers and counters, grids and nudges.

Figure 19.2 To offset the footage counter, Choose Setups > Feet.Frames.

Figure 19.3 Enter a footage (positive only) for the Session Start time.

When working on sound for film, the picture is typically a video transfer from the film. The preferred counter for 35mm film work is feet and frames, with 24 frames per second and 16 frames per foot. Pro Tools lets you display 35mm feet and frames counting from zero. The Session Start time is defined as zero feet and frames plus the offset defined in the Setups > Feet.Frames menu.

To select the Feet.Frames start frame:

1. Choose Setups > Feet.Frames (**Figure 19.2**).

2. Enter the number you would like to use as the Feet.Frames of the Session Start (**Figure 19.3**).

3. Zero is the default. Negative numbers are not permitted.

✔ Tip

■ To perform calculations with the time code or Feet.Frames counters in the location indicator or Event Edit area, select the time field you want to work on, Press + (plus sign) or - (minus sign) on the keyboard, and the time you want add or subtract. Press . (period) to change fields while entering your time. When done entering the number, press Enter to have the result appear in the field. Pressing Enter again will accept the new value. Escape will undo the calculation.

TIME CODE OR FEET.FRAMES COUNTER AND RULER

Working with a Video Deck

The following sections introduce concepts and issues to keep in mind when you work with a video deck.

Synchronizing to time code from external videotape (or audiotape) players

Pro Tools LE can be easily slaved to an external time code stream (also known as LTC or Linear or Longitudinal Time Code). The LTC must be converted to MIDI Time Code (or MTC). MTC is transmitted along with other MIDI data into the computer through a MIDI converter, typically into the computer's USB port. Several third-party USB MIDI converters will accept LTC and pass it to the computer.

The source of the LTC could be a videotape deck or a DAT machine or any other LTC (or MTC) source.

Some LTC to MTC converters

There are several USB MIDI converters that accept LTC. Some are modern MIDI interfaces, such as Mark of the Unicorn Micro Express, or Midiman USB Midisport 8x8/s. There is an LTC to MTC converter, the Rosendahl MIF-3, which will work with a MIDI converter that doesn't accept LTC.

For working to video at least two LTC-to-MTC converters will also generate a synchronous word clock. Mark of the Unicorn's MIDI Timepiece AV (USB) has a range of clock source and pull down options. The Rosendahl WIF-2 requires a standard MIDI to converter but it accepts LTC or VITC (Vertical Interval Time Code, often found on videotapes) and also has a number of clock options.

The Digi 001 and 002 interfaces have MIDI inputs built in and so can work with a straight LTC-to-MTC converter like one of the Rosendahl converters.

Some clocking options

In order to maintain sync over time, it is necessary to have a common clock for your tape deck and your Pro Tools hardware.

The only way to clock a professional video deck to an external source is with a video sync generator. Home video players cannot be clocked to an external source.

Pro Tools LE can only be clocked to a digital audio word clock on the S/PDIF (or ADAT) input.

The traditional and most stable system for clocking a video and audio system is to have a video sync generator feeding all the devices in the system (**Figure 19.4**). There are devices that can do this while producing a synchronous word clock for Pro Tools LE to follow. The Aardvark Aardsync II with UVG option can generate a highly stable synchronous video clock and word clock for Pro Tools at sample rates up to 96kHz.

Figure 19.4 The standard setup for work in sync to a video tape deck with Pro Tools LE. The video sync generator and video sync to word clock generator can be the same device.

If you have a DAT recorder with a video sync input, it can be used to clock Pro Tools LE. Other professional digital tape recorders could be used in this manner, too.

If you have a video sync generator you can clock the video deck and also the Rosendahl WIF-2 to create a synchronous word clock for Pro Tools. The MIDI Time Piece AV can also create a synchronous word clock from a video sync input.

As mentioned earlier, these last two devices can also synthesize a word clock from incoming LTC (**Figure 19.5**). This is the most inexpensive and flexible way to sync to any deck.

Figure 19.5 The setup for work to sync Pro Tools LE to a video tape deck by deriving word clock from LTC. The LTC-to-MTC converter and the LTC-to-word clock converter can be the same device.

Table 19.1

Time Code Format Uses

TIME CODE	USES
NTSC/SMPTE (NON-DROP FRAME)	
30	Film sound location recordings Music studio work
29.97	Sync to NTSC video
NTSC/SMPTE (DROP FRAME)	
30DF	Broadcast TV uses, rare
29.97DF	Sync to broadcast video
PAL/EBU	
25	All uses in PAL-land
CINEMA/SMPTE	
24	Specific cinema uses, rare

Setting up your MTC converter

Follow the instructions supplied by the manufacturer to configure your LTC to MTC converter. You'll need to know the format of the time code on your tape. Configure the computer to receive the MIDI according to the manufacturer's setup instructions. **Table 19.1** lists time code format uses.

Setting up your system clock

The word clock input to Pro Tools needs to be set for the correct sample rate. Bit depth is not relevant for clocking. Set the clock speed to the session's sample rate. Adjusting the clock for pull down (or pull up) can be done at the word clock generator, if you need to pull your audio down or up in Pro Tools AV. Adjusting the pull factor of your word clock on the word clock generator is the *only* way to actually adjust pull down or up in Pro Tools LE. **Table 19.2** lists scenarios for when to pull up or down.

To set up Pro Tools peripherals synchronization:

1. Choose Setup > Peripherals.

2. Click the Synchronization tab.

3. Select Generic MTC Reader from the Device pop-up menu (this is the default).

4. Select Any from the Port pop-up menu (**Figure 19.6**).

Figure 19.6 A Generic MTC Reader is the only synchronization interface available to Pro Tools LE. A Port selection of Any will work with a USB MIDI interface.

Table 19.2

When to Pull Down or Pull Up	
PULL FACTOR	**USES**
No pull	Location recordings for film or video
	All sound for picture shot on video
1% pull down	To sync location recordings to film to NTSC video
1% pull up	Some location recordings for Digital Cinema
	NTSC video origination for film release
4% pull up	Sync 24fps location recordings to film transferred to 25fps PAL video
	24fps film for release in 25fps PAL video
4% pull down	25fps PAL video to 24fps film

Figure 19.7 A word clock or digital audio stream at the selected digital audio Clock Source is the only way to clock Pro Tools LE to an external clock.

Figure 19.8 The Hardware Setup window is an alternate place to change the Clock Source.

Session Setup for Accurate Synchronizing

There are two ways to select the digital word clock input when you want to clock to an external source. There are also two ways to set the Session Start time.

To set the clock source in the Session Setup window:

1. Choose Windows > Show Session Setup.

2. Select S/PDIF (or ADAT) from the Clock Source pop-up menu (**Figure 19.7**).

To set the clock source in the Hardware Setup window:

1. Choose Setups > Hardware Setup.

2. Select S/PDIF (or ADAT) from the Clock Source pop-up menu (**Figure 19.8**).

✔ Tip

■ While switching between analog and digital inputs for recording, Pro Tools automatically switches the clock source from Internal to the appropriate digital clock and back. However, this feature can work against our desire to clock to the word clock source while playing and editing. Be careful to leave the clock source to the correct digital input for your word clock source when playing and editing in sync to your tape deck.

To select Session Start time code value:

1. Choose Windows > Show Session Setup.

2. Enter the appropriate time code value into the Session Start field.

3. If the new Session Start time is earlier than the first region or automation data in any track (whether hidden or not) you will be given the option to maintain time code or maintain relative position. Typically when working with sync sound, you'll want to maintain time code (**Figure 19.9**).

4. If the new Session Start time is later than the first region in any track, you will be given the option to maintain relative position or to cancel the change in Session Start time (**Figure 19.10**).

5. If there are no data in the tracks, the change in Session Start time goes ahead immediately.

Figure 19.9 Making the Session Start time earlier in a session you've begun working on will require you to make a choice.

Figure 19.10 Moving the Session Start time later also requires a choice.

Figure 19.11 Choose Edit > Redefine Current Time Code Position for an alternate method of changing the Session Start time.

To change Session Start time code value by redefining the current time code position:

1. Select a position in a track that corresponds to a known time code location (such as a sync beep).

2. Choose Edit > Redefine Current Time Code Position (**Figure 19.11**).

3. Enter the appropriate time code value into the Desired Time field.

   If the new Session Start time is later than the first region in any track, you will be given the option to maintain relative position or to cancel the change in Session Start time.

4. Otherwise, the change in Session Start time goes ahead immediately.

✔ Tips

- Set the Session Start time to a whole number of hours or minutes. This makes it easier to change and then return to various times, if needed.

- There can be no audio before the Session Start time. This may seem obvious, but it means that any test tones or sync beeps that precede the program must be allowed for when selecting a Session Start time.

- When working in Feet + Frames the Session Start time is equivalent to zero. That means that in Pro Tools your sync beep cannot be before zero feet and frames. The custom in film sound in America is to have the zero feet (and the Session Start time) at an even time code hour, a sync beep at nine feet (or six seconds) and the first frame of action (and sound) at 12 feet (eight seconds).

To check that the frame rate is right for your session:

1. Choose Windows > Show Session Setup.

2. Select the appropriate time code format and rate from the Frame Rate pop-up menu (**Figure 19.12**).

   The frame rate should match the time code being received by the MTC converter.

To set Pull Up/Down for your session (DV Toolkit only):

1. Choose Windows > Show Session Setup.

2. Click the triangle control to the left of Time Code Settings (in the lower left of the Session Setup window) to reveal the Time Code Settings panel.

3. In the Pull Up/Down section, select the appropriate pull amount from the Audio Rate Pull Up/Down pop-up menu (**Figure 19.13**). Note, this setting does not and cannot actually pull the audio up or down. Only the word clock generator setting can do this. This pop-up menu only adjusts the ruler and counters to reflect the speed varying caused by the word clock settings.

Figure 19.12 Usually, when working to NTSC video, you'll want to select 29.97 fps non-drop, or sometimes drop. For PAL video, select 25 fps. Select 30 fps when working with time code from location recordings in NTSC land. There are exceptions to these general rules.

Figure 19.13 You only need to worry about pull down if your video image was originally shot on film. Changing the Pull Up/Down setting in the Session Setup window does not change the pull factor of the audio in the session; it only adjusts the ruler to compensate for clocking to a pulled word clock.

SESSION SETUP FOR ACCURATE SYNCHRONIZING

✔ Tips

■ (DV Toolkit only) Pro Tools defaults to limiting the pull options to those normally required for a given time code frame rate. There are very few times when one would want to change this default, but it can be done to cope with incorrectly prepared material. Selecting Setups > Preferences, Operation tab, and deselecting Limit Pull Ups To NTSC/PAL Film Standards will unlock non-standard pull up/down rates for the frame rate you have selected. This also unlocks the Video Rate Pull Up/Down pop-up menu. Whatever pull factor you use should follow the word clock settings.

■ If you need to pull Pro Tools LE up or down, but don't have the DV Toolkit option, remember that the only thing the Audio Rate menu actually adjusts is the ruler and counter settings. The audio actually follows the word clock settings, whatever version of Pro Tools you have. Since a typical use of audio pull down is working with film sound to NTSC video picture, a workaround is to set the frame rate to 30, instead of the actual 29.97. This results in the same pulled down ruler you'd get with a setting of 29.97 with pull down.

■ When working with time code, one inevitably encounters dropouts. Having a freewheel in the system helps to play over these hiccups. In the Session Setup window, Time Code Settings, Freewheel section you can choose whether to have Freewheel off or on, how many frames of freewheel, up to forever (Jam Sync). The longer the freewheel, the longer Pro Tools will play on after the incoming time code has stopped, so the default eight frames is a good starting point.

SESSION SETUP FOR ACCURATE SYNCHRONIZING

Using the video player as the time code master, with Pro Tools as the slave

Having completed all the setups described above, you should now be ready to play your videotape in the deck, with Pro Tools on-line, have it lock to the incoming time code and play in sync with the video. In this case the video player is the master, and Pro Tools is the slave. Whenever you play the video forward at play speed, Pro Tools will lock on and follow in sync.

To put Pro Tools online with the Transport control:

1. Choose Windows > Show Transport.

2. To toggle the online status of Pro Tools, click the Online (clock) button to put Pro Tools online.

   Pro Tools will play at the incoming time code location for as long as time code is present.

   The status indicator at the bottom left of the edit window shows that Pro Tools is waiting for time code (**Figure 19.14**).

To put Pro Tools online with the keyboard:

◆ To toggle the online status of Pro Tools, press Command-J (Mac) or Ctrl-J (Windows), or press Option-spacebar (Mac) or Alt-spacebar (Windows).

To put Pro Tools online with a menu selection:

◆ To toggle the online status of Pro Tools, choose Operations > Online.

Figure 19.14 The Transport window does not need to show since the status indicator tells you whether Pro Tools is waiting, locking, or locked to external time code. You don't need to take Pro Tools off-line to play normally.

To move the insertion point to the current incoming time code position:

1. Press = (equals sign) on the numeric keypad once to select the Main Time Scale in the location indicator.

2. Press = again to place the incoming time code value into the indicator.

3. Press Enter to move to the new location.

To move the selection to the current incoming time code position:

1. Press the Down Arrow key to move the selection start to the current time code location.

2. Press the Up Arrow key to move the selection end to the current time code location.

3. While Pro Tools is playing online, pressing the down and up keys will create a selection.

Making Pro Tools the Master with MMC

Pro Tools supports MIDI Machine Control which allows Pro Tools to be the master, controlling devices which support MMC, or professional Sony 9 Pin (RS-242) video decks via an MMC to RS-242 interface such as the Mark of the Unicorn Digital Timepiece or the JLCooper MMC/9PIN+.

Depending on the accuracy of your system, this comes closest to a professional sound for picture system involving a video deck.

Digitizing Your Guide Track from the Videotape

In order to test the sync accuracy of your setup, and to have a reference guide track for your editing work, it is necessary to digitize the guide track from the videotape. The true test of the sync capability of your system is if it can maintain sync during playback of a guide track recorded online from the video. The process of recording online is explained here.

Online recording from the videotape

All the components of your time code and clock system must be on and correctly configured for online recording to work properly.

The audio outputs from the deck should be plugged into the appropriate inputs of the Pro Tools system. If the video has analog audio outputs and there are level reference tones on the videotape you should adjust the input gain so the tones are at −20dBFS (typically).

For more information on recording in Pro Tools, see *Chapter 6: Getting Ready to Record*, and *Chapter 7: Recording and Playing Back Audio*.

What is a Guide Track?

The guide track is the audio that has been edited in sync with the picture, played out to videotape or audiotape, or exported as a QuickTime audio track, or audio bounce from the picture editing system. It is an essential reference for the sound editor(s). It should contain a head and tail sync beep.

When the picture editor produces a guide track for the sound editor it is useful to separate production sound from other, added sounds such as music or sound effects. A common solution is to have production sound split onto the left channel of a stereo pair, and music and effects on the right. This can be prepared by the picture editor for playout to videotape or exporting to QuickTime. Sometimes further splitting is useful for the composer, and sound effects editors, to keep temp music separate from the sound effects, but these splits require more playouts or exports, or require the use of a multi-track tape recorder to keep separation of more than two categories of sound.

Figure 19.15 For most applications, you want Pro Tools to lock as soon as it sees running time code.

To define online record options:

1. Choose Setups > Preferences.

2. Click on the Operation tab.

3. In the Online Options section, select Record Online At Time Code (or ADAT) Lock (**Figure 19.15**).

✔ Tip

■ If you select the Record Online at Insertion/Selection option, Pro Tools will only record from the insertion point onward, or into the selected area. This can be useful when recording specific sounds while locked to picture, such as ADR or Foley from an external source, or layered or processed sounds or sound design from within your session.

To record online:

1. Cue the videotape to a location several seconds before the first desired sound, which may be the sync beep.

2. Set the tracks to the appropriate inputs for the video deck outputs.

3. Name the tracks so that the recorded files will have meaningful names.

4. Record-enable the tracks.

5. To put Pro Tools into online record ready mode, click on the Online button of the Transport control, then click on the Record Ready button of the Transport control (**Figure 19.16**).

6. Press Play on the video deck.

   Pro Tools should go into record as it locks and stay there until you stop the video deck. After the tail sync beep has gone by, stop the video deck.

7. When the recording is complete, immediately name the recorded sound file.

8. Take the track out of record.

Figure 19.16 You'll need to enable record after each time you roll. Press Option-Command-spacebar (Mac) or Alt-Ctrl-spacebar (Windows) to quickly put Pro Tools back into online record ready mode.

DIGITIZING YOUR GUIDE TRACK FROM VIDEOTAPE

✔ Tip

■ Troubleshooting online record problems:

▲ To check whether time code is being generated by the deck, plug the LTC out into your monitor somehow. Time code has a distinctive square wave whine.

▲ Make sure the signal is being seen and sent by the LTC to MTC converter. A front panel indicator will alert you to proper time code being received by the unit.

▲ Make sure the Pro Tools Clock Source is set to the correct digital input, and that a word clock signal (or digital audio signal) is actually present at the input.

▲ If Pro Tools will record, but the results lock up out of sync when played from the middle or end of the program, instead of the middle, your clock is running at the wrong speed. If you record a bit of the guide track onto another track just at the end of the program (the tail beep, for example), you can calculate the percent of error, which may lead you to the correct setting.

Visible time code

Make sure you have visible time code in your video image for sync setup and checking, and easy spotting and locating while you work. Most professional video decks allow the time code window to be superimposed while playing. If your deck can't do this, get the picture editor to provide a tape with a time code window burn-in. This is the superimposed time code image recorded onto the tape.

Checking Sync Accuracy

Once the guide track is recorded, it is useful to compare the recording to the picture and audio tracks on the videotape to ensure they are correctly in sync.

To check sync by eye:

1. First check that the head beep is in sync with the correct time code. Typically this is 01:00:06:00, or 9+00 feet and frames (**Figure 19.17**).

2. Play the video while listening to Pro Tools.

   Is the head beep in sync with the visual mark in the leader?

   Is the dialog in sync with the lips?

   Is the tail beep in sync with the leader?

Figure 19.17 It is impossible to check sync without an accurate sync beep at a known frame at both the head and tail of your program.

To check sync by listening for phasing:

◆ Play the video while listening to an equal mix of the recorded guide track and the track coming from the tape.

The head beep should sound as one, not doubling.

The dialog and other sounds from the program should be so closely in sync with each other that the higher frequencies cancel out, creating a distinctive phasing sound. The sound should not be drifting in or out of sync at any time, but rather stay in the exact sync relationship indefinitely.

The tail beeps should also play as one, whether the program has been played from the beginning, or if the beeps are played from nearby.

✔ Tips

■ If there is a clock error, checking sync by playing from the beginning of the program will not reveal it. The clocks in modern video and audio equipment are quite stable, so the same timing errors will be reproduced during playback. A timing error can be revealed most clearly by checking lock and sync late in the program.

■ Because the clocks are so stable, it is often workable to have both the video deck and Pro Tools running on internal clocks. This is possible only when pull down or pull up is not required. This method is not reliable or repeatable enough to be recommended for professional applications.

Editing with the video deck as master

Working with a video deck is only for those who already own the requisite parts. If you don't already own the gear, it is more expensive to purchase, and it is less productive to use to edit to picture. However, it works.

Since there is no direct coupling between a video deck and Pro Tools except at play speed, it is difficult to place sounds at the correct picture hit points without a time code or feet and frames ruler. Thus DV Toolkit becomes an essential part of a system involving an external video deck. Equally important is the visible time code burn in on the videotape.

To sync a sound to picture with a video deck with DV Toolkit involves a several step procedure.

CHECKING SYNC ACCURACY

To put sounds in sync to videotape:

1. Using the jog/shuttle wheel on your video deck, locate a picture hit point.

2. Press = (equals sign) to select the main counter. Press = again to grab the incoming time code to the main counter.

3. Press the Enter key to move the insertion point to the time code location. This usually is close to the current location, but is likely to be several frames off, since LTC can't be read at slow jog speeds.

4. Using the plus (+) and minus (-) keys on the numeric keypad, nudge the insertion point until its time code location matches the visible time code on the video screen.

Figure 19.18 After marking your hit point, line up your sounds. Markers allow you to easily return to your hit points.

5. Record this location by pressing the Enter key to create a Marker. Name the marker so you can find the place again quickly.

6. Once the location is marked, it is easy to place a sound in sync with the hit point (**Figure 19.18**).

7. Roll the video deck back and press Play on the video transport.

Pro Tools will lock to the time code and play across the edited sound. Check the sync relationship, and nudge the sound earlier or later as needed.

✔ Tip

- If you have a VITC (Vertical Interval Time Code) reader, you can grab the time code from the videotape even when it is stopped. The VITC code is embedded in the first few scan lines at the top of the video frame, outside of the viewing area. A VITC reader makes a video deck quite useable.

CHECKING SYNC ACCURACY

Using Digital Video To Sync Pro Tools To Picture

The more elegant way to sync Pro Tools to the picture is by using digital video. Importing a QuickTime digital video track into your Pro Tools session allows accurate and instantaneous sync between the picture and your tracks. There's no question that this is the easiest way to work with sync picture in Pro Tools. Since the availability of Pro Tools LE 5.1, Windows users can also work with QuickTime in Pro Tools. As of this writing (Pro Tools LE 6.1) there are a few remaining limitations for Windows users.

The QuickTime video file can be obtained in many ways. It can originate as an export from Avid (using Apple DV codec), Final Cut Pro, or iMovie. Or you can digitize your file from a DV camera through FireWire (called iLink by Sony), or from a DV to analog video converter like the Canopus ADVC-100. If you digitize your own QuickTime files, you'll need appropriate video digitizing software.

Importing the digital video

Pro Tools will import and play any QuickTime movie at any size or frame rate. For sync to video use, QuickTime movies should be digitized at the same frame rate as the NTSC or PAL videotapes they come from. Imported movies play along in sync with the timeline. Pro Tools can also import the sound from the current movie, or another QuickTime movie. You can have only one movie track, and it can only contain one movie file.

To import a movie:

1. Choose Movie > Import Movie (**Figure 19.19**).

2. Select a QuickTime movie file from the Open Movie dialog (**Figure 19.20**).

   If there is already a movie in a movie track, you'll be alerted that it will be removed if you proceed (**Figure 19.21**).

Figure 19.19 Choose Movie > Import Movie to select the QuickTime file you want to work with.

Figure 19.20 Select the QuickTime file using the standard File Open dialog.

Figure 19.21 Since you can only have one movie file open at a time, you have to confirm your choice of a new movie file.

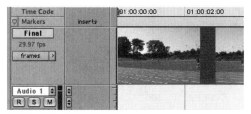

Figure 19.22 An exported QuickTime file can start exactly at the desired Session Start time, but QuickTime files digitized from videotape start at a random frame number after the Session Start. If you have digitized from tape, you'll need to place your movie file at the correct start frame within the session.

To put a movie into the timeline at the correct time code location:

1. Import your movie into Pro Tools.

When it is first imported into Pro Tools, your movie will start at the Session Start (**Figure 19.22**).

2. Using the grabber tool drag or spot the movie to the correct start time.

✔ Tips

■ Spotting the movie to a particular time code location is easiest with visible time code in the picture and with DV Toolkit installed. You can spot the picture to the time code location of the first frame of the file.

■ Without visible time code or DV Toolkit installed you can still sync your 29.97 video to the correct session time code. Make sure your session start time is set to an even hour (zero minutes, seconds or frames). Place a sync mark in the video track at the leading edge of the 2 frame in the countdown leader. Spot the Sync Point of the movie to 0:06.006 (0.1% later than 6 seconds from the start of the session). Even though the Minutes:Seconds time counter will drift slowly out of sync, the time code is correctly handled by Pro Tools. You can see this for yourself by synching to external code, or examining the time stamping of a file recorded in your session.

■ If you zoom in to the Movie Track, in frames mode, with a small height, so that just a one or two frames are visible with a large gap between them, the left edge of the frame you see on the screen is the leading edge of that frame.

Viewing digital video

Once your movie is in place you should hide the movie track since it takes up space in the edit window. Also, if the movie track is showing, and its display mode is frames, extra CPU power is consumed drawing the frames in the edit window. On an LE system, available CPU power is directly related to audio track and plug-in count. For more information on optimizing performance, see *Chapter 20: Optimizing Performance*.

After importing a QuickTime movie, there are several options for viewing it on a screen.

◆ View Movie window on single computer monitor along with Pro Tools.

When working with only one computer screen (unless it's huge) you'll find the movie window is always in the way. To temporarily hide the window, use the Command-9 (Mac) or Ctrl-9 (Windows) (on the numeric keypad only) to toggle the visibility of the Movie window.

◆ View Movie window on a second monitor.

If you have a second monitor, you can probably find a place for the Movie window so it isn't always in the way. The mixer and plug-in windows may also find a good home there (**Figure 19.23**).

Computer Monitor

Video Program   Computer

USB, FireWire, or Proprietary

2nd Computer Monitor (for video only)

Pro Tools Audio Interface

Audio Monitors

Figure 19.23 Working with your video image on a second computer monitor may be the simplest way to work, but it requires a fast computer.

◆ View Movie window on a second monitor with pixel doubling.

If you have a second computer monitor that you can run in 640 x 480 VGA resolution you can use pixel doubling to fill the screen with a 320 x 240 QuickTime image. This provides a very workable environment, and many modern computers come with dual monitor capability built in.

Digidesign has approved the Radeon 8500 dual monitor card for use with Pro Tools on the Mac only. It has the unique feature of supporting an S-Video output for the second monitor. This setup seems to work well for those who have it.

◆ Play DV Movie out FireWire port, convert to analog video, and view on TV or video monitor.

If this command is selected from the Movie menu, the picture will not be shown in the Movie window, but rather will be routed out the FireWire port in sync with the timeline, at any speed (**Figure 19.24**).

Figure 19.24 Using a FireWire DV-to-analog video converter gives excellent picture quality but causes a noticeable delay in the image output, which must be compensated for.

Video Program

TV or Video Monitor

Computer Monitor

Computer

DV-to-Analog Video Converter

USB, FireWire, or Proprietary

Pro Tools Audio Interface

Audio Monitors

USING DIGITAL VIDEO TO SYNC TO PICTURE

You need a FireWire to analog video converter to pass the signal on to a video monitor or TV. Digidesign has tested and approved the Canopus ADVC-100 as well as certain Sony digital 8 cameras for this purpose, but any DV to analog converter should work. All these D to A converters take a fraction of a second to do their conversion, so you need to advance the movie track to compensate for this. This can be done with the Movie > Set Movie Sync Offset command. There you can type in the amount of picture delay introduced by the D to A converter in quarter frames. Digidesign has found that the Canopus ADVC-100 requires a 22 quarter frame compensation (5 1/2 frames) for NTSC video and 18 quarter frames for PAL.

By offloading the display of the DV data onto the Canopus or equivalent hardware, the computer's CPU is actually required to do much less work, so Pro Tools LE feels zippier, and audio performance is increased. The downside of working with DV is that the files are very large: over 200 MB per minute.

This function currently works on Mac computers only, though Digidesign is promising to deliver the same ability to Windows users as soon as they can.

◆ Play movie through PCI card in computer. Digidesign has approved the IgniterX video digitizing card that fits inside a Mac computer with PCI slots. This card will digitize from an analog video source using software such as Final Cut Pro or Adobe After Effects. The IgniterX card creates QuickTime MJPEG-A files can be highly compressed if storage space is an issue. The use of this card will drag down performance on an LE system somewhat. D to A conversion delay is minimal.

Figure 19.25 Choose Movie > Import Audio From Current Movie to get a standard QuickTime track import dialog.

Importing sync sound from an imported QuickTime movie into Pro Tools

The QuickTime format stores audio tracks along with the video image. When digitizing a video program from a DV camera or Canopus ADVC-100, the audio will also be recorded. When exporting an edited program from Avid or Final Cut Pro to the QuickTime format, audio tracks typically form a part of the result. After importing a QuickTime movie into Pro Tools, it becomes the Current Movie. It's easy to import its audio into Pro Tools, where you can drag it into a vacant audio track and sync it to the video.

It's also possible to import the audio from any other QuickTime movie file even if the video portion of the movie has not been imported. The process of importing audio from CD uses the same interface. For more information on importing audio from CD, see *Chapter 8: File Management Basics*.

To import the audio tracks from the current movie:

1. Choose Movie > Import Audio From Current Movie.

   The Track Import window will appear with a listing of the available QuickTime Audio Tracks. Each listing includes a channel count, bit depth, and sample rate (**Figure 19.25**).

2. Select a track or tracks to import. All tracks are selected by default.

3. Click OK.

4. Select a destination folder for the audio.

   Pro Tools displays a progress bar as it converts the audio from the QuickTime format to the session's appropriate format. When the process is complete, the file will be selected in the audio region list.

To import the audio tracks from another movie:

1. Choose Movie > Import Audio From Other Movie (**Figure 19.26**).

2. Select a QuickTime file (or CD track).

3. Follow the steps for importing audio from the current movie in the preceding task.

✔ Tip

■ If the session has the same bit resolution and sample rate as the QuickTime audio, the imported audio will be a clone of the source. Thus, QuickTime movies can be exported by the picture editor and imported into Pro Tools with no loss of quality. This is a simple and straightforward way to obtain audio from the picture editor.

Figure 19.26 Choose Movie > Import Audio From Other Movie to import sound from any QuickTime movie or CD track.

sc.73_7.18.03_CUT
2section.omf

Figure 19.27 The same icon is shared by Avid OMF and AAF interchange files. Even though the icon is labeled with the word "Media," the icon shown here is from a composition or sequence file and contains no media.

Getting Sync Audio from the Picture Editor

The picture editor can provide the following:

◆ Audio from production sound, sequence information from EDL or Assemble List

◆ Audio from NLE, sequence information from OMF or AAF interchange file

◆ Audio (and sequence) from edited audio tracks from videotape or exported audio track files

Getting audio from the picture editor using OMF or AAF (DV Toolkit only)

Several years ago Open Media Framework (OMF) became an accepted format for interchanging files containing edit decisions and other sequence data between editors using systems from different manufacturers. An OMF Interchange (OMFI) file is like an EDL, only it contains descriptions of many more aspects of an editor's work than just cut or dissolve points (**Figure 19.27**). For a sound editor, OMFI delivers a sample accurate duplicate of the sound regions from the picture editor, complete with fades and certain types of automation. The OMFI file can optionally contain embedded media files, or it can refer to sound files you've copied from the picture editor's system onto your hard drive.

More recently AVID, Digidesign and many other workstation and software developers have embraced a newer format for sequence interchange called Advanced Authoring Format. This system is apparently easier for developers to implement, and delivers more details of the exported sequence. AAF is new and not well known yet, but its advocates promise AAF will supercede OMF in the next few years. AAF files with embedded media are not supported by DigiTranslator.

Guidelines for exporting OMF and AAF

The specific methods of exporting OMF or AAF files from a NLE is beyond the scope of this book. Generally, try to use the most compatible interchange format, referring to files in the most compatible form for your hardware, operating system, NLE, and Pro Tools version.

✔ Tip

■ If the picture is completely finished, an OMFI file with embedded media is a single file to export/import, and can save some file management hassles.

However, if the picture may be changed and you anticipate needing another export from the video workstation, you should use OMFI or AAF with external file references. Later, when the picture and sound have been updated, instead of requiring a new embedded audio export, your new interchange file will refer to the audio you already have. The extra audio file management work you'll need to do will pay off. Do not consolidate the media at any time in the NLE or in Pro Tools, or this technique will not work.

Figure 19.28 Select the OMF or AAF file using the standard File Open dialog.

Figure 19.29 Enter a name for your new session file. If you don't change the Session Parameters, the original audio file settings will be used.

Using DigiTranslator to import the OMF or AAF sequence into Pro Tools (DV Toolkit only)

After installing DV Toolkit, DigiTranslator 2 is incorporated directly into Pro Tools LE 6.1. Its functions are seamlessly integrated into Pro Tools' normal operations. DigiTranslator allows Pro Tools to import audio, video and edited sequences from other AAF or OMF compatible applications. It also allows Pro Tools to export audio files and audio tracks to other compatible systems.

Whether you use external or embedded media, you'll need to have the files on a valid audio drive. You'll also need the OMF or AAF interchange file with the sequence data in it.

The benefits of OMF and AAF are lost if the sound in the NLE was not recorded in well. If the sound was recorded on DAT or other digital audiotape format, or if it was recorded on a hard disk recorder, the chances are that the sound files in the NLE are identical clones of the original recordings. However, if the sound in the NLE has been degraded due to poor load in procedures, the efficiencies of sequence interchange are offset by permanent sound quality loss if OMF/AAF techniques are used. In this case audio should be reloaded into Pro Tools from the original recordings.

To open an interchange file:

1. Choose File > Open Session.

2. Select your OMF or AAF document and click OK (**Figure 19.28**).

3. Choose a name and a location for the session file that will be created from the interchange document (**Figure 19.29**).

continues on next page

4. The selections in the Session Parameters section of the dialog reflect the settings in the OMFI or AAF document. You may change the Audio File Type, Sample Rate and Bit Depth now. If you do change any of these parameters, Pro Tools will convert all the referenced audio files to the newly selected format. This happens as a background task as the session is opened.

5. In the Import Session Data dialog which now appears you will see what's in the interchange file. You can adjust many parameters here, but typically you'll want to refer to source media, maintain absolute time code, and convert clip-based gain to automation.

6. Select the tracks you want to import. Shift-click on a track name, and drag through to select all tracks. Option-click (Alt-click in Windows) on a pop-up menu to select Import As New Track for all tracks (**Figure 19.30**).

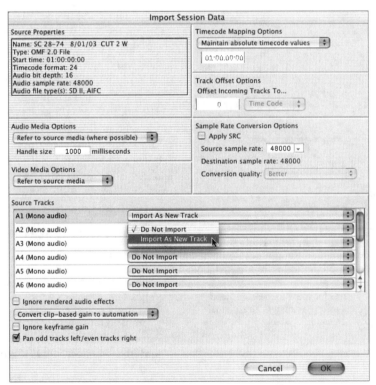

Figure 19.30 Select which tracks you want to import, and many other session parameters in the Import Session Data window.

Figure 19.31 Pro Tools 6.1 can quickly and automatically find and relink audio files on any valid audio drive.

Figure 19.32 The Tasks window is showing the queue of background tasks after opening an OMF file.

Figure 19.33 A cryptic OMF error window. You should save the list of errors, when given the option. Most OMF conversions result in some harmless errors.

7. Click the OK button.

8. Since the audio files may not be where Pro Tools expects them to be, you may get a Missing Files dialog. Select Automatically Find & Relink and click OK to let Pro Tools try to find the audio for you. This happens as a background task (**Figure 19.31**).

Typically the sound files from a video editor need to have their overviews drawn. This is another background task (**Figure 19.32**).

9. When the various background processes are complete, you must save the session again and you are done.

✔ Tip

■ At various stages during this process you might get an error message such as Some OMF parsing errors occurred (**Figure 19.33**). When offered the option to save a report, do so. It may help you track down the source of an important error. More likely, you'll find that OMF and AAF file interchange is still an imperfect art, and small, but typically insignificant errors regularly occur.

Importing Tracks into Pro Tools with DigiTranslator (DV Toolkit only)

Since the extra functionality of DigiTranslator is built right into Pro Tools, many of the standard Pro Tools file and track opening and importing functions work with OMF and AAF files in much the same way that sessions work.

◆ Double-click on an AAF or OMF file in the Finder (Mac) or File Manager (Windows) to open it into a new session.

◆ Choose File > Import Session Data to select an interchange file and import tracks from it into an open session.

◆ Double-clicking on an OMF or AAF file in the DigiBase Workspace browser triggers either opening it into a new session, if no session is open, or importing tracks from the selected file into an open session.

◆ Drag and drop an interchange file from the DigiBase Browser window onto an open Edit window to import tracks.

Reloading from the original recordings

If the production sound was recorded on DAT or other digital audiotape format, it is easy setup to get a digital clone of the sound into Pro Tools. Loading directly from the digital output of a DAT machine into the S/PDIF input of Pro Tools will give you an identical copy (clone) of the original recording, and you can't get better quality than that.

In order to proceed with the loading, you'll need a list of all the sound takes required. The key to efficient tape handling is to go through each tape only once, and load the needed takes in the order in which they appear on the tape. Even if the portion of a take used in a sequence is quite small, you should consider loading the entire take. The editing process is much smoother if you don't have to go back into the tapes looking for extra bits of sound.

The recent introduction of location hard disk recorders have made direct copying from the location recorder into Pro Tools possible. If these recordings were available to the picture editor, the audio files exported from the NLE should be perfect. Otherwise you can just import the audio directly from the location recorder's disk(s), bypassing the chore of real time load in from tape.

Recording from DAT with time code sync

The setup required for recording with time code from a digital source is essentially the same as recording the guide track from a videotape, described earlier in this chapter. The only difference is that Pro Tools maintains sync while clocked directly to the digital audio stream itself, rather than needing an external clock for the system.

Getting time code from the audio deck requires an LTC-to-MTC converter and a time code tape player (**Figure 19.34**).

Figure 19.34 The standard setup for digitizing from a time code DAT deck into Pro Tools with time stamping.

Create a new session for loading with Session Parameters that match the format of your production sound. In the Session Setup window, make sure the various parameters are correctly configured (**Figure 19.35**).

◆ Clock Source = S/PDIF

◆ Ch 1-2 Input = Digital

◆ Time code frame rate matches the time code on the DATs

◆ Under Time Code Settings, a few frames of Freewheel is good, but don't use Jam Sync.

Once you have configured your setup, you should be able to cue up your tape to the first take to be loaded. In order to hear the tape as you cue it, the track you will be recording into must be in record ready, and the session should not be playing. It is helpful to retain the voice ID (at the head of most takes) in the portion of the take that you load. This makes finding correct takes (and troubleshooting) easier.

If the take was recorded onto two channels with different sound on each, load it into a stereo track. This allows naming both tracks at the same time, which is faster and more consistent. However, if the take was recorded onto one track, or with one microphone onto two identical tracks, it is easier to edit if you record that one channel only into a mono track. Editing and mixing is much easier if there aren't redundant copies of your audio involved.

Figure 19.35 Select your digital input, making sure the Input and Clock Source settings are matching.

Figure 19.36 Name your digitized files immediately. It's too easy to forget which take is which after you have a few unnamed files to deal with.

✔ Tips

■ You can't digitize the first few frames of a take, since it takes that long for Pro Tools to lock and go into record. If you cue the tape before the beginning of a take, Pro Tools may go into record and then drop out as soon as the take starts because of a break in the time code.

■ While you are loading the takes, you may notice that some of the takes are excessively noisy, or have other audio problems. Try to find and load some cleaner alternate takes of the lines, and more options when you edit.

■ Pro Tools has a limited range of time code it can lock to. It cannot lock to time code from before the Session Start time. The Load Session Start Time may be set to any arbitrary time before the time code of the takes. But since a Pro Tools session has a maximum length of 12 hours from the Session Start time, you may need to change the start time as you work to accommodate a wide range of source tapes with different time code hours.

To record online:

1. Cue the audiotape to a location after the beginning of the take you want to record, but enough before the section where you want the recording to begin to allow Pro Tools to lock to the incoming time code when it begins playing.

2. Set the track to the appropriate S/PDIF inputs.

3. Name the track so that the recorded files will have meaningful names.

4. Record-enable the track.

5. To put Pro Tools into online record ready mode, press Option-Command-spacebar (Mac) or Alt-Ctrl-spacebar (Windows). Or, click on the Online button of the Transport control, then click on the Record Ready button of the Transport control.

6. Press play on the DAT deck.

   Pro Tools should jump to the location matching the time code from the take, go into record and stay there until you stop the DAT machine, or when there is a break in the time code.

7. When the recording is complete, immediately name the recorded sound file (**Figure 19.36**).

Synchronizing takes to the guide track

In order to reconstruct the picture editor's work in Pro Tools from the newly digitized takes, you need to know what portions of which takes have been used to make up each part of the guide track. Guided by an EDL from the picture editor, it is possible to piece together the audio to match the editor's track. There is a program called Titan, from SynchroArts, specifically designed to automate the matching of the loaded takes to an EDL from the picture editor. This can be done quickly and easily if you have Titan, an EDL, and were able to load from a time code DAT player. However, if you lack Titan, but have DV Toolkit, you can still work through the process manually, reading the EDL (or track Assemble List) and using your eyes and ears to sync up the appropriate regions to the guide track. This is a difficult and tedious process, which is to be avoided if at all possible.

Use the sound from the guide track as your source for sound editing

Getting a series of guide tracks or bounced files from the picture editor is a good workaround for having no OMF/AAF. If the picture editor can provide you with exported audio or QuickTime files of the various tracks in the picture system, you will be able to have perfect sync effortlessly. And if the sound was properly loaded into the system, you will have master quality audio as well.

You'll probably want to get the audio tracks twice from the editor. Once as they were cut, and once with each track split out or checkerboarded, and with its handles pulled out as far as possible. The original track becomes the guide, and the second set of tracks has the head and tail extensions you'll need to smooth out the production sound.

Auto-conforming with an EDL using Titan

The only program for auto-conforming sound to an EDL for Pro Tools is Titan 3 by SynchroArts. It is a very powerful and easy to use tool for the Mac only. A detailed discussion of its use is beyond the scope of this chapter.

For more information on auto-conforming with Titan, see the Titan manual and demo version, available online at www.synchroarts.com.

Also see the comprehensive online tutorial at www.editorsguild.com/newsletter/JulAug01/tip_pro_tools_murray.html.

Editing Dialog (Production Sound)

At the heart of sound editing for video is the cleaning up of the sound from the shoot. This sound often has technical problems that can be repaired in editing or mixing, though some sounds are technically impossible to fix and must be replaced.

The goals of the dialog track

The goals of the dialog track are fairly straightforward, but sometimes difficult to achieve.

◆ All the dialog should be clear and intelligible.

◆ The voices should sound natural and pleasant.

◆ Separate takes edited together within the same scene should sound smooth and continuous.

◆ The lines of dialog should play at a consistent level.

◆ Some sounds will need special treatment, such as reverberation, or futzing to sound as though heard through a telephone, or public address system.

Its impossible to stress enough the importance of clean location sound recordings. Excess environmental noise, distant or off-axis miking, or distortion caused by poor level control ruin the quality of production recordings. These problems can be modestly improved in editing and mixing, but cannot be eliminated. The old adage, "we'll fix it in post," often is true only if you can afford to replace all the sound with new ADR and Foley recordings, and this is not possible in many situations.

In dialog editing, all the sounds are put in the right places and smoothly overlapped, and any new sounds are added to fill unwanted gaps in the track. Momentary clicks, pops and bumps are removed. Alternate takes can be searched for cleaner and clearer renditions of lines, words, or even syllables, which can be used to replace poor sections of sync sound.

Editing and mixing are complementary aspects of all sound work. Since the edited sound is passed along to the mixer to be mixed, you must be sure that your work is properly prepared for the mixer's needs.

Laying out the tracks for dialog editing

Before editing begins you have to have obtain the synch sound from the picture editor. Your next task is to duplicate these tracks. Lock all the regions in the duplicate tracks and make the tracks inactive so they are accessible, but don't use any CPU resources. Now hide them. They'll be available to refer to if needed.

Create enough new tracks to do all your dialog editing. You might need eight to sixteen new tracks. Several will be used for splitting the principal dialog. A couple may be used for alternate takes. Two or four tracks may be enough for fill, or air and movement tracks. If preparing for an alternate language version, extra tracks can be created to hold non-language sounds, or production effects. Create a couple of work tracks that will only be used as a temporary work space, but never to hold finished cut material.

Once you've created the tracks, name them according to their use. Appropriate names might be Dial 1 through 6, Alt 1 & 2, Fill 1 through 4, PFX 1 through 4, Work 1 & 2 (**Figure 19.37**).

Figure 19.37 An example of a simple dialog editing track layout. Notice the inactive duplicate original OMF tracks: A1.dup1 through A4.dup1.

Basic dialog editing tasks

Once you have all the sounds in sync, the three basic dialog editing tasks are splitting, smoothing and filling. This is the basic requirement for delivery tracks to the mix.

When a source take's qualities are very different from the preceding take, it should be split to another track. This allows the mixer to more easily apply a different set of plug-ins or tools, or different settings to the various tracks and not have to change them at every region boundary, which may be difficult to accomplish on a conventional mixing console, and saves time.

On the other hand, if a take's sound qualities match those of the preceding sound, both should be placed on the same track if possible. The mixer should not have to copy the same settings from one track to another in order to match takes on different tracks.

Splitting tracks is the first step in dialog editing. The next steps can only properly occur after the splitting decisions have been made. After splitting, the tracks are smoothed out to obscure the transitions between takes. This involves trimming out the ends of the takes for as far as possible, and then creating long fades in and out over the length of the head and tail extensions of the takes.

Filling holes is the process of coming up with *air* or *room tone* and movement sounds from the location recordings to fill out a scene that has used picture-only, or MOS, takes. MOS (initials spelled out) stands for *Mit Out Sound*, a phrase apparently used by a famous, heavy-accented, German director in the early days of sound.

It is also necessary to fill the track when the synch sound has been eliminated by the picture editor for having the wrong content. There are many reasons for the holes that occur in a dialog track, but the best solution is always to look at the picture for clues and listen to the surrounding sound takes for the most likely candidates for fill.

EDITING DIALOG (PRODUCTION SOUND)

To split dialog:

1. Listen carefully to dialog and background qualities while playing along through the conformed production sound.

2. When you play across an edit and the sound qualities seem to match, leave the takes together on the same track, even if the edit itself is bad. If the takes will require the same treatment in the mix, they should remain on the same track. The bad edit can be repaired now, or after the splitting is complete.

3. If the takes do not match qualitatively, they should be split. With the grabber tool, select the region to be split to another track.

4. Hold down the shift and option keys together (shift-Alt in Windows), and press the return key to select from the currently selected region to the end of the track.

5. In Command Focus mode, press X to cut the audio from the original track.

6. Press P or ; to move up or down to the desired track.

7. Press V to paste the audio, in sync, to the new track. You have now split the track (**Figure 19.38**).

✔ Tip

■ If you'd rather, after selecting the audio to split, you can Control-click on the selection and drag it with the grabber to the desired track.

Figure 19.38 After splitting, these dialog tracks are ready to be smoothed out.

EDITING DIALOG (PRODUCTION SOUND)

Figure 19.39 Drag the "handle," or end of a region, out a ways to see whether there's any air there.

Figure 19.40 Trim the handle back to the beginning of the air. Often this visual approach works well, but always check your work by listening carefully to the results.

Figure 19.41 Create a fade over the length of the handle. You may need more or less handle than is immediately available. Change the fade shape if needed to make a smooth segue with the adjacent audio. Always use your ears.

Figure 19.42 These tracks play smoothly now.

To smooth out transitions between dialog tracks:

1. To smoothly fade into the head of a block of regions, use the trim tool to drag the head out a couple seconds (**Figure 19.39**). (These descriptions work the same way for the tail extension.)

2. Looking at the waveform, you can usually see at a glance where unusable sounds occur. Dialog or distinctive unwanted sounds, such as doors or other effects.

3. Trim the extension back to the apparently useable section of sound (**Figure 19.40**).

4. Listen carefully to the extension and make sure it's innocent of any offensive material.

5. Create a fade up through the extension to the first frame of the original clip (**Figure 19.41**).

6. Listen to the transition through the fade out from the outgoing region and the fade in to the incoming region.

7. If necessary, adjust the shapes and lengths of the fades to make the transition as smooth as possible. Typically, noisier backgrounds will need to be introduced or withdrawn more gradually and over longer times than quieter backgrounds (**Figure 19.42**).

✔ Tip

■ You may find that pulling out the end of the region doesn't give you enough of an extension to make a smooth transition. This is a common problem. Look into the filling holes section below for steps to obtain more of the needed sound than is immediately to hand.

EDITING DIALOG (PRODUCTION SOUND)

To smooth cuts from region to region:

1. To smoothly cut from region to region within a block of regions, you can use a combination of two basic techniques: move the edit earlier or later, or cross-fade between the regions.

2. If the offensive sound is at the end of the outgoing region, use the trim tool to drag the head of the incoming region earlier to cover the distracting sound.

3. If the problem is at the start of the incoming sound, drag the tail of the out-going sound later to cover the problem (**Figure 19.43**).

4. Once the edit point is in the best place, a short crossfade will usually smooth the cut further (**Figure 19.44**).

✔ Tips

■ When cutting from region to region in a track, make sure to listen carefully for subtle sounds which may be interrupted or upcut. Use a high quality, comfortable set of headphones to eliminate room noise. You'll be surprised how much more you'll hear.

■ Putting the edit immediately before an incoming transient will usually mask the cut.

Figure 19.43 The incoming air will bump at the cut, so trim the outgoing air longer to smooth the cut.

Figure 19.44 The cut has been moved slightly later and a crossfade completes the smoothing of the internal edit.

EDITING DIALOG (PRODUCTION SOUND)

Figure 19.45 Track Work 2 contains the regions of useful air from the take in Work 1.

Figure 19.46 Select the smoothed assemblage of regions of air and Choose Edit > Consolidate Selection to save your work as a convenient file. Remember to name the new file immediately.

To find air to fill holes:

1. To find air in a take, lay the take out in a work track. Using visual clues, find a quiet passage in the take, starting at the beginning. Listen to confirm the absence of dialog or distracting sounds. Select the useful portion, staying clear of distinctive sounds at the edges of the selection, and cut it.

2. Paste the section into the other work track.

3. Repeat steps one and two, pasting the air at the end of the previously assembled bits until you have found and assembled all the useful air from the take (**Figure 19.45**).

4. Play through the assembled pieces, listening through the mostly bad edits for the best selections. Discard any clips that don't work well with the others.

5. Crossfades may help smooth out the assembled clips.

6. Once you've created a useful assembly of clips it's easier to handle if you consolidate it. Choose Edit > Consolidate Selection (**Figure 19.46**). After the new air file has been rendered, immediately name it with the take name and the word "Fill" or "Air" or "Mvmnt" or similar description. As always, be consistent with your naming.

EDITING DIALOG (PRODUCTION SOUND)

✔ Tips

- If there is an evolving sound, like a long jet by, through the take, it may be impossible to edit pieces from different parts of the take together.

- A piece of air can be doubled in length by duplicating it and reversing it. This results in one iteration of a "backwards/forwards" loop. Backwards/forwards loops are always smooth since the head and tail always match. However, you can't make an unobtrusive b/f loop from sounds with transients that can't be transparently reversed.

- You may have to search through any number of nearby takes looking for better candidates for useful air.

- Often the best air is after sound has rolled, but before "action" is called, or after the action is over, but before "cut" is called.

- Don't hesitate to use sections of air with light movement in them, but don't repeat short bits of movement or breaths, as the ear picks up the loopiness of it very quickly.

- You can randomize the order of short clips when repeating them in order to minimize loopiness.

- You can stretch the chunk of air you've created using the TCE Trim tool to get a longer piece.

- Look for wild sound recordings of "Room Tone" for the location. When available, this is always the easiest place to look for a long section of clean air. The problem here is that the air is often too "dead." With the camera off, and no movement from the actors, the air may not match the background in the actual takes from the same location.

Figure 19.47 A piece of fill standing by below the hole that needs filling.

Figure 19.48 The fill is selected and ready to copy.

Figure 19.49 The fill has been paste into the hole and the ends have been crossfaded to smooth the joins.

To fill holes with the air:

1. Once you've got a chunk of air in a work track, select and cut it. Paste the air into a work track alongside the area where it is needed (**Figure 19.47**).

2. Select the area you want to fill.

3. Transfer the selection to the work track by pressing P or ; (in Command Focus mode) (**Figure 19.48**).

4. Copy the required amount of the fill.

5. Move the selection back to the track to be filled with P or ; and paste the fill into the selection. This works for a hole of certain length within a take or for a head or tail extension.

6. Crossfading in and out of your fill may smooth out a bumpy cut (**Figure 19.49**).

7. To create a long fill loop to smooth out a rough scene, or to fill for MOS shots, you may need to duplicate the chunk of air many times.

✔ Tips

- You can paste a small fragment of your air into a space, then trim the end(s) out to fill your hole.

- If you need to fill a series of holes, don't always use the beginning of your piece of air. Use other sections of a longer piece of air to avoid repetition.

- When filling a long section, it is advisable to use more than one fill loop. Use a two or three different fill loops on different fill tracks and let the mixer move the faders up and down to vary the sound.

Dialog microsurgery

Once the basics of splitting, smoothing and filling have been taken care of, there are the small clicks and bumps to remove. These sounds are often artifacts of the recording process: mic bumps, electrical crackles, digital glitches. Sometimes they are undesirable sounds recorded on set, like the distracting snap of a piece of gravel underfoot during a close-up of a face. Occasionally a click is actually a desired sync sound, so watch the picture to be sure the click you are about to attack is actually a suitable target. Let's divide these sounds into three categories and describe how to remove them.

Clicks are so short they can be removed without creating a dropout. After removing a longer click, which we'll call a pop, you'll need to fill the resulting hole. To remove low frequency bumps without losing the dialog or other important sound, use an AudioSuite EQ plug-in to attenuate the bump.

To remove clicks:

1. Locate the click precisely. Tab to transient will find many, but not all, of the audible clicks you might want to remove. Scrub to find the click if Tab to transient can't find it.

2. Once located, zoom in to the click until you can clearly see the cycles in the waveform.

3. Select the noise impulse. The selection start and end should be at zero crossing points. You may need to zoom in vertically to clearly see the points where the waveform samples cross the zero line (**Figure 19.50**).

Figure 19.50 Clicks like this extremely short glitch are usually from some sort of digital source. The selected area is ready to delete.

Figure 19.51 The pop is selected.

Figure 19.52 The pop is deleted.

Figure 19.53 A piece of fill shorter than the hole has been pasted at the start of the hole, ready to be trimmed out to fill the hole.

Figure 19.54 Very short crossfades have been made to eliminate the possibility of clicks at the edits.

4. If the selection is less than about 200 samples, it is usually safe to delete it without worrying about needing to fill it. Press the delete key to remove the click.

5. Play across the deletion to be sure that there is no audible drop-out.

✔ Tips

- This technique is fast, but only works when the click is very short.

- Create a zoom preset for microsurgery and use it to instantly get to the working view after finding the click.

To remove pops by editing:

1. Locate the pop as above.

2. Select the pop (**Figure 19.51**) and delete it (**Figure 19.52**).

3. Find a small piece of fill from nearby in the take that will match the sound quality surrounding the deletion.

4. Select a portion of the sound that is slightly shorter than the length of the deletion. Copy the selection.

5. Select the start of the deletion and paste the fill from the clipboard (**Figure 19.53**).

6. Now trim the fill out until it fills the hole.

7. Listen to the repair.

8. If necessary, make tiny crossfades to smooth out the in and out of the fill (**Figure 19.54**).

EDITING DIALOG (PRODUCTION SOUND)

To volume graph pops out:

1. Locate the pop as above.

2. Select the pop and switch to volume graph view by pressing the minus (-) key in Command Focus mode (**Figure 19.55**).

3. Pull the volume level down around the pop. Use trial and error to find the correct attenuation. Try different shapes for the volume graph (**Figure 19.56**).

4. Play through the repair. If the pop is not too long, the attenuated pop makes good fill for itself. This works particularly well within words.

To remove bumps with EQ:

1. Locate the bump by listening and looking at the waveform.

2. Select the bump and perhaps as much as half a second on either side of the bump (**Figure 19.57**).

3. Choose AudioSuite > 1-Band EQ II.

4. Select the High Pass EQ Type and set the frequency to something like 100 to 250 Hz (**Figure 19.58**).

Figure 19.55 This pop is selected and in volume graph mode, ready to be turned down.

Figure 19.56 The center of the pop has been attenuated. The amount and shape of the attenuation is based on trial and error and listening.

Figure 19.57 A phrase of dialog containing a large low frequency bump is selected.

Figure 19.58 Use an AudioSuite EQ plug-in to roll off the lower frequencies.

Figure 19.59 After processing, the bump is much reduced, but the surrounding dialog has been affected by the EQ.

Figure 19.60 Trim the original dialog in towards the bump.

Figure 19.61 Use crossfades to help smooth the EQed section into the take.

Figure 19.62 The mid- and high-range frequencies are still present in the bump, so a little attenuation helps minimize the flaw. Don't go too far or you'll have a dropout instead of a bump.

5. Process the selection (**Figure 19.59**).

6. Listen to the processed audio, the bump will be attenuated, but the dialog will sound thin.

7. Trim the unprocessed audio back to almost cover the peak of the bump on both sides of the bump (**Figure 19.60**).

8. Create short crossfades into and out of the EQed section (**Figure 19.61**).

9. Listen. Be sure not to go too high with the high pass frequency, or let the EQed section play any longer than necessary. Use trial and error to find the best balance of no bump and full voice.

10. If the higher frequencies remaining in the bump are annoying, use a volume graph to attenuate the bump further (**Figure 19.62**).

EDITING DIALOG (PRODUCTION SOUND)

Working with Sound Effects

Adding sound effects can bring the world around the action of the video to life. Atmospheric background can create an off-screen world that can help set and tell the story of the video. Background tracks can mask problems in the dialog recordings and help smooth out bumps in the production sound. Specific sound effects that work in sync with the picture can add presence and character to objects and actions on the screen. The attention of the audience can be focused on a particular thing on the screen by placing a sound effect that syncs with the object of interest.

In addition to sound effects recorded on location during the shoot, sound editors often draw on the many excellent commercially available libraries of professionally recorded sound effects. Whenever feasible, however, it is advisable to record your own custom sound effects which are likely to fit the action and character of your video better than canned effects. Recording Foley sound effects in a studio to picture can help fill out the many detailed sync sounds of movements, small and large, which are nearly impossible to record or edit in any other way. Special sound effects and atmospheres are created by sound designers, who use a variety of techniques and equipment to bend sound recordings to the needs of the video. Sound designers create sounds for monsters and space ships, but they also create sounds to use as an almost musical underscore that has a subliminal and evocative effect on the audience.

Editing sound effects

Whatever the source of your sound effects, there are some basic ways they can be cut in to your sound track.

Backgrounds need to be laid out so they start and stop at the picture cuts that define the scene edges. Spot effects need to line up with the action on the screen. Most sound effects benefit from layering. Balancing the levels of sound effects while editing helps judge their impact while editing, and helps during the mix.

Finding sync and editing sounds to picture, as sound effects editors do, is much easier with digital video than with videotape. Working with videotape requires a lot of playing the tape, rewinding and jogging to find a particular frame you need to spot to establish sync. With digital video, wherever you click, there you are. The picture plays along with the session, and the picture will also scrub with the audio. This makes identifying sync points as easy as possible. Essentially, when you are editing sound to video you have to locate the hit point and then make a sync mark in Pro Tools, often by nudging with trial and error, or typing numbers into the Spot Dialog. Because time code numbers are so important when working this way, DV Toolkit is nearly essential for sound effects editing to videotape. Due to space limitations we'll focus on the processes of sound effects synching using digital video, covering the basic principles most succinctly. You will be able to work out the process of synching sound effects to videotape for yourself with these guidelines.

To play and scrub to find a scene boundary (without DV Toolkit):

1. To edit backgrounds, you must identify the scene boundaries. Play your video to the scene change point. When you get close, stop.

2. Using the scrubber tool, scrub forward or back as needed to locate the leading edge of the first picture frame in the new scene.

3. Place a marker at this location by pressing the enter key.

4. Select Marker from Time Properties, and name the Marker with a short, meaningful name. An example of a name is "EXT courtyard." Click the OK button.

5. Proceed through the video to the end, placing a named marker at each change in location, time or perspective requiring a change of background.

✔ Tip

■ If you don't have DV Toolkit, you can make your own frame line grid of sorts. By careful sample accurate selection between the leading edge of the first two fames, you can then use Edit > Identify Beat to set up a custom bars and beats grid which is aligned to the picture frames. Call the Start Location 1|1|000 and the End Location 1|2|000. Define a 30/32 time signature for NTSC (25/32 for PAL) so that a 32nd note grid will match the rhythm of the frames, and the bar numbers will count seconds of time code from the first defined frame. It is quicker to locate scene boundaries with DV Toolkit.

To play and nudge to find scene boundaries (with DV Toolkit):

1. Set the ruler to time code.

2. Set the edit mode to grid mode.

3. Set the grid to 1 frame.

4. Play to the beginning of a new scene and stop.

5. Click near where you stopped playing. In grid mode, the insertion point is forced to a frame boundary.

6. Use the plus and minus keys on the numeric keypad to nudge forward or back as many frames as needed to arrive at the very first frame of the scene. This is the leading edge of the frame, and thus the scene.

7. Place a marker at this location and name it, as above.

8. Proceed through the video as above.

✔ Tip

■ If there is a fade to black or fade up from black or a dissolve between scenes, you can mark the start and end of the visual effect as a guide to the fades you should make in your background tracks.

To play and scrub to find a hit point:

1. To locate a hit point in the action, such as a door close, scrub the picture, or nudge in frame grid mode, until you have identified the leading edge of the moment of impact of the door against the door frame.

2. Once you have identified a hit point, you can use it immediately, or store it by placing a named marker at the point.

✔ Tip

■ Adding a distinctive first character to the Marker name, such as an asterisk, helps to quickly see the difference between a hit point and a scene boundary (**Figure 19.63**).

Laying out your effects tracks

Before actually editing sound effects, you'll need to create tracks to hold them. It's best to use mostly stereo backgrounds, and mostly mono effects for video sound tracks. You'll probably want at least two, and maybe three or four, stereo backgrounds for each location. You should checkerboard the sounds from location to location, for the same reasons we split tracks in dialog editing: the mixer needs to be able to adjust levels, EQ and other parameters at each distinct new sound or scene. Checkerboarding is the alternating of track usage, switching the edited sounds for each scene back and forth between two (or more) sets of tracks (**Figure 19.64**). You'll also need several mono and several stereo sound effects tracks. These tracks tend to be sparsely populated for most videos (**Figure 19.65**).

Figure 19.63 Marker text gets hidden, sometimes you can only see the first character of the marker name.

Figure 19.64 Checkerboard backgrounds to give the mixer easier control of the tracks. Marking the scene boundaries makes cutting backgrounds much easier.

Figure 19.65 Mono and stereo sound effects and background tracks for a typical Pro Tools LE sound effects session.

WORKING WITH SOUND EFFECTS

Placing, looping, and trimming backgrounds

Once you've marked up your session to identify where the scene boundaries lie, you can fairly quickly lay up your background tracks. If the sound files are long enough and the sounds have no internal problems, you can quickly lay them over the markers, and trim off the ends. The process is a bit more time consuming if the sounds are not long enough to cover the scenes.

A field recording typically has mic handling, voice slates, starts and stops, and other unwanted interruptions. Internal flaws in the sounds can take a while to fix or remove. It can be helpful for your future work to take care of these fixes early on, and then bounce the fixed regions to a single, new, cleaned up file.

Once the regions are trimmed, they need to be smoothed. The smoothing step is the most tedious part of the process. Many sound recordings contain low frequency sounds that can click if they cut off abruptly, so the region ends need to be trimmed out and faded. Other sound anomalies can often occur at edit points and result in annoying bumps or "ffftt" sounds. Like all sounds, each region need to be auditioned in its entirety, paying special attention to the ends. Problems can be corrected quickly.

To lay out and trim the background sounds:

1. Grab a background sound file and drag it to the first available BG track, placing it so that it overlaps the markers defining the in and out of the scene (**Figure 19.66**).

2. Click the marker identifying the in time of the scene to move the insertion point to the head of the scene (**Figure 19.67**).

3. Trim the head of the sound by pressing the A key in Command Focus mode.

4. Click the marker identifying the end time of the scene to move the insertion point to the tail of the scene.

5. Trim the tail of the sound by pressing the S key in Command Focus mode.

✔ Tips

■ Drag two or more sounds at once from the Audio Region list to lay them up together.

■ If you have already cut sounds that come up later in the track you want to place a new untrimmed sound into, you should drag the new sound to a work track and trim it there before dragging it up to the destination track.

Figure 19.66 Drag the background sound file into a free track so that the head of the file can be cut off at the scene marker.

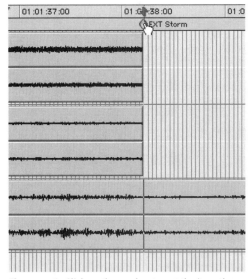

Figure 19.67 Click on the marker to put the insertion point at the scene boundary.

Figure 19.68 Zoom in and trim the background regions out by a frame before fading in or out. If you don't overlap the regions at the boundary, there will be a drop out at the scene change after you apply the fades.

Figure 19.69 The background regions all have a one-frame fade.

To smooth the edges of background sounds:

1. Set the edit mode to grid mode and the grid amount to 1 frame, or 10 milliseconds. This makes it easier to make a consistent small adjustment.

2. Set the tool to Smart Tool for faster operation.

3. Trim the ends of the regions out by a frame (about 40 ms) to give an overlap to fade with. Do this to all the background regions that start or stop at that picture cut (**Figure 19.68**).

4. Apply a one-frame fade into the head of each incoming sound and a one frame fade out to the tail of each outgoing sound (**Figure 19.69**).

✔ Tip

■ While you are pulling the background regions in and trimming them to length, you can nudge the insertion point over a frame and trim the sounds so they have an overlap built in from the start. Then they'll be ready to fade.

WORKING WITH SOUND EFFECTS

To loop background sounds to fill out the scene:

1. When you pull a sound in from the region list, it's likely to be too short to fill the entire scene. Place it so that it covers the start marker for the scene (**Figure 19.70**).

2. We will now loop the sound, so listen to the tail of the region and make sure that it ends while in the midst of the sound. If it doesn't, trim it shorter until it seems like it will be able to be looped.

3. Now find the earliest part of the sound that can be looped with the end of the sound. Select from this point to the end of the region.

4. Choose Edit > Duplicate to duplicate the region and repeat as many times as necessary to fill the scene with the background sound (**Figure 19.71**).

5. Listen to the sound as edited, paying attention to the loop points. If the sound jumps, it may be possible to change the edit points of the start and end to make a smoother loop. Undo and repeat steps 2, 3 and 4 until you get the optimal loop.

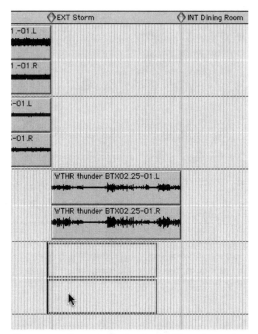

Figure 19.70 The region being dragged from the Region list is shorter than the scene.

Figure 19.71 Duplicate the loopable section to make the sound long enough for the scene.

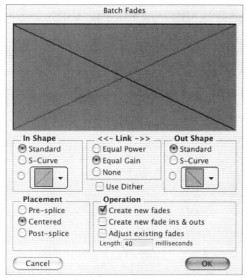

Figure 19.72 Apply a one-frame crossfade to all the edits in a looped region to remove clicks. Longer crossfades may be needed to smooth out a changing background.

6. If the loop point bumps, apply a cross-fade to all the loop points to smooth the joins. Select the entire assembly of regions and choose Edit > Fades > Create Fades.

   This will bring up the Batch Fades dialog (**Figure 19.72**).

7. Select the appropriate fade length and shape settings to smooth out your sound. Don't bother with dither. Then select Create new fades and click OK.

8. Your sound is now longer than the scene and you can trim it to length and smooth it out as described earlier.

✔ Tips

- One of the reasons it is useful to have more than one background track running is that backgrounds frequently need to be looped to get enough length, and different files looping with different lengths sound much less loopy together than alone.

- Backwards/Forwards loops can work with evolving backgrounds that haven't got any transient sounds within to tip off the audience, such as wind that is steadily getting faster.

To internally clean up sound effects:

1. To remove unwanted interruptions in a background sound file, play through it from the beginning, selecting the problem areas as you go. While playing, hold down the down arrow key. When you hear a problem, release it and start holding down the up arrow key. When you hear the problem area end, release the up arrow. Now the problem area is selected. Adjust the selection if necessary.

2. Press the delete key.

   The problem is deleted.

3. Hold down Control (Mac) or Start (Windows) and click on the next region of the sound file to snap it to the end of the first region.

4. Now play on in the sound file, as you did in step one, repeating the steps as necessary until you reach the end.

   You should now have a series of regions that may be able to be played together as a single file, or they may need to be used as separate regions, depending on how different the regions are to each other.

✔ Tips

■ It is likely that the edits you have made will need to be tweaked and crossfaded to make them work.

■ When you have finished, it can be a real time saver to either bounce the new assembly of regions to disk (which preserves automation), or choose Edit > Consolidate Selection to duplicate the regions into one file, which you must rename immediately.

■ Spending the time to clean up and organize your sound effects as they enter your library ensure that you'll never have to do the same job again with the same sounds.

A few methods for editing sound effects

Much of the creativity of sound for picture work is in selecting and assembling sound effects to bring an action or an object to life. Starting with a rich library of sounds is helpful, and recording the required sounds for each project you are involved with is the single best way to build this library. Selecting the perfect sound is an art we will leave to the reader to explore.

When pulling together sound effects for a sequence of shots, it's important to try to create a consistency of sound quality. Also, the recordings should be from an appropriate point of view that matches the picture.

Convincing sound effects must have tight sync to picture. If the sound seems to be in perfect sync with the picture, the viewer will be convinced it actually emanates from the picture. Sound effects must also be in sync with the production sound and with each other. When the production sound contains useful sounds, it is easy to sync your sound effects to the waveform of the guide track. Typically this is done to sweeten the PFX, and create a more consistent sound.

Tying sounds from disparate recordings together is a common problem for effects editors. You may have production sound effects, original effects recordings made in the field and library sounds of various sources. The sound qualities of these recordings are bound to vary, and steps must be taken to blend them together. This often involves long crossfades between sounds, as we've seen in dialog editing. Another useful technique is layering of different sonic textures to create a "fatter" sound, which helps tie everything together.

To add depth and variety to your sounds, cut a second or third layer of sound with more detail or complementary sound qualities.

Figure 19.73 Line up the sync mark with the hit point.

Figure 19.74 Trim the sound and apply fades if necessary to smooth the in and out of the sound.

To sync to picture:

1. If you've already marked up your session with the picture hit points, select one. Otherwise, locate a hit point.

2. Hold down Shift-Control (Mac) or Shift-Start (Windows) and drag a sound onto a sound effects track from the Audio Region list. The beginning of the sound will line up with the hit point. (For more information on the other sync modes, see *Chapter 11: Working with Regions.*)

3. Play through the sound to check sync against picture. If the sound is early or late, nudge it into place (**Figure 19.73**).

4. If the sound is too long, trim it to fit.

5. If the sound is too short, build it out by repeating sections as appropriate, or using the TCE trim mode to stretch to fit.

6. Apply fades as necessary (**Figure 19.74**).

✔ Tips

- The steps are simple and familiar. It is the choice of sound, including placement against picture that takes time and much trial and error leading to refinement.

- Sound effects track selection should follow principles similar to dialog tracks. Keep similar sounds on the same tracks, and split different sound qualities to other tracks. Try to keep it consistent to make life easier for the mixer.

WORKING WITH SOUND EFFECTS

To sync to guide track:

1. To find a hit point in the production sound, scrub the guide track and leave the insertion point at the hit point. Often the hit point is easy to spot by looking at the waveform.

2. Place a marker at the hit point.

3. Drag your sound from the Audio Regions list to the appropriate sound effects track.

4. Position the sound's hit point against the track's hit point by dragging the hit point to the marker (**Figure 19.75**).

Figure 19.75 Click on the hit point in the guide track and mark it for later, or just hold Control (Mac) or Start (Windows) and drag a sound to sync with the guide track.

Figure 19.76 Select the space between the hit point in the guide track and the beginning of the desired sound in the uncut sound effect. Delete the space and pull up the later sound to sync with the guide track.

Figure 19.77 Keep tightening up or pushing back the sound effect to sync with the guide track. When you are finished you'll have to fill any holes you made.

To maintain ongoing sync with picture or track:

1. Maintain ongoing sync between the sound effect and the picture or guide track by pulling up the sync of the sound repeatedly. Sync the beginning of the sound effect to the first hit point.

2. Play the sound effect and leave the insertion point where it goes out of sync. If the sound is too long, select through to the next wanted sound (**Figure 19.76**).

3. Press the B key in Command Focus mode to separate the region, or the delete key to clear out unwanted sound, then drag the later region into its new sync position. If you create a hole, you may need to fill.

4. Repeat steps two and three to maintain sync as long as desired (**Figure 19.77**).

To sweeten a sound by adding another simultaneous sound:

1. After cutting a layer of sound effects on a track, go back and add another layer of sound on another track.

2. Drag a "sweetener" from the Audio Regions list and line it up with the first sound.

3. Add contrasting sounds as additional layers, for example, add high cracks to low booms to create more powerful explosions. Line up the sounds so the sync is tight and the sounds blend into each other.

4. Alternatively, the second sound can add missing details to the first sound. In this case line the second sound up so the hit points work around the original sound (**Figure 19.78**).

Assembling sound effects from various sources

To blend sound effects from different sources there is a range of useful techniques:

◆ As in dialog editing, use long overlaps to blend sounds seamlessly.

◆ Hit hard with a new incoming sound, cutting in on a large transient, so that it overwhelms the outgoing sound, distracting the ear.

◆ Cut layers of sound effects, where possible, weaving tracks from the different material, so that none of the sounds ever fully disappears. All the layers don't have to be doing equal work at all times, but can come to the fore as appropriate.

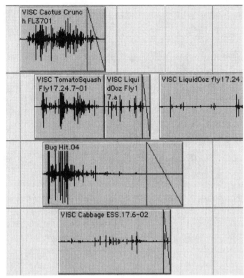

Figure 19.78 Some complementary sound effects layered to create a complex bug squashing sound.

Editing Music for Video

The principles of dialog and sound effects editing also apply when editing music.

Music often enters the project at an early stage, and is used during the picture editing to give a rhythm and tempo to a scene. So the picture is edited to the music.

Just as often, the music is brought to the picture later. In this case the sound editor may be asked to adapt the music to fit the rhythms and hit points of the picture. This is a challenging task, as it calls into play all the tools at the sound editor's disposal, as well as a musical sensibility. Most professional music editors are musicians themselves, which gives them a depth of understanding of musical forms. However, everyone has some musical sensibility and can learn to edit music in effective ways.

Mixing for Video

Film and video have always been mixed in elaborate facilities with expensive audio, projection, and interlock equipment. The field has been the exclusive domain of highly trained engineers and crafts people. Since Pro Tools has become the dominant tool in the industry for post production sound editing, a few forward thinking sound engineers have been adapting the powerful mixing tools in Pro Tools to the mix to picture field. The results have been resoundingly successful, with Larry Blake's work on Steven Soderberg's films at the high end, and innumerable smaller film and video projects mixed partly or entirely in Pro Tools.

The details of mixing for video and film are beyond the scope of this introductory chapter, so we will merely touch on some of the major topics of mixing for video here.

The stages of a mix

The three stages of a mix are

- ◆ Premixing
- ◆ Final Mixing
- ◆ Print Mastering and Versions

A premix is where you focus on getting the details of a particular category of sound just right, without regard to the rest of the tracks.

The dialog premix focuses on getting the dialog clear, clean, smooth and balanced. Reverb and other effects are added as needed to place the dialog into the proper setting. ADR is matched in to the production sound.

The effects pre-mix is where you balance the sounds against each other and against the dialog track. EQ, panning and effects are added. Foley is similarly premixed.

Once the premixes are complete, the final mix begins. In the final mix the dialog, ADR, sound effects, Foley, and music are balanced and final adjustments are made to the EQ and other effects. Since the music is making its first appearance, it often gets most of the attention in the final mix.

During the final mix, the sounds are kept separate by category (dialog, ADR, effects, Foley, and music), using *stems*, which ease mix fixes and later re-purposing of your mix. Stems are summed together and monitored during the final mix, but are recorded and stored separately as the ultimate master for the sound track. From the stems any number of different versions of the sound track can be produced.

The print master is a copy of the stems tailored for the particular release format required. Any number of different print masters can be made for different release requirements. Examples of different release formats with differing audio requirements include IMAX, 35mm film, 16mm film, DVD, VHS, broadcast television, broadband Internet, dial-up Internet, and even cell phone!

Simple mixes can be effectively done in an editing room with a mouse and keyboard. More complex mixes require video or film projection, surround sound monitoring, one or more Pro Tools TDM systems and control surface(s).

For more information on mixing in Pro Tools, *see Part V: Mixing Audio.*

MIXING FOR VIDEO

OPTIMIZING
PERFORMANCE

In Pro Tools LE, every processing task— from the number of tracks you can record and play back at one time to the performance of RTAS plug-ins—depends on CPU power. Thus, using the fastest computer possible is the best way to optimize your system's performance.

But computer speed is not the only factor. The amount of RAM in your computer makes a big difference, too, as does the way you allocate your system's CPU power. Allocating CPU resources judiciously will allow your system to handle audio processing tasks without interruption.

This chapter offers some useful tips for enhancing your computer's performance. I'll show you how to manage CPU power by assigning resources where they're needed. And I'll also provide suggestions for running plug-ins efficiently, and for maximizing limited hard drive space.

If your system's performance starts to lag, you may want to try some (or all) of these tricks. In other words, keep this chapter bookmarked.

Managing CPU Power

Managing CPU power in Pro Tools LE is somewhat of a balancing act. Because you're limited by the host computer's processing power, it's sometimes necessary to juggle CPU resources among different functions, and you may occasionally need to shuffle plug-ins around. The good news is that Pro Tools has many features that can help you manage CPU power quite efficiently.

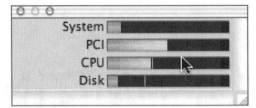

Figure 20.1 The System Usage window helps you track your system's overall performance.

The System Usage window

The System Usage window (**Figure 20.1**) lets you keep an eye on the overall performance of your Pro Tools system. It displays how much CPU power Pro Tools is using. Keep this window open so you can monitor CPU resource allocation and make adjustments, if necessary.

Figure 20.2 The Hardware Setup dialog box lets you set the amount of total CPU power dedicated to Pro Tools.

CPU usage limit

The Playback Engine dialog box lets you set the amount of total CPU power dedicated to Pro Tools. You can allocate up to 85 percent of your computer's CPU power to Pro Tools.

To set the CPU usage limit:

1. Choose Setups > Playback Engine.
   The Playback Engine dialog box appears.

2. From the CPU Usage Limit pop-up menu, select a percentage of CPU resources to allocate to host processing (**Figure 20.2**).

For more information on the Playback Engine dialog box, see *Chapter 2: Software Basics*.

Figure 20.3 The Hardware Setup dialog box also lets you set a hardware buffer size.

Hardware buffer size

The Hardware Setup dialog box also lets you set a hardware buffer size (**Figure 20.3**). This determines the size of audio data blocks that are sampled and processed at one time by the CPU. Larger buffer sizes let you use more plug-ins, but increase latency. Smaller buffer sizes decrease latency, but decrease the number of plug-ins that you can use.

During recording, use a smaller buffer size (128 or 256 samples) to keep latency to a minimum. During mixing, when latency is less relevant, increase the buffer size so you can use more tracks and plug-ins.

To set the hardware buffer size:

1. Choose Setups > Playback Engine.
   The Playback Engine dialog box appears.

2. From the H/W Buffer Size pop-up menu, select the audio buffer size (in samples) for host-processing tasks.

For more information on the Playback Engine dialog box, see *Chapter 2: Software Basics*.

DAE playback buffer size

The DAE Playback Buffer Size option controls the amount of RAM that's allocated as a holding area for data coming into your hard drive. The buffer size determines the length of time that occurs between when the computer receives a signal and the hard drive records it. The higher the buffer size, the longer the time span.

Smaller buffer sizes can increase system responsiveness, but may make recording and playback on slower hard drives less reliable. Larger buffer sizes can make hard drive performance more reliable, but may cause time lags to occur before recording or playback begins.

MANAGING CPU POWER

503

To set the DAE playback buffer size:

1. Choose Setups > Playback Engine.
   The Playback Engine dialog box appears.

2. From the DAE Playback Buffer pop-up menu, select a buffer size (**Figure 20.4**).

For more information on the DAE Playback Buffer, see *Chapter 2: Software Basics* or the *Pro Tools Reference Guide.*

Reducing levels of undo

Pro Tools 6 lets you undo up to 32 editing operations. These operations are stored in a temporary queue inside your computer's RAM. Reducing your system's levels of undo will free up RAM for other uses.

To reduce levels of undo:

1. Choose Setups > Preferences.

2. Click the Editing tab.

3. In the Level of Undo field, enter a number from 1 to 32 (**Figure 20.5**).

Figure 20.4 The DAE Playback Buffer dialog box.

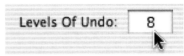

Figure 20.5 Reducing levels of undo can help free up RAM and enhance system performance.

Figure 20.6
Consolidating regions
is another way to save
CPU power.

Figure 20.7 Smoothing and thinning automation
removes unnecessary breakpoints and makes
automation playback less CPU-intensive.

Consolidating regions

Consolidating multiple separate regions into
a single region reduces the number of edits
on a track. This creates fewer edits for Pro
Tools to manage, which saves CPU power.

To consolidate regions:

1. Select the regions that you want to
   consolidate.

2. Choose Edit > Consolidate Selection
   (**Figure 20.6**).

Smoothing and thinning automation

Pro Tools writes automation data as a series
of events called breakpoints. Smoothing and
thinning automation removes superfluous
breakpoints and makes automation playback
less CPU-intensive.

To smooth and thin automation data automatically after an automation pass:

1. Choose Setups > Preferences.

2. Click the Automation tab.

3. Check the Smooth and Thin Data After
   Pass option (**Figure 20.7**).

For more information on thinning automation, see *Chapter 15: Automating a Mix*.

MANAGING CPU POWER

Making tracks inactive

In Pro Tools 6, you can make Audio, Auxiliary Input, and Master Fader tracks inactive. You can also make individual sends, inserts, plug-ins, bus paths, and track inputs and outputs inactive. When items are made inactive, they release their CPU resources (although their setting configurations are saved).

To make a track inactive:

1. Click the track name to select it.

2. Choose File > Make Selected Tracks Inactive.

    or

◆ Command-Control-click (Macintosh) or Control-Start-click (Windows) on the track type indicator in the Mix window (**Figure 20.8**).

    The track becomes inactive. Its name is italicized and the track's channel strip turns a monotone shade of gray (**Figure 20.9**).

For more information on making tracks and other items inactive, see *Chapter 4: Starting a New Session* and *Chapter 13: Mixing Basics*, or see the *Pro Tools Reference Guide*.

Figure 20.8 To make a track inactive: In the Mix window, Command-Control-click (Macintosh) or Control-Start-click (Windows) on the Track Type indicator.

Figure 20.9 The names of inactive tracks (and other items) become italicized and their channel strips become a monotone shade of gray.

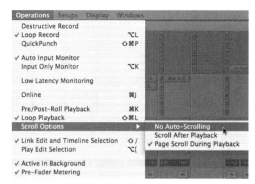

Figure 20.10 Disabling the Page Scroll During Playback setting can help free up processing power.

Disabling page scroll during playback

Disabling the Page Scroll During Playback setting frees your computer's CPU from having to constantly redraw the screen during playback. This can save a lot of processing power that may be better used elsewhere.

To disable page scroll during playback:

◆ Choose Operations > Scroll Options > No Auto-Scrolling (**Figure 20.10**).

Disabling moving faders

Although being able to display automated moving faders is a nice feature, it can monopolize a fair amount of CPU power, as Pro Tools constantly redraws the screen. Try disabling this setting to recover some of CPU power.

To disable moving faders:

1. Choose Setups > Preferences.

2. Click the Automation tab.

3. Uncheck the Faders Move During Playback option.

Disabling Sends View meters

Sends View meters can also monopolize CPU power. Try turning this option off to regain some processing power.

To disable Sends View meters:

1. Choose Setups > Preferences.

2. Click the Display tab.

3. Uncheck Show Meters in Sends View.
   or
   Choose Display > Sends View Shows > Assignments.

MANAGING CPU POWER

Using Plug-ins Efficiently

Real-time DSP plug-ins are undoubtedly one of the most useful features in Pro Tools, but they're also one of the most power-hungry. Here are a few ways to ease the power crunch.

Using AudioSuite plug-ins instead of RTAS plug-ins

RTAS plug-ins consume lots of CPU power because they apply effects in real time. If you're hitting the limit on the number of real-time plug-ins you can use, try using a non-real-time AudioSuite plug-in instead.

Most RTAS plug-ins also come in AudioSuite versions. You can save RTAS plug-in settings and then import them into the AudioSuite version. This lets you find effects in real-time, but apply them in non-real time. For example, if you have a favorite EQ setting created with an RTAS EQ plug-in, import the setting into the AudioSuite version and process your audio while Pro Tools is not playing. This conserves CPU power for other power-intensive RTAS plug-ins such as delays and reverbs.

To switch from an RTAS plug-in to its AudioSuite version:

1. Configure and save the desired RTAS plug-in settings.

2. Remove the RTAS plug-in from the track insert.

3. In the Edit window, select the same track using the Selector or Grabber.

4. Choose the desired AudioSuite plug-in from the AudioSuite menu (**Figure 20.11**).

5. Import the saved setting.

6. Click Process.

   The desired effect is applied to the track.

Figure 20.11 Using non-real-time AudioSuite plug-ins instead RTAS plug-ins is a good power-saving alternative.

USING PLUG-INS EFFICIENTLY

Using fewer CPU-intensive plug-ins

Some plug-ins are more CPU-intensive than others. Generally speaking, RTAS plug-ins consume the following amounts of CPU power:

◆ Delay effects (such as flange, slapback, chorus, and echo) and reverbs tend to consume large amounts of CPU power.

◆ Single-band EQs, gates, compressors, limiters, expanders, and dither require small amounts of CPU power.

Using effects loops

Effects loops let you apply the same effect to multiple channels of audio simultaneously. They work especially well for reverbs and other CPU-intensive plug-ins that are frequently used on more than one track. By making one plug-in available to multiple tracks simultaneously, an effects loop can help you get the most out of power-hungry plug-ins like delays and reverbs.

When you create an effects loop, audio is sent from audio tracks to an auxiliary input, where an inserted effect is applied. The effected signal is then returned to the main mix, where it's combined with the original signal. For more information on effects loops, see *Chapter 14: Adding Effects to a Mix.*

USING PLUG-INS EFFICIENTLY

Using Hard Drives Efficiently

When you're recording digital audio, hard drive space can evaporate faster than you can say "take two." Consider the following methods to get the most out of your hard drive.

The Disk Space window

Similar to the System Usage window, the Disk Space window (**Figure 20.12**) lets you gauge how much space remains on each disk. Keep an eye on this window: You don't want to run out of disk space in the middle of recording.

To view the Disk Space window:

◆ Choose Windows > Show Disk Space Window.

Using disk allocation

Pro Tools lets you record audio tracks simultaneously to different hard drives. Using disk allocation can help ease the workload on individual hard drives. For more information, see *Chapter 6: Getting Ready to Record*.

Figure 20.12 The Disk Space window lets you keep an eye on how much space remains on each disk.

USING HARD DRIVES EFFICIENTLY

Figure 20.13 Removing unused regions is a great way to keep your sessions organized.

Figure 20.14 The Clear Audio dialog box.

Removing unused regions and deleting audio files

Removing unused regions is a great way to keep your sessions organized. And if you're not using the underlying audio files, deleting them from your hard drive can help you recover valuable hard drive real estate.

To remove unused regions or delete audio files:

1. From the Audio Regions List pop-up menu, choose Select > Unused Regions (**Figure 20.13**).

   Currently unused regions are highlighted in the Audio Regions list.

2. Choose Clear Selected from the pop-up menu.

   The Clear Audio dialog box appears (**Figure 20.14**).

3. Click Remove to clear the unused region from the session.

   or

   Click Delete to erase the underlying audio file from the hard disk.

For more information on using the Audio Regions list, see *Chapter 10: Editing Basics*.

Compacting audio files

Another good way to recover hard drive space is to compact audio files. This process deletes unused portions of an audio file that aren't referenced by a region in the session. If an audio file is referenced in the session, compacting erases the entire audio file *except* the referenced portion.

Be careful when compacting audio—it permanently erases audio data from your disk. In fact, it's a good idea to wait until the session is over and the audio is mixed before you compact any files.

To compact audio files:

1. Select the regions you want to compact in the Audio Regions list.

2. Choose Compact Selected from the Audio Regions List pop-up menu.

   The Compact dialog box appears (**Figure 20.15**).

3. Enter the amount of padding in milliseconds.

4. Click Compact.

For more information on compacting audio files, see *Chapter 8: File Management Basics*.

Figure 20.15 The Compact dialog box.

Creating submixes

When you create a submix, you bounce multiple audio tracks down to a pre-mixed mono or stereo track. Once you've created a submix that you want to keep, you can delete the parent audio files and free up additional disk space.

For more information on submixes, see *Chapter 13: Mixing Basics.*

Using lower bit depths and sample rates

Audio file size is determined by the bit depth and sample rate at which it's recorded. Recording at 16-bit/44.1kHz (CD quality) consumes about 40 percent less hard drive space than recording at 24-bit/48kHz. And 16-bit/44.1kHz audio still sounds quite acceptable.

In fact, there's a reasonable argument that recording audio at 24-bit/48kHz and then converting it to 16-bit/44.1kHz actually makes your audio sound worse. The reason? Audio files are truncated in the conversion process and quantization distortion occurs. Adding dither to the converted file is supposed to mask this noise, but don't take anyone else's word for it. Let your ears decide.

For more information on hard drive space requirements, see *Chapter 1: Setting Up Your Pro Tools LE System.* For more information on bit depth and sample rate, see *Chapter 4: Starting a New Session.*

USING HARD DRIVES EFFICIENTLY

CONNECTING YOUR STUDIO

Your studio equipment needs will vary depending on which Pro Tools LE system you're running—Digi 002, Digi 002 Rack, Digi 001, Mbox, or Audiomedia III—and the type of audio source, external hardware, and monitor system you want to connect it to.

If you already have a studio full of great-sounding peripheral hardware, don't worry: You can connect all types of external hardware to Pro Tools LE systems. How many pieces of external hardware you can connect at one time, however, depends upon which Pro Tools LE system you're using.

Connecting Your Studio to the Digi 002, Digi 002 Rack, Digi 001, Mbox, or Audiomedia III

The minimum studio setup needed to record with Digi 002, Digi 002 Rack, Digi 001, or Mbox is a mic and mic cable (or instrument and instrument cable), and a pair of headphones. Audiomedia III is the only LE system that does not include an audio interface; thus, you'll need a separate mixer or mic preamp to send audio into Pro Tools.

Figures A.1–A.5 show basic studio setups for Digi 002, Digi 002 Rack, Digi 001, Mbox, and Audiomedia III systems, respectively.

Figure A.1 A basic Digi 002 studio setup.

With eight channels of analog I/O (including four balanced mic preamps with individual high pass filters) and 24-bit, 96kHz A/D input signal conversion, Digi 002 and Digi 002 Rack give you the best audio quality and most input versatility of the LE systems.

Digi 002 and Digi 002 Rack also give you eight channels of optical I/O, 2 channels of S/PDIF digital I/O, and two alternate analog inputs (RCA plugs) for connecting an external sound source, such as a CD player or tape deck.

Figure A.2 A basic Digi 002 Rack studio setup.

CONNECTING YOUR STUDIO

The Digi 001's eight channels of analog I/O, eight channels of optical I/O, and two channels of S/PDIF digital I/O give you lots of flexibility for connecting multiple audio sources, hardware effects, monitors, and two-track tape machines.

Mbox and Audiomedia III have far fewer I/O options than the Digi 002 and Digi 001. You can, however, connect external hardware using the two channels of analog I/O and two channels of S/PDIF digital I/O provided by each system. Mbox also provides two 1/4-inch line inserts, which let you add external hardware effects during recording.

Figure A.3 A basic Digi 001 studio setup.

Audio source

Laptop computer
(with internal CD burner)

Headphones

Figure A.4 A basic Mbox studio setup.

External hard drive

Audiomedia III PCI card
(inside computer)

Macintosh
or Windows
computer

Monitor

Mixer

Amp and speakers

Audio source
(mic, keyboard,
guitar, mixer, etc.)

Figure A.5 A basic Audiomedia III studio setup.

Making Connections

Connecting audio gear can be confusing: There are many types of connectors and cables, and some even have multiple names. You'll encounter many of the following audio connection terms as you set up your Pro Tools LE studio.

AES/EBU: AES/EBU (Audio Engineering Society/European Broadcast Union) is a professional transmission protocol. It specifies two channels of data through an XLR cable as the standard for digital audio.

Balanced Line: A balanced line is a cable with two conductors and a ground connection surrounded by a shield. Balanced lines are less prone to interference than unbalanced lines; thus, they help keep recordings free of noise.

BNC/Word Clock: BNC/word clock refers to the coaxial cable (resembling video cable) that connects devices that run in sync.

I/O: I/O (input/output) indicates the direction of an audio signal with respect to an audio device. Input is where audio signal enters the device; output is where audio signal leaves the device.

Line-Level: Line-level refers to a nominal pre-amplified signal between +4 dB (pro) and +10 dBV (consumer) that's used to connect certain studio hardware devices such as keyboards, preamps, and mixers. Microphones, speakers, and power amplifier outputs do not operate at line-level.

MIDI Cable: MIDI cables use a five-pin connection standard to transmit MIDI information between MIDI devices such as sequencers, controllers, sound modules, keyboards, and effects.

Optical Connectors: Optical connectors (sometimes called lightpipe) are fiber-optic cables that transmit digital audio signals. They were originally developed to link Alesis ADATs to compatible gear.

Phantom Power: Phantom power refers to a voltage provided by a mic pre-amp for powering a microphone. Most condenser mics require phantom power; dynamic mics usually don't. Phantom power can damage ribbon mics: Make sure the red phantom power light is off before connecting a ribbon mic.

RCA Plug: RCA plugs, which are also called phono plugs, are unbalanced connectors used in most home stereo and video equipment. The tip is audio signal and the surrounding shield is ground.

S/PDIF: S/PDIF (Sony/Phillips Digital Interface) is a transmission format for digital audio devices. It's commonly used in consumer devices. S/PDIF inputs and outputs generally have unbalanced RCA connectors.

TRS: TRS (tip-ring-sleeve) is a 1/4-inch stereo (two-channel) connector commonly found on headphones. The tip is left channel, the ring is right channel, and the sleeve is ground. Sometimes called phone plugs, TRS connectors can be used for balanced inputs and outputs.

TS: TS (tip-sleeve) is a 1/4-inch unbalanced mono connector. The tip is audio signal and the sleeve is ground. It's commonly used for electric guitars, keyboards, and other unbalanced line-level connections.

Unbalanced Line: An unbalanced line is a cable with one conductor and a surrounding shield at ground potential. Unbalanced lines are more prone to pick up interference. As a result, they can add noise to a recording.

XLR: XLR is a three-pin connection usually found on balanced microphone cables. Also called a Canon connector, it's used for analog and digital (AES/EBU standard) audio signals.

Connecting Audio Sources to Digi 002 and Digi 002 Rack

The Digi 002 and Digi 002 Rack's eight channels of balanced analog I/O (including four mic preamps) and 24-bit, 96kHz A/D input signal conversion make them useful for live recording, studio sessions, or any situation requiring multiple high-quality mic or instrument inputs.

The Digi 002 and Digi 002 Rack have identical audio input controls, monitor controls, and status indicators, located on the front panels of their respective hardware interfaces (**Figures A.6** and **A.7**), as follows:

Mic/Line/Inst input controls

Console/Channel View section with controls for pan, sends, and inserts

Fader section with solo and mute switches

Monitor controls

Status indicators

Transport controls

Figure A.6 The Digi 002's front panel includes Mic/Line/Inst Input controls, Monitor controls, and Status indicators (top section). The interface also includes transport controls, level faders with solo and mute buttons, and channel strip controls for sends, inserts, and pan (lower and middle sections).

Mic/Line/Inst Input Controls

◆ **Mic/Line/Instrument Selectors:** These selectors let you toggle inputs between microphone and line-level operating levels. (Note: Toggling to mic position without XLR mic cable attached may introduce low-level noise).

◆ **High Pass Filter Switch:** This switch enables a high pass filter (75Hz, 12db/ octave rolloff) on the input. This filter is useful for reducing low-end rumble from sources such as air-conditioning units.

◆ **Input Gain Control:** This knob lets you adjust input level of Mic/Line Inputs 1-4.

Monitor Controls

◆ **Monitor Level Control:** This knob controls the level of the Monitor Outputs. The Monitor Outputs mirror the Main Outputs (outputs 1-2).

◆ **Monitor Mute Switch:** This switch mutes the Monitor Outputs only. It has no effect on the Main Outputs or Headphone Output.

◆ **Mono Output Switch:** This switch combines output signals 1 and 2 in both the Monitor and Headphone outputs. This is useful for checking phase relationships of stereo material. The Mono Output switch has no effect on the Main Outputs.

◆ **Headphone Jack:** This jack accepts a standard 1/4-inch stereo headphone connector.

◆ **Headphone Level Control:** This knob lets you control headphone output level. Headphones let you monitor the Main Outputs (outputs 1 and 2).

Status Indicators

◆ **Session Sample Rate Indicators:** The Session Sample Rate LEDs indicate the sample rate of the current Pro Tools session.

◆ **Pro Tools Connection Status Indicator:** This LED, marked "1394," indicates that communication has been established between the hardware interface and Pro Tools LE software via Firewire.

Figure A.7 The Digi 002 Rack's front panel includes Mic/Line/Inst input controls, Monitor controls, and Status indicators.

The Digi 002 and Digi 002 Rack's respective back panels (**Figures A.8**) provide the following audio I/O features:

◆ **Mic Inputs 1-4:** These four balanced XLR mic preamps let you boost the input signals from microphones and other low-level audio sources requiring amplification.

◆ **Line/Instrument Inputs 1-4:** These four balanced 1/4-inch TRS inputs let you record line-level audio sources from line-level audio sources, such as keyboards, mixers, and preamps.

◆ **Phantom Power Switches:** These switches let you apply 48V phantom power to Mic/Line inputs 1-2 and inputs 3-4, respectively.

◆ **Analog Inputs 5-8:** Analog inputs 5-8 accept balanced or unbalanced 1/4-inch connectors, and are switchable between −10 dBV and +4 dBV line levels.

Figure A.8a The Digi 002 and Digi 002 Rack's back panels.

◆ **Operating Level switches for Inputs 5-8:** These switches let you switch the nominal line-level of channels 5-8 between −10 dBV and +4 dBV.

◆ **Footswitch Jack:** Lets you connect a standard footswitch to punch in audio or MIDI when recording

◆ **Alt Source Inputs:** This pair of unbalanced RCA-connectors let you input audio from alternate sources such as a tape deck or CD player.

◆ **Monitor Outputs:** These balanced 1/4-inch TRS jacks let you monitor stereo output. These outputs play output routed to analog outputs 1 and 2 in Pro Tools.

◆ **Main Analog Outputs 1-2:** These balanced 1/4-inch TRS jacks output audio routed to analog outputs 1 and 2 in Pro Tools. These outputs are useful for stereo mix-down to an external stereo device (such as a two-track analog tape machine). Output is balanced, +4 dBu line-level.

◆ **Analog Outputs 3-8:** These balanced 1/4-inch TRS jacks output audio routed to analog outputs 3-8. Outputs are balanced, +4 dBu line-level.

◆ **S/PDIF Digital I/O:** These unbalanced RCA jacks input and output 24-bit digital data at sample rates up to 96 kHz. (See the sidebar *Making Connections* for more information on S/PDIF.)

◆ **Optical I/O:** This pair of optical connectors input and output eight channels of ADAT-format or two channels of S/PDIF-format digital audio. ADAT format supports sample rates of 44.1 and 48 kHz, while S/PDIF format supports sample rates up to 96 kHz. Both Optical formats support 16-bit, 20-bit, and 24-bit data resolution. (Select the desired Optical format in the Hardware Setup dialog.) Optical I/O uses standard optical "lightpipe" cables.

◆ **MIDI I/O:** The Digi 002 and Digi 002 Rack's 5-pin MIDI connectors include one MIDI input and two MIDI outputs.

◆ **Footswitch Jack:** Lets you connect a standard footswitch to punch in audio or MIDI when recording

◆ **IEEE-1394 (FireWire) Ports:** These two ports let you connect to your computer and external storage devices via FireWire. The Link LED (located between the FireWire ports) indicates an active connection is established between the interface and the computer.

To connect an analog audio source to the Digi 002 or Digi 002 Rack:

◆ Connect either an XLR cable from a microphone or 1/4-inch TRS cable from a line-level device or instrument to any of the mic/line inputs 1-4 on the interface's back panel. Mic preamps are necessary for microphones and instruments using magnetic pickups (such as electric guitars and other string instruments) that generate lower-level audio signals requiring amplification.

or

◆ Connect a balanced or unbalanced 1/4-inch cable from a line-level audio source (such as a keyboard, preamp, or mixer) to any of the analog inputs 5-8 on the interface's back panel. If necessary, use the adjacent Operating Level switches for inputs 5-8 to switch between –10 dBV and +4 dBV line-level.

To connect a digital audio source to Digi 002 or Digi 002 Rack using optical cables:

1. Connect an optical cable from the optical output of the external digital device to the optical input on the Digi 002 or Digi 002 Rack's back panel.

2. Connect an optical cable from the optical output on the Digi 002 or Digi 002 Rack's back panel to the optical input of the external digital device.

To connect a digital audio source to the Digi 001 using S/PDIF cables:

◆ Connect a S/PDIF (RCA plug) cable from the S/PDIF output of the external digital device to the S/PDIF input on the Digi 002 or Digi 002 Rack's back panel.

◆ Each S/PDIF input and output carries a stereo signal. The following step is required only if you want to send a digital signal from Pro Tools to a digital device.

◆ Connect a S/PDIF (RCA plug) cable from the S/PDIF output on the Digi 002 or Digi 002 Rack's back panel to the S/PDIF input on the digital device.

For more information on connecting analog and digital hardware to Digi 002 and Digi 002 Rack, see *Getting Started with Digi 002* or *Getting Started with Digi 002 Rack*.

CONNECTING AUDIO SOURCES TO DIGI 002

Connecting Audio Sources to Digi 001

Digi 001 lets you record analog and digital audio signals directly into Pro Tools without a mixer. All you need is an audio source (such as a microphone, keyboard, or guitar) and the appropriate cables. The front panel of the Digi 001 I/O box (**Figure A.9**) has the following features:

◆ **Mic/Line Inputs 1 and 2:** These balanced XLR /1/4-inch TRS combo connectors let you input analog audio sources on channels 1-2.

◆ **−26 dB Pads:** This button lets you reduce input level by −26 dB on mic/line inputs 1 and 2.

◆ **Input Gain:** This knob lets you adjust the input level of mic/line inputs 1 and 2.

◆ **Phantom Power:** This button lets you apply 48V phantom power to mic/line inputs 1 and 2.

◆ **Phantom Power Indicator:** This red LED indicates that phantom power is on.

◆ **Monitor Mode:** This button lets you monitor analog inputs 3 and 4. This mode is useful for monitoring external audio devices (such as a CD player).

◆ **Monitor Volume:** This knob lets you adjust the monitor output level.

◆ **Power On Indicator:** This green LED indicates that the Digi 001 I/O box power is on. The computer must be on to power Digi 001.

◆ **Headphone Output:** This jack accepts a standard 1/4-inch headphone connector.

◆ **Headphone Gain:** This knob lets you adjust the headphone level.

Figure A.9 Front panel of the Digi 001 I/O box.

The back panel of the Digi 001 I/O box (**Figure A.10**) has the following features:

◆ **S/PDIF Digital I/O:** 24-bit digital input and output. (See the sidebar *Making Connections* for more information on S/PDIF.)

◆ **MIDI I/O:** Standard 5-pin MIDI input and output connectors.

◆ **Computer Connector:** This port connects the Digi 001 PCI card to the Digi 001 I/O box.

◆ **Footswitch Jack:** This jack lets you connect a standard footswitch to punch in audio or MIDI when recording.

◆ **Monitor Inputs (Analog Inputs 3-4):** These balanced 1/4-inch jacks let you input analog audio sources on channels 3 and 4. You can monitor a stereo audio source, such as a CD player, when used in Monitor mode.

◆ **Analog Inputs 3-8:** These balanced 1/4-inch jacks let you input analog audio sources on channels 3-8.

◆ **Monitor Outputs:** These balanced 1/4-inch TRS jacks let you monitor stereo output. These outputs play output routed to analog outputs 1 and 2.

◆ **Main Analog Outputs 1-2:** These balanced 1/4-inch TRS jacks output audio routed to analog outputs 1 and 2. These outputs are useful for stereo mix-down to an external stereo device (such as a two-track analog tape machine). Output is balanced, +4 dBu line-level.

◆ **Analog Outputs 3-8:** These 1/4-inch outputs let you play audio routed to analog outputs 3-8. Outputs are unbalanced, −10 dBu line-level.

Figure A.10 Back panel of the Digi 001 I/O box.

CONNECTING AUDIO SOURCES TO DIGI 001

The Digi 001 PCI card (**Figure A.11**) has the following I/O connections:

◆ **Optical Input:** Lets you input eight channels of ADAT-format digital audio or two channels of S/PDIF-format digital audio using optical cables.

◆ **Optical Output:** Lets you output eight channels of ADAT-format digital audio or two channels of S/PDIF-format digital audio, using optical cables.

Figure A.11 Digi 001 PCI card optical connections.

CONNECTING AUDIO SOURCES TO DIGI 001

To connect an analog audio source to the Digi 001:

◆ Connect either an XLR or 1/4-inch cable from a microphone or instrument to either mic/line input 1 or 2 on the front of the Digi 001 box (**Figure A.12**). (Both of these inputs contain microphone preamps, which let you boost the audio signal to the desired input level.)

or

◆ Connect a 1/4-inch cable from a line-level analog audio source, such as a keyboard preamp or mixer, to any of the six line-level analog inputs (3-8) found on the back of the Digi 001 box (**Figure A.13**).

Figure A.12 Mic/line inputs 1 and 2. Connect a microphone or instrument to this XLR and 1/4-inch combo connector.

Figure A.13 Analog inputs 3-8. Connect a line-level audio source (such as a keyboard, preamp, or mixer) to these balanced 1/4-inch inputs.

To connect a digital audio source to the Digi 001 using optical cables:

1. Connect an optical cable from the optical output of the digital device to the optical input of the Digi 001 PCI card.

2. Connect an optical cable from the optical output of the Digi 001 PCI card to the optical input of the digital device.

To connect a digital audio source to the Digi 001 using S/PDIF cables:

◆ Connect an S/PDIF (RCA plug) cable from the S/PDIF output of the digital device to the S/PDIF input on the back of the Digi 001 box (**Figure A.14**).

Each S/PDIF input and output carries a stereo signal. The following step is required only if you want to send a digital signal from Pro Tools to a digital device.

◆ Connect an S/PDIF (RCA plug) cable from the S/PDIF output on the back of the Digi 001 box to the S/PDIF input on the digital device.

For more information on connecting analog and digital hardware to Digi 001, see the *Getting Started with Digi 001* QuickStart guide.

S/PDIF digital I/O (RCA plug connectors)

Figure A.14 S/PDIF Digital I/O.

Figure A.15 Mbox front panel.

(diagram labels, top to bottom, left side:)
48V (phantom power) LED
Source selector
S/PDIF LED
Headphone gain
Headphone output (1/8-inch)

(diagram labels, right side:)
Peak LED
Gain controls
Peak LED
USB LED
Mix (ratio) control
Mono switch

(panel text: 48V, mic line inst, source, (1) gain, peak, mic line inst, source, (2) gain, peak, spdif, USB, Input, playback, mix, mono, headphone)

Connecting Audio Sources to Mbox

Like Digi 001, Mbox provides two combination mic/line preamps. These mic/line preamp inputs accept either XLR (3-pin) or 1/4-inch TRS cables. Mbox also provides two channels of S/PDIF digital I/O.

The front panel of the Mbox (**Figure A.15**) has the following features:

◆ **48V LED:** When lit, the 48V LED indicates that 48V phantom power is available at the mic/line input.

◆ **Source Selector:** The Source selector lets you switch between three input level options for the Mbox's mic/line inputs: Mic (microphone), Line, and Inst (Instrument).

◆ **Gain Controls:** Gain controls let you adjust the input level of the mic/line inputs.

◆ **Peak LEDs:** Peak LEDs light up just below analog clipping levels. This warns you that the input signal may be approaching clipping.

◆ **USB LED:** The USB LED indicates that the USB port is active, and audio can pass in or out of the system.

◆ **S/PDIF LED:** The S/PDIF LED indicates that channels 1 and 2 are set to receive digital input (rather than analog).

◆ **Mix (Ratio) Control:** The Mix (ratio) control lets you monitor an adjustable blend of live input signal (with zero latency), and audio playback from disk. To hear the input signal only, turn the Mix knob hard left to Input. To hear Pro Tools output only, turn the knob hard right to Playback.

◆ **Mono Switch:** The Mono switch lets you hear live input signals in mono. You can use this switch to check for stereo phase cancellations. (Typically, out-of-phase tracks sound hollow and lacking in low frequencies.)

◆ **Headphone Gain:** Headphone gain controls the output level of the headphones on both the front and back panels.

◆ **Headphone Output (front panel):** The front panel headphone output is a 1/8-inch stereo mini connector. (Inserting a 1/4-inch TRS connector into the rear panel headphone disables the 1/8-inch headphone output on the front panel.)

The back panel of the Mbox (**Figure A.16**) has the following features:

◆ **Headphone Output (back panel):** The back panel headphone output features a 1/4-inch TRS connector.

◆ **48V Switch:** The 48V switch activates phantom power for use by microphones (especially condenser mics).

◆ **USB Port:** The USB port lets you connect Mbox to any compatible USB-enabled computer.

◆ **S/PDIF Digital I/O:** S/PDIF digital inputs and outputs use RCA plugs.

◆ **Line Outputs:** Line outputs are balanced TRS outputs, which you can connect to a mixer or stereo system to monitor mixes.

Figure A.16 Mbox back panel.

◆ **Source 1 and 2:** Combination mic/line (balanced/unbalanced) audio inputs. Accepts XLR (3-pin) or 1/4-inch TRS connections.

◆ **Inserts 1 and 2:** Inserts 1 and 2 are line inserts, which let you insert an effect into the audio input path of Source 1 and 2 inputs. The inserted effect is added to the analog audio input signal before it's converted into digital audio. These inserts are useful for adding analog effects processors (such as equalizers and compressors) to a track.

To connect an analog audio source to the Mbox:

◆ Connect an XLR or 1/4-inch cable to the Source 1 or Source 2 input on the Mbox's back panel.

◆ Using the Source button on the Mbox's front panel, select the input source type (mic, line, or instrument).

To connect a digital audio source to the Mbox:

1. Connect a S/PDIF cable (75-ohm coaxial cable with RCA plugs) from the digital audio source's S/PDIF output to the S/PDIF input on the Mbox's back panel.

2. Connect another S/PDIF cable from the Mbox's S/PDIF output to the digital audio source's S/PDIF input.

Connecting Audio Sources to Audiomedia III

Unlike the Digi 001 and Mbox, the Audiomedia III card (**Figure A.17**) doesn't have built-in mic preamps. Thus, you'll need an external mixer or mic preamp to boost the signal coming from the audio source into the Audiomedia III card. Or, you can send audio from your home stereo into the Audiomedia III card.

To connect an analog audio source to the Audiomedia III:

1. Plug your analog audio source into a mixer or mic preamp using the appropriate mic or instrument cables.

2. Connect the main stereo outputs of your mixer (or mic preamp) to the inputs of the Audiomedia III card.

   If your mixer's outputs are 1/4-inch jacks, you'll need a 1/4-inch-to-RCA adapter to connect to the Audiomedia III.

To connect a digital audio source to the Audiomedia III:

1. Connect a S/PDIF (RCA plug) cable from the S/PDIF output of your digital device (such as a DAT machine) to the S/PDIF input on the Audiomedia III card.

   Each S/PDIF input and output carries a stereo signal. The following step is required only if you want to send a digital signal from Pro Tools to a digital device.

2. Connect a S/PDIF (RCA plug) cable from the S/PDIF outputs on the Audiomedia III card to the S/PDIF inputs on your digital device.

S/PDIF digital I/O
Analog inputs
Analog outputs

Figure A.17 Audiomedia III PCI card connections.

Connecting Audio Monitors

If you're using Digi 002, Digi 002 Rack, or Digi 001, the easiest way to monitor audio is with headphones plugged into the jack on the front of their respective interfaces (**Figure A.18**). Mbox users have two headphone options: a 1/8-inch stereo mini connector on the front panel and a 1/4-inch TRS connector on the rear panel. Audiomedia III card users will need to plug headphones into a mixer or stereo system.

While monitoring over headphones is useful for hearing accurate stereo mixes, whenever possible, it's best to monitor your audio through a set of speakers as well. Speakers give you a more accurate representation of how most listeners will experience your mixes—In a 3-dimensional space, over an average home stereo system.

Caution: Listening to headphones at even moderate volumes for prolonged periods can cause hearing damage and permanent ringing in the ears, or tinnitus. *Always* make sure your headphone volume is turned down before listening, and turn the volume up slowly and carefully!

Figure A.18 Headphone input on front panel of Digi 001 I/O box.

To connect monitor speakers to the Digi 002 or Digi 002 Rack:

1. Connect 1/4-inch TRS cables to the left and right monitor outputs on the back of the Digi 002 or Digi 002 Rack.

2. Connect the 1/4-inch TRS cables to left and right inputs on your power amp, mixer, self-powered speakers, or home stereo.

   Most home stereo systems use RCA connectors and will require an adapter.

To connect monitor speakers to the Digi 001:

1. Connect 1/4-inch cables to the left and right monitor outputs on the back of the Digi 001 box (**Figure A.19**).

2. Connect the 1/4-inch cables to left and right inputs on your power amp, mixer, self-powered speakers, or home stereo.

   Most home stereo systems use RCA connectors and will require an adapter.

Figure A.19 Monitor outputs on rear panel of Digi 001 I/O box.

CONNECTING AUDIO MONITORS

To connect monitor speakers to the Mbox:

1. Connect 1/4-inch cables to the left and right line outputs on the back panel of the Mbox.

2. Connect the 1/4-inch cables to the corresponding left and right inputs on your power amp, mixer, self-powered speakers or home stereo.

Most home stereo systems use RCA connectors and will require an adapter.

To connect monitor speakers to the Audiomedia III:

1. Connect RCA cables to the left and right outputs on the Audiomedia III card.

2. Connect the RCA cables to the corresponding left and right inputs on your power amp, mixer, self-powered speakers, or home stereo.

✔ Tip

■ During the recording and mixing process, it's useful to listen over as many different sets of speakers as possible. Most studios have small, medium-size and large monitor speakers (some even have ultra-tiny and extra-large speakers), which can help you gain perspective on the frequency balance and overall sound quality of your mixes.

CONNECTING AUDIO MONITORS

Connecting MIDI Devices

The Digi 002 and Digi 001 system's built-in MIDI ports make it easy to connect MIDI devices (such as MIDI keyboard controllers, MIDI instruments, and sound modules). A MIDI driver for these ports is installed with Pro Tools LE and recognized by Windows Multimedia (Windows) and Audio MIDI Setup (Macintosh).

Audiomedia III and Mbox users will need a third-party MIDI interface to record MIDI into Pro Tools LE.

For information on recording and editing MIDI in Pro Tools 6 LE, see *Chapter 17: Recording MIDI* and *Chapter 18: Editing MIDI.*

To connect a MIDI device to the Digi 002 or Digi 002 Rack:

1. Connect a standard five-pin MIDI cable from the MIDI Out port on your MIDI device to the MIDI In port on the Digi 002 or Digi 002 Rack's back panel.

2. Connect a standard five-pin MIDI cable from either of the two MIDI Out ports on the Digi 002 or Digi 002 Rack's back panel to the MIDI In port on your MIDI device.

3. Connect the audio outputs of your device to an available audio input on the Digi 002 or Digi 002 Rack's back panel.

To connect a MIDI device to the Digi 001:

1. Connect a standard five-pin MIDI cable from the MIDI output on your MIDI device to the MIDI input on the back of the Digi 001 box (**Figure A.20**).

2. Connect a standard five-pin MIDI cable from the MIDI output on the Digi 001 box to the MIDI input on your MIDI device.

Figure A.20 5-pin MIDI I/O ports on rear panel of Digi 001 I/O box.

Connecting External Hardware Effects

Pro Tools lets you route both analog and digital audio signals to external hardware effects (such as equalizers, compressors, reverbs, and delays). Using the Digi 002, Digi 002 Rack, or Digi 001's 1/4-inch analog inputs and outputs, or S/PDIF digital inputs and outputs, you can run several external hardware effects with your system.

Mbox has two 1/4-inch TRS inserts, which let you place effects into the path of analog audio entering Source 1 and Source 2 mic/line inputs. The inserted effect is added to the incoming signal before it's converted into digital audio. These inserts are useful for adding effects such as equalizers and compressors to tracks during recording.

Connecting external analog hardware effects

To connect an external analog hardware effect to the Digi 002 or Digi 002 Rack:

1. Connect a mono (single) or stereo (pair) output from analog outputs 5-8 to the corresponding inputs of the hardware effect.

2. Connect the outputs of the hardware effect to the corresponding analog inputs on the Digi 002 or Digi 002 Rack's back panel.

To connect an external analog hardware effect to the Digi 001:

1. Connect a mono (single) or stereo (pair) output from analog outputs 3-8 to the corresponding inputs of the hardware effect.

2. Connect the outputs of the hardware effect to the corresponding analog inputs on the Digi 001 box.

To insert an external hardware effect on the Mbox's input signal path:

1. You'll need a TRS Y cable (a TRS connector that splits into two unbalanced connectors).

2. Connect the unbalanced connector that corresponds to Tip to the input port of the hardware device.

3. Connect the unbalanced connector that corresponds to Ring to the output port of the hardware device.

4. Insert the TRS connector into the desired insert port on the Mbox.

Connecting external digital hardware effects

To connect an external digital hardware effect to the Digi 002 or Digi 002 Rack:

◆ Connect the S/PDIF (RCA plug) inputs and outputs on the Digi 002 or Digi 002 Rack's back panel to the corresponding inputs and outputs of the external digital hardware effect.

or

◆ If the hardware effect has optical inputs, connect the optical inputs and outputs on the Digi 002 or Digi 002 Rack's back panel to the corresponding optical inputs and outputs of the external digital hardware effect.

To connect an external digital hardware effect to the Digi 001:

◆ Connect the S/PDIF (RCA plug) inputs and outputs on the back of the Digi 001 box to the corresponding inputs and outputs of the digital hardware effect.

or

◆ If the hardware effect has optical inputs, connect the optical inputs and outputs of the Digi 001 PCI card to the corresponding optical inputs and outputs of the digital hardware effect.

To set up an effects loop between an external digital hardware effect and Digi 002, Digi 002 Rack, or Digi 001:

1. Connect the digital inputs and outputs of the external digital hardware effect to the appropriate connectors (S/PDIF RCA connectors or Optical ports) of the Digi 002, Digi 002 Rack, or Digi 001.

2. In Pro Tools, choose Setups > Hardware Setup.

3. Under Digital Input, select one of the following options:

   ▲ If the external effects device is connected to the S/PDIF RCA jacks, select "RCA = S/PDIF."

   ▲ If the external effects device is a S/PDIF device connected to the Optical ports, select "Optical = S/PDIF."

   ▲ If the external effects device is an ADAT Optical device, select "Optical = ADAT."

4. Choose Internal from the Clock Source pop-up menu.

5. Click OK.

For more information on setting up effects loops, see Chapter 14: Adding Effects to a Mix.

✔ Tips

■ You can send signals to external hardware effects using the S/PDIF digital I/Os and analog I/Os on both the Audiomedia III and Mbox.

■ The I/O Setup dialog box lets you label channel inputs and outputs. This can help you keep track of sends and inserts during a session. For more information on I/O Setup, see *Chapter 4: Starting a New Session.*

■ Most external hardware effects have 1/4-inch connectors. Higher-end units generally include both XLR ands 1/4-inch connectors.

CONNECTING EXTERNAL HARDWARE EFFECTS

SETTING
PREFERENCES

Figure B.1 The Preferences dialog box's seven tabbed windows.

Figure B.2 Choose Setups > Preferences.

The Preferences Dialog Box

The Preferences dialog box contains seven tabbed windows (**Figure B.1**), which let you specify settings for many Pro Tools session parameters.

To open the Preferences dialog box:

◆ Choose Setups > Preferences (**Figure B.2**).

The Preferences dialog box opens.

Display Preferences

The settings under the Display tab (**Figure B.3**) let you customize many Pro Tools viewing features. Preferences include:

Recompute Invalid Overviews: This setting prompts Pro Tools to recreate overviews of missing or corrupted waveform display data.

Draw Waveforms Rectified: This setting shows waveforms summed together in a single positive direction starting at the bottom of the track. This lets you see more waveform detail in reduced track height views. It's especially useful when you're editing volume-level automation data.

Draw Grids in Edit Window: This setting displays grid lines in the Edit window. To define a grid size, enter a value in the Edit window's Grid Value field.

Mix Window Follows Bank Selection: This setting automatically updates the view of banks in the Mix window whenever you switch banks on an external MIDI controller.

Edit Window Follows Bank Selection: This setting automatically updates the view of banks in the Edit window whenever you switch banks on an external MIDI controller.

Figure B.3 Display preferences.

Show Meters in Sends View: This setting displays the level meters of individual send controls in the Sends view. The Show Meters preference can tax CPU power, so disable it if you have a slower computer.

Edit Window Default Length: This lets you set a default recording length for the Edit window in hours, minutes, seconds, and frames. The maximum session length is 13 hours.

Zoom Toggle Track Height: The Zoom Toggle Track Height preference lets you set a default track height when using Control-Minus to toggle audio tracks between Waveform and Volume view, or to toggle MIDI tracks between Notes and Regions view.

Edit Window Color Coding: This setting lets you determine how colors are assigned to waveform displays in the Edit window. Options include:

♦ **None:** Turns off color assignments to waveforms.

♦ **Tracks and MIDI Channels:** Assigns colors to waveforms according to the track number and MIDI channel assignment.

♦ **Tracks and MIDI Devices:** Assigns colors to waveforms according to the track number and MIDI device type.

♦ **Groups:** Assigns colors to waveforms according to group ID.

Peak Hold Options: These options determine how long the peak indicators on the track meters stay lit after a peak is detected. Options include:

♦ **3-Second Peak Hold:** Displays last peak level for three seconds.

♦ **Infinite Peak Hold:** Displays last peak level until you clear it by clicking the level indicator.

♦ **No Peak Hold:** No hold; meter moves freely.

DISPLAY PREFERENCES

Operation Preferences

The settings under the Operation tab (**Figure B.4**) determine the function of various Pro Tools recording and playback features. Preferences include:

Timeline Insertion Follows Playback: When this setting is checked, the cursor automatically updates to the track location where playback stops.

Edit Insertion Follows Scrub/Shuttle: When this setting is checked, the cursor automatically updates to the track location where scrubbing stops.

Support Background Record Applications: This setting lets you run other audio recording applications in the background concurrently with Pro Tools.

Sends Default to "–INF": This sets the initial fader level of newly created sends to infinity (no audible signal level).

Audio During Fast Forward/Rewind: This setting makes audio audible during fast-forward and rewind.

Latch Record-Enable Buttons: This setting lets you record-enable multiple tracks simultaneously.

Latch Solo Buttons: This setting lets you solo multiple tracks simultaneously.

Link Mix and Edit Group Enables: This setting links the enabling and disabling of Mix and Edit groups. For example, enabling Group A in the Edit window automatically enables Group A in the Mix window.

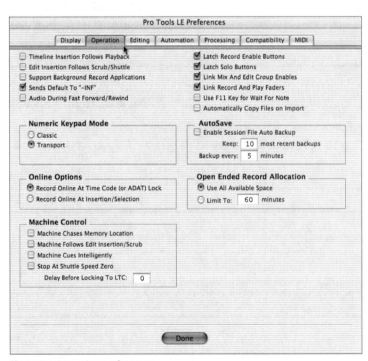

Figure B.4 Operation preferences.

Use F11 Key for Wait for Note: This setting lets you use the F11 key to put MIDI recording in Wait for Note mode.

Numeric Keypad Mode: This setting lets you determine the function of the numeric keypad (options include Classic and Transport). For more information on the Numeric Keypad mode, see the *Pro Tools Reference Guide*.

AutoSave: This setting lets you enable the AutoSave feature, and select the frequency and quantity of saves.

Online Options: This setting lets you determine how recording is initiated when Pro Tools is set to receive time code from external source. Options include:

- **Record Online at Time Code (or ADAT) Lock:** Online recording begins as soon as Pro Tools receives and locks to time code or ADAT.

- **Record Online at Insertion/Selection:** Online recording begins at a chosen insertion point in a track. Recording continues until Pro Tools stops receiving time code. If you make a selection, Pro Tools records online for the length of the selection.

Open-Ended Record Allocation: This setting lets you determine how much hard drive space is dedicated for recording. Options include:

- **Use All Available Space:** Allocates the hard drive's entire available space. This can slow down performance on some hard drives.

- **Limit To:** Sets the maximum allowable recording duration (in minutes). This can improve performance on some hard drives.

Machine Control: This setting lets you determine how a connected transport responds to Pro Tools. Options include:

- **Machine Chases Memory Location:** The connected transport chases to a selected memory location.

- **Machine Follows Edit Insertion/Scrub:** The connected transport follows to a new insertion point, or chases to a location where scrubbing begins.

- **Machine Cues Intelligently:** When you move a new cue point, the connected transport follows to the new cue point.

Remote Mode: This setting lets you set an offset in frames to compensate for both punch-in and punch-out timing delays.

Auto Regions Fade In/Out: This lets you set a default length for automatic fade-ins and fade-outs on region boundaries. Values range from 0 to 10. A zero (default) value means that no automatic region fading will occur.

Calibration Reference Level: This lets you set a default calibration reference level in dB when Pro Tools is in Calibration mode.

OPERATION PREFERENCES

Editing Preferences

The settings under the Editing tab (**Figure B.5**) determine the function of various Pro Tools editing features. Preferences include:

Track Selection Follows Region List Selection: When this preference is chosen, selecting a region in the Audio Regions list also selects it in its corresponding track.

Region List Selection Follows Track Selection: When this preference is chosen, selecting a region in a track also selects it in the Audio Regions list.

Auto-Name Separated Regions: This setting automatically names newly separated regions by appending a number to each region's name.

Auto-Name Memory Locations When Playing: When this preference is selected, Pro Tools gives default names to new memory locations based on their time locations.

Recall Original Track Selections: When this preference is selected, memory locations that recall a selection also recall the track in which the selection was made.

Crossfade Preview Pre-Roll: This setting lets you specify the amount of pre-roll added when you audition crossfades in the Fades dialog box.

Crossfade Preview Post-Roll: This setting lets you specify the amount of post-roll added when you audition crossfades in the Fades dialog box.

Figure B.5 Editing preferences.

Default Fade Settings:

- **Fade In:** Selects the default envelope shape for fade-ins.

- **Crossfade:** Selects the default envelope shape for crossfades.

- **Fade Out:** Selects the default envelope shape for fade-outs.

Conversion Quality: This setting lets you select the sample rate conversion quality for several Pro Tools conversion features including converting, importing, bouncing, and saving audio.

ìMatching Start Time" Takes List: Command-clicking (Macintosh) or Control-clicking (Windows) in a track displays a list of regions whose start times match the current cursor location. The following preferences determine which takes appear in this list:

- **Take Region Name(s) That Match Track Names:** Only regions that share names with the track/playlist appear in the Takes List pop-up menu.

- **Take Region Lengths That Match:** Only regions that match the length of the current selection appear in the Takes List pop-up menu.

- **"Separate Region" Operates On All Related Takes:** Editing a region with the Separate Region command affects all other related takes with the same user time stamp. This helps you compare different sections from a group of related takes.

QuickPunch Crossfade Length: This setting lets you specify a default length for crossfades created during QuickPunch recording. Crossfades occur before punch-in and after punch-out.

Levels of Undo: This setting lets you choose the maximum number of actions (up to 16) that can be undone with the multiple undo feature.

EDITING PREFERENCES

Automation Preferences

The settings under the Automation tab (**Figure B.6**) determine the function of various Pro Tools automation features. Preferences include:

Faders Move During Playback: When this preference is selected, automated faders will move on screen.

Smooth and Thin Data After Pass: When this preference is selected, automation is smoothed and thinned by the amount specified by the Degree of Thinning option.

Mutes Follow Groups: When this preference is selected, muting a track that belongs to a Mix group mutes all the other members of the group.

Solos Follow Groups: When this preference is selected, soloing a track that belongs to a Mix group solos all the other members of the group.

Send Mutes Follow Groups: When this preference is selected, muting a Send that belongs to a group mutes all the other members of the group.

Send Levels Follow Groups: When this preference is selected, adjusting the level of a Send that belongs to a group adjusts all the other members of the group.

LFEs Follow Groups: When this preference is selected, adjusting or editing an LFE (low-frequency effect channel) control that belongs to a group adjusts all the other members of the group.

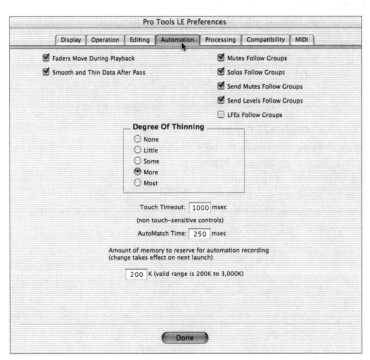

Figure B.6 Automation preferences.

Degree of Thinning: This setting lets you specify how much automation data thinning is applied when automation is recorded.

Touch Timeout: This setting lets you specify how quickly automation recording stops or times out after you stop moving a MIDI controller in Touch mode.

AutoMatch Time: This setting lets you specify how quickly a fader or other control returns to its previously automated level after automation recording stops.

Amount of Memory for Automation Recording: This setting lets you specify an amount of memory to reserve for recording automation. If you have dense automation data or a large number of automated tracks, increase this amount. You must restart Pro Tools for this setting to take effect.

Processing Preferences

The settings under the Processing tab (**Figure B.7**) determine the function of many Pro Tools DSP (digital signal processing) features. Preferences include:

AudioSuite Dither: Dither is randomized noise added to a digital audio signal to help reduce distortion. For more information on dither, see *Chapter 14: Adding Effects to a Mix*. Pro Tools lets you customize the following AudioSuite dither functions:

◆ **Use AudioSuite Dither:** When this preference is selected, dither is applied to specific audio processing tasks.

◆ **Dither Plug-In:** This setting lets you specify the plug-in used for dither processing when the Use AudioSuite Dither option is selected.

◆ **Edit Settings:** This setting lets you apply either normal or noise-shaped dither to Digidesign's dither plug-in.

◆ **Bit Depth:** This setting lets you select a bit depth for dithered audio.

AudioSuite Buffer Size: This setting lets you set a memory buffer size for audio processing and for previewing AudioSuite plug-ins. Smaller buffers are recommended for previewing plug-ins; larger buffers for processing files.

Figure B.7 Processing preferences.

Compatibility Preferences

The settings under the Compatibility tab (**Figure B.8**) determine how Pro Tools handles various imported file formats. Preferences include:

Convert All Imported .WAV Files to AES31/BroadcastWave: This lets you make imported .WAV files compliant with AES31/EBU broadcast standards.

Figure B.8 Compatibility preferences.

MIDI Preferences

The settings under the MIDI tab (**Figure B.9**) include:

Play MIDI Notes When Editing: When this preference is selected, MIDI notes will sound when you insert them with the Pencil tool or drag them with the Grabber tool into a MIDI track.

Default Note On Velocity: This setting lets you specify the default Note On Velocity for MIDI notes inserted in the Edit window and MIDI Event list.

Pencil Tool Resolution: This setting lets you specify a default resolution for MIDI controller data created with the Pencil tool. Lower resolutions help avoid creating unnecessarily dense controller data. The value range is 1 to 100 milliseconds.

Global MIDI Playback Offset: This setting lets you specify an offset in samples to compensate for MIDI latency.

MIDI Note Display: This setting determines how pitches for MIDI notes are displayed in the Edit window and the MIDI Event list.

Default Thru Instrument: When this preference is selected, Pro Tools routes all incoming MIDI data to a Default Thru Instrument. This saves you the trouble of creating a MIDI track to hear a particular MIDI device and channel.

Figure B.9 MIDI preferences.

GLOSSARY

A

AES/EBU: Audio Engineering Society/ European Broadcast Union. A professional transmission protocol that specifies two channels of data through an XLR cable as the standard for digital audio.

Audio region: A visual representation of a Pro Tools audio file. Regions can be whole audio files or segments of audio files, and are usually displayed during editing as audio waveforms.

Audio Regions list: A list, found in the Edit window, that lets you manage the flow of audio regions in and out of a Pro Tools session. When you record, import, or create a new audio region, it appears in the Audio Regions list.

Audio signal flow: The path that audio takes through a mixer. In Pro Tools, this path is generally fixed, moving from top to bottom through audio track, auxiliary input, and master fader channel strips.

Audio track: In Pro Tools, a channel that holds and controls recorded or imported audio files.

AudioSuite plug-ins: Digidesign's non-real-time plug-ins. They process audio directly to disk, creating a new audio file that includes the effected signal.

Automation pass: In Pro Tools, automation recorded during the playback of a session.

Automation playlist: In Pro Tools, a snapshot of a track's automation parameters (such as volume, mute, and pan). Pro Tools creates a separate automation playlist for each parameter that you write.

Auxiliary input: In Pro Tools, an input that lets you add mono or stereo effects to bused signals. It's also useful for submixes and other audio-routing tasks.

B

Balanced line: A cable with two conductors and a ground connection surrounded by a shield. Balanced lines are less prone to interference than unbalanced lines; thus, they help keep recordings free of noise.

Binaural auditory system: The two-ear auditory system that lets us locate sounds in space.

Bit depth: The number of bits used to describe each individual sample taken during recording. For example, if you're recording at 24-bit resolution and a sample rate of 44.1kHz, there will be 44,100 individual 24-bit representations of the sound recorded each second. Also known as bit resolution.

BNC/word clock: The coaxial cable (resembling video cable) that connects devices that run in sync.

Breakpoints: Breakpoints indicate changes in the amount of an automation parameter. They're displayed along a graphic curve, which you can grab and move when performing edits.

Bus: An audio bus carries audio signals from different tracks and delivers them to a single destination track, much as a city bus picks up people from different stops and delivers them to a bus depot. In Pro Tools, buses are used mainly to send audio signals from one or more audio tracks to a single auxiliary input, where a DSP effect is added.

C

Cardioid mic: A heart-shaped mic pick-up pattern that accepts sounds from the front (on-axis), and attenuates signals that are 180 degrees off-axis.

Channel: The physical inputs and outputs of the Pro Tools system.

Channel strip: Each track in a Pro Tools session is displayed in the Mix window as a channel strip. Channel strips let you control the mix functions of a track, such as level, mute, pan, and sends. There are four types of channel strips: audio tracks, auxiliary inputs, master faders, and MIDI tracks.

Click track: An absolute time reference that can help you produce takes with a steadier feel. It can also help you properly align tracks when you're overdubbing, editing, and mixing.

Clipping: Digital distortion that occurs when you record a signal at levels that overload your system's inputs. When a signal clips, it distorts, and the peaks of its waveform are literally clipped off.

Condenser mic: More sensitive, accurate, and expensive than dynamic mics, condenser mics are used frequently in recording studios.

Conductor ruler: In Pro Tools, a ruler that indicates important track locations within a session.

Controller: Any device that's used to send MIDI without necessarily making a sound on its own.

Crossfade: An overlapping fade-out and fade-in placed between two adjoining audio regions. Crossfades let you smooth transitions between separate audio regions on a track.

D

Delay time: The length of time it takes for a sound to return to its source. The delay time tells you how big a space is.

Destructive editing: Editing functions in Pro Tools that permanently alter the parent audio file on disk.

Dither: A form of randomly generated noise that helps smooth out fade-ins or fade-outs from silence. Dither can also help smooth crossfades between low-level audio regions.

DSP: Digital signal processing. In Pro Tools, DSP refers to the manipulation or processing of digital audio. In Pro Tools LE systems, all DSP tasks are handled by the host computer's CPU. The system's total DSP power thus depends on the processing power of the host computer.

DSP plug-in: Software that lets you add effects such as reverb, compression, and EQ to audio signals within the Pro Tools environment.

Dynamic mic: The least expensive type of mic. It can handle lots of volume, and is durable enough to survive most live settings. It tends to accentuate mid-range and can sometimes make tracks sound boxy.

Dynamic range: The difference between the softest and the loudest volume produced by a sound source.

E

Edit playlist: In Pro Tools, a snapshot of a track's current arrangement of regions. An edit playlist can contain a single region or multiple regions.

Edit selection: In Pro Tools, the actual audio region and/or track space that's highlighted when you make a selection. Edit selections can include a single region or multiple regions, and can include the space before, after, and in between regions.

Effects loop: An effects loop lets you add an effect to multiple tracks simultaneously. Also known as a send-and-return submix.

EQ: Equalization. The process of cutting or boosting the volume level of specific frequencies of an audio signal. EQ is used to open up frequency ranges, and thus enhance the clarity, spaciousness, and blending of sounds in a mix.

F

Fade: A volume curve that controls the rate of increase (fade-in) or decrease (fade-out) of a region's volume. Fades let you smooth the entrance and exit of audio during a mix. Fade-ins are placed at the start of regions; fade-outs, at the end.

Feedback loop: Created when an active microphone picks up its own signal from a loudspeaker and amplifies that signal again in a self-perpetuating cycle.

Figure-8 mic: A figure-8 mic picks up sound from both the front and back. Also known as a bi-directional mic.

G

Gain stage: Any point in an audio signal path where the audio signal is amplified (boosted) or attenuated (cut). The volume knob on your stereo, for instance, is a gain stage. Likewise, every amp, pre-amp, fader, and effect in your Pro Tools system is a gain stage.

Gain staging: The process of setting all gain stages in a system to their optimal values.

H

Handle value: In Pro Tools, a preserved segment of the original audio file before and after each region. It can be useful for fine-tuning the boundaries of a region.

I

Input selectors: Controls that let you assign audio input from external sources (via the Pro Tools interface) or from internal buses.

Inserts: Controls that let you add effects on channel strips. You can assign internal software effects and external hardware effects to inserts.

Interleaved stereo files: Single-file stereo files.

I/O: Input/output. The direction of an audio signal with respect to an audio device. Input is where audio signal enters the device; output is where audio signal leaves the device.

K

Keyboard workstation: A keyboard that includes an onboard synthesizer, sequencer, and effects, and often, a sampler. Originally conceived as "one-stop shopping" for full audio production, keyboard workstations are more often used today as hot-rod controllers and for onstage performance.

L

Latency: The lag time between audio entering and leaving your recording system. Pro Tools LE systems are susceptible to latency because of the heavy processing load placed on the host computer's CPU.

Line insert: In Pro Tools, a line insert applies its effect only to the track on which it's inserted.

Line-level: A nominal pre-amplified signal between +4 dB (pro) and +10 dBV (consumer) that's used to connect certain studio hardware devices such as keyboards, preamps, and mixers.

M

Main paths: In Pro Tools, logical groupings of inputs, outputs, inserts, or buses, such as a stereo (two-channel) output.

Master controller: A device, usually a keyboard or synthesizer, that's used to play back all of the other MIDI equipment in the studio.

Master fader: In Pro Tools, a master fader controls the level of a session's main outputs. Mater fader inserts let you add effects post-fader to the main mix.

Mastering: The process of preparing mixes for duplication. It involves optimizing dynamics and tonal balance, matching the volume levels of all of the songs, and sequencing tracks.

Memory locations: Settings in Pro Tools that store information about specific edit points and selected track ranges.

Metadata: Metadata refers to general data that describes the attributes of a file, such as file name, creation date, file size, etc. DigiBase collects metadata about audio files and other Pro Tools session-related files during the indexing process and stores this information in an associated database file.

MIDI: Musical Instrument Digital Interface. A communication protocol originally designed to allow synthesizers created by different manufacturers to communicate with each other.

MIDI cable: A cable that uses a five-pin connection standard to transmit MIDI information between MIDI devices such as sequencers, controllers, sound modules, keyboards, and effects.

MIDI interface: A hardware device that connects to a computer to send and receive MIDI.

MIDI keyboard: A device with piano- or organ-style keys that sends MIDI information when played.

MIDI Regions list: In Pro Tools, a list that displays MIDI regions. You can use it to add regions to a session, as well as move and rename them.

MIDI track: In Pro Tools, a channel that holds and controls MIDI note, instrument, and controller data.

Mixdown: The process of combining all tracks, edits, effects, and automation events into a final two-track master.

Modulation: A parameter of many delay effects that lets you adjust changes in delay time over time. Effects such as phase shifting, flanging, and chorus use short delay times with modulation.

N

Non-destructive editing: In Pro Tools, editing functions that let you change audio regions without altering their parent audio files.

The Nyquest Theorem: A basic rule of digital audio. It states that the sample rate must be twice the value of a sound's highest frequency for that sound to be accurately reproduced. For example, CD audio is sampled at 44.1kHz, while the human hearing range extends to only 20kHz.

O

Omni-directional mic: A mic that captures sounds from all directions.

OMS: Open Music System. A Mac-only utility that properly identifies and routes MIDI devices.

Optical connectors: Fiber-optic cables that transmit digital audio signals. They were originally developed to link Alesis ADATs to compatible gear. Also known as lightpipe.

Output selectors: Controls that let you route audio output to internal buses or external destinations (via the Pro Tools interface).

P

Parametric EQ: A tonal control (equalizer) that lets you target specific frequency ranges.

Performance volume: A performance volume is a storage volume that has been designated as suitable for recording and/or playback of media in a Pro Tools session.

Phantom power: A low-level electric current sent from the mic preamp to the condenser mic.

Phase cancellation: A type of audio interference that occurs when sound waves overlap and cancel each other out. This can cause frequencies to lose clarity or drop out.

Playlist: In Pro Tools, an arrangement of regions on an audio or MIDI track. A playlist can include a single region or multiple regions.

Precedence effect: The process by which humans locate sounds in a three-dimensional space: The ear that first hears a sound perceives it as significantly louder than the other ear does. Our two-ear auditory system uses this difference in perceived loudness to automatically triangulate the location of the sound source.

Punch recording: In Pro Tools, pressing (punching) the Record button in or out of Record mode at precise track locations. Used frequently during recording to redo unsatisfactory vocal or instrumental segments.

Q

Q: An adjustable parameter that determines the range of frequencies selected by a parametric EQ. The Q represents the number of octaves that the applied EQ affects.

Quantization distortion: Noise that occurs as a result of errors introduced when low-level audio signals are sampled, or when digital audio is converted from higher to lower bit depths (such as when converting 24-bit audio to 16-bit for CD mastering).

Quantizing: The process of automatically changing the timing of a group of MIDI notes.

R

RCA plug: Unbalanced connectors used in most home stereo and video equipment. The tip is audio signal and the surrounding shield is ground. Also called phono plug.

Region: In Pro Tools, a visual representation—usually a waveform—of a parent audio file stored on disk. A region can be any length—from an entire audio file to a single verse, hook, bar, or note.

Reverb: A natural property of any enclosed room that occurs when sound waves bounce off walls, ceilings, and floors. Its three basic sound components are direct sound, early reflections, and reverberations.

Ribbon mic: An expensive and fragile mic that can produce a unique silky tone—the result of a slight roll-off that tends to occur in the high end. Ribbon mics were popular from the 1930s to the 1960s, but were pretty much replaced in the studio by condenser mics.

GLOSSARY

557

RTAS plug-ins: Digidesign's Real-Time AudioSuite plug-ins use your computer's CPU to process audio non-destructively in real-time. They don't change the original audio file saved on disk; effects are applied only during playback or when bouncing to disk.

S

Sample rate: The number of times per second that sound wave information is gathered, or sampled, during the digital audio recording process. Measured in kilohertz (kHz). Sample rate determines a recording's frequency range and, thus, its accuracy. Higher sample rates generally produce more accurate audio recordings.

Sampler: A sound generator that plays back individual sounds, or samples, when triggered by a MIDI note.

Scrub: A term borrowed from analog recording, scrubbing refers to running the tape manually back and forth over the playback head. It's useful for locating edit points that might be difficult to find visually.

Sends: Channel strip controls that let you route audio to an internal bus or external output for effects processing or submixing.

Separation: The technique of using left/right panning to spread tracks out across the stereo image. Separation lets you hear tracks with more clarity, and introduces the perception of width in the stereo image.

Sequencer: Hardware devices or computer programs that are used to record, edit, and play back MIDI data. Sequencers can work with not only MIDI notes, but controller and sysex data as well.

Session: A Pro Tools session is analogous to a session in a real-world recording studio: It contains all the elements you need to record, edit, process, mix, master, and store audio recordings.

Session file: When you start a new Pro Tools project, you create a new session file. A session file maps all the elements in a session, including audio files, MIDI data, edits, and mix information.

Side-chain processing: Audio signal routing that involves an effect on a track being triggered by audio from a different track.

Signal path: The way that audio is routed in, out, and through a Pro Tools session.

Sound module: A MIDI synthesizer without a keyboard.

S/PDIF: Sony/Phillips Digital Interface. A transmission format for digital audio devices. It's commonly used in consumer devices. S/PDIF inputs and outputs generally have unbalanced RCA connectors.

Splice point: In Pro Tools, the location where two cross-faded regions join.

Stereo image: A simulation or image of a three-dimensional acoustic space that's constructed during the creation of a stereo mix. Techniques such as left/right panning, spatial effects (reverb, delay, chorus, and flange) and EQ shaping help trick our two-ear auditory system into perceiving sound in the three dimensions of width, depth, and height.

Sub-paths: In Pro Tools, these are signal paths within the main path. For example, a main path stereo output has two mono sub-paths.

Submix: Created by merging multiple tracks of audio into a single track.

Synthesizer: An electronic instrument used to make sounds. There are many different kinds of synthesizers and different methods for synthesizing sounds, including analog, sample playback, wavetable, granular, physical modeling, and virtual analog synthesis.

Sysex data: System-exclusive data. Specialized MIDI data that vendors can use to define MIDI events and messages that work only with their MIDI devices.

T

Timeline ruler: In Pro Tools, a ruler that provides a timing reference for track material.

Timeline selection: In Pro Tools, a selection of a range of time in a Timebase ruler. Timeline selections automatically apply across all tracks in a session.

Track: A designated space in a recording system that's assigned to carry a single audio signal. In Pro Tools, tracks let you direct the flow of audio into your system, through DSP effects, and then back out to your ears and/or mix-down machine.

Transfer volume: Transfer volumes are storage volumes that cannot be used by Pro Tools for recording or playback, such as a CD-ROM or network storage volume.

Transient: A sound that occurs for a brief time period, such as a drum hit, a piano note, or a guitar strum.

Transient peak: The instance of strongest attack in a transient. For example, a snare drum hit consists of a strong initial attack— a transient peak—followed by a period of decay.

TRS: Tip-ring-sleeve. A 1/4-inch stereo (two-channel) connector commonly found on headphones. The tip is left channel, the ring is right channel, and the sleeve is ground. TRS connectors can be used for balanced inputs and outputs. Sometimes called phone plugs.

TS: Tip-sleeve. A 1/4-inch unbalanced mono connector. The tip is audio signal and the sleeve is ground. It's commonly used for electric guitars, keyboards, and other unbalanced line-level connections.

U

Unbalanced line: A cable with one conductor and a surrounding shield at ground potential. Unbalanced lines are more prone to pick up interference. As a result, they can add noise to a recording.

W

Waveform: A graph of an audio signal's sound pressure level (in decibels) versus time.

X

XLR: A three-pin connection usually found on balanced microphone cables. It's used for analog and digital (AES/EBU standard) audio signals. Also called a Canon connector.

Z

Zero crossing: In Pro Tools, the point at which a waveform crosses its center line, and the waveform's amplitude is zero.

Index

audio files. *See also* files
  adding, 148
  auditioning, 184, 185
  backing up, 163
  batch-loading, 151
  compacting, 160, 512
  conversion quality, 152
  converting, 148, 150, 152
  copying, 148, 150
  cross-platform, 59
  deleting from hard drive, 124, 161, 511
  described, 12, 13
  displaying information, 214
  duplicate names, 158
  exporting audio regions as, 157–158
  file ID, 144
  finding, 144–146
  importing, 147–151, 188–189
  location of, 123
  managing. *See* DigiBase
  missing, 144–145
  mixed, 63
  names, 80, 158
  relinking, 144–145, 190–194, 467
  sample rates, 152
  size of, 512
  spotting, 189
  storing, 178
  waveforms and, 13, 15
Audio Files folder, 178
audio gear, connecting, 520
audio input format, 23–24
Audio Media options, 153–154
audio monitors, connecting, 535–537
audio regions. *See* regions
Audio Regions list
  clearing regions, 124, 217
  described, 553
  displaying file info, 214
  finding regions, 215
  importing audio files into, 188
  renaming regions in, 272
  selecting regions, 216–217
  sorting regions, 215
  using, 213–217
audio signal flow, 303–305, 553
audio signals, 66, 104
audio sources
  connecting to Audiomedia III, 534
  connecting to Digi 001, 526–530
  connecting to Digi 002, 521–526

connecting to Digi 002 Rack, 521–526
connecting to Mbox, 531–533
audio track channel strips, 27–28, 88, 303
audio tracks. *See also* tracks
  assigning inputs, 81, 82, 306
  assigning outputs, 81, 83, 306–307
  described, 14, 78, 553
  displaying inputs/outputs, 83
  exporting, 157–158
  importing from movies, 162, 461–462
  importing from OMF/AAF files, 468
  importing with Import Session command, 153–156
  line inserts, 321
  looping playback, 137
  mixing and, 303–304
  multiple, 125
  No Output option, 83
  playback scrolling options, 136
  playing, 135–139
  record-enabling, 100
  recording, 123
  scrubbing, 139
  transferring from CD, 162
  vs. MIDI tracks, 380
  zooming, 45
audio/video synchronization
  basics, 431
  checking accuracy of, 452–455
  getting sync audio from picture editor, 463–472
  head/tail leaders, 432
  importing digital video, 456–457
  peripherals, 440
  session setup for, 441–447
  Session Start time, 435, 442–443
  synchronizing sound effects, 495, 496, 497
  synchronizing to time code, 436
  syncing takes to guide track, 472
  video deck, 436–440
audio volumes, 176–177
Audiomedia III
  audio input levels and, 104
  basic studio setup, 519
  connecting audio sources to, 534
  connecting hardware, 9
  connecting monitor speakers to, 537
  connecting studio equipment to, 516–520
  described, 4
  external hardware effects, 540
  input gain, 106

INDEX

MIDI Event list, 383, 421–423
MIDI events, 383, 398, 421–423
MIDI feedback loops, 388, 390
MIDI files
    described, 12
    exporting from Pro Tools, 402
    importing to sessions, 400–401
    working with, 400–402
MIDI interface, 378, 556
MIDI keyboard, 379, 556
MIDI Machine Control (MMC), 447
MIDI Merge feature, 393–394, 397
MIDI notes, 49, 409–411
MIDI Regions list, 53, 397, 401, 556
MIDI Thru command, 387
MIDI Time Code. See MTC
MIDI Time Stamping (MTS), 418
MIDI track channel strips, 30, 381
MIDI tracks
    adding MIDI regions, 404–405
    described, 14, 78, 556
    discarding, 401
    displaying, 381, 382
    punch-recording, 393–394
    record-enabling, 100
    Record-Ready mode, 34
    recording, 389–394, 424
    viewing, 406–407
    vs. audio tracks, 380
    zooming, 45
MIDI velocity, 412–414
Minimum Strip Duration slider, 290
Minutes:Seconds ruler, 221, 222
Missing Files warning, 144–145
mix groups, 40, 93, 317
Mix Groups list, 40
Mix window, 26–40
    audio track channel strips, 27–28
    auxiliary input channel strips, 31
    illustrated, 26
    Inserts view, 39
    master fader channel strips, 32
    MIDI track channel strips, 30
    Mix Groups list, 40
    Sends view, 38
    Show/Hide Tracks list, 40
    Track Comments view, 39
    track controls, 34–37
mixdown, 365, 367–371, 556
mixer strip, 17

mixes
    automating, 351–363
    bounced, 367–371
    effects. See effects
    equalization, 332–334
    key inputs, 339–340
    plug-ins. See plug-ins
    reverb, 343–345
    stereo. See stereo mixes
    submixes. See submixes
mixing. See also stereo mixes
    assigning inputs/outputs, 306–307
    assigning sends, 310–311
    audio signal flow, 303–305
    audio tracks and, 303–304
    auxiliary inputs and, 303–304
    basics of, 295–317
    bouncing to disk, 367–371
    creating width, 297
    described, 295
    final mixdown, 365, 367–371, 500, 556
    input selectors, 306
    inserts, 308–309
    master faders, 304–307
    mastering, 365, 372–373
    monitoring mixes, 302
    output selectors, 306–307
    Output windows, 312–314
    process for, 301
    submixes, 315–317
    for video, 499–500
mixing groups, 40
MMC (MIDI Machine Control), 447
Mod Delay plug-in, 342
modulation, 340, 556
monitor latency, 110–111
monitor speakers, 536–537
monitors
    audio, 535–537
    system requirements, 5, 7, 8
mono compatibility, 300
mono sound effects, 488
MOS (Mit Out Sound), 475
movie tracks, 78
movies. See also QuickTime movies
    importing, 456–457
    importing audio tracks from, 162, 461–462
    playing, 458–460
    spotting, 457
MP3 format, 13, 147, 369
MTC (MIDI Time Code), 436

INDEX

R

Radeon card, 459
RAM. *See* memory
RCA plug, 520, 525, 530, 557
Real-Time AudioSuite. *See* RTAS
RealAudio files, 369
Record button, 99, 123
Record-Enable button, 34, 36, 100, 121, 388
record-enabling tracks, 100–101
record faders, 108
record modes, 98–99
Record-Ready mode, 120, 121, 123
Record Safe mode, 37, 101
recording
  ADAT input, 134
  analog audio, 430, 431
  audio input levels, 104–107
  audio tracks, 123
  auditioning takes, 131–132
  canceling takes, 124
  with Click plug-in, 115–118
  to click tracks, 115–118
  clipping, 107
  cloning recordings, 468
  DAT input, 134, 469–471
  Destructive Record mode, 98, 99, 125, 127
  from digital sources, 134
  feedback loops, 125
  at half-speed, 125
  hard drive allocation, 112–113
  latency during, 110–111
  limiting allocation, 114
  loop-recording audio, 130
  microphones. *See* microphones
  MIDI, 389–394, 424
  modes, 98–99
  monitor latency, 110–111
  monitoring audio, 108–109, 110
  Non-destructive Record mode, 98, 99, 125,
    126
  to playlists, 133
  plug-ins and, 323
  preparing for, 97–118
  punch-recording. *See* punch-recording
  record-enabling tracks, 100–101
  sysex into Pro Tools, 398–399
  with time code sync, 469–471
  Transport window, 120–122
  video. *See* video

Redo command, 218
Region End Pad slider, 290
region number, 80
Region Start Pad slider, 290
regions
  aligning, 252–253
  auto-created, 204, 274
  capturing, 243
  changing breakpoint values in, 361
  choosing for takes, 132
  clearing, 217, 264, 275
  compressing, 257
  consolidating, 505
  copying, 262–263
  creating, 16, 243–245
  creating sync points in, 254
  cutting, 262–263, 478
  described, 16, 203, 557
  duplicating, 262, 264
  edits and, 202
  expanding, 257
  exporting as audio files, 157–158
  fades. *See* fades
  finding, 215
  hiding, 274
  importing, 147, 149–150
  length of, 16
  locking/unlocking, 269
  managing, 271–275
  MIDI, 397, 401, 404–407
  moving, 46, 219–220, 251, 264
  muting/unmuting, 270
  names, 80, 207, 243, 271–273, 291
  nudging, 51, 260, 261
  offline, 146, 204
  overview, 203–204
  padding, 159
  pasting, 262, 264
  placing in tracks, 246–247, 251
  placing sync points in, 255
  quantizing, 268
  ranges of, 216
  rearranging, 219
  removing from Audio Regions list, 217
  removing from sessions, 159
  removing from tracks, 262
  removing unused, 275, 511
  renaming, 271–273
  repeating, 266
  restoring, 245
  scrubbing, 47

regions *(continued)*
  selecting, 46, 216–217, 234–235, 238–239
  separating, 244–245
  shifting, 267
  shuffling, 249
  sliding, 248–251
  slipping, 248
  smoothing, 489, 491
  snapping, 219, 220, 246, 251
  sorting, 215
  spotting, 250
  stereo, 204
  stripping silence from, 290–291
  sync points, 254–255
  synchronizing, 219
  time locations, 207–208, 219
  time stamps, 208, 219
  trimming, 46, 256–259, 489
  types of, 203–204
  unused, 217, 275
  user-defined, 204
  viewing, 205–210
  waveforms, 203
  whole-file, 203
  working with, 231–275
  zooming, 208–210
Regions view, 406
Relative Grid mode, 220, 251
Relink window, 145, 167, 191–192
Remove Memory Location option, 229
Render Sources folder, 178
Repeat command, 16, 265
resolution, 61, 370, 513
Resolution option, 370
Restore Performance function, 408
Return to Zero button, 120, 123
reverb, 321, 343–345, 557
reverb plug-in, 321, 344
Revert to Saved command, 61
Rewind button, 120
rewinding, 120, 135
ribbon microphones, 102, 557
room miking, 103
room tone, 475
RTAS (Real-Time AudioSuite), 19
RTAS Compressor plug-in window, 325–328
RTAS effects, 19
RTAS plug-ins
  described, 320, 558
  dynamic effects, 335–337
  offline regions and, 146

performance and, 320, 350
settings for, 12
switching to AudioSuite plug-ins, 508
TDM and, 75
vs. AudioSuite plug-ins, 508
rulers, 221–222
  Bars:Beat, 221
  Conductor, 221, 554
  deleting, 222
  Feet.Frames, 434–435
  Markers ruler, 221
  Meter, 117, 221
  Minutes:Seconds, 221, 222
  Samples:Seconds, 221
  Tempo, 117, 221
  Time Code, 434–435
  Timebase, 221
  timeline, 559
  track, 221–222

S

S/PDIF cables, 520, 525, 530–534, 558
S/PDIF input format, 23, 24
S/PDIF Mirroring input format, 23, 24
Safe mode, 36, 359
Sample Rate Conversion options, 155
sample rates
  changing, 21
  choosing, 21
  conversion quality, 152
  converting bounced files to, 370–371
  default, 21
  described, 61, 558
  for sessions, 59, 62, 63, 163
  using lower sample rates, 513
  for video, 431–433
  word clock, 440
sampler, 378, 558
Samples:Seconds ruler, 221
saving items
  I/O Settings files, 70
  sessions, 60–63
scrolling options, 136, 507
Scrubber tool, 46, 47, 139, 487
scrubbing
  audio regions, 47
  described, 558
  identifying hit points, 488

INDEX

INDEX

X

Z